AIRY PERSIFLAGE

AIRY PERSIFLAGE

Occasional thoughts on film, television and culture

Neil Rattigan

Fastnet Books

2015

Fastnet Books
227 Donnelly Street
Armidale, New South Wales, 2350
Australia

www.fastnetbooks.net

publishing@fastnetbooks.net

First published 2015

National Library of Australia
Cataloguing-in-Publication entry:

Rattigan, Neil —1946–
Airy Persiflage: Occasional thoughts on film, television and culture

ISBN-13: 978-0-9874587-1-1
ISBN-10: 0-9874587-1-X

Ko-Ko. Nonsense! A terrible thing has just happened. It seems you're the son of the Mikado.

Nanki-Poo. Yes, but that happened some time ago.

Ko-Ko. Is this the time for airy persiflage?

(W.S. Gilbert, *The Mikado*, Act II)

Persiflage: Light banter or raillery; frivolous talk.

(Shorter Oxford English Dictionary)

Contents

CINEMATIC BEGINNINGS

THE AVAILABLE ENVIRONMENT: THOUGHTS ON THE AMERICAN FEDERATION OF ARTS SEASON, 'BEFORE HOLLYWOOD: TURN-OF-THE-CENTURY FILM FROM AMERICAN ARCHIVES'[1]

It only slowly dawned on early American film makers that the 'great outdoors' could serve other purposes in films than merely being the place in which some aspect of real life as 'obvious' as a fire (e.g., *The Burning of Durland's Riding Academy* [1902]) or as 'unexpected' as the aftermath a disaster (e.g. *Scenes of Wreckage From The Waterfront* [1900]) took place and in which perforce such films had to be made. Even so, the reality of the great outdoors had to be reasonably accessible. A disaster in Galveston was apparently considered accessible; Manila Bay in the Philippines was not (perhaps not unreasonably). Thus the patently (and painfully) obvious models in *The Battle of Manila Bay* (1898).

Some sense of the photographic and dramatic possibilities inherent in the great outdoors of America, the environment which was available to film makers, began to impinge despite the fact that the influence of vaudeville and the theatre seemed to be an immovable 'mind set' for early film makers. In *What Happened on Twenty-Third Street* (1901), it is clear that the environment suggested itself as a source of the gag, the existence in this case of a vent blowing air upwards into the street—anticipating Billy Wilder, Marilyn Monroe and *The Seven Year Itch* by over half a century. This gag, which is a long time coming in the film and which significantly is built up to as if the film were just another street scene *actualitie* is dependent totally upon the existing environment. It could not have been incorporated into a vaudeville style gag without elaborate build up. It relies upon availability of an environmental phenomenon—the blowing vent—and a knowledge of the environment—the city street in general—by the audience. The film is just another slightly risqué comic situation, or a risqué situation rendered comic to avoid being only risqué (comparable in this with the rather more obvious *Trapeze Disrobing Act*. That its inspiration was probably the environment rather than the other way round is significant in attempting to trace a course to see if the environment would become a determining factor in the sort of narratives the American cinema came to make.

The influence of the theatre combined with (in the case of the Edison Company) the bulkiness of the camera no doubt served to make it difficult for the embryonic film production industry to see the possibilities of utilizing the environment as location for action and as inspiration for stories. The possibilities of using real locations for fictional films, even at the level of simple gag films (despite the hint provided by Lumiere with *L'Arraseur arrose'),* were still governed by a certain satisfaction with the artifice of theatre on one hand

2

and by economics on the other. In the-first case, it would seem that audiences were not disturbed by the patently obvious theatre-style back-drops, props, and very limited three-dimensional sets nor indeed by crude models and even cruder art work, e.g. *Raising Old Glory Over Morro Castle* (1899) in which the nvironment suggested an endless manner of ways in' which the simple flight and pursuit may be varied: existing objects, buildings, terrain may be utilized to impede or progress flight or pursuit, to offer temporary sanctuary and so on. Thus *Meet Me at the Fountain* (1904) is almost 'pure' cinema. Its simple structure of a man pursued by a 'monstrous regiment of women' is so fundamental that it has been used many times since although perhaps never with more success than by Buster Keaton in *Seven Chances* (1925). *Meet Me at the Fountain* does not make any real use of the possibility of moving the camera to follow action and indeed it seldom moves from the then conventional front-on position. Most action takes place, once the chase begins, from background to foreground with participants running out of shot either side of the camera. In this at least it breaks away from the studio/theatre-based entrance and exit to the side through the non-existent wings. But the break with theatre is most complete in the manner in which the film moves around the environment *between* shots. A variety of locations are utilized; it is difficult from this time distance to discern whether the variety of locales were deliberately selected to give an impression of the chase moving further and further out into the country away from the city. That *Meet Me at the Fountain* was released in the same year as *The Great Train Robbery* and somewhat before Griffith seems to have locked (or 'lucked') onto the cinematic possibilities of the chase in action/melodrama suggests that rather than the later comedies (especially those of Sennett and his Keystone Kops) getting their impetus from Porter and Griffith, it may well have been that even earlier comedies provided inspiration for Griffith and others.

It can only be conjecture that the possibilities of the environment suggested themselves as suitable for filming chases, or whether the idea of filming chases preceded the using of the environment in which to shoot them. It would seem plausible, however, to state the environment provided the impetus. Other than for the chase films, there is little evidence in the earliest American comedy films that anything other than small gag films or single joke 'acts' (all within vaudeville, burlesque or theatrical conventions) suggested themselves to the film makers. Even *The European Rest Care* is little more than a series of short sketches designed to show the never-ending series of disasters that beset the 'innocent abroad' with only the location-shot opening and closing sequences extending slightly the theatricality. *Rube and Mandy at* Coney Island (1903) is heavily dependent on the actual environment of Coney Island for all of its jokes and situations, but still only uses Coney Island (or its fairground anyway)

3

as a setting for a series of gags (a running joke about a pair of yokels constantly being disconcerted by fairground attractions). Coney Island is, in any case, a form of theatre, open-air theatre with, occasionally, audience involvement. (In relation to this film, it may be that the film was also intended as a promotion for Coney Island, a suspicion which is increased by Edison's *Coney Island at Night* [1905] which is an almost an *avant-garde* film celebrating the spectacularity of the use of electric light at Coney Island—and we know where that electric light was coming from!)

With *What Happened On Twenty-Third Street* and more especially through *Meet Me at The Fountain)* it is possible to see a glimmer of the way in which environment was going to start to impinge more and more upon early film makers. Even though their story inspirations were going to depend for quite a while (and still do) upon other established sources, the theatre, the short story and the popular novel, there would be an increasing (if painfully slow) use of environment as setting and, consciously or unconsciously, a use of setting to provide the structures of these narratives. *The Great Train Robbery* is almost too obvious an example but could or indeed would it have been made without the possibility of using real locations? If indeed *The Great Train Robbery* is the inspiration for the later development of the Hollywood Western (a problematic claim if ever there was one), its inspiration is not simply the provision of a very thin narrative framework but also the provision of the concept of using the great outdoors as settings for a particular type of story which was in turn dependent upon the great outdoors.

The environment represented a freedom from restriction, the restriction of the theatre and its cinematic successor, the studio, and their limited space for action. Comedy film makers grasped this perhaps earlier than their more serious minded brethren. Although the greatest of them, Chaplin, would, in his insatiable quest for perfection return or retreat to the studio, most of the others, great and small, would continue to use and expand the use of the environment. Sennett's Keystone Kops were almost totally dependent upon the embryonic city streets for their comic mania. Keaton, for all his fascination with things mechanical and his interest in the integrity of story, used the environment for unparalleled inspiration even to the extent of driving a real locomotive off a burning bridge into a ravine (*The General,* [1925]). Indeed, Keaton is the great outdoor comedian of the silent film, and the environment supplied the setting and the inspiration for many extended comedy routines such as the town in the grip of a hurricane in *Steamboat Bill Jr* (1928) or the waterfall in *Our Hospitality* (1923). And Harold Lloyd, the great comedian of the city environment, hanging off a clock face at the top of a skyscraper (*Safety Last* [1923]), or from the power pole of a tram car (*Girl Shy* [1924]), or just standing in the street with the crank

4

handle of the car just demolished by a passing locomotive still in his hand (*For Heaven's Sake* [1926]), sought and found in the environment comedy that endures as fresh today. Add Laurel and Hardy attempting to deliver a piano up a seemingly an endless flight of steps from street to house[2] or demolishing Jimmy Finlayson's house while he demolishes their car (*Big Business* [1929]), or starting a riot in a jam of cars which leads to a scene of escalating destruction (*Two Tars* [1928]). All these, and the work of less well-known and lesser comedians, point to the singular importance of environment in determining the type of films, the type of narratives, the type of situations, gags and humor.

The Great Train Robbery is instructive in another sense. It demonstrates not only the way in which the environment may have affected the narrative—although perhaps not providing the environment depicted in the film with any qualities beyond the 'real' place where such actions can (and did) take place—but it also demonstrates another form of narrative which was going' to lead to another popular genre once Hollywood got under way: the Crime film. These, ultimately, were to utilize another environment altogether. The city/urban environment of early American film making suggested material for 'quickie' stories other than comedy in perhaps an overly obvious way: the criminal event. As early as 1898, with *Burglar on the Roof,* crime is seen as the 'natural' story material of film. Shot on the roof of the Morse Building in New York (Musser 1983, 48), standing in for a tenement building, the film depicts a burglar helping himself to possessions through a skylight. The scene rapidly turns to a slapstick comic turn of the crudest type when the burglar is seen and quickly assaulted first by a group of women, one wielding a broom, and then by a group of men. The resulting brou-ha-ha is unstructured knockabout; it lacks the *finesse* (or at least the comic choreography) of, say, Chaplin's *The Immigrant* (1917) and the pummelling handed out in that film by Eric Campbell and his bevy of enraged waiters to the diner who attempts to welsh on his dinner check. The story of *Burglar on the Roof* does not have an end; it simply stops when, presumably, the film in the camera was all used up. That Vitagraph, in looking to use that part of the environment most readily available—their own roof—should then have the idea of shooting a burglary is instructive.

There is demonstrated in *Burglar on the Roof,* the grip of vaudeville on the imagination of the early film makers. *Burglar on the Roof is* a vaudeville sketch and a remarkably unsubtle one at that. Good vaudeville would surely have required more structure, more choreography and a satisfactory conclusion. Still in the vaudeville vein but more rounded as a gag is *How They Rob Men in Chicago* (1900). This film represents, on one hand, simply another vaudeville sketch on celluloid, but on the other, an early 'fascination' with urban crime that was to remain a constant theme of American cinema from then on. *How*

They Rob Men in Chicago is more subtle than *Burglar on the Roof* even to the extent of containing social comment and perhaps a 'dig' at Chicago's expense by the New Yorkers who produced it. A top-hatted toff is hit a couple of times on the head by a cudgel-wielding villain, and his unconscious form (which falls almost out of sight at the bottom of the frame) is robbed of his wallet. Mugger exits left. A cop enters from the right of frame, trips on the unconscious victim, leans down and takes the victim's watch. The gag is good enough to raise a genuine laugh in a 1980s audience. The setting is still a painted studio set; the inspiration however is the real environment of the *fin-de-siecle* American city streets.

It is generally conceded that the environment is an important physical and thematic structuring aspect of the Gangster/Crime genre of the 1930s and beyond—even if that environment is (re)presented by studio sets. (See for example McArthur [1972] and Mitchell [1976].) These two films, which between them hardly add up to five minutes of screen time, suggest an understanding of that environment and its narrative possibilities had already been appreciated before the turn of the century. Further, although restricted by the technology and by the ill-formed aesthetics of the early cinema, that they revealed an embryonic fascination with crime and criminal activity (as did *The Great Train Robbery*) as a source of story material and, especially *Burglar on the Roof*, in the way in which crime and environment are symbiotically linked.

By the time that D.W. Griffith came to make *The Musketeers of Pig Alley* (1913), the link between environment and crime-narrative was fully established. *The Musketeers of Pig Alley* is a narrative informed, as in so much of Griffith's work, by Victorian sentimentality but at the same time it is clearly cognizant of the realities of New York's lower East side. The street scenes, or some of them at least, are shot in real locations. More than this, the effect of environment is to alter the narrative. A Victorian melodrama of this type— suffering, 'pure' heroine, dying mother, brother seeking to alleviate the family's plight but being robbed, etc—would have demanded that virtue be rewarded and villainy punished. Instead of which 'Snapper Kid' who has done much to make 'The Little Lady's' life even more unbearable is able to escape, with her active intervention, the long arm of the law. There is a sympathy, understanding, even admiration for the criminal (which would be a hallmark of many of the '30s films) which is, I would argue, derived from the effect the environment had upon the narrative. The environment in *The Musketeers of Pig Alley* is not neutral; it is not simply photographic description of where certain actions took place. It takes on a social dimension and effectively modifies the simple good-and-evil morality of the story to permit finer shading between these two positions. The environment signifies: the moral tones have different resonances because of what the environment 'means'. (This can seen to be still true, even more impressively so, in Francis Ford Coppola's *Godfather* films [1972, 1976 and 1991] especially in those sections dealing with Vito Corleone's early life in *Part Two* and nearly all of *Part One*). When the film uses the 'real' world for its background, the moral certitude of the theatre is being modified to come closer to the moral ambiguity of the real world; and thus the real world comes out of the background, resisting being simply an alternative for a painted backdrop and impinging upon the very central processes of story-telling.

In both *The Burglar* and *The Musketeers of Pig Alley*, while the environment provides a set of conditions which affect the sort of story that may be told, it is used to greater dramatic and cinematic effect in *The Musketeers of Pig Alley*. (This should hardly surprise us since nearly a decade-and-a-half of film making has taken place between the respective production of these two films.) There is a greater sense of verisimilitude to *Musketeers*—although the indoor scenes are nearly all governed by the still-powerful theatrical conventions of straight-on camera, entrances and exits stage right and left, and so on. Outside, the street with its crowded sidewalks, stalls and store fronts give a depth to the recreation of the environment—whether they are 'real' streets or sets is actually difficult to determine. The alley in which the near-climactic gun-fight takes place certainly looks real. The movement of the actors through the alley is different from the way they move through the various interior sets, suggesting that the demands of a real location forced Griffith to accept action in depth rather than laterally and may well account for the startling use of close-up when 'Snapper Kid' sidles along a wall almost right into the camera.

Griffith's interest in crime relied upon two simple themes. First, the crime which motivated (in the narrative sense) the last minute rescue (of which none are present in this season but are along the lines of *The Lonely Hills* [1909]). Second, social crime as 'explored' in *The Usurer* (1910) and even more fully (and more melodramatically in *One is Business; The Other Crime* (1912). Out-and-out use of crime as the narrative core as it was to become the basis of the Gangster genre with the sound film seems to have been rare with Griffith, *The Musketeers of Pig Alley* being an exception, and one in which the crime story is no more important than the melodrama surrounding 'The Little Lady'.

The codes of theatrical convention and modes of theatrical presentation maintained a Herculean grip on the imagination of early film-makers, relaxing but rarely during the first two decades. This is even true to the point of a 'cut-away' set—a door but no wall—being used in *Foul Play: or A False Friend* (1906). The 'simple' cutting between two juxtaposed locations while presenting simultaneous action (such as had already been done in, for example, *Life of An American Fireman* [1905]) was either not considered or considered to be

7

unnecessary. Simultaneous action which the narrative required to take place on either side of a closed door was shot exactly as it would have been presented on the stage, the wall between the two pieces of action being 'presumed' to exist. This suspension of credulity as demanded by the stage is of an entirely different order to that the cinema would demand once it established its own aesthetic of verisimilitude.

Despite the evidence before their eyes (and lens) of the possibilities of outdoor locations as *settings* for fictional narratives, or at the very least as alternatives to and escape from the artificiality of theatre scenery, these early film-makers seemed to blind to these potentialities. Or, charitably, to be wearing blinkers. The ambiguity, already noted in relation to *The European Rest Care,* is continued in a rather curious film, *The Hold-Up of the Rocky Mountain Express* (1906). Here the landscape *is* used and may indeed be the Rocky Mountains to judge by the terrain. The film, however, commences as if it were simply an *actualitie;* the first several minutes of the film is unbroken footage taken from a camera positioned on the front of a locomotive as it pulls out of a station and commences a journey out of the switching yards and into a mountain pass. In this it resembles the same company's[3] *Interior New York Subway 14th Street to 42nd Street* (1905). This unchanging camera view of the tracks and passing landscape is finally interrupted for a sketch of vaudevillian knockabout in a patently studio-set railway carriage. The shot from the front of the train returns and continues for a while before the actual hold-up is initiated by a log lying on the tracks stopping the train. The robbers enter the carriage (back to the studio set), rob the passengers and leave. The rest of the film—the robbers fleeing first on a hand cart and then on a horse drawn carriage on the road next to the railway line—is all filmed from the camera fixed to the front of the locomotive (albeit that the camera does pan slightly on occasion). Presumably the drawing power of the film was felt to be the long tracking shot from the locomotive.[4] The story (such as it is) is played out totally within the view of that camera other than for the two cutaway scenes inside the train. Part of that drawing power was the scenery which indeed is quite, spectacular: mountains, ravines, running streams. The producers of *The Hold-Up of the Rocky Mountain Express* must have thought that scenery would hold an audience's attention. They must also have felt (after the example of *The Great Train Robbery'*) that a robbery story would also be of interest. Was it expediency or lack of imagination that prevented them from seeing that the environment might have been used to much greater effect as setting if the camera had been 'free'? In contrast, but equally as exemplary of 'tunnel vision' is *The Miller's Daughter* (1905). Here the outdoors is utilized in place of theatrical scenery. A highly theatrical melodrama of a type which must have been only too familiar to audiences for the popular theatre of the day—

8

girl seduced, abandoned, thrown out and finally forgiven and reunited with her family—is played out, with only one or two exceptions, in 'real' locations. Like most films of the time, each scene is shot from one camera position and like a scene on the stage from beginning to end without interruption. The intriguing question is, why did the Edison Company choose to make such a thoroughly theatrical piece out-of-doors? With the exception of a couple of scenes in which characters arrive and depart by horse or horse-and-carriage, there is no narrative 'need' for the action to take place outside. The use of real locations, however, gives the film's clichéd sentimentality a surprising and refreshing sense of verisimilitude. But again, this is undercut in the most extraordinary manner in one scene which is meant to be outdoors but which is enacted on a stage set of the most blatant and obvious kind: the heroine throws herself into a river which is clearly a stage setting of paper-maché rocks and painted backdrop; rescued by the hero, both emerge completely dry! Even the interior scenes of the family home have greater attention to authenticity that this.

Neither *The Hold-Up of the Rocky Mountain Express* nor *The Miller's Daughter* reveal any sense, even an embryonic sense, of the possibility of integrating the environment into the narrative. But they do point to a willingness to move between the two more freely. Curiously *The Miller's Daughter,* while it gains from being shot al fresco, need not have been while *The European Rest Cure,* crying out for exterior shooting, loses by being studio bound. A film which does suggest a degree of integration between location and narrative but which is still heavily dependent upon vaudeville for its inspiration is *Getting Evidence* (1906). With the exception of the opening and closing scenes, this film is shot in a variety of real locations—parks, gardens, the beach and so on. Its construction is rather like *Rube and Mandy at Coney Island* in that it is a series of knockabout sketches in which a private detective continually tries and fails to photograph what he takes to be a couple engaged in an adulterous tryst. The possibility of film to do more than record complete scenes one at a time is, however, utilized in a chase sequence which takes place on a beach. Again the chase as a purely cinematic form! The chase, which is quite long, is the only action within the film which is 'broken up', that is to say, not played from beginning to end in one shot. The chase too is the only scene/sequence in the film which takes advantage of the environment. The other scenes might have as easily been shot in a studio; they are vaudeville slapstick sketches.

It is difficult not to be surprised that a decade and more after the first films were made and shown, the possibilities of breaking with theatrical convention (both in terms of location shooting *and* in terms of editing within scenes) did not seem to be being explored rather more. On the evidence of the films discussed so far it is not surprising that Griffith should have gained

9

the reputation as a genius which film historians have given him. There are, nonetheless, tantalizing inklings of a gathering sense of cinema's difference from theatre here and there. For example, the rather macabre *Terrible Ted* (1907). This film still consists of a series of sketches *a la* vaudeville, but most of these sketches are dependent for their effect on taking place out-of-doors. Indeed, the first exterior scene involves—yes—a chase as 'Terrible Ted' puts to flight a handful of pre-Keystone New York cops. Although *Terrible Ted* is childish nonsense (and blood-thirsty enough to require Rambo to look to his laurels) there is a sense in which it is cinematic in a way which few of the previously discussed films are, and it is unlikely to have been workable on the stage. This is not to claim that the environment provides more than setting, nor that the settings are especially concerned with verisimilitude (in terms of 'logical' places for the action to occur), but it is to claim that the ability to shoot outdoors was realized in constructing the narrative and was probably a determining factor in that narrative construction.

The 'perils' of shooting outdoors in real locations was demonstrated unintentionally in *The Black Hand* (1906), a film surprising in its utter theatricality even for its time. One scene—the kidnapping of a child—is enacted in a street in New York. Not only do the passersby react to the presence of the camera (thus indicating there had been no attempt to 'stage-manage' the location) but the actual snatching of the child promotes a reaction from those same bystanders that might very well have disrupted the filming. The reaction of the bystanders may well have added authenticity if it were not for the fact that their (genuine) reactions were clearly at odds with the exaggerated theatricality of the actors. The real tension in the scene—at least for a 1980s audience—is whether the real people are going to interfere, inadvertently, with the filming. The remainder of the film takes place, for all its claims that it is based upon details of a real arrest in similar circumstances, on the 'conventional' stage sets—of which the kidnap gang's set does not even attempt the superficial authenticity of a butcher's shop set seen earlier in the film.

In discussing early American film, it is impossible from 1908 onwards to ignore D.W. Griffith. But even as his films demonstrate (in perhaps a rather more random fashion than some histories would imply), a gradual development of awareness and demonstration of the aesthetics of the cinema (or a particular set of aesthetics), they also demonstrate strikingly the power of theatre in providing the types of narratives to be told and the 'understanding' of how narratives were to be told through the cinema. A film such as *The Usurer,* directed by Griffith in 1910, differs in practically no way from films such as *Foul Play or A False Friend,* made by Vitagraph some four years earlier. The subject matter is inescapably theatrical—a sentimental morality tale of a heavily melodramatic

10

nature—and it is enacted in front of sets which are no more 'realistic' than any in the earlier films. It is true that the narrative contains a number of sub-plots structured around the central idea of a usurer getting his just desserts for oppressing the poor: Griffith provides scenes of the decadent, spend-thrift social life of the usurer, a view of his working methods, and separate views of three of his 'victims'—a widow with a sick-daughter, a young married couple, a single man. In the complexity of plot, *The Usurer* is an 'advance' on more single-plotted films both earlier and around the same time. But its reliance on studio-bound sets of the usual crude theatrical type is in contrast with the external locations of *ATin-type Romance* (1910) or the greater verisimilitude of *A Friendly Marriage* (1911)—both single-plot narratives.

It would seem that the grip which the theatre had on Griffith's imagination manifest itself in his stories long after his film-making practice had grasped the possibilities of transcending the limitations of tiny, unauthentic sets by constructing realistic sets (sometimes of enormous magnitude as in *Intolerance)* or by judicious use of the environment. If *The Usurer* is a film which looks as if it was 'old-fashioned' even when it was made in 1910, *The Informer* made a mere two years later, stands out as ahead of more conventional (for the time) films such as *The Dream* (1911) or *A Friendly Marriage* by an almost immeasurable degree. Of course, it is the case that Griffith directed some 153 more films between July 1910 when he made *The Usurer* and October 1912 when he made *The Informer* (Henderson 1970, 193-215), and it is difficult to say the degree of commitment he may have had to the former film; he may have simply dashed it off.

Of greater pertinence here is the extent to which Griffith did (or did not) permit the environment to influence the types of stories he would tell in his films and, equally importantly, the manner in which his narratives may have been influenced in their very construction by the environment. Linda Arvidson (Griffith's first wife) has told how Griffith was 'always overly fastidious about "location". His feeling for charming landscapes and his use of them in the movies was a significant factor in the success of his early pictures' (Henderson 1970, 112). Staying for the moment with the instructive contrasts between *The Usurer* and *The Informer,* it is clear that environment (real or imagined) plays no part in the inspiration neither for the story nor for the settings of the former. The latter, however, is an entirely different kettle of fish. *The Informer* is one of Griffith's many films which deal with aspects of the American Civil War, or which at least take their time location from within that period of American history and which include at some level conflict between soldiers of the North and South. Indeed, the greater part of the narrative of *The Informer* is a 'rehearsal' for the climactic ending of *The Birth of a Nation*, especially in its cross-cutting between the women and a wounded confederate besieged in 'the old negroes quarters' by the union soldiers, and the confederate cavalry charging to the rescue. (In *The Birth of the Nation* the cross-cutting is among rather more ambitious but the narrative situation is almost identical substituting rampaging blacks for union soldiers.)

The almost dual personality of Griffith as demonstrated in the startling manner in which his films alternate between 'progressive' works of cinema as in the case of *The Informer* and those which, even for the time of their production, looked 'old fashioned', such as *The Old Actor* (1912), may be explained by the fact that Griffith's various contracts with Biograph always specified from the outset that Griffith would receive in addition to a salary a 'commission for each linear foot of positive motion picture film' sold by Biograph (Henderson 1970, 47), a percentage that was increased with each subsequent contract. This must have encouraged Griffith to churn out as many films as he could, and may account for the pot-boilers of no particular artistic or cinematic merit which *The Usurer* and *The Old Actor* represent.

The Old Actor is, however, still interesting in light of Griffith's use of interiors and exteriors. The quality of the sets show a marked improvement over the painted canvas backdrops which were considered good enough for *The Usurer*, there is a greater attention to verisimilitude in the set of the 'the Old Actor's' home even though it is never used as more than a simple stage for actors to enter and exit in stage fashion (except 'the Mother' who sits, as immobile in her chair as Whistler's Mother). The 'Old Beggar's' home is perhaps less concerned with realistic construction but the theatre, which is presumably a real stage (Biograph's?), registers as far more real than either. In nearly every interior scene, however, the hidden fact that the stage was open to the elements is revealed by the manner in which the curtains, antimacassars, table-cloths and so on blow about in the wind. (Both *The Old Actor* and *One is Business; The Other Crime* were made in California where the 'studio' was open to the air unlike the fully enclosed Biograph New York studio.[5]) Restricted (by choice?) to the stage sets, Griffith makes no attempt to break with the stage traditions of actors entering and exiting stage left and right, nor with the cinematic 'tradition' of single camera placement throughout the action. No interior scene is interrupted by cutting. Indeed, had later films not survived, if Griffith's reputation was based on these films, that reputation might not have been any greater than Porter's.

It is clear from the written histories that Griffith was using a variety of locations for his films. What is not quite clear is—why? It seems to have involved considerable inconvenience and organization. But it does not seem unreasonable to assume that stories were written (in as much as they were 'written' at all)

12

to take advantage of location shooting. In this way the environment was a determining factor in the films which were made. The famous Griffith last minute chase-and-rescues (perhaps not quite as prevalent as is claimed [e.g., Slide 1970, 102]) were a product of the capacity for mobility (to and between different locations) that the camera had and which the theatre stage did not. Further the plethora of 'Indian' films that Griffith made (none of which were in this season) were no doubt inspired by the availability of suitable landscapes.

While it may be that Griffith was more sensitive to the pictorial possibilities of landscape than were many of his competing film producers working for other companies, his own set of obsessions seem to have governed his choice of stories to make in those landscapes. Thus the prevalence of melodramas, of overly simplistic moral parables, and stories of women threatened with rape (and worse?) requiring last minute rescue, and the frequent use of Civil War themes.

Griffith's use of the environment, at least by Henderson's (1970) analysis, was to extend the grammar of cinema that he was, consciously or unconsciously, developing. The possibility of landscapes inspiring the sort of films Griffith was making seems secondary to Henderson's analysis. It is true that Griffith tended to make the same four or five films, with variations, over and over again, the differences being in setting and of techniques (more close-ups, panoramic shots, cross-cutting, changes in lighting, etc). Yet it would seem that almost despite himself, the environment did impinge to some extent, modifying the typical Griffith melodrama and the last-minute rescue in subtle ways, and in some cases, 'taking over' for short moments. Thus the 'appearance' of the panoramic shot that has a group in the foreground and a vast scenic view beyond them (the most famous example: the family group on the edge of a ridge overlooking a panorama of Sherman's army 'marching through Georgia' in *The Birth of a Nation*; a similar composition but without movement in the vista exists in the scene of 'the trysting place' in *The Informer*.) These shots take on meanings derived from the landscape that perhaps were not fully intended or realized by Griffith.[6] The landscape has become truly a *character* in the narrative; no longer simply a picturesque setting or a celebration of cinema's difference from and 'superiority' to theatre.

Griffith was to put his faith finally not in the great outdoors but in the authentically constructed set: *Intolerance* and especially the Babylonian sets being the epitome of this. Given his interest in historical locations for his melodramas this is not surprising. It is true his skill at getting (with Billy Bitzer's help) the cinematic composition that was part of his 'genius' meant that the landscape when he used it was more striking in his films than in the films of most of his contemporaries but the environment was, like really everything else, put by

Griffith at the service of his narratives which remained in turn melodramatic and theatrical even when they took epic scope.

The exteriors in *The Old Actor* do show that Griffith was capable of permitting (or requiring) his actors to move diagonally across the camera view, to leave past the camera, and in general to break with the invariable lateral movements of the interiors, and establish another dimension to off-screen space; behind the camera/spectator. Here he also breaks action up into shots rather than keeping unbroken scenes; there is an attenuated Griffith chase towards the end in which, somewhat uncharacteristically, the geography is rather random. We can only assume that Griffith knew quite well that actors need not enter and exit laterally, and we can assume since the sets used the same daylight that the exteriors did that the reason for action being restricted to the lateral plane was not a limited depth of field due to poorer interior illumination. Rather that in essence Griffith was really not bothered by the theatricality of these films.

Equally it would seem, neither were other producers of the time. *The Passer-By* (1912) is just as stage-bound as these films by Griffith. *The Passer-By* contains, however, two startling tracking in and reverse shots but despite these, all action takes place on stagey sets—probably the same one for a majority of the scenes. There is a quality, possibly of restraint in the action, to *The Passer-By* which makes it possible to concur with Anthony Slide when he states, 'Apfel's direction is masterly...and it is strange that he never really achieved any real importance as a director' (Slide 1970, 102)[7]. This is even more obvious when compared with a much less 'masterly' film such as *How Men Propose* (1913) which not only returns in story-style to vaudeville but which displays the sort of exaggerated histrionic style that most directors had managed to modify to some extent by this time. (It is possible that the director was sending up *that* style of acting although there is little in the film to give credence to such an interpretation other than the comic tone of the whole piece.)

It still remains a puzzle from this distance why film makers were able to realize the enormous liberation in narrative construction provided by the cinema's ability to divide up time and space and re-construct them—nearly all the films dating from 1910 onwards in the season are constructed of many more scenes, and of short duration, than could have been considered for the stage—and yet not comprehend how unnecessary it was to have action played out before a fixed camera with lateral stage-bound movement. So *The Vampire* (1913), which has a lengthy plot involving frequent changes of location (between a fixed set of locations nonetheless) and covers a considerable time period often by ellipsis, still follows the pattern in its interior scenes of front-on camera in fixed position and entrances from the side. Is it possible that while Griffith's 'innovations' were teaching cinematic art to other directors, the 'laziness' manifest in his pot-boilers was equally holding them back? Griffith's role as *teacher* is out of the scope of this essay; the idea is, however, intriguing.[8]

On the other hand, there were films which were made totally in exterior locations—*The Water Nymph* (1912) is one such. It doesn't seem unreasonable to think that such films were made out-of-doors because the Keystone Company (this was one of the first films they made) lacked studios. Thus the first two scenes take place outside for no discernible reasons and even in the case of the second (the son prevented from eloping) in the face of all but the flimsiest logic. While the basic plot of older man attracted to young girl outwitted and forced to concede to the marriage of his son to the girl in question was undoubtedly a staple of the vaudeville stage, there are changes wrought upon it by the use of exteriors. The most obvious of these are the shots taken of Mabel Normand cavorting in the water, diving from a diving board. Bathing belles, like comic cops, were to become a staple of Sennett films. The implication, then, is that the possibility of an aquatic location inspired the story (old hat as it might have been at the bottom line) rather than the other way around. It may be that exterior locations were not simply in lieu of studio sets; even later when Sennett had a studio of his own (which he was quite capable of sending up in his own comedies), the lure of the outdoors remained seemingly irresistible. It provided not simply places but *possibilities*.

A certain wariness needs to be taken when extrapolating from exterior scenes in early American film to an argument that suggests that the film-makers had some concept of the narrative and/or scenic cinematic potential of landscape. *The Girl of the Golden West* (1915) opens with a panoramic view of a wagon train winding its way through the Sierra Madre Mountains. Comparable with panoramic views from Griffith's films, it seems to be an inspired cinematic moment of locating figures in the landscape with all the mythic connotations which would become more fixed as the Western genre flourished in the hot-house conditions of the studio system of Hollywood production. It would appear, however, that the director, Cecil B. de Mille, was not exercising a cinematic eye but simply putting onto film almost verbatim as it were the very opening *The Girl of the Golden West* as when it was originally staged in the theatre by David Belasco:

> Perhaps the most striking of all the mobile, camera-affecting stagings occurs in the Prologue to *The Girl of the Golden West*. Belasco rolls a painted backdrop in a lengthy 'pan' down from a peak in the Sierras, from mountain slope to a cabin, down a footpath to a miner's camp, then 'trucks' into the exterior of the Polka Saloon… The stage then fades to black. With the fade-in the set is the saloon's interior, and action commences. (Fell 1986, 21)

15

Other than for the fact of the opening 'prologue' of the film version being filmed in a real location rather than being a moving painted backdrop, and thus having not only the veracity of actual landscape but having 'movement' in the form of men and animals, and other than for a brief cut in this panoramic shot to show a family mourning at a rough-and-ready graveside as the cavalcade of covered wagons pass by, the two prologues, stage and screen, are almost identical. Here the theatre has not only dominated the shape of the narrative that follows, much of which takes place in a limited number of stage-like sets, but has, in fact, provided the inspiration for the exterior scenes as well. It is perhaps worth noting at this point that *The Girl of the Golden West* does point to the fact that 'legitimate' theatre rather than vaudeville was the more important source of inspiration for film narrative in form and content.

Instead of what would otherwise seem to be a film adaptation of a play in which the landscape has been used to *open out* (i.e., make cinematic) the essential theatricality of the piece, *The Girl of the Golden West* is a film which largely puts onto the screen that which has previously been held back because of the limitations of the stage: panoramic environmental reality. Arguably *opening out* still occurs: around the scene in the stage coach hold-up and the subsequent movement of groups of men on horseback through the landscape. But this attempt to permit the cinema to do that which theatre with all its artifice can only suggest—have real landscapes with 'real' action within them— is, surprisingly, undercut by a shot in the cabin when, in a 'cut-away' set similar to that in *The False Friend,* both the main room and the attic above are shown together—an essential stage-bound convention[9] and one which the film itself reveals as unnecessary when, a few moments later, it adopts a camera angle from above showing both the attic and, through gaps in the floor of the attic, the action below. (This shot stands out even more so since it is one of the few occasions, if not the *only* occasion that the camera deserts its straight-on, eye-level view point.)

A far more modest film which shows, however, a closer link between environment and narrative is *Maiden and Men,* (1912). Somewhat like *The Water Nymph,* this film *is* shot entirely out-of-doors, even some scenes which need not have been so. Although an overly-simplistic morality tale and one in which the moral has little to do with the setting, it nonetheless reveals interesting links between the landscape and the shape taken by the narrative. This is particularly true of the opening sequences in which the isolation of the girl's home is demonstrated, not simply by scenic panoramas (although at one level these sequences are *just* that) but by linking the environment to the (foolish) romantic notions that the girl has about 'love'. Coupled by the titles 'Will I find my love o'er the sea' and 'Or in the mountains', the panoramic views of sea and mountains take on diegetic meaning: they are signs of the isolation the girl suffers from, and they are sources for the romantic novel-inspired love she seeks. Unfortunately, *Maiden and Men* fails to capitalise on the possibilities of its opening sequences and wanders into a hackneyed, and not entirely comprehensible, parable something along the lines of the Prodigal Daughter together with a confused warning about aroused women's sexuality. One wonders a little about the western ranch setting with its groups of cowboys standing about in the background; there is a nagging feeling that Allan Dwan, the director, may have wanted to say something about Western/masculine existence but the melodrama got in the way.[10] As it stands, the ranch settings are no more than this—settings—in much the same way as *The Miller's Daughter* some seven years earlier. They may have been sufficiently novel to please the contemporary audience, of course, and to have acted something like a new plate upon which to serve the same old recipe.

A more satisfactory mix of interior and exterior exists in *Who Pays? Episode Seven; 'Blue Blood and Yellow'* (1915), although even here there is a sense in which the exteriors serve more as visually interesting settings, rather than as inspiration for the action that takes place within them. The one exception to that generalization is, perhaps, when the heroine falls from a ledge and slips down the side of a mountain. Placing the heroine in this 'perils of Pauline' situation is only truly possible with use of the available environment—especially once the aesthetic of realism/verisimilitude had been widely embraced by early film makers. By 1915, it would have been inconceivable that a set such as the paper-maché water-fall and bridge used in the suicide scene in *The Miller's Daughter* would have sufficed in *Who Pays?*. The environment then serves to provide a space, an appropriate space for heroics, for the true man to reveal his manliness. The environment in *Who Pays?*, underutilized as it is, does provide an early instance of the narrative opposition nature/culture which is to become a dominant structuring opposition in many Hollywood films but especially the Western. The 'true-blue' hero is defined by and through his relationship with and place in the natural environment; the villain (almost a cardboard cut-out theatrical melodrama villain—he doesn't quite get around to twirling his moustaches) is defined both by his place within the city environment and by his mis-fit in the mountain environment, *Who Pays?* is essentially a theatrical melodrama but one taking on the form, through its serial production and exhibition, of a sort of prototype for the television soap operas as yet half-a-century away. It does not capitalize on the scenic possibilities (as Griffith might have done) of its mountain environment in which part of its action takes place other, and with the exception of the one exciting rescue scene, might as well have taken place anywhere. But it again demonstrates the curious ambiguity which I have discussed in relation to other films of the relation of the theatrical and the cinematic in early American films. Nearly all interior scenes are shot in single head-on camera angle with characters entering and exiting 'stage right' and 'stage left'. Although in the exterior scenes, the camera still tends to take on a head-on point of view (but not exclusively so), movement of characters is much freer—they move towards and way from the camera, even passing it. The environment sometimes 'insists' on changing camera angles and positions—e.g. a series of high angle shots of a group of characters riding down the mountain, or the necessity to shoot the 'falling off the mountain' scene from the side. The 'lessons' do not seem to have been translated back into studio shooting practices. The existence and use of literal off-screen space behind the camera does not seem to have prompted the recognition of or 'creation' of a similar, implied off-screen space in the studio.

The final film of the season, *Young Romance* (1915) displays all these rigid theatrical conventions still at work. The story is straight theatre: a girl and a boy, neither (improbably) aware of each other existence despite working in the same department store, both decide to fulfil their romance magazine-inspired fantasies of moving in the upper circles by spending one week at a leisure resort for the rich and famous. Of course, they find not magazine romance but each other—eventually and after many complications. Although the story flits about between a number of locations, and indeed between a number of characters, the sets remain just that, *sets*—with the camera still taking its fixed gaze through the invisible but inescapable proscenium arch (albeit that cinematic practice had by this time 'permitted' the camera to be normatively somewhat closer than the existence of a real proscenium arch might have allowed). There is little editing within scenes even while there is considerable cross-cutting between scenes (especially in the opening sequences which parallel the similar existence and aspirations of the films hero and heroine). The film really only comes to 'life', in a cinematic way, when the action moves into real locations. Even something as simple as shooting on the veranda of a hotel forces the makers to require action to move diagonally across the screen rather than the theatrical side-to-side action of the studio scenes. At the same time, the image 'opens out', taking in action in depth; there is a background in which people are seen to exist and move. The characters, little more than comic theatrical characters, also seem to come to life when placed in real locations. The beach where the girl and boy meet for the first time provides an authenticity to their characters previously missing. He is seen at first dodging the waves running up the sand but these same waves, having 'trapped' the girl on a rock, will provide an environmentally-inspired gag as he at first continues to try and avoid getting wet *and* rescue the girl. Even the villain (another moustachioed nasty) becomes slightly more 'human' in the location scenes where he abducts the heroine and maroons her on a 'desert' island. Perhaps slightly more attuned to the possibilities of using the environment than, say, *The Girl of the Golden West,* it may also be that, like a number of other films in this season, the great outdoors were used not because they inspired the narrative but because they were there—and they were cheap. The interiors were, to judge by the wind-blown props, shot on an open-air stage, indicating the Lasky organization was not yet in a financial position to own purpose-built film stages.

Overall, it is tempting to re-title this essay, 'The Ignored Environment'. The grip of the theatre is so evident for the most part in these films that it is difficult not to feel that these early film makers seemed blind to possibilities for use of the environment that were right before their eyes. But hard and fast conclusions should be avoided. It is difficult to know from this distance in time just how representative of *typical* film practice this season of film may be. But even more difficult is to try and assess from the evidence of the *films themselves* the conditions of their production, to tell, in other words, what other factors— economic, industrial, indeed environmental—may have affected their choice of subject matters *as well as* their choice of how, when and where they would shoot those stories. What does remain tantalisingly apparent though is that some of the aspects of the way in which environment was to influence future film form and future film narratives can be seen, if fleetingly, in some of these films: the use of scenery for epic spectacle, the setting up of the thematic opposition of nature and culture, the opportunity for action-dominated scenarios, and, perhaps, most importantly in the short-term, for the development from the simple chase film of a unique, and uniquely cinematic, comic form. The grip of the theatre on the imaginations and the 'industrial' practices of the early film makers, combined with economics, led American cinema to seek authenticity *through* rather than *despite* artifice, and to re-create the environment with studio stages. For all that, the environment, though often marginalised, would not be denied. These early films reveal that much at least.

NOTES

1. Details of individual files screened in this season of films are available in the Filmography at the conclusion of this essay.
2. The film I am thinking of here is *The Music* Box, made in 1932 and thus a sound film, but it was in turn a remake of a silent film made by Laurel and Hardy in 1927, *Hats Off,* which worked the same gag but with a washing machine rather than a piano.
3. American Mutoscope and Biograph Company.

4. Kristin Thompson cites research by Robert G. Allen which indicates that 'audiences regretted to some extent the replacement of scenics and topicals by narratives' which was taking place right around the time of the release of this film (Bordwell, Staiger and Thompson 1985, 161). The increase in demand for more footage may also account for the length of the unbroken 'shot' from the locomotive.

5. This California studio is described in some detail in Henderson (1970, 36ff).

6. For example, the idea of actually including a battle in any of his civil war films does not seem to have occurred to Griffith—or at least been executed by him—until *The Battle* (1911). Whether this was because Griffith failed to perceive of landscape as anything beyond 'authentic' background, or the logistics and economics of the cinematic battle were too overwhelming prior to this, cannot now be ascertained with any certainty.

7. Apfel directed the camera work in de Mille's *The Squaw Man* (1914)—another adaptation of a well-known stage play—and went onto direct a number of films for the Lasky Company about the same time, according to MacGowan (1965, 163 and 168).

8. Griffith's position in the history of the development of film language and film narrative has been re-assessed. For example, Kristin Thompson makes a convincing case for the need to look to wider causes than simply Griffith's 'genius' for explanations as to how, when and why changes in film narrative came about in the so-called 'primitive' period of cinema history (Bordwell, Staiger and Thompson 1985, 157ff).

9. This particular theatrical device seems to have had a tenacious grasp on life so to speak. Even long after the ruling aesthetic of realism had established itself firmly in Hollywood, and authentically constructed and decorated sets were treated (by the camera) as if they had the three-dimensional, concrete integrity of real buildings, there were occasions when the theatrical convention of the wall that-is-and-isn't there appeared in films. This seems to have been particularly the case with directors whose styles leaned towards mobile camera-work. For example, *Caught*, directed by Max Ophuls in 1949, contains several instances where the camera 'violates' the verisimilitude of sets in this way, the most notable (and noticeable) being when it follows (by tracking parallel with) the heroine's husband as he enters her East End apartment from the corridor outside, and then, at the end of the sequence, reverses the camera movement as they both come out of the apartment into the corridor. The camera in each case passes not through the door but 'through' the wall. This contrasts instructively with the famous scene in *Citizen Kane* (1941) in which the camera 'respects' the solidity of the 'El Rancho' set when, in an ambitious crane shot it passes through a large neon sign and into the club 'through' a plate glass skylight. The actual 'passing through' of the latter is accomplished by a rapid dissolve accompanied with a simultaneous 'flash of lightning'. An interesting variant appears in Hitchcock's *The Lodger* (1926) where a man pacing the floor is shot from below—actually through a sheet of glass. This does not violate the verisimilitude of the set so much as suggest an impossible angle—but an appropriately expressionistic angle in the context of the file's aesthetic style.

20

10. There is a noticeable tinge of misogyny in the whole piece, or at the very least, an undertone that male grouping is much more positive than any 'silly' romantic man/woman pairings. This, too, would become a convention of the Western as it evolved.

BIBLIOGRAPHY

Bordwell, David, Staiger, Janet and Thompson, Kristin. *The Classical Hollywood Cinema: Film Style & Mode of Production to 1960.* New York: Columbia University Press, 1985.

Ellis, Jack C. *A History of Film,* second edition. Englewood Cliffs, NJ: Prentice-Hall, Inc., 1985.

Fell, John L. ed. *Film Before Griffith.* Berkeley: University of California, 1986.

----- 1986. *Film and the Narrative Tradition.* Berkeley: University of California, 1983.

Henderson, Robert M. *D. W. Griffith: The Years at Biograph.* New York: Farrar, Straus and Qiroux, 1970.

MacGowan, Kenneth. *Behind the Screen: The History and Techniques of the Motion Picture.* New York: Delta, 1965.

McArthur, Colin. Underworld Films. London: Martin Secker & Warburg/British Film Institute, 1972.

Mitchell, Edward. 'Apes and Essences: Some Sources of Significance in American Gangster Films,' *Wide Angle,* No. 1, 18-23. Reprinted in Barry Keith Grant, ed. 1986. *Film Genre Reader.* Austin: University of Texas, 1976.

Musser, Charles. 'The American Vitagraph, 1897-1901: Survival and Success in a Competitive Industry', in John G. Fell, ed. *Film Before Griffith.* Berkeley: University of California, 1983.

Slide, Anthony. *Early American Cinema.* New York: Barnes & Co 1970

Wagenknecht, Edward, *The Movies in the Age of Innocence.* New York: Ballantine Books, 1971.

FILMOGRAPHY

Program I: An Age of Entertainments

Annabelle Butterfly Dance (Edison Manufacturing Company. 1896). Photographed by W.K.L. Dickson and William Heise. With Annabelle Moore.

Annabelle Serpentine Dance (Edison. 1895). Photographed by W.K.L. Dickson and William Heise. With Annabelle Moore.

Annabelle Butterfly Dance (Edison. 1896). With Annabelle Moore.

Serpentine Dance (Edison, 1896).

The Passion Play of Oberammergau (Select Scenes): Salome's Dance,' 'The Messiah's Entry into Jerusalem.' and 'The Ascension' (Eden Musee, 1898). Produced by Richard Hollaman and Albert Eaves.

The Battle of Manila Bay (American Vitagraph Company. 1898). Produced by J. Stuart Blackton and Albert E. Smith.

Soldiers at Play (William Selig, 1898).

Raising Old Glory over Morro Castle (Vitagraph. 1899). Produced by J. Stuart Blackton and Albert E. Smith.

Burglar on the Roof (Vitagraph, 1898). Photographed by Albert E. Smith. With J. Stuart Blackton as the burglar.

A Visit to the Spiritualist (Vitagraph, 1899). Photographed by Albert E. Smith and J. Stuart Blackton.

The Tramp's Dream (Sigmund J. Lubin, 1899). Produced by John F. Frawley and Jacob Blair Smith.

Searching Ruins on Broadway, Galveston, for Dead Bodies (Vitagraph, 1900). Produced by J. Stuart Blackton and Albert E. Smith.

Scenes of the Wreckage from the Waterfront (Lubin, 1900). Photographed by J. Blair Smith.

Beheading the Chinese Prisoner (Lubin. 1900). Produced by John F. Frawley and Jacob Blair Smith.

How They Rob Men in Chicago (American Mutoscope and Biograph Company, 1900). Produced by Wallace McCutcheon.

An Unexpected Knockout (A.M.B.C., 1901). Produced by Wallace McCutcheon.

He Forgot His Umbrella (A.M.B.C., 1901). Produced by Wallace McCutcheon.

A Mighty Tumble (A.M.B.C., 1901). Photographed by James Congdon.

Next! (A.M.B.C., 1903). Produced by Wallace McCutcheon and Frank Marion.

Smashing a Jersey Mosquito (Edison, 1902). Produced and photographed by Edwin S. Porter.

The Burning of Durland's Riding Academy (Edison, 1902). Photographed by Jacob Blair Smith or Edwin S. Porter.

Electrocuting an Elephant (Edison, 1903). Photographed by Jacob Blair Smith or Edwin S. Porter.

What Happened on Twenty-third Street, New York City (Edison, 1901). Photographed by Edwin S. Porter.

Trapeze Disrobing Act (Edison. No date). Produced and photographed by Edwin S. Porter.

What Happened in the Tunnel (Edison. 1905). Photographed by Edwin S. Porter. With Gilbert M. 'Bronco Billy' Anderson.

Pull down the Curtains, Suzie (A.M.B.C., 1904). Produced by Wallace McCutcheon.

Meet Me at the Fountain (Lubin. 1904). With female impersonator Gilbert Saroni as the Successful Woman.

Rube and Mandy at Coney Island (Edison. 1903). Produced and photographed by Edwin S. Porter.

The European Rest Cure (Edison. 1904). Produced and photographed by Edwin S. Porter.

Program 2: Pleasures and Pitfalls

Interior N.Y. Subway. 14th Street to 42nd Street (A.M.B.C., 1905). Photographed by G.W. 'Billy' Bitzer.

Coney Island at Night (Edison. 1905). Photographed by Edwin S. Porter.

The Hold-up of the Rocky Mountain Express (A.M. B.C., 1906). Produced by Frank Marion. Photographed by G.W. 'Billy' Bitzer.

The Miller's Daughter (Edison, 1905). Directed by Edwin S. Porter and Wallace McCutcheon. Produced and photographed by Edwin S. Porter.

Getting Evidence (Edison, 1906). Produced by Edwin S. Porter and Wallace McCutcheon. Photographed by Edwin S. Porter.

Photographing a Female Crook (A.M.B.C., 1904). Produced by Wallace McCutcheon.

The Black Hand (A.M.B.C., 1906). Produced by Frank Marion. Photographed by G.W. 'Billy' Bitzer.

Foul Play; Or, a False Friend (Vitagraph Company of America,). With Leo Delaney and Florence Turner.

The Thieving Hand (Vitagraph, 1908).

Terrible Ted (A.M.B.C., 1907). Directed by Joseph Golden. Photographed by G.W. 'Billy' Bitzer.

Three American Beauties (Edison, 1906). Produced by Edwin S. Porter and Wallace McCutcheon. Photographed by Edwin S. Porter.

Program 3: America in Transition

First Mail Delivery by Aeroplane (Powers, 1911).

Ancient Temples of Egypt (Kalem Company, 1912). Directed by Sidney Olcott. Photographed by George Hollister. Shot at Luxor, Egypt.

Princess Nicotine: Or, the Smoke Fairy (Vitagraph, 1909). Produced by J. Stuart Blackton. Photographed by Tony Galidio.

A Tin-type Romance (Vitagraph, 1910). Directed by Larry Trimble. With Jean (the Vitagraph dog), Leo Delaney, and Florence Turner.

A Friendly Marriage (Vitagraph, 1911). Directed by Van Dyke Brooke.

The Usurer (Biograph Company. 1910). Directed by D.W. Griffith. Photographed by G.W. 'Billy' Bitzer.

Winning an Heiress (Essanay Film Manufacturing Company, 1911).

The Dream (independent Moving Picture Company. 1911). Directed by Thomas Ince. Script by Mary Pickford. With Marv Pickford. Owen Moore.

The Informer (Biograph, 1912). Produced and directed by D.W. Griffith. Photographed by G.W. Bitzer. With Mary Pickford, Henry B. Walthall, Lionel Barrymore, and Lillian Gish.

Program 4: Domestic Life

The Old Actor (Biograph, 1912). Directed by D.W. Griffith. Photographed by G.W. Bitzer. With Mary Pickford.

The Passer-by (Edison, 1912). Directed by Oscar C. Apfel.

The Water Nymph (Keystone Company, 1912). Produced and directed by Mack Sennett. With Mack Sennett, Mabel Normand.

One Is Business; the Other Crime (Biograph. 1912). Directed by D.W. Griffith. Photographed by G.W. Bitzer. With Blanche Sweet.

How Men Propose (Crystal, 1913).

A House Divided (Solax, 1913). Produced and directed by Alice Guy-Blache.

The Vampire (Kalem. 1913). Directed by Robert Vignola, Photographed by George Hollister. With Alice Hollister as Sybil, the vampire.

Program 5: The Frontier Spirit

Maiden and Men (American Film Manufacturing Company, 1912). Directed by Allan Dwan. With Pauline Bush.

The Ruse (New York Motion Picture Company, 1915). Scenario by A.P. Johnson and Thomas Ince. Photographed by Robert Doeran. With William S. Hart.

The Girl of the Golden West (Jesse L. Lasky Feature Play Company, 1915). Directed by Cecil B. DeMille. Scenario by DeMille, based on the play by David Belasco. With Mabel Van Buren.

Program 6: Love and Misadventure

Dreamy Dud: He Resolves Not to Smoke (Essanay, 1915). Directed by Wallace A. Carlson. Animation.

Who Pays? Episode Seven: 'Blue Blood and Yellow' (Balboa Amusement Company, 1915). Directed by Harry Harvey. With Ruth Roland and Henry King.

Young Romance (Lasky, 1915). Produced and directed by George Melford. Written by William deMille, based on his play, after a story by O. Henry. Photographed by Walter Stradling. With Edith Taliaferro, Tom Forman.

OF HORSES AND CENTENARIES: NOTES ON ONE HUNDRED YEARS OF AUSTRALIAN CINEMA

The thirty-sixth running of the Melbourne Cup took place in 1896, as usual, on the second Tuesday (the 3rd) in November at Flemington Race Course. In addition to the racing itself, the social rituals that had gathered around the event since the 1860s were indulged. Notably, Melbourne's social elite and those whose aspired to or wished to be thought of as belonging to this class be-sported themselves in their fashionable finery, particularly the women, of whom the prevailing attitude as that they had no interest in the masculine pursuit of racing but overwhelming interest in the fashions of that year. The bulk of the 95,000 who attended were more ordinary citizens of Melbourne and further afield, prepared to enjoy the spectacles both on and off the race track itself. The race was won by "Newhaven", ridden by H. Gardiner, both of whom won the Melbourne Cup for the first (and only) time.

There was at least one other unique occurrence at the 1896 Melbourne Cup. This was signified by the presence of a motion picture camera for the first but far from only time. This particular camera was Lumière cinématographe, invented, manufactured and owned by Lumière Brothers of Lyon, France, and was operated by a cameraman (although the term was not then in common use) employed by them, a Frenchman, Marius Sestier. Sestier was but one of a number of operators employed by the Lumière brothers to travel the world, shooting films (*actualités*) which were then returned to France to become part of the Lumière library of exhibition films but which were also, where opportunities presented themselves, exhibited to paying audiences in their country of origin.[1] With Sestier at the 1896 Melbourne Cup, and possibly the driving force behind his presence and 'directing' the filming, was an Australian society photographer H. Walter Barnett. The cinematic result of the afternoon's shooting was ten short films (thus about ten minutes of film at silent film speed: approximately 16 frames per second) which cover the event quite comprehensively from the arrival of racegoers at the train station through to the winner and including the start and finish of the race, the arrival of the Governor of Victoria and, thanks to Barnett's efforts, plenty of footage of the fashionable members of the crowd. These films, or some of them at least, were exhibited in a charity screening in Melbourne on November 19, 1986. The films were subsequently screened in Sydney and it may be presumed in other parts of Australia. Indeed, they may well have been seen more widely overseas than in Australia as they were sent to France (or returned there with Sestier in early 1897), where they entered the Lumière catalogue.[2]

There has developed a belief that these films (often discussed as if they were one) were the first ever shot, processed and screened in Australia, and therefore Melbourne Cup Day in 1996 represented the exact moment of the one-hundredth anniversary of Australian cinema. (Strictly speaking, as the Melbourne Cup was run on Tuesday 5th November in 1996, the previous Sunday would have been the actual calendar anniversary day.) It is not clear where the idea comes from that the film of the 1896 Melbourne Cup was the first film shot in Australia. None of the standard histories of Australian film3 make such a claim. Now, due to the excellent and painstaking research undertaken by Chris Long[4], this particular furphy can be laid to rest. While there is a clear cultural attraction to the idea that Australia's first film(s) should be of an event of such popular folk and historical potency, the fact is that the films of the 1896 Melbourne Cup are not the first cinematic films shot in Australia. Indeed they are not even the first motion picture footage of a horse race in Australia. As Long points out, the previous Saturday in 1896, at Flemington racecourse, Sestier and Barnett shot three short films of scenes of the VCR Derby, including footage of the Derby itself.[4]

Further, and no doubt to the disappointment of Melburnians, it is now abundantly clear that Australia's first motion picture film was not of the Melbourne Cup, nor was it shot in Melbourne at all but in Sydney. A couple of weeks prior to the shooting of the Derby and the Melbourne Cup, Sestier, who had been exhibiting Lumière films for or in partnership with Barnett and C. B. Westacott in Sydney, shot a film of passengers disembarking from a ferry at Manly. This film, probably shot on October 25, 1896 and shown in Sydney on October 27, 1896 is thus the first motion picture film shot, processed and exhibited in Australia, and it is from October 25, 1896 that the first one hundred years of Australian cinema ought more properly to be counted. This footage seems to no longer exist.

The shooting, or rather the screening of this film also brought about the first appearance in Australia of one of the great and enduring urban myths associated with the cinema. Chris Long quotes *The Bulletin* of November 14, 1896:

> There is one Sydney man who curses loud and long the cinématographe. In his amiable, husbandly way he took his wife to see the new cin. [*sic*], and in the Sunday embarkation scene at Manly, his better half saw what she believed to be her husband coming ashore with another lady. To be more convinced, she saw the tableau fully half-a-dozen times with the aid of opera glasses. The accused male indignantly denies everything, but, as he cannot prove a complete alibi for that particular Sunday afternoon, and

his wife won't entertain the idea of an 'extraordinary likeness', there is a big storm in the once happy 'ome. The possibilities of the cin. [*sic*] as a worker of mischief to supposedly upright people are great.

Although at first no doubt simply an indulgence in journalistic licence (of what originality is as yet uncertain), the instantaneous appearance and promulgation of this urban myth is fascinating in itself. The myth retained its potency throughout the period in which actuality films become formalised into newsreels and then was substantially revitalised with the arrival of television, especially outside broadcast television. It has a number of variants, of course, notably the one in which an employer sees in the newsreel or television coverage of a sporting event an employee to whom he has given time off (usually to attend a funeral of a close relative). The wife/other woman version remains popular.

Thus, although it was scarcely noticed at the time, October 1996, saw the centenary of two significant events in the history of popular culture in Australia: the first Australian motion picture, and the first public appearance (in Australia, anyway) of one of the cinema's long-serving urban myths. The first truly indigenous narrative motion picture was a few years away—and it was not *The Story of the Kelly Gang* (1905) as is often thought. Thanks to the researches of Chris Long, that honour can be given to a film produced by the Salvation Army in 1903, *Sensational Rescue from Drowning at Queenscliff*. Even so, and not ignoring *Highlights of the Musical Comedy "Florodora"*, produced in 1901, or the more famous biblical-narrative film inserts in the Salvation Army's *Soldiers of the Cross* (1901), *The Story of the Kelly Gang*, with its quintessential Australian subject matter, may well prove to be the first Australian fictional motion picture to contain a fully-structured narrative story, and thus (purists notwithstanding) the more appropriate date for celebrating 100 years of indigenous Australian cinema may have to wait until 2005. Especially as the opportunity for a suitably commemorative ferry ride to Manly on October 25, 1996 passed unseized.

NOTES

1. Or sometimes in between. Sestier, for example, gave exhibitions of Lumière films and perhaps some he had shot in India on board the ship that carried him to Australia in August 1896.
2. Copies were eventually obtained by the National Film Archive in Australia in. It seems that not all the films were exhibited as a set as some did not receive a Lumière catalogue number and at least one has a catalogue number at considerable variance with the others which are in numerical sequence for the most part.

3. Shirley and Adams, Eric Reade, Pike and Cooper. In my own, *Images of Australia* (1991), I hedge my bet by stating that this footage is the "earliest extant" Australian motion picture footage.

4. Published progressively in the pages of *Cinema Papers* as "Australia's First Films: Facts and Fables" since issue no.91, 1993. The particulars of the filming of the 1896 Melbourne Cup are in "Part Three: Local Production Begins", *Cinema Papers*, no. 93, May 1993, pp 34-41, 60-61. Any scholar delving into the early history of cinema in Australia must register a debt of gratitude to Chris Long for his careful and detailed research and to *Cinema Papers* for their publishing of it. I am pleased to acknowledge that debt here.

MUSICAL NOTES

DANCING THE REDS AWAY: THREE COLD WAR MUSICALS

INTRODUCTION

The ways in which the Cold War (which here I am reducing to the period 1945-1960, although historically it existed from 1945 to the fall of Soviet communism, in the late 1980s) affected Hollywood have been well documented, although they can still be a source of controversy and argument. This was witnessed as recently as two years ago when Eli Kazan, a noted Hollywood director who was 'tainted' by the testimony he gave to the House Un-American Activities Committee (HUAC) naming names of 'communists', was awarded a Lifetime Achievement award at the Academy Awards. His award was by no means universally acclaimed and many of those present refused to join in the applause; old bitterness remained, positions were taken, even by those too young to have been involved.

While the ways in which the industry and individuals within the industry acted and reacted to Cold War conditions and politics are recorded in studies, biographies and histories, there has been less attention paid to the way in which the films themselves, the products of that industry and those individuals, were affected by the Cold War, in both its manifest and its veiled socio-cultural conditions and perceptions. Such work as there has been has often, perhaps too often, focussed on those films which directly addressed the more obvious 'issues' of the immediate Cold War, namely communism in both its international and domestic 'existence'. There were a small number of such films, made it is usually argued by Hollywood studios in order to directly counter any impression arising from the HUAC inquiries and other right-wing sources that Hollywood was soft on communism. An example of this source of examination can be found in Leo K. Adler's *The Red Image: American Attitudes toward Communism in the Cold War Era*[1]. In a chapter headed 'The Counter-Subversive Screen: Hollywood and the Red Image' Adler discusses, albeit briefly, a number of 'anti-communist' films but the films he mentions all display overt (and often remarkably unsubtle) wearing of their anti-communist credentials on the their sleeves.

It is necessary however look further or deeper to find the effects of the Cold War in other films than those which are 'about' the Cold War. In fact, to assume or imply no matter how inadvertently that the only way in which the Cold War was examined in Hollywood films was in those films which advertised themselves as engaged in such an examination, is to be misled into thinking that what these films 'say' is all Hollywood had to 'say' about the matter. It is also essential to recognise that the Cold War had, to put it broadly and perhaps over simplistically, two dimensions: the perceptions which America and Americans had (or were provided) of the Soviet Union and communism—an outward dimension—and the effect the idea of a Cold War had upon the American psyche—an inward dimension.

Given the atmosphere in Hollywood during the period of the Cold War—witch-hunts, blacklists, fear of accusations of communism or communist influence, investigations by HUAC and others—it is scarcely surprising that the majority of motion pictures produced (barring those with a deliberate, and usually crass, anti-communist content) were anodyne and almost self-consciously uncontroversial in any social sense: to comment in any even mildly interrogatory way upon American life and society was seen as being 'communist' or un-American. The studio executives had 'collaborated' with HUAC and contributed by their public actions to the general anti-communist hysteria, many actors, directors and others had given 'friendly testimony' supported and even contributed to the blacklisting of fellow actors, writers, directors and others (often without justification, but in contradiction to the vaunted American ideals of 'liberty' and 'freedom' in any case). Even future President of the USA, Ronald Reagan while in 'training' as the president of the Screen Actor's Guild 'insured the blacklist was fully enforced against his fellow actors'.[2]

Films which seemed to contain a 'social message' were subject to scrutiny and often condemned just because they had a social message—unless it was one which affirmed (or could be interpreted to affirm) the basically reactionary notion of 'American ideals' which were wielded as weapons against anything 'different'. Musicals, the (assumed) least likely form of motion pictures to contain disturbing or even thoughtful reflections on American society or culture (let alone anything remotely subversive) were pretty unlikely candidates for examination for 'un-American' content. And probably pretty unlikely candidates in the first instance for anything 'Un-American' to find its way into these structures, surface or sub-textual. These seems little evidence that anyone associated primarily with musicals was suspect except, oddly enough, Gene Kelly, despite his very screen personas being far more those of an 'all-American guy' than the more urbane and (suspiciously) Europeanised Fred Astaire. (Suspicion fell on Kelly, not for his screen roles, but for his initial support for some of the Hollywood accused.)

The Cold War was, in the USA at least, really two 'wars'. Firstly, the international 'war' of foreign policy, foreign relations and nuclear bluff and brinkmanship together with 'traditional' military violence as in Korea, the Lebanon and Guatemala. Secondly, the internal war within the United States, a civil war, where the rhetoric of the ideology of 'democracy' (as completely distinct and oppositional to communism as it was imagined) was used, socioneurotically, to conduct warfare against difference. It was a war for the American psyche. 'Difference' of almost any sort was the 'enemy', but basically difference was what was or could be interpreted as distinct, contrary, or tangential to a conservative or reactionary ideology, and thus anything different was demonized by being labelled 'un-America' and or 'communistic'.

What is interesting to try and locate in Cold War era films is not out-and-out or even thinly disguised representations of communist and 'subversion' but films which were structured narratively around difference, especially around social difference. The difference of being literally alien was often explored in regard to Horror and Science-fiction films and has often being explored in studies of those genres.[3] More subtle forms of being different have been located in examinations of film noir, although film noir's dominant reflection of the Cold War era is in its representation of paranoia, a clear 'effect' on the American psyche of the conditions and perceptions of the Cold War.

Social difference—the difference manifest through different sets of values and different social and even personal behaviour—is what many Cold War era films unconsciously react to, reflected and represented within their narratives and their thematics. And within this representations, and often underpinning them were the two conditions of the domestic or 'civil' Cold War in the USA: irrational fear (often inchoate, often hysterical, nearly always paranoid) and violence. This is not a study of history but it does not seem to be drawing an impossibly long bow to suggest that violence as a social and personal solution, if not exactly engendered as cultural philosophy during the Cold War in the USA, certainly was greatly enhanced and profoundly publically and ideologically confirmed then. The latter condition, violence, may seem at odds with the normal temper and condition of the Musical, but I would like to consider its place in two of the three films I am examining here as Cold War Musicals: *Brigadoon* (Vincente Minnelli, 1954) and *Seven Brides for Seven Brothers* (Stanley Donen, 1954). The primary aspect of Cold War culture that I find reflected and represented in these films is, however, difference. This is the motivating narrative factor on all three films—fear and violence are however the precursor to and result of this condition of difference in the previously named two films.[4]

SILK STOCKINGS

Of the three Musicals which I suggest are worth analysis as representing in some way or another the Cold War (or Cold War attitudes, sensibilities and perceptions, *Silk Stockings* (Rouben Mamoulian, 1957) can be discussed first and most easily. *Silk Stockings* is a film which concerns itself, in ways which are blatantly obvious, with the external aspects of the Cold War (from the American point of view). The anti-Communism of the film is directed outwards, at the

Soviet Union, rather than inwards, at American society. It is unconcerned with 'Un-American' attitudes or behaviours; rather with 'anti-American' attitudes and behaviours. These anti-American attitudes and behaviours only exist in *Silk Stockings* as a contrast to the positive views of America (and capitalism which is defined as Americanism) and in order to be dismissed as mistaken, delusional, and fragile when faced with the 'truth'. They are, moreover, an aspect of the general anti-communist/anti-Russian ideology of the film, which extends beyond simply representing communism as being anti-American but details its many other 'flaws' as well. These flaws are, of course, defects in the communism system, the communist way of life, because they are, the film implies, precisely what does not happen in America under the capitalist system and the American Way of life.

Silk Stockings, although produced in the fifties at the height of anti-communist hysteria in the USA, is actually a relatively straightforward adaptation of an earlier film, *Ninotchka* (Ernst Lubitch, 1939) which contained basically the same attitude towards the fundamental differences between communism and capitalism as they impose themselves (or are imposed) on individuals. *Ninotchka* was first adapted successfully as a Broadway musical in the mid-1950s[5] (where, presumably, its anti-communist sentiment was felt to be appealing) and then the Broadway version was further adapted for the film version of *Silk Stockings*. What has been retained from 1939 to 1957 is, as Adler says of *Ninotchka,* its anticommunist message in which logic, reason, ideology and the artificial structures of twentieth century thought all yield before the sweep of human emotion. Western natural openness and feeling are sharply contrasted with Communist repression and denial of all emotion except devotion to the cause.[6]

Expression of emotion is, arguably, the key defining characteristic of the Musical; song and dance, no matter whether integrated to the narrative or justified by the diegesis, are almost inevitably demonstrations of emotional states, personal and communal. A Musical which accepts as a given the perception, the ideology, that communism represses emotion, or channels it only in high proscribed directions at the service of the state, is bound then to only too easily demonstrate the desirability of a 'system' in which emotions are free to be expressed. The music (the expression) is all on the side of the free; how can whatever 'side' is identified with this not clearly be the morally, philosophically and emotionally desirable one? With one exception, all the musical numbers in *Silk Stockings* 'belong' to the West, and that one exception, 'The Red Blues', which takes place within a 'typical' crowded, shared accommodation in Moscow, is itself an expression of Western 'ideas' brought back from outside. That it is not acceptable behaviour is indicated when the singing and dancing, which has spread throughout the tenement is abruptly halted when a fellow-sharer who is obviously a dyed-in-the-wool communist (and probably informer), enters.

Repression of emotion (which seems more Freudian than Marxist) is not the only way in which *Silk Stockings* is anti-communist. Of equal, if not greater importance, is the contrasting materialism of the West and the East, and this is significant given the timing of the film. Post-war America, in which it might be argued expression of emotions were equally proscribed—or there were attempts to apply proscription or restriction—was embracing materialism in the form of consumerism as never before. It is the clear abundance of these in the West, and the opportunities that exist to easily take advantage of them, that is contrasted with their lack in Russia. The most important (in the thematic sense) number in *Silk Stockings* is the 'Silk Stockings' number itself. An extended balletic solo by Ninotchka, it reveals the extraordinary potency of the materialism of the West to totally overpower the entrenched ideology of Communism which Ninotchka has heretofore not simply represented but seemingly embodied, physically and mentally. In what is an elegant 'strip-tease', Ninotchka, alone her hotel room in Paris, discards the mundane Russian 'uniform' she has worn to the point, and brings out of hiding places a series of 'feminine' garments—silk stockings, underwear, shoes, dress, hat—which she dons, and, as the choreography dictates, delights in. (The film is silent on how she manages to pay for them, or the expensive hotel suites she and the three commissars occupy in Paris.)

This transformation, in story terms, is not because she no longer wishes to be Russian and/or a communist, although the effect is to make her no longer look or act like one. Tying in with the opposition that the ideology creates between American freedom (of action and of emotion) and Communist repression and denial, this transformation in appearance is linked with Ninotchka's emotional attraction to Steve Cranfield, an American film producer. As Ninotchka 'stands for' Russia and communist, so Steve 'stands for' America and capitalism. This is blatantly stated on many occasions, including sequence where they tour Paris together, each finding ideological reflection in the sites they visit. Of course, the way in which capitalism is expressed by Steve—mainly through interest in excesses of consumerism (expensive jewellery, fashion garments)—it is never given the sense that it is a 'system' in the way communism is. Capitalism, expressed through the irrepressible *joi de vivre* of Steve, is simply 'natural' development of freedom, especially the freedom to express oneself. Indeed, in 'Paris Loves Lovers', the implication is the capitalism exists for the express purpose of providing opportunities for emotional/sexual freedom of expression.

While the anti-communist 'message' is hammered home mainly through the demonstration of excesses of consumerism and through the attractions of being able to engage in free enterprise in order to (easily) afford those excesses—Steve is a film producer who is actually seen 'at work' a couple of times, three absconding Soviet commissars open an expensive nightclub—there is something rather disturbing about the nexus between American freedom and what it can buy. The film's demonstration of consumerism is nearly all through the representation of expensive material goods designed for, although not necessarily designed to be bought by, women. In fact, the consumerism of the West seems to only exist to allow men to 'buy' women, or to allow women to attract, even 'entrap' men. The number 'Satin and Silk' takes place within an expensive fashion salon and serves to allow Peggy Dainton, the American film star to seduce Peter Boroff, the Russian composer whom Steve is attempting to keep in the West. Unlike the three Soviet commissars, ironically sent to get him to return, Peter actually is not interested in defecting, at least not for its own sake, but wishes to remain in the West because (he thinks) it is an opportunity to get his music heard outside the Soviet Union. In a one of those curious moments of contradiction so likely in so many films, a clear criticism of America is made when Peter becomes (justifiably) outraged at the way his music has been Americanised (that is, popularised) out of all recognition. This cultural piracy is denounced by Peter and it is this which sends he and Ninotchka (and the three commissars) back to Russia; that, and the belief by Ninotchka that Steve does not love her, which is linked to this blatant act of American 'free enterprise'. This contradiction is compounded by the way in which, perhaps inadvertently, the film, for all its attack on communism, cedes to it the ground of 'high' culture: Peter's serious music is vulgarised by crass commercialism[7] (and Steve's defence of this sounds desperate rather than convincing but is specifically cited as 'the American way'); Ninotchka is the only one who 'dances' in ballet-style (in the 'Silk Stockings ' number) while all other 'dances' are American Musical style (jazz, tap, ballroom). In terms, then, of what is often considered to be 'civilised'—art and high culture—Russia and Russians seem to be the exemplars, the West and Americans represent art (beauty) 'reduced' to luxury consumer items (jewellery, fashion clothes), and music 'reduced' from classical seriousness to popular triviality.

By and large, through both the narrative and the song-and-dance, *Silk Stockings* confirms what Adler has said of pre-war films, that the Russian characters are 'merely garden-variety westerners' albeit they don't know it or reveal it until the freedom of the West gives them an opportunity to display it. The opportunity extends as well to others who have not been privileged to visit Paris—all the young, vital Muscovites who join in the spirited 'The Red Blues', initiated and inspired by Ninotchka, Peter and the three commissars. The film does not suggest that Russian and communist are synonymous; rather that communism is a system that imposes a repressive ideology and regime on people who would otherwise be indistinguishable from Americans. The American way or life, albeit transposed for purpose of the story to Paris (which is hardly French at all in any meaningful sense), is celebrated through song and dance. Song and dance become political in *Silk Stockings* in ways which are transparent, even self-conscious. Although there would seem to be few if any intellectually tenable points of comparison between *Silk Stockings* and *Cabaret* (Bob Fosse, 1972), in terms of the political 'use' of song and dance, uses that provide a political message within the number as well as through contrasting the 'text' of the number (whether lyrics, music or choreography) with the context (whether narrative or thematic), *Silk Stockings* clearly suggests itself, perhaps subconsciously at the level of production, as a precursor of *Cabaret* and may be other more strident socially conscious Musicals of a later era.

It must be noted, nonetheless, that in *Silk Stockings*, the anti-communist jibes, attitudes and denigrations, for all that they are present as comic, are crude and relentless. Save, that is, for the occasional time out for a distastefully sexist development of the romance between Steve and Ninotchka—many of the 'misunderstandings' of which are based upon her rigidly ridiculous ideological attitudes or her failure to respond in suitable 'feminine' ways (she is not attracted by diamonds and facials—at first). Dance, in the form of dancing with Steve, overcomes all these ideological attitudes and communist brainwashing—as dancing with Fred Astaire as whomsoever always does overcome the specific partners objections in all his films. In *Silk Stockings,* Ninotchka's objections are only partly overcome by dancing with Steve, and as consequence being physically intimate with him. Her ideological objections have to be removed not only by physical seduction ('decadent' American rhythms, dance styles and so forth) but by materialistic seduction (by fetishistic feminine objects, including the eponymous silk stockings).

There is an occasional uneasiness with the politics of *Silk Stocking* (as there often is in many films). It shows itself through the 'over-kill' of its demonstration of the 'badness' of communism (in Russia) and the 'goodness' of capitalism. But it appears momentarily in other places. In Ninotchka's rejection of Steve before she returns to Moscow (from which she has to be 'rescued' by Steve) there is a moment of 'subversion' or contradiction when she rejects him with the words 'It's always your opinion. It is always what you think. Everything I do is wrong and everything you do is right. You leave me nothing of my own'. This might very well be a suitable epigraph for *Silk Stocking*'s approach to its own audience.

Silk Stockings, like all Musicals, is structured around particular dominant binary oppositions. The most important of these is Male : Female (or 'Boy' :

'Girl'), which is the binary opposition that most Musicals set out to resolve by removing the 'conflict' through song and dance, This binary opposition usually favours the Male side. What might be considered subsidiary oppositions follow on and are 'controlled' by the primary Male: Female opposition; one of the most frequent is Spontaneity: Rigid Conformity. This can be seen in *The Pirate* (Vincente Minnelli, 1948), for example, as well as rather obviously in *Silk Stockings*. In *Silk Stockings*, this pattern of binary opposition is furthered by the binaries: Capitalism : Communism; America : Russia. Others might be added, such as Emotionally Expressive: Emotionally Repressed, Freedom : Repression, Individual(ity) : Group, and also in light of my comments about some of the contradictions which perhaps do not show America/capitalism is such a good light, Frivolous : Serious, and Popular Art : High Art.

Thus, following the lead suggested by Jim Kitses' examination of the Western[8], these structural or binary oppositions would form a pattern. (The first two are conventional to the Musical, the others are specific to *Silk Stockings* although they may be found in other Musicals as well).

Male : Female
'Boy' : 'Girl'
Capitalism : Communism
America : Russia
Individual : Group
Freedom : Repression/Oppression
Spontaneous : Rigid Conformity
Emotional expression : Emotional repression
Frivolous : Serious
Popular Art : High Art

I don't wish to here deal with each of these in detail. Instead, I want to take the opposition Capitalism : Communism and its immediate 'subsidiary', America : Russia, and list how the numbers in *Silk Stockings* relate to these.

Number	Performed by	Type	Relationship to Oppositions: Capitalism : Communism America: Russia
'Too Bad, We Can't Go Back to Moscow'	The 3 Commissars, Steve, and 3 'chorus girls'	Comic song leading to ensemble dance	Celebration of seduction powers of the West, especially women and wine.

'Paris Loves Lovers'	Steve (to Ninotchka)	Song – solo	Western 'civilisation' exists for emotional freedom
'Glorious Technicolor'	Peggy and Steve	Song and dance - duet – display/ performance	No immediate relevance (although it may be celebrating technical advances of American film)
'It's a Chemical Reaction, That's All'	Ninotchka (to Steve)	Song – solo	Demonstrates repression of emotion by 'science' under communism.
'I Like the Looks of You'	Steve (to Ninotchka)	Song– solo – leads to dance – duet	Argument for sexual attraction found in individuality (capitalism) and personal attraction, counters emotional repression of communism. Dance expresses freedom.
'Sain and Silk'	Peggy (to Peter)	Song and dance – solo	In favour of materialism/ consumerism – and seduction of Russia composer by sexual freedom of West
'Silk Stockings'	Ninotchka	Solo dance (ballet)	Magnetic/inescapable attraction of Western materialism in form of 'feminine' personal apparel and accessories.
'Without Love'	Ninotchka (to Steve)	Song	Acceptance that capitalism/ individualism frees repressed sexual desires
'Fated to Be Mated'	Steve and Ninotchka	Song leads to dance (latter stage of dance to 'The Looks of You' tune)	Prompted by Ninotchka's claim that in Russia her relationship with Steve would not be permitted – Western freedom emphasised.
'Josephine'	Peggy	Song (as part of film being produced with narrative)	Vulgarisation of (unheard) Russian serious classic music.
'Siberia'	The 3 Commissars	Song and Dance	Reference to arbitrary totalitarian punishment under communism in Russia
'The Red Blues'	Nine, Peter, the 3 Commissars and 'chorus' of Russian men and women	Song and large-scale dance (Production number)	Incursion of West/American values instantly celebrated as demolishing restriction/repression of life under communism.
'The Ritz Roll and Rock'	Steve and chorus line	Dance – production number	Unrelated production number – narratively illogical as Steve is a film producer not a professional dancer

Reprise 'We Can't Go Back to Moscow'	Steve, Ninotchka and the 3 Commissars	Song and Dance	Celebration of triumph of Capitalism over Communism

Silk Stockings is probably the only Cold War Musical to directly concern itself with the politics of the era, the only one to offer representations of communists and communism in an unmediated (except by ideological prejudice) manner. That it did so without any aura of seriousness only confirms that perceptions of communism that it uses so blithely although, as I have indicated, not without an occasional moment where it suggest an uncertainty with its own certainties. That a Musical could be overtly political perhaps also revealed that Musicals could be serious; that Musical did not automatically imply Musical Comedy. Later Musicals would develop this further and Musicals of the later decades would frequently become serious, even tragic (*West Side Story, Camelot, Cabaret,* among others). A propensity for seriousness is not apparent in *Silk Stockings* it is true; indeed, it tends to make frivolous matters which ought to have been treated more seriously, perhaps. In so doing, it directs attention to an aspect of the Cold War Musical which is more fully apparent in *Brigadoon*.

BRIGADOON

Brigadoon would seem to be miles apart from *Silk Stockings*; it barely takes cognizance of the modern, 'real' world at all. Nary a communist as such exists, nor is the idea of communism ever mentioned. It is a fairy tale in the most literal sense. But *Brigadoon* is more typical of the Cold War Musical, or the way in which the Cold War is 'felt' in Musicals of the period than *Silk Stockings*. Firstly, and most obviously, this is because it is not concerned with the external situation of the Cold War but with the internal conditions of the American psyche of the period and some of the external manifestations, the symptoms of that socio-cultural 'psychological' condition.

As Michael Wood, in his flippant way, puts it: 'It's no news to anyone that Americans in the fifties were not as happy as they pretended to be'.[9] Wood, in a chapter entitled 'Darkness in the Dance' offers a case for Gene Kelly's musicals (before *Brigadoon* which he does not mention) as revealing, through Kelly, a deep seated anxiety about the confidence in self and in America Musicals have usually expressed. It is odd that Wood does not cite *Brigadoon* as it seems to be irrefutable proof of his claim of a Kelly (the character is called Tommy Albright) who has the open-faced brashness usually associated with Kelly's brand of all-American male (and masculinity), which at a crucial moment fails him. Fortunately, for the story's happy ending, he recovers his American confidence, indeed to such an extent that it triggers a miracle. But *Brigadoon* touches upon another, seemingly fundamental aspect of the American psyche in the Cold War era that Wood describes in relation to other films. Without, I hope perverting the argument that Wood is making (maybe strengthening it), I want to quote from Wood but substitute *Brigadoon* for the films he cites (*Picnic* [Joshua Logan, 1955], a non-Musical, *It's Always Fair Weather* [Gene Kelly, Stanley Donen, 1955])

> And the loneliness was there in the fifties in [*Brigadoon*]. It was muffled by then other emphasis we chose to give to the film, but we did see its hopeless and frantic gestures, we did hear its angry and embittered words, and this is precisely the function I am proposing for popular movies. They permit us to look without looking at things we can neither face fully nor entirely disavow. We usually don't notice this function, but then it is because we don't notice—because the distress lurking in [*Brigadoon*] merely lurks but never pounces – that these movies work so well as myths. When we see them as myths, it's too late, because we are already living among new myths we have yet to recognise.[10]

Brigadoon's relationship to the Cold War psyche—the internalisation of Cold War fears that so affected the way American thought about and, in many cases, acted towards, each other—is two-fold. The demonstration of this is also a demonstration of how it is that films reflect their times not through their surface narratives or their apparent explicit meanings, but implicitly, or (as is surely the case here) symptomatically. *Brigadoon* especially reveals that contradiction that so often lurks below the surface of popular films. *Brigadoon* supports the Cold War neurosis of American society, that America was threatened by alien doctrines to which the people would have no resistance—the very foundation of reactionary right-wing attacks on Hollywood, that somehow communism would be inculcated into the films and that the audiences would be unable to resist the effects. The same attitude was, of course, applied to almost all aspect of American public and private life. This hysterical fear of communism attributed to it enormous power so persuasion with the corollary that the American people were somehow unable to resist it (why they would find it so attractive was not often spelled out as this may well have questioned the basis of American society). This peculiarly Cold War attitude is offered in *Brigadoon* as an explanation for why Brigadoon itself takes the form that it does—isolated from the real world, save for twenty-four hours every one hundred years. In a lengthy monologue delivered by the village's schoolmaster, it is explained that Scotland, the geographical site of Brigadoon in its earthbound moments, was plagued by witches, wicked sorcerers who were taking the people away from the teachings of God and putting the devil into their souls. This is Cold

War-speak at its most obvious, barring the references to witches and sorcerers, which nonetheless encapsulates something of the way in which communism and communists were presumed to work: 'bewitching' people. More than this, the schoolmaster's explanation also makes clear that these influences were internal: 'It did not matter that they were not real sorcerers [Russian or foreign communists]...but their influence was very real indeed'.

The schoolmaster's explanation offers two views of the baleful influence of communism. First, by taking Brigadoon itself to be a metaphor for the United States, then the encroachment of communism is described by the impending arrival of the witches who, elsewhere, were taking people away from the teachings of God, and which the people of Brigadoon or, more precisely, those who had the place and authority to make decisions on their behalf (as the people are apparently easily influenced) have reason to fear. Thus communism is seen as an external and baleful threat, and it seems an unstoppable one. There is no assumption on the part of the schoolmaster nor on the part of the minister, Mr Forsyth, who according to the story, recognized this threat and (without it would seem consulting the villages) took steps to counteract it, that the changes that would be wrought were anything but evil. This, too, is part of the conservative attitude towards the possibility of domestic communism in the USA.

Second, taking Brigadoon not as representing metaphorically all of the USA, but as part of it, there is the implication that the purveyors of communism/witchcraft are externally imposed or an alien threat but, worse still, are from within: 'The Highlands of Scotland were plagued with..' is how the story begins. The fear of the alien within is endemic in Cold War attitudes and their reflection and representation in popular culture, including films.

The solution to the threat of communism/witchcraft and its seemingly irresistible attraction to the 'people' is for those in authority to intervene (without it any due democratic process) and to literally (if in fairy tale fashion) remove Brigadoon from the possibility of contamination. As the schoolmaster points out, by returning only for one day once very one hundred years, they would not be long enough in any one century to be touched by it. This is social paranoia taken to an extreme. *Brigadoon* shows a very real connection with the Cold War culture of the United States by demonstrating the 'possibility' of escaping from the threat of communism and, much more pertinently, by the fear it engenders of change (somehow but not self-evidently for the worse), by denying the possibility of change, by freezing the social structure and the status quo in time, of defying history. It is, of course, a demonstration of wishful thinking rather than of course a practical plan of action. The point is not that *Brigadoon* is somehow a 'solution' for the social ills of the 1950s, but that in postulating this explanation for its very narrative, the diegetic explanation is one which derives its 'sense' and its explanatory power from the socio-cultural situation, perceptions, attitudes and ideology of the time.

Yet, *Brigadoon* is far from secure in its self-isolation. This has not brought the unbounded boons that, for most of the time, the film is determined to suggest the inhabitants of *Brigadoon* do enjoy. Like most Musicals, these things are celebrated through song and dance, whether communal (production numbers) or personal, solo and duet song and dance, especially by the two romantically-entwined principals. There are no numbers which contradict or reverse the feelings of joy, pleasure and community spirit, save one. At the celebration of the marriage of Jean and Sandy, the revelries (choreographed chorus dancing) are disrupted by the arrival of an embittered and rejected suitor of Jean's, Harry Beaton.

Harry Beaton serves to represent a contradiction, intended or otherwise, to the joys of communist-free existence. He sees Brigadoon not as a Garden of Eden, free of the (original) sin of communism, but as representing the dimensions of his gaol. The price of being beyond the influence of witchcraft/communism is that it is impossible to leave, or to change or progress, individually or communally. There is no suggestion that Harry wishes to leave to have the opportunity to embrace witchcraft, but his desire to leave, narratively-motivated by his failure to win Jean's hand, is expressly because there is no point to his staying. His leaving is prevented by the condition that if anyone leaves, 'then night shall fall upon us forever'. Of course, there is a whole subplot built around this, to add excitement, suspense and to explain why Fiona does not simply leave with Tommy when they fall in love. But there are echoes of Cold War attitudes here too. Indeed, it is intriguing to postulate in what way Harry differs from many Americans who were denied the right to leave America even when (especially when) accused of communist sympathies—the case of the famous singer Paul Robeson, whose passport was confiscated is a clear example.

Harry is not a character who is intended to be view with much sympathy, yet, although his outbursts are couched in bitter and extremely self-pitying terms, some of his arguments do not seem without foundation, and in effect, challenge some of the apparently unassailable explanation for the condition of Brigadoon. Certainly, it seems that no-one asked him if he wanted to be a part of this magically inspired, never-ending isolation. Although Harry is the only citizen of Brigadoon who expresses dissatisfaction and although much time (and singing and dancing) is devoted to showing how happy the Brigadunians are, this raises a sort of thematic itch. The people seem *too* happy; the jollity seems at times rather forced. There are musical moments which support this uneasiness: the sombre, militaristic beginnings to the marriage ceremony seem threatening and aggressive rather than communally celebratory.

Harry Beaton also represents an internal threat, however. He is a symbolic red-under-the-bed, his attempts to escape are, as he and the entire village know, an attempt to destroy Brigadoon, to plunge it into that eternal night. He is the domestic communist menace, the individual who cannot accept the American way of life and who would just as soon destroy it than come to any such accommodation—destruction of the American way of life is, of course, the charge that was made against the domestic communists (or those so designated). In a moment in which the mask of comedy slips aside, Harry is shot 'while trying to escape', albeit by accident and by an outsider. But prior to his 'execution', he has been hunted by his fellow villagers who have, however, taken on some of the appearance of savages—the men are stripped to the waist, wearing only kilts and brandishing swords and axes. He is demonised and hunted down literally. Even his father seems satisfied with the outcome.

In another way, and a much more direct rather than allegorical way, *Brigadoon* also realises the uncertainty, the challenges to confidence that Wood discusses. On one hand, ignoring the metaphorical possibilities of Brigadoon representing a view of America, frozen in the (non-communist, non-fearful) past, Brigadoon is also a foreign, non-American place (albeit the Schoolmaster is dressed in knee breeches, white ruffled blouse, hose and buckled shoes, very much like popular images of early American colonists; he might almost be just taking a break from drafting the American Constitution), and thus is a non-American culture and society which proves irresistible to an American. (To balance this, Jeff, Tommy's cynical and jaded friend, feels no such attraction—but he is not attracted to contemporary American culture either.) On the other hand, what is seen of the 'real' America is far from positive either. While this is reduced to one sequence, it is a sequence which demonstrates but far from celebrates American capitalism and consumerism: a crowded bar in which American executives (Wall Street? Madison Avenue?) and women associated with them, jostle and shout, but whose entire conversation, even *raison d'être*, seem to be making money—or spending it. It is hardly surprising that Tommy wants to return to Brigadoon, a Brigadoon which ought to be beyond his grasp but which his love for Fiona (and his rejection of both modern American capitalism and communism) brings back into existence.

Brigadoon is a Cold War Musical not so much through its music—it is difficult to find any specific numbers that are connected to the sort of Cold War attitudes I have discussed beyond those numbers which celebrate 'simple' folk culture and community—as through the implications of the very basis of its narrative and some of the actions of its characters. It is because of this that *Brigadoon* is vaguely unsettling, despite having some extremely attractive numbers provided through the collaboration of Jay Lerner and Frederick Lowe, and some wonderful and spirited dancing, and the balletic attraction of Cyd Charisse and, of course, Gene Kelly. It has, and here the musical numbers do contribute, a certain sense of desperation, a sense that it is trying too hard to convince its putative audience. But convince it of what—that it is possible to have fun, despite the Cold War? But in order to so, the film seems to argue the necessity to run and hide, to escape, and this surely is contrary to the American mythos? There is, I detect, a slight hysterical edge to *Brigadoon*. To take, once again, a remark by Michael Wood about another film of the time, '...there is a frantic *will* to be happy'. Or, in connection with yet another film: 'In the world as it is, in order to sing and dance, you have to be outside America'.[11] I have changed Wood's line from 'you have to be drunk' to 'you have to be outside America'. To see how the Cold War affected Musicals in deep, sub-textual ways, and used America itself to do so, I want now to turn to *Seven Brides for Seven Brothers*.

SEVEN BRIDES FOR SEVEN BROTHERS

Peter Biskind mentions some six Musicals by title within his extensive discussion of Hollywood's fifties films.[12] They are *Carefree* (actually a 1930s film and only mentioned for comparative purposes), *Singin' in the Rain, Kiss Me Kate, Rhapsody in Blue, Seven Brides for Seven Brothers* and *Jailhouse Rock*. Of these, only *Seven Brides for Seven Brothers* receives more than a short sentence. This would seem to suggest that Musicals certainly managed to avoid being 'controversial' or socially relevant during the period, but it would also suggest that *Seven Brides for Seven Brothers* somehow differed from the mainstream musicals, enough at least for Biskind to take particular note of it.

The discussion I have made above about *Brigadoon* should indicate the way in which an analysis of *Seven Brides for Seven Brothers* might proceed. That is, to examine the structure of the narrative to detect ways and places in which the social imaginary of the Cold War period (which I have defined as 'neurotic' and 'paranoid'[13]) has affected that narrative, has provided motivations and 'explanations' for the actions of characters. In *Brigadoon*, there is a clear and unambiguous statement that it was a fear of outsiders (who represented and even proselytized an alien 'ideology') which brought about the very condition of Brigadoon and its inhabitants. *Seven Brides for Seven Brothers* suggests very much the same thing, less directly and with not quite the same intentions.

Woody Haut, in a discussion of aspects of the popular literature of the Cold War claims that much of the fiction he examines, demonstrates 'irrational concerns regarding an alien invasion'.[14] This finds expression in *Seven Brides for Seven Brothers*, and in fact the concerns turn out to be not quite 'irrational', as first Adam Pontipee and then in a far more literal way, all the Pontipee brothers 'invade' a town, and carry off seven young women (only one, Milly, willingly). Later, reversing the narrative focus upon just who is concerned about an alien invasion, or who has every right to be so concerned, the Pontipee farm/community is invaded by outsiders from the town. It is particularly noticeable that while the Pontipee 'invasion' is aggressive, but only hostile to a very limited extent, the townsfolk's invasion is hostile, armed and quite clearly directed towards killing the Pontipees.[15] This certainly serves to suggest that the Pontipees are right to desire isolation and separation (rather like the inhabitants of Brigadoon) from outsiders who would do them harm (unlike Brigadoon, of course, the Pontipees have brought some of this upon themselves). There is, then, a doubled view of (or paranoia about) 'invasion' here. If it is taken that the town is invaded or threatened by 'aliens' whose 'culture' is opposed to that of the town (i.e., simply carrying off women rather than the more 'moral' behaviour of controlled/repressed courtship), then the town's reaction may be seen as that of the USA's in the 1950s with the invasions of Guatemala and Lebanon, and the involvements in Korea and, later, Vietnam to 'preserve its way of life'. On the other hand, if the 'invasion' of the Pontipee land is seen as the justification of *their* paranoia about the outside, then it can be seen that their way of life is threatened by outsiders who do not share their culture and their perceptions and wish to destroy them (the Cold War view of communism).

The film then seems to be uncertain as to which 'side' is alien, and which represents normality. What it actually does is shift the perception to suit itself, but the perception remains one informed by paranoia. The 'side' which shows the most paranoia is that of the town. From the outset Adam, and by extension his whole family, is marginalised. They are not 'of' the town, being 'slummucky backwoodsmen' according to the shopkeeper's wife. And as Adam leaves with Milly, a townsman opines, 'I never did like them Pontipees'. The basis for this dislike seems to be that of difference—the Pontipees are different from the townsfolk. Although the same individual does continue, 'And now I know why'—suggesting it is Adam's ability to immediately attract Milly (a towns woman) where no townsman has been able to that measures in some way the difference the man felt but could not previously articulate. Combined with the notion of difference is the fact that the Pontipees are, in large measure, unknown to the townsfolk (beyond this one individual and presumably the storekeeper and his wife). The Minister, asked to marry Adam and Milly, objects on the grounds, 'I don't know you or anything about you', to which his wife adds confirmation of Adam's status as an alien: 'We meant you to marry one of our young men, Milly'. The fact that the Pontipees are unknown is further reinforced at the barn raising, when some of the young ladies (instantly attracted) note, 'I don't recall seeing them before', or 'They're all strangers to

45

me'. The fact that the Pontipees are strangers and/or act differently is a reason for instant hostility from the townsfolk, it seems. This is with the exception of the young women but even here it is after the brothers are 'civilised'—shaved, washed, laundered and dressed. On the first visit of the brothers, other than Adam, to town, an attempt to speak with women is rebuffed and leads, instantly, to violence instigated by men of the town. Difference in appearance and, especially, behaviour (or what is considered acceptable behaviour within the culture of the town) is met with attempted violence; paranoia lurks very close to the surface in this town.

This attitude that treats the brothers as strangers, as unknowns, as both alien and 'other' is somewhat uneven. As I have mentioned at least one townsmen does know (and dislikes the Pontipees), and at the barn-raising one man knows Frank's full name (Frankincense, a running gag in the narrative, and usually the cause of a fight) while others claim never to have seen them before. That the Pontipees are at a barn-raising, even at Milly's instigation, suggest they are sufficiently part of the community to be considered part of this fundamental community activity (akin, surely, to the church raising in *My Darling Clementine* [John Ford, 1946] in the way it is a metonym for civilisation). Still, they are known to some there and treated with suspicion by just about everyone, except the young women instantly sexually attracted. Perhaps sexual attractiveness is a measure of difference—and there may well be resonances in the way the right-wing attitudes to communism were that it was, by some unexplained mechanism, instantly and irresistibly attractive—which is why it had to be hounded out, hunted down and destroyed. It is certainly the case that the townsmen instantly set out in armed pursuit of the brothers after the abduction, and later are all set to execute them without due trial and process (and supervised by the minister) when they finally invade the Pontipee land. This flexible perception of the Pontipees as 'aliens', outsiders and strangers parallels attitudes to domestic or native communists (or those who, for whatever reason were thought to be or could be charged as being), and in this *Seven Brides for Seven Brothers* does utilise aspects of the paranoia that was so clearly a defining characteristic of the Cold War psyche.

Difference, the difference of the brothers (from the rest of the community/ population), is reinforced visually throughout the film. In the first instance all the Pontipee's have red hair (and red beards until Milly causes them to be removed). This is the first of a number of ways they are distinguished from, are different to, the men of the town. By and large, they are also taller on average—Gideon, the youngest, may slip marginally below the average (his hair is less red as well, as maybe befit his youth, his 'immaturity; he will grow and 'redden' presumably). This is further apparent at the Barn Raising Sequence. In this sequence, as nowhere else in the film, the visual/appearance difference of the Pontipees and the townsfolk is clearly registered. The brothers are all dressed in a Western/Pioneer dress, particularly a double-button shirt (a different colour for each brother), that owes something to the conventions of the Western genre (rather like the one worn by John Wayne in *Stagecoach* [John Ford, 1939] albeit suitably modified for a Musical). Nonetheless, it is a tough, outdoor, masculine look. The men of the town, especially those with whom they compete (via dance and feats of strength) are all dressed in the fashion of 'dudes' or citified dandies (in the Western sense—suits, string bow ties, some even have small neat pencil-line moustaches).[16] It should be noted that at the end, in the mass wedding ceremony that takes place under the guns of the townsfolk (although of course desired all along by the brothers and the brides), the brothers' dress has moved substantially towards that of the townsfolk. They still wear their western shirts but now they submerged below jackets and string ties, a process of enculturation (began by Milly) is nearing completion. Their difference is being removed—at gunpoint.

The hostility towards the Pontipees is based as much in the fact they are different (and flaunt the difference) as in the sexual rivalry that develops for the young towns women. The common purpose—the communal one of cooperative barn-raising—only exacerbates rather than reduces the differences between the two groups, especially as the Pontipees have not really come to be neighbourly (and probably would not have gone at all but for Millie's urging) but to meet/court women, a fact not entirely lost on the townsfolk, especially the young men. Difference, in the Cold War atmosphere in America, is another cause for fear, hatred and paranoia; the different (whether truly communist in any meaningful sense or not) are un-American.

Cold War paranoia was not entirely located within fear of the outside nor 'merely' rampant xenophobia or of the aliens within. Biskind argues that, in various forms, 1950s films demonstrated a paranoia about women (patriarchy was 'afraid of sex and menstrual women' and Biskind makes a case for how often 'Reds' (represented metaphorically as fantastic creatures) are also women ('monsters from the id').[17] While Biskind initially makes his case around Science-fiction films, his claim that these provide a paranoid fantasy of a world dominated by predatory females'[18] is not widely removed from *Seven Brides for Seven Brothers*. It should not be overlooked that the six future brides initiate the advances of the brothers and later, continuing the process begun by Milly, dominate (or at least domesticate) them; Milly and the abducted 'brides' are also responsible for sending the 'king', Adam (the first man?) into exile and taking over the farm house. It is noticeable that the women in the town are largely ineffectual, and while still in town Milly is a much-put-upon servant

47

(as well as a sexual object of desire). Once married and residing at the brothers' house, after some minimally skirmishing with Adam, she quickly imposes a female regime, insisting on table manners, personal hygiene, and 'gentlemanly' behaviour, and achieving all these goals with the minimum of effort. The film may not exactly indicate these changes are undesirable, and certainly does not make Milly out to be a monstrous female, nonetheless, the ruling patriarchy is challenged successfully; eventually even Adam (after at first being exiled) is brought to heel by the combination of Milly and a female baby.

What is perhaps being represented in the 'triumph' of femininity (or of women at least) is not so much paranoia about women (this is better demonstrated in Film Noir as well as Science- fiction and Horror films of the time) as it is a demonstration of another Cold War concern: the need for social control. The irony that America, whose ideology was built upon the myth of individual freedom, became obsessed with social control during and because of the Cold War has often been commented upon: 'Once again, the problem was social control: how to deal with the troublesome groups in society'.[19] Rather than a paranoid fear of what women represent (threats to patriarchy and masculinity), *Seven Brides for Seven Brothers* rather 'uses' women to impose social control and order on a troublesome group—the heretofore uncontrolled brothers—and so doing reduce the distance between them and the rest of society. Like the gangs in *West Side Story* (Robert Wise, 1961), the Pontipee 'gang' is simply enacting behaviours which are anti-social (or to be fair to the Pontipees, *un*social); unlike the *West Side Story* gangs, however, the brothers are not in rebellion against society (simply letting their libidos get out of control, slightly), and are also not fully cognizant of the rules of that society.

There is, then, a clear irony in the fact that the cause of the brothers kidnapping the 'brides' (and justifying the paranoia of the townspeople and their hostility to then Pontipees) is actually Milly's fault. That is, it is information that Milly has brought with her into the valley as part of her 'civilisation' that incites the brothers; in fact (through the number, 'Sobbin' Women') the brothers get the idea for an action they would not have thought of themselves. It is Milly's copy of Plutarch's *Lives* that provides the story of the Sabine Women whose abduction and subsequent disinclination to return to their husbands, is joyfully interpreted, considered in song and dance, and acted upon by the love-lorn brothers—at Adam's instigation. (The film politely declines to suggest that what Plutarch tells is of 'rape' not simple abduction.) It does not seem that the Pontipees would have thought of, let one carried out, wholesale abduction without the example of the book, although their willingness to do so after they consider the historical example places them, presumable outside the definition of 'normal' behaviour.

It is Milly who brings the outside world, or more properly, brings its values, into the valley, and most of what she brings is clearly shown to be good: cleanliness, organisation, domestic and, more importantly, social skills— all of which she is willing, able and, when she gets over the shock of not one male to tame but seven, eager to import and impose. Her 'power' to do so is demonstrated in Musical genre fashion through song and dance, specifically, the number 'Goin' Courtin'. Milly also has contributed from the 'normal' world understandings that are apparently unknown or not considered by the Pontipees: she knows what love is, how it manifests itself, and how it is expressed. This she also teaches to the Pontipee males, especially Adam ('When You're in Love'.) Once ensconced as the source of social control, Milly is immovable. Contrary to Biskind's assertion[20] it is not Milly who leaves but Adam. He leaves her after she denies him her bed, following the abduction—punishment for social aberration. He spends at least six months in exile, in a cabin in the mountains.

All this is, of course, within the conventional framework of a Musical, but *Seven Brides for Seven Brothers* is considerably different from many of the Musicals that preceded it, and most of its contemporaries. Noticeable in *Seven Brides for Seven Brothers* is the 'domesticity' of Milly, which is only partly explained by the underlying socio-cultural concern with social control characteristic of the Cold War psyche in America. Although some years after the end of World War Two, *Seven Brides for Seven Brothers* replicates the very social trajectory for women which (patriarchal) American society was anxious to see followed (and presumably by the 1950s if followed then confirmed as the correct path); that of the removal of women from paid employment and the 'public arena' and the placing (or replacing) of them into secure marriage and family 'employment' (which was, of course not seen or considered to be employment at all). Milly moves from being an employee (a servant in a tavern) to being a housewife, but more than this: she clearly becomes personally validated by this. (She expresses her joy in this in 'Wonderful, Wonderful Day'.) Within the house, Milly rules absolutely and because of this she is able to tame (socialize) the males in terms of behaviour both within and outside the domestic situation, to indeed inspire them with the desire not simply for sexual partners (although the film does give emphasis to this) but for domesticated women. All of the chosen brides are, in any case, pre-domesticated to a greater extent than Milly, most are seen doing 'women's place is in the home' activities at one time or another (and confirm their attitude with 'June Bride' later). With the exception, then, of Milly and the shopkeeper's wife, all the women sighted in *Seven Brides for Seven Brothers*, others as well as the brides, are or seem to be thoroughly domesticated. The Cold War period saw an increased emphasis on 'family values', probably as a result of the disruption of (the hot) World War Two as any fear about alternative social/personal relationships being 'alien'` or un-American. Family values, too, are the cornerstone of conservative and reactionary ideology—it is no accident so many television programs, especially early situation comedies, were based entirely within situations which consistently and relentlessly made this point.

It is observable, moreover, that Musicals before the war—for example, the Astaire-Rogers Musicals and the backstage Musicals of the Depression—were populated with women who, while they were apparently seeking marriage, were not after domesticity at the same time. It is difficult to imagine any of the characters played by Ginger Rogers in the Astaire-Rogers Musicals as being or even becoming a housewife, let alone a mother. Equally, 'Fred' (in his various characters) and even 'Gene Kelly' in his, seem anxious for marriage (some 'Kelly' characters perhaps less so), anxious for a wife but not for a *house*wife. Fred and Ginger more often seem as interested in a professional as well as a sexual partnership. On the other hand, of the three films I have examined here, this is precisely what the love/courtship narrative, truncated in *Seven Brides for Seven Brothers* (for Milly and Adam anyway) and extended in *Brigadoon*, is headed towards. (Fiona in *Brigadoon* seems already thoroughly domesticated as a daughter seen to be fully and happily occupied keeping house for her father, and will presumably continue to do, even or especially for/with her 'alien' husband, Tommy. *Brigadoon*, set in a frozen-in-time past, hardly offers any alternative.)

This place of women in society and male/female relationships is a clear shift in the conventions of the Musical from pre-war to Cold War Musicals. This shift seems accountable through reference to Cold War attitudes. Those attitudes are also found in other aspects of the Cold War Musical. Films, like other popular cultural artefacts (and perhaps more so than many given the complexity of film narratives), 'reveal much about their culture, particularly its needs, values, and the contradictions to which both often give rise'.[21] Musicals often seem to elude this generality because of their 'energy, exuberance, and emphatic tales] of harmony'.[22] While it is certainly demonstrable that the Musical, for most of its history, has been less obviously concerned to deliberately provide social comment, it is no more 'free' of the effects of the social subconscious, no less a (changing) creature of its times than any other film form. The Cold War was felt throughout practically every aspect of American life, culture and institutions, communal and personal. It would be highly unlikely if it was not felt in some way in Musicals made at the time. My argument is that it was and in the ways which I have outlined, and probably others as well.

NOTES

1. Leo K. Adler, *The Red Image: American Attitudes toward Communism in the Cold War Era*, Garland Publishing, New York, 1991.

2. Stephen J. Whitfield, *The Culture of the Cold War*, The John Hopkins University Press, Baltimore, 1991, p. 142.

3. Examinations of this aspect may be found in Peter Biskind, *Seeing is Believing: How Hollywood Taught Us to Stop Worrying and Love the Fifties*, Pantheon Books, New York, 1983.

4. Violence is a characteristic which separates pre-war Musicals from post-war Musicals. I can think of no '30s Musical with death in its narrative, certainly not death by other than natural causes. Post-war Musicals which do include *Brigadoon, Oklahoma!* (Fred Zinnemann, 1955), *West Side Story* (Robert Wise, 1961), *Cabaret* (Bob Fosse, 1972), *South Pacific* (Joshua Logan, 1958), *Jailhouse Rock* (Richard Thorpe, 1957), *Camelot* (Joshua Logan, 1967) among others.

5. The film's opening titles do not credit the 1939 film or its writers but cite 'Suggested by Ninotchka by Melchior Lengyel', who also seems to have provided the story adapted for the film version.

6. Adler, *The Red Image*, p. 431.

7. The lyrics of this song especially are so 'vulgar' as to suggest a deliberate parody of American popular song (especially the 'Tin Pan Alley' type of song found in Musicals), and thus confirm that the film is actually saying something negative about American capitalism attitude to 'art' and 'music'. Steve's claims confirm rather than deny this.

8. Jim Kitses, *Horizons West*, British Film Institute, London, 1989.

9. Michael Wood, *America in the Movies*, Basic Books, New York, 1975, p. 161.

10. Wood, *America in the Movies*, p.163.

11. Wood, *America in the Movies*, p.155. (Italics in original). Wood is discussing *On the Town* (Gene Kelly, Stanley Donen, 1949) in the first instance and *It's Always Fair Weather* (Gene Kelly, Stanley Donen, 1955) in the second.

12. Biskind, *Seeing is Believing*.

13. These are, of course, far from my own individual interpretations but are an attempt to encapsulate the claims and assertions of historians and social scholars generally.

14. Woody Haut, *Pulp Culture: Hardboiled Fiction and the Cold War*, Serpent's Tail, London and New York, 1995, p.15.

15. The brothers are armed when they go to town—the guns prove useful to start of the avalanche that isolates them from the town—but this seems more a convention borrowed from the Western than because they are willing to kill for the women.

16. For fairly obvious reasons, the Pontipee brothers are all much more physically attractive than the men of the town. As Milly says, you're all mighty fine looking boys, every one of you.

17. Biskind, *Seeing is Believing*, p.133.

18. Biskind, *Seeing is Believing*, p.133.

19. Biskind, *Seeing is Believing*, p. 229. Biskind uses Science-fiction and the Western as the genres in which 'directors who wanted to examine intolerance turned'. *Seven Brides for Seven Brothers* has at least some of the iconography of the Western—time and place—as well as a hint of some of the thematic—taming the wilderness, the bringing of civilisation.

20. Biskind, *Seeing is Believing*, p 289.

21. J.P. Telotte, 'Dancing the Depression: Narrative Strategy in the Astaire-Rogers Films', *Journal of Popular Film and Television*, Vol. 8, no. 3, 1980, p.15.

22. J.P. Telotte, 'Dancing the Depression: Narrative Strategy in the Astaire-Rogers Films', p.15.

MAGIC IN THE AIR: MOTION PICTURE MUSICALS AS FAIRY TALES

To many folklorists, the status of the fairy tale is conditional, at best. The wide circulation of fairy tales since the 18th century through print, with concomitant editing, bowdlerising, and other types of modification and codification, renders the fairy tale suspect as a folk object. It has become also the 'property' of litterateurs, or at least a small body of them, and this has led to practices in analysis, criticism and theorising which many folklorists treat with suspicion, and sometimes downright hostility. The purist folklorist position is best summarised by Alan Dundas:

> The first thing to say about fairy tales is that they are an oral form. Fairy tales, however one may choose ultimately to define them, are a sub-genre of the more inclusive category of 'folktale' which exists primarily as a spoken traditional narrative. Once a fairy tale or any other type of folktale, for that matter, is reduced to written language, one does not have a true fairy tale but only a pale and inadequate reflection of what was originally an oral performance complete with raconteur and audience. From this folkloristic perspective, one cannot possibly read fairy tales: one can only properly hear them told.[1]

This is an essentialist position from which there is little room to manoeuvre and which, if adopted completely, would place the fairy tale outside the purview of the folklorist, and permanently in the literary camp. Again, as Dundas argues,

> [a] vast chasm separates an oral tale with its subtle nuances entailing significant body movements, eye expression, pregnant pauses, and the like from the inevitably flat and fixed written record of what was once a live and often compelling storytelling event.[2]

Overlooking the rather tendentious implication that all 'storytelling events' were 'compelling' and that all 'written records' are 'inevitably flat', Dundas is still making a vital argument about the condition of the fairy tale as part of folk culture. It is not my intention to make an intervention into this argument, and Dundas notwithstanding, it is by no means clear that all scholars accept that fairy tales are or must be an oral form. My purpose will be to make the outline of a case for the 'orality' of performance of the fairy tale finding equivalence in the motion picture. On the face of it, to allow fairy tales to exist in motion picture form would seem to further invalidate the 'legitimacy' of the fairy tale, perhaps even more so than simply to be written down and published in books. Mass culture and the mass culture industry, particularly that of the twentieth-century, are often considered to be the antithesis of everything or anything folkloric, 'natural' or 'organic' in cultural terms. They are equally considered to be the antithesis of 'high' culture as well. Theodore Adorno and others of the 'Frankfurt School' of social and cultural criticism are but eloquent (if dour) spokespersons for this attitude toward the culture industry. Cinema, especially as epitomised by Hollywood, is the arch-purveyor of 'de-humanised' mass culture; or it was until the arrival of television. It is impossible to argue that cinema is not, in terms of its techo-economic organisation, an 'industry' (although world-wide, many of its products are produced in what might be argued to be 'cottage industry' rather than factory industry conditions). But the circumstances of the production of a 'story' (whether fairy tale or not) do not, *ipso facto,* make the story itself inevitably and inescapably a reflection (and nothing more) of the ideological practices of the socio-economic circumstances of its production (as Adorno would argue). And even if the ideological circumstances of its production are of significance, to what extent is this not also (if not more so) the case with an individual storyteller, narrating a folk/fairy tale to an audience? The difference between the mass culture product, a motion picture, and the 'limited (?)' culture product of the narrated fairy tale becomes even less clear when it is demonstrated that most fairy tales are, in fact, widespread and not isolated to one area or community, or to one time. The idea that any individual motion picture is exactly the same throughout the world (if it is lucky enough to be so distributed) is a cornerstone of the idea of mass culture, but even here it can be demonstrated that the 'same' motion picture is frequently different in different places; it may be modified for all sorts of reasons to meet perceived local demands, tastes, attitudes, and so forth, and further modified for release in video form or for television and so on. The differences in the versions of a motion picture may not be quite as great as, say, the differences in a telling of the 'Cinderella'-type folk/fairy tale in twelfth-century China and a telling in nineteenth-century Russia (let alone versions in collected and published fairy tale books), but differences there are likely to be that can be accounted for by the different cultural and social conditions of different markets.

The basis of my argument here is not, however, that motion pictures are not products of a culture industry based in commodity production, although I wish to argue that being so does not invalidate their functioning in ways akin to 'genuinely' folk-culture artefacts. I am more interested in making a case that motion pictures are the equivalent of the narrated story-telling event, or demonstrably more so that a written version of a fairy tale is; and to further this notion by arguing that certain motion pictures are so close to fairy tales in form as perhaps to be considered 'evolved' fairy tales. That is, to borrow an analogy from palaeontology, whereas the dinosaurs certainly became extinct, it is generally considered one branch evolved into birds (and thus dinosaurs still 'exist', so to speak), so fairy tales as orally narrated events have become extinct (in the West at least), they too evolved into different forms—the written fairy tale and, more particularly, the motion picture 'fairy tale'. This is a rather crude analogy, perhaps, but in the same way as one might look at a bird and not see a dinosaur, so one might look at a motion picture and not see a fairy tale.[3]

Motion pictures are irrevocably implicated in the reproduction of tangible materiality in ways which strongly correlate the re-presentation of things with their appearance in the real world. Cinema adds to this re-presentation the 'reality' of movement of things and the sounds that they make. Notwithstanding that there are conventional ways in which this re-presentation is made, and that all motion pictures are illusions, motion pictures have what film theorist Joseph D. Anderson calls 'veridicality'[4]. This is the manner in which motion pictures re-present tangible materiality in ways that human perception 'operates' upon them as it does upon objects in the actual world; perception confirms the 'truth' of the world it senses and operates upon. Motion pictures are patterns of light and sound which are perceived and comprehended as if they were things in the perceived 'real' world. This does not mean that cinema spectators cannot tell the difference; human perception is capable not only of 'veridicality' but also of illusion, and of recognising the existence and difference between the two. Nonetheless,

> The motion picture has... [a] fundamental avenue of accessibility. It presents to the visual system an optical array and to the auditory system a pattern of molecular disturbance that, for lack of an alternative, is processed as information from the natural world. In so doing, perception itself confers upon the fictional world of the film the status of a world that can be seen with one's own eyes and heard with one's own ears.[5]

This being so, it follows that the 'experience' of any narrative motion picture is going to be akin to witnessing the events for one's self, certainly more so that a written version would be so experienced, and perhaps even more so than hearing a story-teller narrate the story, no matter how 'compelling' a 'storytelling event' it may be. At the same time, however, a motion picture is a storytelling event. A motion picture is a narrative *and* a narration without any obvious narrator—and most motion pictures are just that: stories told by a 'non-existent' storyteller. This, of course, enhances the sense of their being correlates with 'reality'. The verisimilitude that is the consequence of cinema's ontological nexus with the (re)production of material reality can be extraordinarily powerful in (re)presenting the appearance of the fantastic, marvellous or magical aspects of fairy tales—or, in some way, of cinema having its fairy-tale cake and eating it by giving a technically-based approximation of oral storytelling (although narrative fictional films are stories being told that have no storyteller as such) and visualization of the magic itself, which no storyteller could emulate.

Cinema is, by and large, a mimetic art. Its basis in verisimilitude, in the accurate reproduction of tangible materiality (even where that tangible materiality has no existence in the real world)[6] and in the cognitive processes of human beings who perceive motion picture images and sound in the same way as the real world, ensures this is so. On the face of it, this may seem inimical to motion pictures being fairy tales, or successfully adapting fairy tales (other than in animated form, as with the Disney films). In fact, these two factors are crucial in making fairy tales a truly motion picture form, in the 'evolution' of the fairy tale via the otherwise despised mass culture industry. It may be argued that fairy tales continue to exist in motion pictures in forms closer to their origins than they do in literary forms.

It is not simply the 'condition' of motion pictures as mimetic art and as visual/oral storytelling that is important. The nature of the fairy tale itself is equally significant.

The fairy tale is a narrative genre with numerous examples that manifest in common the basic characteristics of:

- the incorporation of magic or fantasy in such a manner that its epistemological and ontological validity is affirmed,

- the incorporation of a quest, adventure, or problem, which entails interaction with the unknown or magical realm.[7]

Herein lies an apparent contradiction. The reliance of the fairy tale on 'the incorporation of magic or fantasy' and the 'interaction with the unknown or magical realm' would seem to be opposed to the basic quality of the motion picture, mimesis—except in certain clearly self-defining categories perhaps: Science-fiction, and the Horror film. What is important here is the notion that magic and the magical is 'incorporated' into the fairy tale, that the fairy tale narrative shifts between some level that equates to the quotidian to some level of the marvellous or fantastic without finding any disparity between the two existing simultaneously. While individual fairy tales may have to find a motivation for a character to move into (and out of) a magical realm (although this is not a necessary characteristic of all fairy tales), the existence of a magical realm and its indispensable part in the narrative is taken for granted. This is

56

not to claim that many fairy-tale protagonists do not have to undertake special actions in order to enter the fairy-tale realm, that it is not occasionally 'guarded', but that its existence is continuous with the ordinary world and that existence is no more 'extraordinary' than is that of the ordinary world.

Fairy tales 'serve to unite the people of a community and help bridge a gap in the understanding of social problems in a *language and narrative mode familiar to listeners' experience*'.[8] Whatever one might feel about the social function of fairy tales, the idea that they are told in ways familiar to their audience is important to any claims that motion pictures are, or occasionally are, fairy tales; the motion picture (and its close cousin, television) is obviously in the late 20th century a 'narrative mode familiar to listeners [spectators] experience.'

•

Excluding those motion pictures, animated or live action, which are made from already known or established fairy tales, there is one genre of motion picture which is arguably the 'evolved' fairy tale form which I have claimed. That is, the Musical Comedy. The Hollywood Musical Comedy is very much a genre which has narrative and mise-en-scene conventions like fairy tales. Indeed, the manner in which musical numbers in musical comedies segue into unreal or 'magical' states is highly reminiscent of the way fairy tales simply take the place of the magical in the real world for granted. Such shifts of register are noticeable, for instance, in the musical comedies of Busby Berkeley (as director or as choreographer), in which apparently realistic stage performances become 'magical' through the means of the camera and editing. In these instances, however, the shift in register between an unlikely but nevertheless 'realistic' performance of song-and-dance upon a theatrical stage to a performance which is cinematic in both mise-en-scene and its cinematic rendering (camera position, space, movement, and editing) does not signal a shift in the diegesis between a 'real' world and a magical one. Such shifts in register as these are basically formal and stylistic. This is exemplified in Ken Russell's *The Boyfriend* (1971) in which there are a number of such shifts of register, or different 'planes of reality', which do not, however, constitute the 'incorporation of magic' into the diegesis. The changes within and to various musical numbers being performed, initially, by the rather shabby theatre company are all (with the possible except of the very last) motivated by the imagination of a character within the diegesis, especially the character of De Thrill, a Hollywood director who is watching the performance. Thus, when the performances transcend the physical limitations of the stage and the cast, it is not that all have entered or been transported to a fairy world, but that the narrative simply presents the visualization of the imagination of a character. Within this mimetic structure, wherein most musical 'numbers' are part of (a) the stage version of *The Boyfriend* being undertaken by this particular company in this particular theatre on this particular Saturday afternoon, and (b) transformed in the imagination of characters within the diegesis, there is also one musical number which is more routinely that of the musical comedy. This is when, Polly, the assistant stage manager, watches Tony, the leading male and object of her unrequited love, and 'sings' a song. There is no change of register cinematically speaking here. Within the 'reality' of her physical situation, Polly sings a song, which, given she is looking longingly at Tony at the time, is thus about her love for him. I assert it is precisely when this sort of situation occurs in a musical comedy, that the musical comedy demonstrates its affinity with the fairy tale.

It is especially in musical comedies in which performance is not diegetically tied to literal performance that the magical aspect of characters singing and dancing is even more pronounced.[9] Any number of musicals would suffice, and I wish to use one in particular in some detail but initially I will just cite as evidence a couple of favourites: practically all *of Seven Brides for Seven Brothers* (1954) (even the name has a distinct fairy-tale ring to it) functions in this way, but especially the barn-raising dance number; *Singin' in the Rain,* with its title number which brings the magical into everyday reality. As Anderson points out, '... signals... are necessary within a film/video narrative to introduce any shift from one realm to another.'[10] Anderson cites flashbacks, hallucinations, and so on, but this is also true when the realms are 'normality' and 'magic'. Musical comedies contain such signals—as obvious one is when the hitherto non-diegetic music seems to become diegetic without quite being so—to become extradiegetic, in fact. So, for example, does the cop hear the 'magic music' in the 'Singin' in the Rain' number from the same film? No, because within the diegesis, it is magic music only Don Lockwood (the character singing and dancing) can hear. Of course, the spectators hear it also, as they can see and hear both the ordinary and the magical worlds as a continuum, as do, in most instances, the characters. The question does Don Lockwood dance in this number from *Singin' in the Rain* is equally answerable by yes, he does, he is seen to do so (by the audience) and no, as he is not seen to by anyone else, although the absence of others is partly explained by the lateness of the hour and the rain. Even though the cop arrives (presumably) only at the very end, what he sees is a grown man splashing in puddles. Lockwood 'appreciates' the cop's perception is different from his—the cop may think Lockwood is drunk, perhaps. He does, without any great sense that it will be believed, state to the cop (repeating a line from the song, of course) that he is 'singin' and dancin' in the rain' before walking away. This example both supports my claim—that magic is present in the musical comedy through the way in which characters break into song-and-dance without disturbing the reproduction of a coherent and, usually, quotidian world—and challenges it because there is no sense in this particular instance that the diegetic quotidian world is aware of the magic. In this latter regard, it touches on a perennial problem of the analysis of musical comedy conventions: do characters 'really' sing and dance, or is this a visualisation, a representation of an emotional state, a metaphor for how they feel, usually, to be in love?

In order to demonstrate my assertion that the breaking out into song and dance is not an interpolation of a different register (metaphor instead of mimesis), I am going to use a recent Woody Allen film, *Everyone Says I Love You* (1997)[11]. Woody Allen is not a director to whom one would initially turn to find fairy-tale characteristics within his films. Since *Annie Hall* (1977), Woody Allen's *oeuvre* has been largely one of highly mimetic narratives, usually located within the identifiably quotidian existence of middle-class professional and/ or creative New Yorkers. That said, it needs to be recognized that Allen has a limited but significant strand of fairy tales within his overall canon; films like *A Midsummer Night's Sex Comedy* (1982) (which has actual fairies in it), *The Purple Rose of Cairo* (1985) (in which Allen wittily exploits the very aspect of film's simultaneous reality and illusion I have been discussing), his foray into German expressionist cinema, *Shadows and Fog* (1991), and perhaps *Stardust Memories* (1980). Nonetheless, Woody Allen films are, at first glance, possibly the least likely to contain that essential characteristic of the fairy tale, 'the incorporation of magic or fantasy in such a manner that its epistemological; and ontological validity is affirmed'. *Everyone Says I Love You* is important for precisely the reason that it is, on one hand, another of the mainstream Woody Allen films, a naturalistic drama based in observation of the lives of a group of 'quintessential' middle-class Americans, and on the other, a film in which the quotidian and the magical are freely intermingled without apparent disruption to the diegesis or the singly out of the magical as a different register or level of reality.

Three sequences from *Everyone Says I Love You*, of its twenty or twenty-one musical sequences, will serve to illustrate my argument. The film's narrative commences with a young man singing to a young woman, next to a fountain. This sequence is significant because it does three things which implicate fairy-tale magic in the structure of the film. Firstly, the young man is clearly singing *to* her; this might of course be mimetic. Secondly, and indicating that, on one hand, the young man *is* singing (this is not a visual metaphor for some other level of communication), and on the other, that there is an acceptance of the magic or marvellous, the young man is unaccompanied by an unseen orchestra. I say 'unseen' to separate it from a *non-diegetic* orchestra, the type that usually provides the music on the soundtrack of a motion picture, music that has no diegetic connection only an emotional or dramatic one. The absent/present orchestras of musical comedy are extradiegetic in as much as they are part of the diegesis—they accompany singing and dancing—while not existing in the visual manifestation of the world of the narrative. Thus, this is an extradiegetic or 'magic' orchestra; it 'knows' that the young man is singing, and what he is singing. Whether the young man (or the young woman for that matter) hears the orchestra is undeterminable. If they do (or even if they do not) they take it for granted—in the same way as the putative spectator might. Music in musical comedies is nearly always 'magical' to the extent that it skirts between diegesis and extra-diegesis in ways in which the music on the sound track of other dramatic motion pictures does not. Thirdly, this is all taking place in a palpably real location, part of New York (identifiable as such even by those who do know Manhattan well), and not a sound stage or a set on a back lot. As this song continues, it transferred from the young man (who is identified as a character in the narrative about to unfold) and is taken up by anonymous individuals (three women pushing prams, an old lady out walking with a nurse, a beggar, etc.) in equally as real parts of Manhattan. Here, like most musical comedies but with the added aspect of being within obviously everyday reality, magic or fantasy is incorporated into the narrative without any specific corralling of the magic. There is even a more magical moment when three mannequins in shop window briefly come to life and dance, an event that surprises no one (in the film). The extra-diegetic nature of the music is revealed when the same melody continues via the soundtrack, under a narration by a character within the diegesis and then re-surfaces to synchronise with the visual track, being played at a party by the well-known violinist Izaak Perlman (as himself?).

Later in *Everyone Says I Love You* a more obviously magical or fantastic sequence takes place. The family who are the narrative focus of the story have gathered in a funeral home to view the corpse of the recently deceased Grandpa. As they sit and pass increasingly fatuous 'philosophical' comments which lead to arguments, the ghost or spirit of Grandpa arises from the open coffin and offers his own philosophy which is also the versified preamble to a song. The visualisation of Grandpas ghost is in keeping with cartoon ghosts—white, translucent, ethereal but clearly in the physical form of Grandpa. He is seen and heard by the living people gathered in the room, who, along with the ghosts of others in other coffins, join in the song and dance into what becomes in musical comedy terms, a production number. Not only do the living, mimetically visualised, and the dead, stylistically visualised, dance but at one point the ghost of Grandpa tips out the contents of an urn and the ashes transmogrify into a human form, sparkling and ethereal but without features, which also dances. The number ends with the ghosts dancing out of the funeral chapel and into the (real) street. This rather self-evident interaction of the quotidian and the magical, which nobody present finds in anyway unusual, is rather rare in musical comedies. But it further underlines my point that in musical comedies, nobody finds it unusual that individuals and groups sometimes sing and sometimes dance in the ordinary course of events, in the same way that characters in fairy tales talk with animals, go to balls in magically converted pumpkins, climb bean stalks and find giants, fly on carpets, and so on, as a matter of course. But the appearance of the 'immaterial' is not unknown in musical comedy. In *Swing Time* (1940), Fred Astaire dances with three of his shadows, which come alive to walk off when his steps become too complicated for them to follow. And there are the examples of Gene Kelly in *Anchors Aweigh* (1945) dancing with Jerry the cartoon mouse, or dancing in impressionist paintings which come to life in *An American in Paris* (1951). The world of the musical comedy, like the world of the fairy tale, is replete with this demonstrable free-flow between ordinary and magical.

Finally, at the very end of *Everyone Says I Love You,* another dance sequence occurs—a direct homage to several Paris-based Hollywood musical comedies[12]—where Joe dances with his ex-wife Stephie on the banks of the Seine. The dance is, seemingly, one of those metaphorical dances whereby the characters express their emotions, the mood of the moment and their attitudes to each other (and maybe to Paris) by dancing rather than enacting or speaking those things. As the dance progresses, Stephie does 'impossible' (i.e., magical) things. She hovers in the air longer than gravity would permit; she flies across the ground but inches above it; Joe holds her up above his head on his fingertips and pushes her into the air where she floats. At one level, this is intended to be comic, Woody Allen's sly dig at the type of musical dance number he is both affectionately saluting and sending up. But it also draws attention to the way in which the magical exists in other dance numbers in other, earlier Hollywood musical comedies. That is, those exceptional performers who seem to do the impossible. I think of the athleticism of Gene Kelly and the Nicholas brothers in *The Pirate* (1948). Or the barn raising sequence in *Seven Brides for Seven Brothers,* with its breathtakingly gymnastic choreography. Or Donald O'Connor dancing up a wall in *Singin' in the Rain.* In these and innumerable other examples, 'impossible' dance actions and movements are usually performed in diegetic reality. But as a final example, and to demonstrate the way in which 'special effects' can be used to produce the magical dance, there is the dance number in *Royal Wedding* (1951) where Fred Astaire dances completely up the walls and across the ceiling of a room.

Everyone Says I Love You draws on specific examples from musical comedies and the conventions of the musical comedy generally and generically but in so doing it provides a demonstration of just how musical comedies resemble fairy tales. In fact, my argument is that musical comedies *are* fairy tales in the way in which they incorporate magic or fantasy, in the way in which they (in Jones's terms) validate magic epistemologically and ontologically. Song and dance are essential to the meaning and existence of musical comedy; they validate the genre and in turn validate the genre's manner of making meaning. Even in the case of the apparently earth-bound backstage musical, the reality of musical performance almost inevitably shifts from the mimetic to the magical and those shifts are taken as integral to the diegesis. How much more this is demonstrably the case with later musical comedies, such as *Paint Your Wagon* (1969) and, now *Everyone Says I Love You,* where the locations of the action are not merely accurate re-presentations of actuality, but are palpably real. 'The power of story-telling is in the re-presentation of experience at once to our intellect and to our emotions. The cinema co-opts this power by presenting a surrogate reality structured as narrative.'[12] In the musical comedy, as in the fairy tale, that surrogate reality intertwines the quotidian and the magical without implying or indicating that they are in any discontinuous, rather the reverse. Magic in the fairy tale is everyday; the everyday is magical in the musical comedy. The everyday is 'made' magical in the musical comedy by its essential defining characteristic of song-and-dance.

NOTES

1. Alan Dundas, 'Fairy Tales from a Folklorist Perspective' in Ruth B. Bottigheimer, ed., *Fairy Tales and Society: Illusion, Allusion, and Paradigm,* University of Pennsylvania Press, Philadelphia, 1986, p.259.
2. Dundas, 1986, p.259.
3. Of course, some motion pictures are adaptations of pre-existing fairy tales and so are dearly fairy tales to that extent.
4, Joseph D. Anderson, *The Reality of Illusion: An Ecological Approach to Cognitive Film Theory,* Southern Illinois Press, Carbondale, 1996.
5. Anderson, p. 126
6. The obviousness of this is, paradoxically, proved by the animated motion picture. Animated motion pictures 'work' only because of the photographically precise reproduction of drawings, later combined with the psychological and cognitive process in the human brain which 'demand' that sequences of animated drawings, photographed and projected, are perceived as moving (animated). It is no accident that many fairy tales have been adapted for this particular form of motion picture.

7. Steven Swarm Jones, *The Fairy Tale: The Magic Mirror of the Imagination*. New York: Twayne, New York, 1991. p 30. Jones list five characteristics of the fairy tale genre. The others are 'thematic' and not of immediate relevance here.

8. Jack Zipes, *Breaking the Magic Spell: Radical Theories of Folk and Fairy Tales.* Heinemann, London. 1979, p *A*. My emphasis.

9. Some musicals are more clearly fairy tales than others. *Brigadoon* (1954) is a fairy tale in which characters move into a fairy realm even without singing and dancing. But singing and dancing is still magical within my terms both inside and outside the dearly delineated magical world of the enchanted village of Brigadoon. *The Wizard of Oz* (1939) is another such musical with a fairy-tale narrative. The situation is slightly confused by Ric Altman, in his extended analysis of the Hollywood Musical, postulating a subgenre he calls the 'Fairy Tale Musical'. In doing so, seemingly he is not asserting the existence of magic within such films (although some do have) but rather he seems to define 'fairy tale' as he describes one such film: "Set in aristocratic Europe, from its vaguely recognizable outline of Paris to the conventional big white set of Ruritanian royalty, the film draws its situations, sets, costumes and props from a typically American storybook version of Old World Kings and Kingdom". *(The American Film Musical,* Indiana University Press, Bloomington, 1987. P. 142)

10. Anderson, p. 122.

11. *Everybody Says I Love You* actually has a diegetic narrator who tells the story rather like a fairy tale. But unlike most fairy tales, this narrator is part of the story. But my assertion that motion pictures are storytelling events without a storyteller holds true: who narrates the narrator? (In this particular instance, because Woody Allen is both writer and director—key creator in other words—it might be said he does. But is there any sense that the spectators for this story are aware of his 'presence' as narrator, especially given Woody Allen plays a character in the narrative?)

12. But especially *An American in Paris* (Vincente Minnelli, 1951).

AUSTRALIANA

'YOU COME OUT HERE A WOG. YOU STAY ONE OR YOU DON'T'[1]: ETHNICITY AND IDENTITY IN THE NEW AUSTRALIAN CINEMA

Of the 500-plus feature films made in Australia since 1970, overwhelmingly by Australians with Australian money and creative input, until recently few have placed any emphasis on the issues of ethnicity (or multiculturalism)—the condition, situation and histories of immigrants in Australia.

For the first fifteen or so years of the new Australian cinema, any possibility of exploring or representing ethnic diversity in Australia through the feature film was swamped by the torrent of representations of a more singular, monocultural Anglo-Australian definition of national identity. Arguably there was little to indicate that 'ethnic' films (films *about* ethnics, not *by* ethnic filmmakers) would be considered favourably by the dominant film financing organisations, which at the time were all federal or state government instrumentalities.

With the introduction of an 'experiment' in privately-funded, tax-incentive financing—the 10BA period from 1981 to 1988—there was a temporary waning of the importance of government bodies in influencing or determining the types of films being made. This did not lead to in a burgeoning of 'repressed' interest in representing the ethnic experience of Australia. This suggests (but may do no more) that there was no compelling social or cultural interest in doing so. It may also suggest that those who may have wished to do so continued, albeit under different conditions and restraints, to be unable to gain access to the means of production.

Since the Bicentennial celebrations in 1988, the obsession with representing, reproducing and exploring Australian identity from within the dominant, Anglo-Australian definitions has faded (but not disappeared) from Australian films. The celebration, if it is such, of Australian identity which many post-bicentennial films reflect, no matter with what clarity (or lack of it), is of diversity rather than singularity. What is of interest here is just how ethnicity is represented in a small group of films that may be designated 'ethnic films'.

Not surprisingly, these films represent ethnicity through the narrative structuring device *of difference*. Put simply, to be ethnic in these films is to be different. But it is the registering of this difference that is important in understanding how ethnicity is represented within and across this body of films. From what position is difference registered? In other words, what is the 'normality' against which difference is measured, to which it is contrasted, with which it is compared?

The overriding structuring antinomy[2], again not surprisingly, is between those characters who are designated 'Australians' (ESB) and those who are designated 'ethnics' (NESB).[3] A defining Anglophone/non-Anglophone distinction is maintained by these films; I have only been able to identify one, *Sunstruck* (James Gilbert, 1972), which represents the condition of, or finds a dramatic narrative based on, recent British migration to Australia. For that matter, Irish ethnicity is equally ignored, although Irishness does exist, usually in stereotyping of minor characters in films that are not specifically ethnic films. To a lesser extent, the structuring difference is between Australia itself (rather than Australians) and the country or culture of origin of the Nesbee characters. This is present in films such as *Silver City* (Sophie Turkiewicz, 1984) and *Kostas* (Paul Cox, 1979), but it is not often the cause of narrative structure or dramatic incident. It is the fact of being ethnic that is the signifier[4] of difference, and that difference is the underlying narrative motivation for the dramatic story.

This is encapsulated in the film *Moving Out* (Michael Pattinson, 1983). The protagonist Gino, the teenage son of an immigrant family, born in Italy but growing up in Melbourne, at one point makes an impassioned speech about being 'a wog'. In a scene entirely in shot/reverse shot close-ups between Gino and his distant cousin who has arrived more recently from Italy, Gino aggressively argues the futility of maintaining Italian cultural identity in the context of living in Australia. Gino's *angst* at being caught in a cultural situation where he is neither one thing nor the other and both things simultaneously, leads him to make a lengthy speech (in clear distinction from his usual monosyllabic utterances), which concludes: 'You come out here a wog. You stay one or you don't. It's as simple as that.'

The narrative structure of *Moving Out* places Gino in a position of alienation. He is alienated from his family because of the cultural pressures of dominant Australian culture different and antagonistic to his Italian culture. (Or so it is implied since Australian culture is barely represented in the film except by inference and by the part played by Dorothea McKellar's poem 'My Country', which thus serves a metonymic function.) The film supports this either/or position—to be wog or not to be a wog—and in spite or perhaps because of an ambiguous ending, it does not indicate that difference in these terms is resolvable. Immediately following this scene, there is a sequence in which 'wogs being wogs' is fully represented, a birthday celebration in which all those present are (seemingly) of Italian origin, in which the behaviour, speech, manner of dress and the decor of the house are all clearly designated as being ethnic (specifically Italian). And further along in the narrative development, Gino reveals that he is still held by the 'power of origins' when he affectionately recalls his early childhood in Italy, especially time spent with his grandfather (who did not migrate to Australia).

Difference is thus not denigrated or condemned in *Moving Out*—or at least not unequivocally so. Gino's 'wog speech' combined with his function as the protagonist—the central character with whom the putative audience is expected to identify—clearly indicated the manner in which he is psychically torn by the knowledge of his 'difference', his ethnicity (which he would partly wish to deny), and the way in which this inhibits him from becoming 'Australian'. His adolescent *angst* is intensified by his ethnicity, his difference from the (understated) normal condition of being Australian. And yet, as Gino's speech reveals, he considers himself *to* be an Australian. This is the closest *Moving Out* comes to actually expressing a definition, a 'working' definition, of multiculturalism as lived personal and social experience.

Yet even given that in the usual process of cinematic/dramatic identification a spectator might reasonably empathise with Gino in the personal anguish he feels through his sense of difference, *Moving Out* still represents ethnicity negatively, at least in the sense of what it means to be different, alienated or out of place. It seems to be arguing for the recognition of the need for assimilation—'you stay a wog or you don't'—and therefore to be implying that the multicultural policy of integration, in contradistinction to assimilation, can be personally and psychologically damaging. Thus in *Moving Out to* stay culturally Italian is to invite personal alienation, to leave the individual, particularly the second generation ethnic, in a psycho-social no-man's land.

But *Moving Out* is far from clear in the 'message' it is sending out. Not least because any sense of a demonstration of what is Australian culture, what it might mean to be a fully encultured Australian, is absent from the diegesis. It is implied inasmuch as it exists as a set of understandings, perceptions, that it is assumed the putative audience share. It shares this with almost all other ethnic films: the dominant definitions of Australia form an unstated set of positions from which the various degrees of ethnicity and types of difference are measured. In this specific instance the only representatives of Esbee-Australian culture given dramatic and/or filmic space are two teachers. One is an 'old-fashioned', elderly teacher, locked in a monocultural and nostalgically recalled past. It is he who insists that Gino learn by heart that erstwhile icon of Australian cultural identity, 'My Country'. The other is Gino's form teacher, who gives no other sense of Australianness beyond his name (Mr Clarke), his ability to speak only English, and as the representative of the (Anglo-Australian) education system.[5]

Locations in *Moving Out* are iconically Australian of course, including the appropriately typical 'Italian-migrant' architecture of the house where the birthday party takes place. Other than a brief appearance of police officers in one short incident, as well as two of a small group of friends Gino hangs around with, the only other Australian character of any narrative significance is an Australian girlfriend whom Gino has for a short time. Here the film does not explore any conflict arising from his cross-cultural personal relationship—unlike many other ethnic films, especially those which might quite reasonably be nominated as 'Romeo and Juliet' stories.

Moving Out (with other ethnic films) fails to provide any clear sense of what the desirability of being Australian might actually mean, or of being a full member of Australian society (that is, if Australian society is seen to be singular rather than functionally multicultural), or of being a fully encultured Australian. It only suggests that a knowledge of not being any of these things fuels Gino's sense of personal and (perhaps) social alienation.

On the other hand, the film's representations of what it means to be ethnic (in Australia) are frequently confused by seeming to be based in dominant Australian (or Esbee) stereotypes of what ethnicity means. Much of the film does strike an Anglo-Australian (me) as having a considerable ring of authenticity in its reproduction of ethnic lifestyles, familial structures and everyday appearance. This is particularly brought about by its disinclination to provide subtitles when Italian is being spoken, and also through the mise-en-scene (although again perhaps this corresponds to what is 'known' or 'believed'—a sort of social imaginary—of how and where migrants live, how they dress, decorate their homes, work and so on).

Strictly Ballroom (Baz Luhrmann, 1992) is particularly instructive in the examination of the way ethnicity is constructed and represented in the new Australian cinema for it emphasises something which is often no more than implied, and at times is only unconsciously 'present'. The narratives of nearly all ethnic films base their sense of difference—the source of dramatic incident and characterisation—on an absence. Or perhaps, upon that which is not fully articulated: an assumption about what constitutes 'normal' Australian culture. Most ethnic films of the new Australian cinema at best do not do more than hint at that normality or typicality of Australian culture against which the culture, conditions, characteristics, and actions of ethnic protagonists are depicted as different. Australian culture is a field or the (back)ground on which the ethnicity of Nesbee characters is stitched. Continuing the metaphor, ethnicity provides the patterns or the designs that form the structure of the narratives of these films. The field is the essential background which throws ethnicity into relief.

Strictly Ballroom draws attention to this by, for once (albeit metaphorically) setting up Australian culture as the opposing culture and demonstrating its failure to be a satisfactory culture, at least in terms of permitting space for the Esbee-protagonist Scott Hastings to exercise freedom of choice and full expression of his personality and talents. The bureaucrats of the ballroom dance culture (which I take to be a metaphor for Australian/Esbee culture) are characterised in two ways. First, through the mise-en-scene, they are represented as a carnival of grotesques: over-dressed, be-wigged, and heavily made-up (men and women), often shot in wide-angle, distorting, extreme close-up. This highly-stylised mise-en-scene continues beyond characterisation to be true of the cinematic presentation of all scenes associated with ballroom dancing/Australian culture. Second, these same figures are all 'old', traditional, hidebound, uncompromising and ruthless in their demands that the established tenets of ballroom dancing (of metaphorically traditional singular Australian culture) be adhered to by the members of its 'culture' without the right of argument or objection: Dance this way or don't dance at all. That is, live in Australia their way or don't live here at all. Assimilation not integration—again. In *Strictly Ballroom,* however, there is a statement that difference in the form of ethnicity is desirable because it is different, and not just for the attractive protagonists as the applauding multitude reveals at the conclusion when all— bar the defeated representative of outmoded, irrelevant, traditional culture— cheer on the 'mix' of old and new, the multicultural-in-practice that Scott and Fran demonstrate personally and through their dancing style. This conclusion is far from being unambiguous about who is assimilating whom, or whether this is actually integration in practice.

A more extended, more negative, indeed vitriolic, critique of Australians and Australianness is found in the earlier *Silver City.* It is not going too far to assert that to be 'Australian' in the diegesis of *Silver City is* to be different, to be 'Other'. Not only does the film resolutely take the position, the point-of-view of the Polish immigrants upon whose imagined (if well-researched) biographies and experiences the narrative is structured, but there is barely an Anglo-Australian character within the diegesis who is sympathetically portrayed. The film suggests that Australians are, variously and together, officious, lacking in tact and feeling (e.g., they address post-World War II Polish refugee migrants in German), are pompous, unsympathetic and give credence and positions of authority to ex-Nazis, are racists and rapists (often at the same time), or if in any way friendly to immigrants they are broadly comic, slow-witted and (by comparison) unsophisticated. There is also no ground for seeing *Silver City's* representation of Australia (in the 1940s and '50s at least) as a society or Australians (Esbees) as acceptable in any terms—save that Australia does provide opportunities for personal betterment to both first and second generation ethnics (as the enveloping opening and concluding scenes state).

Other ethnic films-are far from definite in defining or representing ethnic or Nesbee culture as strong and admirable. For example, those films whose diegesis are within Greek immigrant culture routinely show ethnic Greek culture to be not merely different but to be undesirable in many of its manifestations.

In terms of representations of ethnicity in recent Australian films, it is possible to schematically contrast ethnics and Anglo-Australians:

Nesbee	Esbee
Reactionary/conservative	Sympathetic/'liberal'★
Inflexible	Hostile
Bigoted/insular	Bigoted/xenophobic
Ignorant (of Esbee culture)	Ignorant (of Nesbee culture)
Dismissive (of Esbee culture)	Uncomprehending/uncaring
Sensual, passionate, romantic	Restrained, inhibited
Patriarchal, authoritarian	Democratic
Phenotypically ethnic	Phenotypically Anglo-Celtic
	★ Exception: *Strictly Ballroom*

Clearly there are internal inconsistencies in this list. Even within one film it is possible for some Esbees to be sympathetically inclined towards ethnic characters and some Esbee characters (usually peripheral ones or representatives of the law) to be hostile and aggressive. Similarly not all ethnic characters are reactionary and so on. Nonetheless, this taxonomy reflects detectable trends across these films.

The list importantly includes physical appearance and characteristics which usually denote ethnicity in both 'real life' and, more particularly, in fictitious representations. Phenotypes provide much of the actual and fictional recognition of ethnicity, and characterising by physical appearance is universal in these films, even if the ethnicity is somewhat interchangeable. For example, Italian actors play Greek characters and vice-versa; Greek actors play Turkish characters—the same actor plays a Greek father in *The Heartbreak Kid* (Michael Jenkins, 1993) and a Turkish one in *Death in Brunswick* (John Ruane, 1990) and so on. The mise-en-scene carries this notion of ethnic 'type' into the inanimate. Architecture, decor and dress are other important signifiers of ethnicity, used normatively in these films and thereby reproducing stereotyped perceptions drawn from Australian 'actuality' as well as Esbee prejudices.

In the absence of a value-system based in and supported by representations of what it means personally and communally to be a member of Australian (Esbee) culture and what advantages, boons, rights and responsibilities accrue as such, then ethnic values provide these things, deliberately or not, within individual films. By default ethnic culture is a culture, whereas Australian culture takes on something more along the lines of simply being. Thus these films, grounded in the conflict of difference and drawing their various dramatic materials from this, at the same time suggest that ethnic cultures are more supportive, are more 'alive', life-affirming, communal; that they are built upon and exist through a set of structures by which individuals and the group are located, given roles and functions that are mutually understood, and the parameters are communicable to and between the individuals who, as a group, constitute and share the culture.

Paradoxically, at the same time a number of films are concerned to locate their dramatic structures in representations of just how restrictive, rigid or inappropriate (for Australia, for the late 20th century) some (if not all) these ethnic cultures can be. This is particularly true of those films which take as their Nesbee focus group Greek communities and families. *The Heartbreak Kid* and *Death in Brunswick* demonstrate this most clearly. Throughout both, but particularly the former, the ethnic protagonists are presented narratively as 'victims' of an oppressive, rigid, traditional, alien social structure—especially one which oppresses women, or which places them in highly circumscribed social roles. *The Heartbreak Kid* is interesting in that although the dramatic conflict is located within a "Romeo and Juliet" narrative, both parties to the romantic relationship are of Greek ethnicity; as distinct from *Death in Brunswick, Nirvana Street Murder* (Aleksi Vellis, 1991) and *Kostas,* where the couples are actually mixed—one Australian, the other ethnic.

In postulating the existence of basic ethnic values within and across these ethnic films, I am simply expanding upon the implication of the Nesbee characteristics listed above. That is, I am responding to the seeming implication of these films that there is little to distinguish between different ethnicities: ethnicity is ethnicity is ethnicity and its primary criterion of definition is ethnicity's difference from Australian culture. The most obvious demonstration of this occurs in *Cathy's Child* (Donald Crombie, 1979), which draws its narrative from the actual events surrounding an immigrant woman aided by a Sydney newspaper in regaining custody of her child, who had been taken illegally out of Australia by her husband. Without going into the intricacies of the plot, it is enough to point out that although the 'Cathy' of the tide was, by origin, Maltese, and her husband and family are Greek, and that some of the various contributors to the drama are of Italian origin, the film (as routine) sets up the clear demarcation line as being between ethnicity (Cathy) and Anglo-Australianism (Dick Wordley, the journalist who helps her, and others, notably politicians and bureaucrats). In the initial investigatory section of the narrative, while Wordley tries to get the full picture of Cathy's story, the film's representation of ethnic/migrant communities makes (and demonstrates) a couple of assumptions. First, that the Greek community of Sydney (who are supportive of Cathy's husband's rights as father and as a Greek) is assumed to *be* coherent, homogenous, in easy communication with all its members, and these all accept that 'to be Greek' overrides 'to be Australian' (Cathy's husband is a naturalised Australian, her child an Australian for having been born here). Second, that the ethnic community consists of a whole non-Anglo-Australian 'world' made up of intermingled Southern European migrants who share many of the basic assumptions attributed to the Greek community and also a suspicion of and/or self-imposed isolation from the Anglo-Australian society.

All this does suggest, consciously or unconsciously, that the filmmakers have a deep suspicion of ethnic groups which are perceived to be too tight knit, and it is imagined that ethnicity (otherness/difference) itself has sufficient in common to bind all ethnic groups irrespective of actual ethnic origin. *Moving Out* has little sense of any social existence beyond that of the Italian ethnic community; *The Heartbreak Kid* also demonstrates this even though part of a significant subplot is concerned with the tensions and open conflict between Esbee students and Nesbee students at the school. Outside the school, the society represented in *The Heartbreak Kid* is exclusively Greek but is sufficiently 'extended' to include representations of a thriving and consciously maintained class structure within the Greek community. This sense of self-contained isolation, of course, adds to the manner in which, typically, the larger Australian social and cultural context is an unarticulated given. This designation of a key aspect of ethnicity also adds to the perception of ethnicity as stifling and rigidly authoritarian, closed off to 'liberating' influences of Australian culture, *Strictly Ballroom* notwithstanding.

Even so, it is not enough to simply postulate a fundamental dichotomy— 'them and us'—to these films. Certainly there are strong suggestions that the 'them' are defined by an overriding ethnicity and thus 'they' are located as being different from 'us'. But on an individual film-by-film basis, it is by no means clear just who the 'us' might be. Given the classic identificatory processes of film narrative, many of the protagonists of these narratives are both 'us' and 'them'. That is, the central character with whom putative spectators are expected to identify, whose motives, actions, and so on are mostly clearly those which the same putative spectators are expected to follow, to understand, and whose 'fate' is a matter of imaginative concern and investment, is often an ethnic character.

Therefore, it is possible to assert a degree of schizophrenia in these films. The assumption that difference is understood by being contrasted to an unspoken or under-determined sense of 'normality', which is dominant Anglo-

Australian culture and society, is challenged or contradicted by the presentation of empathetic or imaginatively engaging characters who are defined in turn by that very difference. The lack of a clear set of attitudes is complicated by the fact that many of these films are ambivalent about both Australian (Esbee) culture and ethnic (Nesbee) culture, finding aspects of each to both valorise and condemn.

Self-evidently, representations of ethnicity are fundamental to these films as the condition and situation of being ethnic or, more precisely, of being within an ethnic cultural, personal, domestic and/or community situation is a determining factor of the narrative of each of these films—with the possible exception of *Romper Stomper* (Geoffrey Wright, 1992), where the existence of such a community is still the driving factor in setting the narrative in motion.

The ethnic films manifest their representations, or vision, of ethnicity most clearly through narratives centred in the drama of personal relationships—particularly within the family (represented as a special site of ethnicity). This means only certain aspects of ethnicity are emphasised again and again. With their narrative structures so routinely concerned with interpersonal relationships—often of the sexual kind—these films set Anglo-Australian culture against the ethnicity of the chosen migrant culture through the dramatic device of the two partners being of either Esbee or Nesbee background. But in so doing, the films only occasionally suggest that social cohesion—real or mythical, of an allegedly singular Anglo-Australian culture -is challenged or threatened by ethnicity. The realm of the personal never becomes fully conflated with the realm of the social. In the sense of its function as allegory, the exception once again is *Strictly Ballroom*.

Ethnicity is narrowly defined in these films, very much within the contemporary public discourse of multiculturalism. That is, ethnicity is seen to be a matter of external cultural attributes—physical appearance, dress, language and behaviour—of certain cultural practices—dance, music and cuisine—and of separateness through closed communities that maintain their own tradition and sense of identity drawn from their origins. By and large, ethnicity is associated with rather simple definitions of cultural pluralism, but these are very much the cornerstone of the public discourse of multiculturalism. It may be unreasonable to expect films to do otherwise. Nonetheless, these films do provide 'versions' of multiculturalism in social practice, even if together and individually those representations tend to be less than certain. This too may be a close correlation to the public discourse of multiculturalism.

NOTES

1. The quote is from *Moving Out*, a film released in 1983, directed by Michael Pattinson.

2. This term is used in the sense of opposed meanings and attitudes which structure the theme that shape or inform the narrative. As the term implies, these are able to be expressed as binary oppositions, although in any film their expression may be both explicit (as indicated by the quote used in the title of this essay) and implicit (available through analysis).

3. (ESB stands for English-speaking background and NESB for Non-English speaking backgrounds. Hence, for the purposes of this article, 'Esbees' and 'Nesbees'.)

4. I am using this term in the sense usually applied in structuralism and semiotics, that is, 'the *signifier* is the physical form of a sign as we perceive it through our senses... The signified is the user's mental concept of what the sign refers to'. (O'Sullivan et al, *Key Concepts in Communications and Cultural Studies*, 1994.)

5. It is interesting to note that the actor who plays this role has some of the physical characteristics of ethnicity and his real name is Ivar Kants (is this an unconscious and unintended demonstration of multiculturalism?)

THE CINEMA OF ALAN MARSHALL

Even making allowance for journalistic hyperbole, it is possible that Alan Marshall may well have agreed with reporter Don Petersen who asserted in a 1975 interview in *The Sun* that 'Alan is now head over heels [in love] with the film makers. And they, in increasing numbers, with him'.[1] For a while, it looked as if Marshall, 'the patriarch of Australian story tellers' in Petersen's words, was about to become a dominant influence in the fledgling Australian film industry—or at least his writings a dominant source of material for films.

Before Australian filmmakers, in the first flush of what was to become an Australian film renaissance in the mid-1970s, discovered Alan Marshall (or were directed towards him as will be noted below), his writing had the source of inspiration for a feature film. This first connection (as far as can be judged) between Marshall and the cinema took place a long way from Australia, geographically and culturally. In 1970, the Czechoslovakian director Karel Kachyna produced *I Can Jump Puddles*[2], a relatively faithful adaptation (given its translocation to Czechoslovakia—or rather Moravia in the Austro-Hungarian Empire—around the beginning of the twentieth century) of the first of Marshall's autobiographical trilogy (first published in 1955). There is a tantalising, yet in fact only potential, symmetry about Marshall's writing becoming a Czechoslovakian film in the 1970s. The term 'New Wave', first used in relation to post-war French cinema, was subsequently used (or over-used) to encapsulate each 'new' or re-emerging cinema to appear from European (and later Asian and African) countries—usually the 'sudden appearance' of each new wave coinciding with films shown at film festivals. So pervasive were these appearances and the use of 'new wave' to herald each discovery that David Stratton, writing of Australian cinema's later re-emergence, (rather prematurely) entitled his 1980 book *The Last New Wave*.[3] Marshall looked set, in the early 1970s, to be a prominent figure in this Australian 'new wave', while continuing to be a presence in the on-going Czechoslovakian version. It turned out otherwise on both counts.

The reason why Karel Kachyna chose to adapt an Alan Marshall story is far from clear (or perhaps only available in accounts in Czech). One account of Czechoslovakian cinema makes the intriguing remark that Kachyna 'has a reputation of a "progressive" due to his friendship with left-wing Australian writers'.[4] While this comment may be intended, within the context of the book concerned, with explaining aspects of the Czech cinema and the Czech state (especially post-1968), it still raises intriguing questions as to why Marshall was chosen, and what other Australian writers may have been considered (in Czechoslovakia let alone Australia) as 'left-wing'. Certainly Marshall provided himself with some left-wing credentials in the 1930s, contributing articles to the local communist paper, the *Worker's Voice*. These articles inevitably described the appalling conditions of the employed but exploited, the unemployed, and the poor. He was also a member of the Writers' League in Melbourne, deemed a radical group in the context of the 1930s. Marshall was never a member of the Communist Party and his common interest with them seems not to have been doctrinaire or ideological, but based on observation and experience, on a genuinely engaged (and enraged) social conscience. It may well be the social realism of Marshall's later writing, a term usually understood, if not always fully articulated, to be *socialist* realism, is what attracted Kachyna to the material.

Even so, and allowing for the fact that Marshall's left-wing reputation may have been known in the Soviet Union and its satellite states (possibly assisted in this by Frank Hardy and Stephen Murray-Smith—the latter lived in Prague for a few years after the Second World War), it remains intriguing that it was *I Can Jump Puddles* that first interested Soviet publishers and then Karel Kachyna. It is not the most left-wing or the most critical of the capitalist social situation of Marshall's writings. *I Can Jump Puddles* was certainly translated into many of the languages of the various Eastern Bloc countries (as well as some Western European countries) and was presumably well known in Czechoslovakia. How the book came to be translated and published in the Soviet Union is unclear and it seems Marshall only found out by accident. He wholeheartedly approved and offered other of his books for translation as well.[5] Marshall made two invited trips to the Soviet Bloc in the early 1960s.[6] The first of these certainly involved a visit to Czechoslovakia, where he visited at least one institution for the treatment of crippled children (the quality of which organisation considerably impressed him). It is possible he met Kachyna while in Prague.[7]

Marshall's involvement in the adaptation and the film itself seems to have been minimal, although he did correspond with Kachyna and also supplied photographs of his childhood that enabled him to select an child actor who resembled the young Marshall.[8] Although invited, Marshall was unable to attend the film's premiere in Prague; his daughter Cathy went in his place (and was able to use some of Marshall's accumulated royalties that could not otherwise leave the country). Marshall did not see the film until local distributor Natalie Miller imported a print and provided a private showing.

There is little in the film that suggests an ideological motive (no matter how well hidden) and it succeeded by a combination of its technical excellence and charmingly undemanding narrative. In fact, it presents so successfully a child's-eye view of the world, that the concluding remark by a British reviewer may be considered appropriate: 'The temptation to read a political allegory into crippled Adam's struggle to assert his independence is probably best avoided.'[9]

It was variously reported after *I Can Jump Puddles Again*, Karel Kachyna was intending to make feature films of the second and third parts of Marshall's autobiography. There is no evidence that either of these films was produced.[10] The vagaries of film production, in Czechoslovakia as in Australia or anywhere else, are such that many projects flounder at any of the many stages between scripting and distribution. The same thing seems to have happened in Australia, perhaps at an even earlier stage, with the suggestions (by Petersen in *The Sun*) that Australian directors Tim Burstall and Tom Cowan were 'also working on Marshall-inspired ideas'. Burstall and Cowan, although different in filmic temperament and approach—Cowan being the more socially and politically committed—were both early directors in the Australian film revival, but, given the considerable difficulties in getting feature film productions underway (let alone undertaken) in the beginning of that revival, it is not surprising that no matter what they may or may not have been intending to do with 'Marshall-inspired material', nothing seems to have eventuated.

One of the major contributing factors to the rebirth of the Australian film industry was the establishment by the Commonwealth government in 1973 of the Australian Film, Television and Radio School (AFTRS).[11] One of the requirements of the first students was that they produce a short fictional film based upon the work of Australian writers. (The AFTRS had approached a number of living writers seeking their permission and even asking for suggestions.) One of the first directorial students in the AFTRS's interim program was Gillian Armstrong and the film she made to meet this requirement was *One Hundred a Day* (1973), based upon an incident in Marshall's 1949 novel *How Beautiful Are Thy Feet*. Armstrong and Marshall met and, according to Armstrong, Marshall 'was very encouraging and told me the details because he really did work in a shoe factory as a young man in the 1930s, so he gave me great background details to think about visualising it'.[12] The film concerns itself with a young, single woman, employed in a shoe factory, who, given her economic and social circumstances, has to have a backyard abortion. Supported by two friends from the factory, she undergoes the abortion (not seen) and returns to work.

Another student in the interim program of the AFTRS, Chris Noonan, also chose a Marshall story for his short fiction subject.[13] *Bulls* (1974) was adapted from a short story of the same name and is this time placed in a rural setting. Significantly, *Bulls* too has a female protagonist, this time a young girl. The film was screened at the 1975 Melbourne Film Festival.

The relationship Marshall established with Gillian Armstrong bore further fruit when he sent another of his stories which he felt might interest her. This was a recent short story, 'Old Mrs Bilson', and unlike *I Can Jump Puddles* and

One Hundred a Day, not necessarily set in the past[14]. Armstrong, looking at the time for a project to take to the Australian Film Commission, showed an early draft of the adaptation to them. She received a $20,000 grant but then realised that 'it wasn't something I was passionate about'.[15] At the instigation of her co-writer, John Pleffer, and with the agreement of Marshall, the story was changed to replace two small boys with a young woman, Charlie, who meets and develops a relationship with the old, apparently senile Mrs Bilson. They discover, despite the generation gap, a great deal in common, especially in terms of their unfaithful partners, Mrs Bilson's late husband, and Charlie's current boyfriend. The title reflects a further commonality: unfilled ambitions to be a singer (Charlie) and a dancer (Mrs Bilson). Marshall, happy with what was a fairly fundamental change, left the writing of the young couple to Pleffer and Armstrong but contributed material around Mrs Bilson. (The extent to which he actively collaborated in the screenplay is not clear; he received no credit on the film.)

The completed film, *The Singer and the Dancer* (1976), was a *succès d'estime* and, inasmuch as a short film with its limited release potential can be, a commercial success as well. It was taken up by Columbia Pictures and had limited release, notably in Sydney and Melbourne. In Sydney it was doubled with another recent Australian short film, *Love Letters from Teralba Road* (Stephen Wallace, 1977). It was screened more widely at film festivals, both in Australia and overseas, and won a number of awards.

Marshall may well have been optimistic about future film adaptations, especially feature films, coming from his writing, especially following the reception of *The Singer and the Dancer*—for which he received a tiny fee and a small percentage. But any thoughts that Armstrong would continue the collaboration were disappointed. With her two Marshall adaptations, Armstrong had already indicated a trajectory towards 'the woman's film' and a feminist approach to film production and the content of her films. This was apparent from the significant changes wrought on 'Old Mrs Bilson'—the introduction of the young woman (replacing two boys) and the consequent increased emphasis on themes to do with the women's roles, attitudes and conditions. It is not surprising and perhaps even logical that Armstrong would turn to an Australian woman writer for her feature film debut, Miles Franklin's *My Brilliant Career*. This was the film that established Armstrong's reputation beyond doubt and launched her own 'brilliant career'. Yet Marshall's 'credentials' in this area were hardly lacking. He had, in the 'thirties, contributed a regular and highly successful column, *Alan Marshall Says*, to the magazine, *Women* —a column basically about women. Later this column was transferred to the *Argus* as *Alan Marshall's Casebook*, where it continued up until the demise of that newspaper in the 1950s. The column was essentially 'about' women's matters—prompted often by letters he received—and had a strong following. His credentials as an emphatic and insightful writer about (and for) women and the place in society were probably as strong as Franklin's. Ironically, it may well be that he lacked a sense of fantasy-romance, or his writings did, whereas *My Brilliant Career* had *that* potential for cinematic exploitation.

From the mid-seventies until the early 1980s, the burgeoning Australian cinema showed considerable interest in narratives which explored and celebrated traditional perceptions of national identity. This involved a degree of 'plundering' Australian writers for period narratives that met this unstated policy. In addition to Miles Franklin, sources were found, for example, in Henry Handel Richardson (*The Getting of Wisdom*, Bruce Beresford, 1977), Elizabeth O'Connor (*The Irishman*, Donald Crombie, 1978), Mrs Aneas Gunn (*We of the Never Never*, Igor Auzins, 1982)—notably all women writers. Later, more recent (and male) writers provided material for adaptations, although literary adaptation has been more of a trend than a tradition in Australian cinema over the past thirty years. Marshall, however, was not a writer to whom Australian filmmakers turned, despite the clear demonstration by Kachyna and Armstrong of the suitability of his work for cinematic adaptations. Not, that is, until some time after his death in 1985.

There is a pleasing symmetry and a slight touch of irony that the only feature film (to date) produced in Australia from Marshall's writing is *Hammers Over the Anvil* (Ann Turner, 1991), adapted from a collection of short stories that Marshall was writing at the time of his involvement in *The Singer and the Dancer*. Indeed, 'Old Mrs Bilson', Marshall's 'new' story supplied to Gillian Armstrong and which became the basis of *The Singer and the Dancer*, is one of the stories that make up the *Hammers Over the Anvil* collection, itself published in 1975. Once again, it is a woman director who is attracted to Marshall's writing, even though this work follows the usual Marshall path of being, to a greater or lesser extent, autobiographical, and has therefore a central character who is a crippled adolescent boy and whose path to adulthood is partially mapped by various incidents he is involved in, or more significantly, that he observes. It has, interestingly, a romantic (or at least sexual) narrative (observed by but not involving the boy). At the same time, this romantic plot is considerably darker than that in *My Brilliant* Career. The film had a modest release in Australia (contrary to the ill-informed opinion of an Adelaide journalist who thought it had been screened once and then dumped[16]) and it garnered modified praise from reviewers (none of whom, even the inestimable David Stratton, noticed the Mrs Bilson/*The Singer and the Dancer* link).

Marshall's most popular success on the screen, however, was not on the large cinematic screen but on the smaller television one. In the 1980s, there was a boom in the production of mini-series made for television, led inevitably by the Australian Broadcasting Commission (ABC) but taken up (as favourable tax concession were applied) by the commercial networks.[17] A nine-episode (of sixty minutes each) series was made of *I Can Jump Puddles* in 1981 by the ABC. This time, with the luxury of eight hours of screen time, the second part of Marshall's autobiographical trilogy, *This is the Grass*, and the earlier *How Beautiful are Thy Feet* were included, and the narrative takes Marshall from his childhood through his early adulthood and into the Depression. Although Marshall died just before *I Can Jump Puddles* was broadcast for the first time, he did see the completed production and had been present during much of the shooting. The series has been sold by the ABC in a number of international markets, one of which was Russia prior to the collapse of communism[18]. As a footnote to Marshall's television 'career' it is worth noting that in the early days of Australian television, a semi-animated series of two minute films, *The Ballads of Bull-Ant Ridge*, was made from Marshall's bush yarns; it apparently served as a filler between programs. It is in these rather than the more extensive adaptations that his work as a folk-lorist and folk-storyteller is given a screen presence—if an ephemeral one.[19]

Marshall's contribution to Australian cinema and, considering the Czech version of *I Can Jump Puddles*, international cinema has not been great. The same can be said of many Australian literary figures, of course, with a mere handful contributing more than one adaptation to Australian cinema.[20] Social (or historical) realism has only occasionally been in favour in Australian cinema. It may be argued that the attraction of *My Brilliant Career* to Gillian Armstrong, after two Marshall adaptations, was not simply that the story came from a woman writer but because of the possibilities (fully realised in the finished film) of a romantic (even melodramatic) narrative, an aspect not easily associated with Marshall's writing. It had to be teased out (and in large part further invented) from *Hammers Over the Anvil* for the film version. Yet, as noted, his material has attracted women directors in Australia rather than men. Marshall's position as a teller of tales of both the bush and the urban experiences of Australia has been, as yet, under-utilised. At the same time, it must be noted, that the ABC mini-series *I Can Jump Puddles*, did Marshall great service in successfully bringing his essential Australian yarn-telling style to a wide television audience at home and abroad, albeit in the form of a dramatic narrative.

NOTES

1. Don Petersen, 'A Place in the Sun', *The Sun* (Melbourne), June 12, 1975.

2. The title, in unreproducible Czechoslovakian, seems to vary with different releases. In Britain, where it was released initially in 1973, it was known as *I'm Jumping Over Puddles Again,* which seems to be a translation of its Czech title—although a literal translation seems to be *I am Jumping Muddy-Puddles Again.* It is not clear why, for release in Anglophone countries, it was not titled *I Can Jump Puddles,* even in Australia (where it was released in 1974) and it might be assumed the title would be better known.

3. David Stratton, *The Last New Wave: The Australian Film Revival.* Sydney: Angus and Robertson, 1980. Of course, with this title Stratton was not really suggesting no new cinemas would ever appear but playfully referring to the 1977 Australian film, The Last Wave— part of that 'new wave'.

4. Josef Skvorecky, *All the Bright Young men and Women: A Personal History of the Czech Cinema.* Toronto: Peter Martin Associates. 1971.

5. Harry Marks, I *Can Jump Oceans: The World of Alan Marshall.* Melbourne: Thomas Nelson (Australia) Limited, 1976, pp. 258-259.

6. These were between the crushed Hungarian Revolution (1956) and the 'Prague Spring' attempt at reform of the Czech communist party in 1968 (also put down by Soviet military force). Neither seems to have affected Marshall's attitudes to the 'use' of his works. It is the post-Prague Spring atmosphere in Czechoslovakia that Skvorecky seems to be referring to above.

7. A letter Marshall wrote when in Moscow in 1963 suggests that what may have fascinated some at least of the Soviet writers was the portrait of Alan's father in *I Can Jump Puddles.* (Marks, pp.295-296.)

8. A version available for classroom use in Australia contained a prologue consisting of childhood photographs and a voice-over narration by Marshall.

9. David Wilson. *Monthly Film Bulletin.* Vol. 40, no. 475. August 1973. p. 177.

10. Harry Marks, in his biography of Marshall, *I Can Jump Oceans,* suggests there was only one film planned, to be called *We Danced the Foxtrot Again.* No film of this title appears in Kachyna's filmography.

11. Initially the Australian Film and Television School, radio was added later to the curriculum and the title.

12. Peter Malone. *Myth and Meaning: Australian Directors in Their own Words.* Sydney: Currency Press, p.3.

13. The information contained in Screensound catalogue (National Film and Sound Archive, Canberra) credits three directors: Robert Lee Chittick. Janet Isaac and Chris Noonan. Although Noonan has gone on to direct several feature films, his career as a feature film director does not match Armstrong who has a considerable body of work both in Australia and overseas, importantly including *My Brilliant Career* (1979).

14. Like much of Marshall's writing, it was semi-autobiographical and by this criterion it *was* set in his childhood. However, nothing about the story insists this has to be the case, and a filmic adaptation can (and did) easily avoid period location.

15. Sue Mathews. *35mm Dreams: Conversations with Five Directors about the Australian Film Revival.* Ringwood, Vic: Penguin, 1984. p.132.

16. See Samela Harris, "SA on Six", *Adelaide Advertiser,* Tues. Feb 1, 1994, p.6.

17. Many Australian authors, living and dead, provided material for mini-series made in the 1980s and early 1990s before the boom bust. Katherine Susannah Pritchard (*Intimate Strangers*, 1991), Kyle Tennant (*The Battlers*, 1994), Louis Stone (*Jonah*, 1982), Ruth Park (*The Harp in the South, Poor Man's Orange*, both 1987) are just some.

18. Albert Moran, *Moran's Guide to Australian TV Series.* Sydney: AFTRS, 1993, pp.235-236.

19. Some at least seem to have survived miraculously and are preserved in the film archives at ScreenSound.

20. For example, Frank Moorhouse (*The Coca-Cola Kid*, 1985; *The Everlasting Secret Family*, 1988); Colin Theile (*Storm Boy*, 1976; *Blue Fin,* 1978; *The Fire in the Stone*, 1983). The most 'adapted' Australian writer is David Williamson, whose plays have been the source of seven feature films. Novelists and short story writers do poorly by comparison.

FILMOGRAPHY

The Ballads of Bull-Ant Ridge. Unknown date. (1957 ca.?)

I Can Jump Puddles 1970. Dir. Karel Kachyna. Barrandov Film Studios (Prague). 92 minutes. From *I Can Jump Puddles* (1955).

One Hundred a Day 1973. Dir: Gillian Armstrong. Australian Film and Television School. 8 minutes. From *How Beautiful are Thy Feet* (1949).

Bulls 1974. Dir: Chris Noonan. Australian Film and Television School. 17 minutes. From short story, 'Bulls'.

The Singer and the Dancer 1976. Dir: Gillian Armstrong. 60 mins. From short story 'Old Mrs Bilson', in *Hammers Over the Anvil* (1975).

I Can Jump Puddles 1981. Television series. Dir: Kevin Dobson, Keith Wilkes. 9 x 60 minutes. Australian Broadcasting Commission. From *I Can Jump Puddles* (1955), *This is the Grass* (1963) and *How Beautiful are Thy Feet* (1949).

Hammers Over the Anvil 1994. Dir: Ann Turner, South Australian Film Corporation and Hammer Films. 97 mins. From *Hammers Over The Anvil* (1975)

COUNTRY TOWNS IN AUSTRALIAN CINEMA

The Bush, the Australian Outback in its multifarious environments and ecologies, was from the outset of cinema in Australia and remains a potent site of inspiration for narratives, themes and characters and thus locations for Australian films, exercising a power over the imagination of film makers out of proportion to its reality and place in the everyday lives of Australians. The country town, a curious cultural and psychic site, culturally situated uneasily between the bush and the city has also proved to have a magnetic attraction for Australian film makers. The country town has, like the bush which surrounds it explicitly or by implication, provided both the physical context for narratives and the dramatic content of those narratives as well. Indeed, it is not going too far to argue that it is the very conditions of country towns—their social and cultural as much as their environmental conditions—which supply the shape, structure and specifics of the narratives which locate themselves in them. No matter what the particular dramas and conflicts, or the specific characters which make up individual 'Country Town' film, it is the country town itself, the very nature of its existence, the very act of living or trying to live in it, which determines the narrative in terms of both the types of conflicts and issues that structure the narrative, the way in which these are developed and played out, and significantly the resolutions to the narrative.

Country towns in Australian film vary in the degree and quality of their awfulness; but with rare exceptions they are all represented as irredeemably awful. This awfulness may be as 'harmless' as being merely (if unrelievedly) dull, or, at the other end of the spectrum, this awfulness may be undeniably destructive. The denizens of these towns may be little more than comic, they may be just limited in the sense of their understanding and outlook on life, or they may be distorted, socially deformed. Whatever, they are products of their culture, circumstance and environment rather than producers of it. In this at least Country Town films subscribe to the overall myth of Australian identity: that this identity is formed by the environment. Here, as well as in their mise-en-scene, the Country Town films implicate themselves in the myth of the power of the bush. Even so, particular films make it clear that the environment brings out or exposes latent aspects of the specific subculture of the country town—usually associated with untrammelled and untroubled masculinity—which the isolation, the closeness and closed-ness, the limited size of the community exaggerates.

There is a sense, then in which all Country Town films are the same. But then there is a sense in which all bush films are the same. This sameness lies at the base of the narratives and this commonality may be said to drive the

Country Town narrative in the way in which an engine drives an automobile: an engine needs both to be turned on (a point of ignition; in narrative terms, the point of disruption) and fuel to keep it going. How an engine (or the automobile it powers) is driven varies according to time, place and driver(s), yet the engine (in this—perhaps laboured metaphor—the physical and social condition of existence in country towns) remains basic and unchanging and ultimately determining of what can be done, and what cannot. This analogy (like all analogies) should perhaps not be taken too far but it affords a sense of how a generalised notion of the condition of country town-ness features between and across individual Country Town films.

METAPHORS FOR AUSTRALIA

In representing an aspect of the Australian experience, the country town in film functions in a number of key ways as a metaphor for Australia. This metaphorical Australia is less the Australia of the time of the film's production, especially of the Australia of the time of the New Australian Cinema, than it is of the Australia of the past.

Isolation is one of the fundamental ways in which this metaphor is activated. Australia is, or imagines itself to be, geographically and ethnographically isolated from, firstly, the rest of the world, and secondly, from the sites of the ethnic origin of most of the population. Nearly all Country Town films stress the environmental isolation of the town of their specific narratives, through images that place the town within a mise-en-scene that consistently emphasises the extent to which they are small, lonely places of human making in an otherwise barely habited and barely habitable landscape. *The Year My Voice Broke* (John Duigan, 1987), for example, is punctuated with such images, in this instance motivated or justified by the central character (who narrates the story from a point in the future) escaping the claustrophobic confines (more social than physical) of the town to a spot which is both some distance from it and elevated in the landscape, that looks down upon it as if the bush itself is watching and so emphasises the town's isolation in the landscape.

The mise-en-scene of country town films is replete with recurring images of this sort of panoramic *gaze* from the surrounding countryside or the bush, images which also draw attention to the roads or tracks which lead to or from the town (although seeming to come from and go to nowhere). These are images which stress the limits of the town, its diminutive size in the expanse of the bush, and which emphasise how the town is out of place, being *in* but not *of* the Australian landscape. While also suggesting by their presence that the town may be a place of community and thus of sanctuary from the emptiness and the threat of the Australian landscape, these images are far from comforting;

they imply the communities huddle in these towns not from choice but from a need for mutual support and security.

The isolation is not only physical, although though it is nearly always that. Equally importantly, the isolation is social. The community of the small town is isolated in the sense that its attitudes, mores and behaviours are isolated from a real or implied mainstream—that of the outside, inferentially that of the large cities or more generally of a broader spectrum of Australian society. The small country town in these films is isolated from the knowledge contained within and functioning in the outside world, sometimes as a result of its physical isolation but often as an act of will. The community does not wish to have that knowledge. Or it wishes to have only a particular aspect or version of that knowledge. In *Break of Day* (Ken Hannam, 1976), the internalised conflict which threatens to destroy the protagonist is the knowledge of the reality of war, the First World War, a reality so terrifying that it leads him to wound himself in order to escape further involvement with that reality. On the other hand, the community's knowledge of that same 'reality' is that of the ritual of Anzac Day and collective memory, enhanced (or undermined in the film's attitude) by the drunken anecdotes of returned servicemen. The impossibility of the community accepting or understanding a knowledge and experience that could encompass cowardice isolates the central character from the town, despite his standing in the community, and further motivates the manner in which he embraces the outsiders who bring disruption in their wake.

Country towns in Australian films also act metaphorically through their emphasis on, for the most part, a monocultural community. The advantage then to placing so many of these films in the past is that the monocultural make-up of the community can be justified as being somehow true to the realities of the past. The essence of Australian-ness can thus be imagined without the complicating reality of contemporary multicultural Australia. *Weekend of Shadows* (Tom Jeffrey, 1978) constructs its narrative around this by having the men of the community engage in a manhunt for a Pole—an outsider, a non-Australian—believed, for no reason except that he is a foreigner, to have murdered his landlady. Significantly, Aborigines barely appear in these period country town films. Where they do appear is in contemporary narratives, and not in all of these. Here the very drama is often the conflict between Euro-Australians and Aborigines, particularly emphasising the role of the police in such films as *Deadly* (Esben Storm, 1992) and *Dead Heart* (Nick Parsons, 1996).

There is a sense in which these films, period or not, are nostalgic for an imagined past. This places such films within that broad category of films that might be designated 'nationalist'. These films, almost always period films, take particular perceptions of Australian identity and in one way or another celebrate them. These perceptions are flexible to an extent but tend to be based in conceptions of Australian identity which coalesced at the beginning of the twentieth-century and which have retained their potency since. This nostalgia is, however, tempered and even overturned by the routinely negative attitude the films evince towards country towns and, especially, the communities that inhabit them.

There is barely a film that makes use of a country town locale, and more significantly of a country town as source of its narrative, that does so in a favourable or positive way. Unlike the majority of bush films, the Country Town films express considerable uncertainty over the dominant perceptions of Australian identity. This is not surprising given that country towns, in the Australian cultural mythos, function as sites of transition and mediation between the 'purity' of the bush and the 'corruption' (or worldliness) of the city. Depending upon from which end of the spectrum the gaze is made, the country town is seen as either compromising the ethical clarity of the bush or exemplifying the simplicity of communal existence that the city has lost or bartered away. Thus, the country town community can represent the last bastion of the sense of Australian-ness that was, allegedly, a lived experience in the past, or may represent the quintessence of that Australian-ness, preserved perversely by the very isolation of which it is victim.

MASCULINITY AND XENOPHOBIA

That these films interrogate some (if not all) of the tenets of that dominant perception of Australian identity can be demonstrated in the attitude these films have towards notions of masculinity, and particularly that cultural icon of Australian-ness, mateship. Mateship, which in a 'Bush' film such as *Gallipoli* (Peter Weir, 1981), is extolled as a virtue exceeding all others, is ruthlessly and iconoclastically attacked in the first of the Country Town films of the New Australia (and one of the first films of the New Australian Cinema altogether), *Wake in Fright* (Ted Kotcheff, 1971). Here, the visit to a country town—larger and more populous than is usual for country towns in Australian film—of a naive young man, originally from the city, painstakingly and painfully unfolds as an unrelenting descent into Hell, the descent greatly facilitated by the equally unrelenting, unasked for, and for the most part unwelcome aggressive 'hospitality' of mateship; a mateship originating in and generated by little other than the external conditions of existence and the commonality of maleness.

The aggression, the hostility, the 'evil' which exists in the country town is stirred from its latent state or brought to a higher level by the arrival of an outsider. John Grant, the naive schoolteacher who arrives for an overnight stay in the "Yabba" (*Wake in Fright*), the return after absence of Sam in *The Crossing*

(George Ogilvie, 1990), the enforced stay of Asta Cadell in Ginborak in *Shame* (Steve Jodrell, 1988), the presence of the two mates in *The Settlement* (Howard Rubie, 1984)—these and many other outsiders are the triggers that set in motion events which are, however, attributable to the condition of existence, to the structure of social and power relations in the country town in question. The outsiders are catalysts. Certainly, what they represent—less rigid gender attitudes, greater freedom of word and action, greater 'promiscuity', knowledge and education—are disturbances in and threats to the established order of the communities they 'invade'. But in nearly every instance, that established social order is demonstrably inflexible and constricting, a mixture of narrow-mindedness and rigidly enforced limits to 'acceptable' behaviour, morals and values. Faced with a challenge or a threat to this order, the community, in whole or in part, responds typically with violence: Adam/Felicia in *The Adventures of Priscilla, Queen of the Desert*, (Stephan Elliott, 1995) is beaten up; John Grant in *Wake in Fright* is sexually assaulted and driven to attempt suicide; Lizzie in *Shame* is murdered, Sam in *The Crossing* dies in an accident which may possibly be suicide. Violence is at the very core of the existence of Paris in *The Cars That Ate Paris* (Peter Weir, 1974). The town lives off the violence of engineered road 'accidents' and that violence finally and apocalyptically is turned upon the town itself in a devastating demonstration that those who live by the sword will die by the sword.

The country town's hostility to the outsider is often centred upon a guilty secret, one which the community or some members of it share, and self-evidently which they wish to keep hidden. The outsider brings that secret out into the open, often with devastating consequences for him or herself, for the town, and for a major character who is of the town but who is in the process of 'freeing' him or herself from its grip. Bigotry, prejudice, narrow-mindedness and ignorance stalk the streets of country towns in the New Australian Cinema—even those few films which are comedies. The secrets, often sexual in nature—rape, incest, or ordinary but unacceptable promiscuity—are based in the very nature of the community and its values. For these reasons, most Country Town films represent country towns as social confining and personally stultifying. Only a very few suggest that existence in a country town might by fun, free or life-enhancing—*Blue Fin* (Carl Schultz, 1979), *Dimboola* (John Duigan, 1979), *Frog Dreaming* (Brian Trenchard-Smith, 1986), *Rikky and Pete* (Nadia Tass, 1988)—it is no accident two of these are children's films, and the 'adult' films are comedies. In the less 'happy' Country Town films, those protagonists who survive frequently leave, indeed do so by leaving, and it is often a main character who is close to the protagonist who dies. Death or exile, both represent, if in rather different ways, an escape from the town and what it represents. Only rarely is the town itself changed in ways which might be said to be 'better'—*Shame* is the only clear example, *Warming Up* (Bruce Best, 1984) allows a comic change which may be little more than cosmetic. Escape seems the only genuine option; the generalised condition of existence of and in the country town remains.

CONFLICT
The conflict, the source of the drama that drives the narratives of country town films, is based in general terms upon the combination of the incompatibility of the presence of a 'stranger' and the hidden secret, and is exacerbated by the rigid behavioural codes which the stranger does not accept or recognise, and which have served to create and maintain the secret. These various conflicts, however, frequently are based in generational conflict or gender conflict. The former, not surprisingly, are coming-of-age narratives (*The Year My Voice Broke, The Delinquents* [Chris Thompson, 1989], *The Mango Tree* [Kevin Dobson, 1977], *The Fringe Dwellers* [Bruce Beresford, 1986]) in which sexual maturity is paralleled with social maturity, a distinct getting of wisdom. Some others within this category are less coming-of-age than growing-up stories (*Blue Fin, Frog Dreaming*). The latter, as if to underline the difference between merely growing-up and coming-of-age, tend to find the country town experience more personally rewarding; growing-up means growing into the social conditions and relationships of the town, coming-of-age almost inevitably means that with sexual experience comes a falling of scales from the eyes— sexual knowledge is almost biblical, he (and it is nearly always a male) who partakes of that particular tree of knowledge must leave and venture into the wilderness, except of course these country towns are no Gardens of Eden other than through their institutionalisation of ignorance. In generational conflict, rather self-evidently, the conflict occurs between the older generations who, whether they have a guilty secret or not, wish to maintain the status quo and the younger generation who find that status quo confining, depersonalising, and some cases personally threatening.

Gender conflict is usually the result of masculine dominance of the social structure of the country town and is caused by the manner in which the restricting social codes of the country town have the specific manifestation of denying women their sexuality or their right to their sexuality—or, on the case of *The Adventures of Priscilla, Queen of the Desert*—men their right to a non-heterosexuality. In many cases, this conflict is that of the oppression of 'blokedom', of patriarchy in its particular form of that of the Australian country town. In comedies such as *Dimboola, Warming Up* and to a lesser extent *All Men Are Liars* (Gerard Lee, 1995), the conflict is based in the ockerism of the men, which when carried far enough (as for the purposes of story and humour it always is), brings about opposition and sometimes open 'revolt' by the women (or some of them). This is almost exactly what happens in tragic form in *Shame*. *Shame*, however, also mixes issues of sexuality with more serious intent. Here the conflict is over the 'right' of men to physically impose their sexual demands upon women and the denial of women a sexual identity, reserving for those women who express a sexuality assault justified as 'they were asking for it'. Patriarchy leads to the hidden secrets in many of these narratives, and it in turns demands the complicity of silence from both men and women, a silence which is then threatened by the outsider or by a member of the younger generation or both. Gender conflict, based in the double standards of blokedom and the repression of patriarchy, is not the only outcome of masculinity in these films. Violence is inherently masculine in Country Town films. The mindless but non-directed violence of the male-only group of *Wake in Fright* becomes the mindless violence of the male pack in *Weekend of Shadows*, so palpable that even the feeble-minded 'Rabbit' realises killing the hunted (and innocent man) is preferable to leaving him to the 'mercies' of the male mob.

The pub is the social locus of the male-dominated country town, the power base from which men generate and mutually reinforce their attitudes and behaviours. The pub is a recurring icon of the Country Town film and becomes then the *sign qua non* of the male dominance of the country town. Even in *The Adventures of Priscilla, Queen of the Desert*, the comedy of the scene in which Bernadette, a male-to-female transsexual, defeats a woman in an arm-wrestling contest in a pub depends for its humour upon the masculinisation of the woman (who physically resembles a man, and 'acts' like a bloke) and, of course. the 'feminisation' of Bernadette (who rather more justifiably resembles a woman). Almost inevitably, the pub is a male-only domain; women are excluded beyond performing the role of servant (barmaid). The pub in Ginborak (*Shame*) is where the males of the town inevitably gather. Indeed, many are never seen anywhere else. It is the male-only tribal cave from which the young men go out to stalk their prey, young women, and to which they return.

As ubiquitous an icon in the country town film is the policeman. If the pub is the source and centre of male power in the town, then the 'local copper' is its institutional representative. Rather than being the representative of an abstract and 'absent' (or distant) system of law and justice, another outsider so to speak who represents the outside world to the extent that he embodies *its* codes, the policeman is often fully implicated in the codes of the town. In *Wake in Fright* it is the police sergeant who introduces John Grant to the masculine ethos of the pub and the two-up game (although it is other men who then take over as Grant's guides and 'mentors'). In *Shame*, the policeman (another sergeant) is fully implicated in maintaining the male charade that the institutionalised sexual assaults by the young men are just men "doing as nature intended" and, indeed, goes further in intimidating the father of one such girl into maintaining the male solidarity. Even in the comedies, the policeman is a major character. In *Warming Up*, the policeman (yet another sergeant) is the coach of the football team, the group of young men who again, although in humorous fashion, embody the male values that the female protagonist (an outsider, recently arrived from the city) must strive to overturn. The policeman is doubly if not trebly empowered: he is a man, he is the agent of the law, both the cultural patriarchal 'law' of the community and the remote, institutional patriarchal law of the Australian legal system, and almost inevitably he has a rank within the police hierarchy. *The Mango Tree*, a film slightly more complex or subtle in its delineation of the ways in which patriarchy functions within a country town community which is, nonetheless, barely less repressive than any other found in Australian Country Town films, the police sergeant is provided the status of a community 'elder', a sort of wise man of the 'tribe' with a position in this sense similar to that of the Professor (a educated if alcoholic English remittance man) and that of the protagonist's grandmother (a rare example of a matriarch with community power). The police sergeant is killed in this narrative, arguably in a clash of patriarchal value systems, by the old Testament obsessed 'Preacher'.

Occasionally, the policeman straddles the divide that forms the source of the conflict and thus the drama in country town narratives. His role as agent of both forms of the law forces him, sooner or later, to face the need to decide which he truly represents. In *Deadly*, the failure of the community cop to recognise his duty towards the abstract laws of the nation rather than the demands of the community is partly the cause of the outsider, another policeman, coming to the town in the first instance. Somewhat similarly, in *Dead Heart*, the policeman is caught, as a third force of the outside law, between the two conflicting systems of the community, white and black.

In terms of other accepted representatives of the wider institutions of society—wider that is than those which provide the particular, idiosyncratic rules of the community of each specific country town and, cumulatively, of country towns in general in Australian film—the clergyman and the school teacher are much less evident. There are less than a handful of schoolteachers. John Grant in *Wake in Fright* is one but he is not of the town, and does not function as school teacher while he is there. Others, such as the teacher in *The Mango Tree*, exercise their own form of repression, not always in keeping with and, in this instance, exceeding that of the community itself. Equally, it should be noted in *The Mango Tree*, it is a younger and female teacher who initiates the hero into the mysteries of sex, but *The Mango Tree* is atypical in that its protagonist is guided, indeed, governed by women, and he is on more than one occasion 'feminised'. If school teachers are occasionally present, and if they occasionally confirm and occasionally counter the prevailing attitudes and ideologies of the country town community, clergymen are almost but not entirely absent. There are several in *Dimboola*, both for different reasons figures of fun and, in one case, ridicule. The status of 'Preacher' in *The Mango Tree* is less certain as to whether he is an ordained or recognised clergyman in any meaningful sense. He is, however, driven by an incestuous lust and finally murders the police sergeant before he is shot down rather like a mad dog. Rather obviously he has transgressed community rules but, of course, he has transgressed the law in a much broader sense. The possibilities of the church and its appointed agents acting to mitigate the actions and behaviours of the communities are avoided by most narratives not allowing them a place. Thus, no matter how perfectly self-contained a community may be, where it would present an irreconcilable narrative (and thematic) difficulty to have a church and clergy as part of the community (for example, *Shame*), they are absent. Indeed, it should not be overlooked that the clergyman in *The Cars That Ate Paris* is specifically not a resident, that Arthur Waldo, the protagonist, is warned particularly about talking to him about the town, and that his killing by the 'village idiot' helps precipitate the destruction of Paris.

CONCLUSION

The country town in the New Australian Cinema is, with few exceptions, an unhappy place where the residue of an anachronistic set of Australian 'values' is represented to be not a dream of a simpler, golden past but a nightmare from which Australia may or may not have awoken. Even the contemporary narratives imply country towns exist in a sort of time-warp, and although these film may deal with contemporary 'issues', they place their narratives in social sites that are 'out-of-date', and which by their isolation and extremely limited size serve to highlight and simplify those issues. Thus there is a more than passing Lawsonian tone to these films—the contradiction of a respect for the inhabitants as true or dinkum Australians, as battlers, as pioneers, and a distaste for their patriarchal philistinism, aggressive ignorance and the closed nature of their outlook on life.

CROCODILE DUNDEE: APOTHEOSIS OF THE OCKER.

In box-office terms alone, *Crocodile Dundee* is the most successful film of the New Australian Cinema. Although box-office figures for films made in Australia prior to 1970 are extremely difficult to locate and would provide few points of valid comparison if they were, it is unlikely that there can be any dispute that *Crocodile Dundee* is the most successful Australian film ever, at home or abroad. It established box-office records in Australia, the United States (where it was the second highest grossing film of 1986), and elsewhere.[1] The big question that faces even the most ardent, Australiophilic scholar of Australian cinema is, why should *Crocodile Dundee* have been so successful? Any answer is presumably only partly related to the film's quality as a film. Although it is a better than competent piece of cinema with a tighter, more well-constructed script than many other contemporary Australian films, it is still at best only a good, workman-like film. The blatant attempt to be thoroughly 'commercial' (making *Crocodile Dundee* the Australian equivalent in this regard of, say, *Raiders of the Lost Ark*) cannot be overlooked. Nor can it be doubted that within Australia (where he has been a major television star with a series of comedy shows of his own for close to a decade), and to a lesser extent outside Australia (thanks to a series of commercials for the Australian national airline QANTAS and Foster's Lager), part of the box-office appeal is the appearance in the film of Paul Hogan.

But the presence of a well-known and well-loved Australian 'personality' in a basically well-made but far from inspired production cannot of itself provide a satisfactory insight into the extraordinary appeal of *Crocodile Dundee*. The main answer to why *Crocodile Dundee* should be such an outstanding box-office and, indeed, critical success is to be found within two related aspects of the film. First, this arguably the most Australian film of the New Australian Cinema. This is a bold claim to make of any film, especially of only one of some three hundred films made in Australia since 1970. Further, the claim risks implying that conceptions and perceptions of Australian-ness are unproblematic. It is also a bold claim given that two-thirds of the action of the film take place not in Australia at all but in Manhattan.

I shall argue here that *Crocodile Dundee* represents the culmination of an inclination by the New Australian Cinema to redefine the cultural identity of Australians in a way that, although contemporary, is solidly based in a traditional and essentially conservative ideology. In their examination of the Australian identity, the films that preceded *Crocodile Dundee* tended to present their myths couched either in terms of 'this is the way we were,' or 'this is the way we may be.' *Crocodile Dundee* eschews any of this sense of tentativeness about presenting the image of Australians: it says simply 'this is what we are.'[2] (Of course, to a non-Australian audience the film says, 'this is what *they* are.')

Second, *Crocodile Dundee* wins its audience over by its very unpretentiousness. It is a simple film, almost naive, certainly unsophisticated in narrative, theme, and characterization. It is, in a very real sense of the word, innocent. Innocence is the key note to Australian cultural perceptions of self-identity—that is, innocence defined as a closeness to nature and a (culturally implied) lack of the compromised morality, corrupted or debased social structure of the 'Old World,' enhanced by the 'pure' air of a (perceived) unspoilt land: '. . . this very primitivism is what the jaded nomads from pluralist Europe and New York find so refreshing, indeed inspiring, in Australian cinema.'[3]

It should, however, be noted in this context that *Crocodile Dundee* is very flattering to Americans at the same time. The cultural opposition of innocent/ debased is not activated in the narrative journey from Outback Australia to Manhattan. Indeed, any negative aspects of the antinomy Australia = innocent/ America = debased are effectively masked in the overwhelmingly positive view of America that *Crocodile Dundee* promotes. Instead, this structuring opposition, so vital in the cultural context of Australia's view of itself and of other cultures, is retained by modifying one polarity of the antinomy, the negative aspect. Innocence is retained (because of its cultural significance), but debasement is changed to a less negatively charged quality: sophistication. The implication then is that Americans *were* like 'us' (Australians) but through an unfortunate distancing from nature they have exchanged *innocence* for *sophistication* defined in this case as a form of pretentiousness; the contrast (opposition) is between 'down-to-earth' Michael Dundee (a natural/innocent man) and New Yorkers (Americans) who, in Barry McKenzie's immortal Australian colloquialism, are 'up themselves.' In this positive view of 'the other culture,' *Crocodile Dundee* offers an instructive contrast to *The Adventures of Barry McKenzie* (1972),[4] a film to which it owes no little debt.

I shall return to *Crocodile Dundee's* view of America. It needs to be noted that this innocent/debased antinomy can be expressed in a number of ways but particularly through other narrative structural oppositions that reiterate this same cultural ideology—for example, in *Crocodile Dundee* this antinomy is further defined by its mirror image structure: nature/ culture.

The Australianness of *Crocodile Dundee* is firmly located, as with many films of the New Australian Cinema, in two aspects of its filmic construction: landscape and character. The film continues the aestheticization of the Australian landscape familiar from the earliest films of the Australian film revival (e.g., *Picnic at Hanging Rock,* 1975) and that persists up to the most recent (e.g., *Burke and Wills,* 1986). The Outback section of the film, the first third of the narrative, although important for setting the character of Mick Dundee, is equally significantly concerned with displaying the exotic beauty of the ancient Australian landscape. The camera frequently lingers on the vistas of the landscape long after the action has moved out of frame, or begins a sequence with carefully composed images that could belong as easily in *National Geographic*. This emphasis on the beauty of the Australian Bush is enhanced by self-consciously constructed shots of scenic panorama, sunsets, and so on, all in widescreen format. The mystery of the Australian Bush (its 'otherness' when compared with the familiar landscapes of the Northern Hemisphere) is deliberately emphasized—as when a tracking shot, following Dundee's moving vehicle but locating it at the left side of frame reveals a foreground of skeletal trees that seem to have strange white foliage—foliage that is revealed in turn to be a flock of white cockatoos that suddenly bursts into flight.

As is so often the case in Australian cinema, 'the not-quite-different filmic landscape is always there, claiming priority of place as a point of fascination, as the central character'[5]—at least for the first third to one-half of the film—but here (unlike many other recent Australian films) the landscape is neutral, benign even (crocodile attacks not withstanding). Even so, the Bush has the dramatic *function* in *Crocodile Dundee* of being a place of seeming danger; water buffalo, snakes, and crocodiles are all introduced into the narrative as potential menaces only to be despatched with nonchalant ease by Mick Dundee (in much the same way when in New York he despatches urban menaces in the form of muggers, pimps, guard dogs, and drunken boyfriends). The lingering shots of landscape in *Crocodile Dundee* do function at one level as picturesque backdrop, but in the Australian context there is really no such thing as unmediated depiction of the Bush: '. . . once such geography is visualized and emphasised within a diegesis, it stands as something other than simple description; it has been transmuted into an element of myth, into a sign of supra-social Australian-ness.'[6] Landscape's other functions are, as always in Australian narratives, to provide an explanation of the characters who are located within it and the dramas in which they find themselves. Landscape's function is mythic.

In *Crocodile Dundee*, the explanation of character by and through landscape is more important than the explanation of drama. Mick Dundee is characterized in the film in two ways, ways that a familiarity with Australian cinema might at first lead one to suppose are mutually contradictory. He is both a Bushman and an Ocker. The chronological order of the construction of his characterization is important. On first meeting him, Mick is very much an Ocker; his antics in the Walkabout Hotel, his speech, his attitudes—all of which are contrasted both with Sue Charlton, the American journalist (thus a woman and outsider) and with Wally, Dundee's partner/mate, who attempts a 'refinement' in explaining both Mick and the Outback to Sue—these mark Dundee as an Ocker within the prevailing ideologically determined definition.

This prevailing cultural image of the Ocker tends to be one that emphasizes 'typicality' and 'distinctively Australian,' but this definition is one that has been determined in no small measure by the New Australian Cinema itself. Through a range of films since 1970, the changing cultural perception of the Ocker can be traced along a straight line trajectory from early films based upon gross exaggerations of Australian vulgarity and boorishness through more 'realistic' images to the final acceptance of the Ocker as *the* image of national identity in *Crocodile Dundee.*

The social 'sanitization' of the Ocker is achieved in *Crocodile Dundee* by an interesting sleight of hand in the characterization of Mick Dundee. Introduced in the Ockers' traditional stamping ground, the pub, Dundee's first characterization is that of an Ocker, and he will retain those Ocker characteristics when he goes to New York. But they are quickly overlaid by the more 'positive' cultural attributes of the Bushman.[7] (The Bushman is the most potent culture-hero of Australia, of Australian literature, film, and popular imagination, and is the equivalent in this regard of the Westerner in American mythology.) Once in the Outback, the mythic qualities of the Australian Bush, those qualities that make of the men who can survive it Australian cultural heroes, extend the characterization of Dundee beyond that of a stereotypical Ocker. It is as if Dundee was the amalgam of both Archy (the Bushman) and Frank (the Larrikin/Ocker) from *Gallipoli* (1981).

In no other film has there been such a complete rendering of the character of the mythically typical Australian. Despite and because of Dundee's Bushman status, in *Crocodile Dundee* we see the apotheosis of the Ocker. No longer is he a figure who carries a certain stigma of cultural embarrassment; by showing that the Bushman and the Ocker are not simply opposite sides of the same coin but can actually be the same side, *Crocodile Dundee* reconciles two important cultural perceptions of Australian identity—and implicitly recognizes that the 'pure' Bushman image is an anachronistic one. By absorbing the Ocker, or being absorbed by him, the Bushman is made culturally contemporary without losing his legendary and ideological status.

Although the synthesis of Bushman and Ocker is complete in the characterization of Mick Dundee, the film itself still offers a certain ambivalence about that character. There are moments within the narrative—such as the sequence in the fashionable restaurant in New York—when it is intimated that Dundee himself is playing the role of a 'professional' Ocker. This is an interesting confusion between the fictional character, Dundee, and Paul Hogan whose reputation, whose professional image, has been deliberately built upon a similar confusion to what extent Hogan is the Ocker he inevitably portrays. This slight hesitancy about committing the characterization of Dundee to be unequivocally an Ocker (albeit with the cultural accolades of being a Bushman to legitimize his cultural status) may be because, even yet, there remains a certain hesitancy in Australian culture to fully embrace the untrammelled Ocker as *the* image of national identity.

Australia has a long history of cultural schizophrenia regarding its national image.[8] The development of the image of the Ocker, historically, represents a way in which recent attempts have been made to resolve that 'split personality' and in *Crocodile Dundee* that synthesis has been demonstrated as complete.

Arguably, however, that synthesis has always been present in Australian narratives, and thus in Australian culture. Certain aspects of the mythical Australian character may have been emphasized, others played down at particular moments, but the characteristics have nearly always been present in total for a long time (in relation to the overall existence of [white] Australian culture). For what unites both 'sides' of the Australian character is a basic innocence. An innocence sometimes defined as being child-like (as with Barry McKenzie, and Mick Dundee on occasion), sometimes as being unsophisticated, even naive, and sometimes as being closer to nature (again, true of Dundee). This innocence, as I indicated earlier, is often implied to exist in contradistinction to the assumed decadence and corruption of the outside world, especially Europe. It is the innocence of youth contrasted to the wisdom and worldliness of old age. Australia, in its own mythical perception is a youthful culture; Europe an ancient one. The Australian perception of the United States is, as yet, an ambivalent one—as *Crocodile Dundee* demonstrates.

For the most part the characterization of Dundee is consistently that of an Ocker. In this regard, it is interesting to note the extent to which Mick Dundee's overseas journey parallels that taken some fourteen years earlier by the quintessential (until Mick Dundee) Ocker, Barry McKenzie, and to what extent the journey differs.[9]

The most significant similarity been Dundee and McKenzie is in the essential innocence, the naiveté of both. Whereas Barry McKenzie is innocent to the point of being barely above moronic (providing opportunities for satire on both Australians and the English and opportunities for broader, farcical, and slapstick comedy), Mick Dundee is much more a sort of holy innocent. The film rides, and rides successfully, on a very fine line between allowing Mick to appear dim and suggesting he is not quite as naive as he appears. (An aspect of the ambivalence as to whether Dundee is playing the role of an Ocker I suggested above.[10])

But it is inescapable that Mick Dundee and Barry McKenzie share many narrative incidents in their Candide-style journey through essentially alien cultures. For example, in *The Adventures of Barry McKenzie*, McKenzie does not recognize that 'Claude,' the older woman who is living with Gaylene/Lesley (a childhood friend now in a lesbian relationship) is a woman in men's clothes, nor that the 'women' in the pub to which he and Gaylene/Lesley go are men in women's clothes. Dundee, in a bar in New York, also does not recognize a transvestite even though everyone else in the bar knows. In *The Adventures of Barry McKenzie*, these men/women characters are grotesque caricatures obvious to everyone except McKenzie; in *Crocodile Dundee* the transvestite is much more subtle. (Indeed, I am by no means sure that the actor in the role is not a woman.) This incident in *Crocodile Dundee* leads (as with *Barry McKenzie*) to further comic situations. Dundee later meets a woman who, while dressed like a woman, looks and sounds masculine and he repeats his 'checking by touch,' adding to the image of Dundee as thoroughly out of place in 'sophisticated' (i.e., non-Australian) society.

The sophisticated New York party—which is one of the few moments in the film in which caricature threatens to take over—is clearly intended to contrast with the aboriginal corroboree that takes place in the Bush (both are social rituals and of a secular rather than religious nature—as Nev's attitude to the corroboree makes clear), and with the bar at Walkabout Creek (another social ritual, but again, as befits the image of Australia the film is promoting, a much more down-to-earth 'genuine' one). It is a lack of worldliness that figures both Mick Dundee and Barry McKenzie and at the same time it is unworldliness that gives them heroic status in the terms of Australians' perceptions of themselves. The most significant difference is that whereas McKenzie journeyed to England (a culturally appropriate destination in the early 1970s), Dundee goes to the United States (an appropriate destination in the late 1980s). Australia has had a love/hate relationship with England that goes back nearly as far as the first colonization of Australia in the late eighteenth century. For nearly two centuries, then, this fluctuating relationship has been a cornerstone of Australian cultural identity—for reasons that are too complex to attempt to elucidate here.

The gradual eclipse of the importance of England in Australian cultural perceptions that many Australian films have hinted at and a few documented more fully (e.g., *Breaker Morant* [1980], *Gallipoli*, etc.) is completed by *Crocodile Dundee*. There is evidence to suggest that Australia, culturally speaking, is beginning to develop a dependency relationship with the United States similar to that which previously existed with Britain, although as yet there are only a few films that raise this cultural perception. In a recent critique of the politics and ideology of *Crocodile Dundee,* Veronica Brady stated in no uncertain terms that an obvious reading of *Crocodile Dundee* indicated a 'desire to win the approval of Big Brother, in this case Big Uncle Sam, [which] is perhaps a reflection of the mental colonisation that is delighted to be part American military strategy and finance and admires most things American.'[11] It seems indisputable that *Crocodile Dundee* with its obvious positive attitude toward America represents a considerable change in the previous characterization of the Ocker, a characterization that insisted that the Ocker shows little respect or admiration for anything outside of his own narrowly defined terms of what is acceptable—terms equated with Australianism.

The popularity of *Crocodile Dundee* in Australia is not only because it so accurately holds up the mirror of cultural myth to its home audience, but clearly that is a large part of the reason. *Crocodile Dundee* is also a film that demonstrates what seems to be a curious paradox: It is inescapably *Australian,* yet its construction cinematically speaking, is American. That is, it is a *Hollywood* film—aesthetically speaking. This may partly explain why the film has been equally popular in the United States. *Crocodile Dundee* does not challenge by its otherness; it confirms by producing an image of Australia, for Americans, that is distinct but not different, other but not alien.

There are, however, other reasons why *Crocodile Dundee* should prove to be so phenomenally successful in the United States.[12] Some of these I have touched upon. *Crocodile Dundee* is extremely flattering to America and Americans. In this alone it is unusual. Foreign films are seldom as positive about Americans and 'the American way of life' as *Crocodile Dundee.* The New York sequences of the recent French film *'Round Midnight* (1986) serve as an example. In the broader cultural sense (and emphasizing this is an outside view), it frequently seems that the United States obsessively seeks to be loved (or at least appreciated) by other nations, other cultures, and not infrequently acts with considerable cultural petulance to find that it is not. A foreign film that retains the flavour of its national origin but also has nice things to say about the United States would seem to be an obvious candidate for popularity.

The thematic structure of *Crocodile Dundee* contains other suggestions as to why it might be popular in the United States. Put simply, *Crocodile Dundee* follows the theme of the outsider (stranger but not alien) who enters a community (even one as big as New York) and who, through his actions, reminds the members of that community of important aspects of their culture they have lost sight of, forgotten, or foolishly laid aside. This is not a particularly startling theme for American audiences to confront. It appears, for example, in such diverse films as *Hoosiers* (1986) and *Coogan's Bluff* (1968),[13] and was, in various guises, a perennial theme of many Hollywood Westerns. Mick Dundee reminds the people of New York of the simple truths, simple moralities, of which they have apparently lost sight. In a confusing world the simplicity of Mick Dundee offers the example of axioms once known but momentarily forgotten.

These axioms are related to the concept of innocence. These themes of the stranger, reared in a simpler, less materialistic, less morally confusing culture, arriving in a situation in which others have lost sight of the fundamental values link *Crocodile Dundee* obviously with the films of Frank Capra, most notably *Mr. Deeds Goes to Town* (1936), *Mr. Smith Goes to Washington* (1939), and—perhaps a trifle obliquely—*It's a Wonderful Life* (1946). Caution must be taken to avoid drawing too close a parallel between Capra's heroes and Mick Dundee if only because Dundee does not bring himself into *direct* conflict with his new environment, unlike Deeds and Smith. (That is, although the film is based upon the country/city or nature/culture antinomy that is familiar from Capra's films as well, it does not activate the conflict inherent in this dialectic.) Again, it is difficult to argue for any political analysis of *Crocodile Dundee* along the lines that have been made of the Capra films—although *Crocodile Dundee* may be as purposeful a construction of cultural mythology as any of these Capra films. Equally, Dundee is not the representative of American heartland (of Capra's 1930s nor present day) but is representative of another (albeit sympathetic) culture entirely. But it is still innocence bordering upon naiveté that links Dundee and Jefferson Smith, Longfellow Deeds, and George Bailey. It is not unreasonable to assume that the innocence of Mick Dundee is as appealing to Americans as to Australians, and for the same reasons.

Crocodile Dundee's popularity in the United States would seem to be based then upon its lack of pretension as a film, the manner in which it effectively manages to be Australian without being alien, that it offers an extremely flattering outsiders' view of the U.S., and that its narrative provides the thematic construction of the 'innocent' protagonist who reminds (without confrontation) the community he enters from outside of its own known but forgotten values and provides representatives of the community with the ways and means of regaining those lost values.

In the context of Australian cinema, it is appropriate and yet ironic that *Crocodile Dundee* should appear when it did. After a number of years of loss of direction by the New Australian Cinema, *Crocodile Dundee* proved that Australian film was, in fact, on the right track with the nationalistic films of the late 1970s. *Crocodile Dundee* completes the journey toward re-establishing within the traditional definitions the cultural identity of Australians and Australian-ness begun by the New Australian Cinema over a decade and a half ago. It has been an intensely interesting journey commencing with an interrogation of these cultural perceptions through films such as *Wake in Fright* (1971) or through satirizing films like *The Adventures of Barry McKenzie* and *Don's Party* (1976), but then tracing a continuum in which the questions were either dropped altogether or answered by confirming the traditional myths of Australian cultural identity to the point where *Crocodile Dundee* celebrates, in a way unequalled by any film of the New Australian Cinema (except perhaps *Gallipoli)*, the dominant traditional view of the Australian.

There is a fascinating irony then that *Crocodile Dundee* creates the most perfect rendering of the mythic 'typical' Australian, that it completes the journey of revitalizing the image of Australian national and cultural identity and yet clearly points to a failure in confidence in the strength of that national image through its shift toward a mooted cultural dependency on the United States. In this *Crocodile Dundee* both culturally canonizes the Ocker, provides the most positive acclamation of the mythic Australian character, and simultaneously denies him (and by implication Australia) the strength to exist independently in the world. Paradoxically, it is possible to be uniquely Australian and at the same time a willing colony of another culture. This paradox is, however, one that has been at the heart of Australian attempts to define themselves since the beginning of white settlement nearly two hundred years ago. *Crocodile Dundee's* implicit acceptance of this further demonstrates the extent to which it is the most Australian film of the New Australian Cinema.

NOTES

1. In its first week of release in the United States, *Crocodile Dundee* went to number one in the weekly top grossing films compiled by *Variety,* taking $3,027,100 in box-office receipts *(Variety,* 8 October 1986). In March 1987, after twenty-three weeks in release, it was still in the top-ten grossing films in the United States, having taken some $153,720,911 in box-office receipts *(The Hollywood Reporter,* CCXCV1, No. 15, 10 March 1987).

2. There are, of course, other films that do not have any difficulty in presenting Australians 'as they are,' but few of these are as brashly assertive of the mythic perception of the 'true' Australian as is *Crocodile Dundee*.

3. Ross Gibson, 'Camera Natura: Landscape in Australian Feature Films,' *Framework* 22/23 (Autumn 1983), p. 50.

4. *The Adventures of Barry McKenzie* is a Candide-style narrative in which the eponymous hero is characterized as the quintessential Ocker: a beer-swilling, chauvinistic, vulgar lout whose single ambition (other than to drink as much 'amber fluid' [beer] as possible) is to achieve sexual intercourse, this latter desire being constantly frustrated by his sexual ignorance and inexperience, or by the interventions of factors beyond his control. Written by Australian arch-satirist, Barry Humphreys, the film takes delight in aiming its satirical broadsides at targets both

Australian and English—McKenzie makes the trip to England as a condition of his late father's will 'to further the cultural and intellectual traditions of the McKenzie dynasty.' In this journey, the fictional McKenzie repeats a journey undertaken by many Australians. This visit to 'the old country' is, or was, living evidence of the cultural dependence upon England that was pan of the Australian cultural perception; a perception that *Crocodile Dundee* suggests has been abandoned or at least modified by replacing England with the United States. McKenzie himself is not a *realistic* figure (by comparison with Dundee) but a gross exaggeration, a clown who nonetheless manages to represent both the best and the worst of the *typical* Australian: the Ocker. (See also Note 10 below.) The second Barry McKenzie film, *Barry McKenzie Holds His Own,* is a blatantly commercial sequel/re-make, the main difference being that McKenzie travels to continental Europe.

5. Gibson, p. 50.

6. Gibson, p. 49.

7. The parameters of this image, indeed its very validity, are a constant source of argument in Australian historical and cultural writing. Three extremely valuable discussions are available in Russell Ward, *The Australian Legend* (Melbourne: Oxford University Press, 1958), Richard White, *Inventing Australia: Images and Identity 1688-1980* (Sydney: George Allen and Unwin, 1981), and John Carroll (Ed.), *Intruders in the Bush: The Australian Search for Identity* (Melbourne: Oxford University Press, 1982).

8. Refer to Richard White, p. 136.

9. There are other major differences between Mick Dundee and Barry McKenzie, the most important of which in any examination of their status as culture-heroes is that McKenzie is a suburban Australian, a fact that instantly diminishes his heroic status—real Australian heroes come from the Bush, or most certainly did in 1972 when *The Adventures of Barry McKenzie* was made. McKenzie's suburban background is, of course, important to the satirical purpose of the film. His character is that of Ocker as moron, a characterization that could not be successfully applied to an Australian Bushman without considerable risk—as *Wake in Fright* a year earlier demonstrated.

10. This ambivalence may also be due to the fact that although innocence is a characteristic of the dominant cultural perception of Australian identity, innocence has an opposite side: scepticism. In a *rounded* character like Dundee, and unlike the one-dimensional character of McKenzie, this scepticism enables Dundee to *appear* naive while actually being (to use an Australian colloquial expression) 'more of a wake-up.'

11. Veronica Brady, 'Evading History,' *Australian Society,* V.7, No. 3 (1987), 33.

12. These are speculations as it ill-behoves an Australian scholar of Australian cinema and Australian culture to be dogmatic over the readings of a film, Australian or otherwise, made in another cultural location by another cultural audience.

13. Regarding this latter film, it would seem that this theme is a particular favourite of Clint Eastwood. It appears, for example, in *High Plains Drifter* (1972) and *Heartbreak Ridge* (1987), and is present in a modified form in the *Dirty Harry* films.

DEFENDING LINDY: *EVIL ANGELS* AND TRUTH

Evil Angels (Fred Schepisi, 1988. USA: *A Cry in the Dark*) is a significant, perhaps even crucial intervention in the megatext of Lindy Chamberlain. Although it was preceded by John Bryson's book of the same name[1]—and the film gives a credit of 'based upon'—and also preceded by less available defences of Lindy and Michael Chamberlain, published in book[2], booklet or pamphlet form by various supporters, its timing was just right in terms of what might be called the rehabilitation period of Lindy's image. The principal shooting for *Evil Angels* took place at the same time as the Commission of Inquiry which ultimately exonerated Lindy, and its release was about six months after that Commission's findings were presented. What started as a cinematic project of 'outrage' over Lindy's incarceration became both a protest and a celebration by the time it was finished. Lindy claims in her autobiography[3] that she received many hundreds of letters after the release of the film in which the writers admitted to changing their opinion on the basis of the film. (This cannot be readily substantiated as Lindy, having deposited her papers in the National Library of Australia, has placed an embargo on them for fifty years after her death.)

As the first part of the film's function as a defence for Lindy Chamberlain, of a declaration of her innocence (of the crime, other parts argue for her innocence of many of the other 'charges' made, via the media and/or gossip), the film shows the event which triggered everything else: the 'loss' of baby Azaria. The film offers the event as the truth, not as a version of it. Within the diegesis of the film, this is the event as it takes place; there is no suggestion that the film is reconstructing an event (although extra-diegetically, it may be assumed that the film's putative audience is aware that this is not a fictional event—that is, one that has both never taken place and at the same time is taking place and will take place in the same manner whenever and wherever this version of the film is seen). The sequence offers the event from the point-of-view of the omniscient absent/present narrator (the *sine qua none* of most fictional narrative films), and with the exception of two very short shots, never suggests that any part of this event is being seen/told from the point of view of any diegetic character. (And those two shots may not do what I suggest, as my images come from a video release version in which the sides of the frame are missing.) Thus, Lindy is in all the shots, both those which view the actions at the tent and those reverse shots which view Lindy (as if from the tent or from the side and including the tent). Thus, the event unfolds in 'real' time and in a way which, since it includes the figure of Lindy, precludes (or inhibits) this as being seen as the diegetic 'Lindy Chamberlain's' version.

Of course, what the film is careful to avoid in this manner of constructing/narrating the event, and by including a figure who is diegetically Lindy Chamberlain, is to raise the very basis upon which the sequence *is* in fact founded: that it is the *real* Lindy Chamberlain's version of the actual event that the film is offering as the unarguable truth upon which the whole narrative of *Evil Angels* will depend. In narrative structural terms, this is the disruption which sets the narrative sequence of complications and consequences in train. By thus occupying a familiar narrative-formula position, the sequence encourages the spectator of the film to accept it, at the very least diegetically, as what happened. This will in turn make sure that the attempts by the police, experts and various interested parties to offer alternative versions (especially the one which has Lindy killing Azaria in the family car) will be rejected (or never even considered as possible) by the film's putative audience, who *know* the truth because the film has shown it to them. Again, in conventional narrative filmic tradition, the audience is positioned to side with the protagonist, not necessarily because the protagonist is so overwhelming appealing or sympathetic (this is particularly so in this film, it seems to me) but because the protagonist is the individual in whom the narrative and audience have invested their energies (psychic, emotional)—an investment that is dependent upon accepting a 'truth', the narrative truth. The protagonists 'version' of reality is *the* reality of the diegesis in this case. The audience is required to accept that; not to accept it makes nonsense of any individual spectator's viewing of the film.

And yet, the film does not show clearly and unambiguously that a dingo took Azaria. It could have done so by showing that very act taking place, showing the dingo clearly instead of a partly hidden or swiftly moving blur at the edge of the frame. (There are plenty of quite clear shots of dingos in other parts of the film.) Instead it leaves it to a sort of impression of the event, akin presumably to Lindy's impression of the event. But as I have said, it carefully makes sure that the film sequence cannot be interpreted as being *only* Lindy's version (a version which could be false in terms of it being imagined or even total fiction on her part). And much later, fleeting images of the dingo in and near the tent are inserted in the only place where the film makes such a disruption to linear time and space: during Lindy's cross-examination during her trail. This reconfirms the truth by reminding the audience that, like Lindy, they too know what happened.

Yet, I must register that, like much about this film, there is a vague feeling of contradiction or uncertainty here in both instances. The flashback/memories *could* be interpreted to be simply Lindy's version. But the first sequence is the more important. On one hand, it provides the incident in a way which cannot be gainsaid, or at the very least contradicts the attempts by public, police, press and persecutors to offer an alternative version that has Lindy killing Azaria. On the other hand, it perhaps subscribes to the view which is now, presumably, the widest accepted view: that Lindy Chamberlain did not kill Azaria and that a dingo probably did.

The film functions for the defence by clearly showing that Lindy did not kill Azaria. It also of course provides much circumstantial evidence to show that Lindy would not be capable of such an act anyway. It shows the event through a series of images which support but do not positively confirm beyond all doubt that a dingo killed and took the baby. But, of course, it is not interested in merely declaring Lindy Chamberlain innocent of the crime of murder. It is equally as determined to defend her reputation as an innocent. The final words heard in the film are in fact a statement of the films thesis in this regard. Spoken off-screen by Michael Chamberlain (that is, the diegetic character 'Michael Chamberlain'), they are: 'I don't think a lot of people realise how important innocence is to innocent people.'

If the film did not leave this crucial aspect of its 'story' slightly vague, then the efforts of whomsoever it is to have Lindy prosecuted and found guilty of the murder of her own child would make no sense at all. Clear and uncontroversial film presentation of a dingo taking Azaria would then demand that the film spell out a clear set of motives for the prosecution (or persecution) of Lindy Chamberlain which the narrative then proceeds to develop. There is a certain irony here as in real life the prosecution could not and expressly denied its responsibility to provide a motive for what it alleged Lindy had done. It is my argument that the film is almost as vague in finding a motive for the actions of the police and their political masters, the politicians of the Northern Territory. Some suggestions are there but they are almost hidden. I will return to these, or at least to moments in the film which suggest them.

But the vagueness of the scene depicting the actual incident has another, and possibly unintended, effect in the film. If it taken that the film's makers (or some of them at least—since it seems that the original screenplay by Robert Caswell dealt only with the factual incidents as they related to the Chamberlains but with Schepisi's involvement, the part played by the press and the public was added; the press's part is explored slightly differently in Bryson's book) was to present as negatively as possible and thereby condemn the uninformed, ignorant and prejudiced nature of ordinary Australians, then it actually offers an excuse. It does so because it avoids showing fully and with clarity that a dingo did take the baby. If the film's putative audience saw that was unmistakably the case, then the indignation (and/or shame) which Schepisi wishes to arouse in his audience over the ignorant bigotry of the great Australian public would be even more potent. As it is, those anonymous individuals pilloried by the film because of the disbelief that a dingo did it are, in part, excused because the film itself does not state this emphatically. The putative audience is told that Lindy did not do it; it is less clear through the cinematic construction I have referred to that a dingo did it—although that same cinematic construction does not provide any suggestion of any other rational alternative explanation.

Having effectively demonstrated the truth by representing—or reconstructing in documentary terms—the event upon which the narrative depends, at a much later stage the film addresses the question of the untruth. That is, it addresses but clearly cannot reconstruct (as it did not occur) the version of the incident which is offered by the Crown in its attempt to convict Lindy (of a crime she did not commit). In a way, the whole film is addressing this very issue but there is a specific moment of clarity in which Lindy is used to demolish the Crown's version by having Lindy articulate it and by so doing exposing to the glare of logic, which of course demolishes it. In this scene, Lindy simply outlines the Crown 'story' to herself and her solicitor (and of course to the putative audience). This is also a remarkable piece of acting by Meryl Streep as she not only catches the essential 'fantastic' logic of the Crown's story but does so within a remarkably convincing characterisation of, if not Lindy herself (I cannot judge that), a personality defined by the very mode of speech and expression. However, this scene is *redundant*, not simply because the putative audience already knows the truth, nor simply because the parameters of the Crown's case is going to be revealed in the courtroom drama which follows, but because it has no motivation. It is going nowhere in terms of the narrative development nor the narrative structure. The 'narrative' the Crown is attempting to substitute for the true narrative is doubly demolished: It is untrue, and it is an impossible narrative—its events could not possibly have taken place. At the risk of being redundant myself, the audience knows what events took place and they were patently not these. Thus, as this scene makes it perfectly, plainly and even playfully clear that the alternative version is unfeasible (even to those within the diegesis who do not possess the extra-diegetic knowledge of the audience), and as the film has *from the outset* indicated this to be the case, the narrative and structural logic of this scene *ought* to be to raise, offer or even explain the reasons why this patently false version of events is being made the basis of (as the scene says) a ludicrous case against Lindy. But it does not do so. It leaves it dangling, still born, as is inevitably the situation when the film is required to or offered an opportunity to raise the issue of *why*.

Thus, one of the real questions that may be asked about the way in which the film acts as a statement in defence of Lindy Chamberlain is that given it posits her (and Michael) as victim of a clear miscarriage of justice, how does that miscarriage come about? And as a corollary to that question, who is it that perpetrates the miscarriage of justice and why? In one of the first reviews of *Evil Angels*,[4] Felicity Collins states in her second paragraph 'Only problem is the film fails to tell us *how* the media, myth and the judiciary did it', *it* being what it was that was done to Lindy and Michael Chamberlain. Reviewing, even when it is for a quarterly journal rather than to meet the demanding deadline of a daily newspaper, is usually carried out on the basis of one viewing of the film in question. Thus if (as in this case) some aspect of the film (and in this case it is understandably a crucial aspect) is too subtle, too understated or too obscure, it can be hardly surprising it is not picked up by a reviewer. For this reason (and a number of others), I am usually wary of turning to reviews for an insightful analysis of a film.

In writing my own comments on *Evil Angels* in a book on Australian cinema published in 1991,[5] I relied upon several viewings of the film. Although it was probably the last entry I wrote and the film would have been less familiar to me than others I included, I feel sure my familiarity with the film would have been potentially greater than that of any reviewer 'making do' with one viewing before rushing to judgement. Even so, and allowing that my interest in and approach to the film was driven in part by my overall thesis of the book, I did note that '*Evil Angels* is oddly ambiguous in its attempt to suggest that Lindy Chamberlain was the victim of the media, of the legal system, of public opinion, and possibly political expediency. The film is fairly certain that she *was* the victim of these things; it is uncertain *how* she was the victim of them'.

If I would today modify that opinion it is that the film is subtle to the point on near invisibility about why the actions of those instrumental in bringing about the miscarriage of justice were undertaken. They are there but seldom move beyond the level of implication—or via an oblique reference easily overlooked or registered as yet another non-narrative piece of dialogue a la the *vox populi*—to which I will return.

Having established, albeit without absolute clarity, that a dingo was responsible and, more importantly, that Lindy was not responsible, the film is at some difficulty in establishing the importance of the first inquest, which found a dingo did it. The first inquest, in terms of the narrative, only confirms that which is knowable and that which is known (to the putative audience). Nonetheless, it is at this point that the film offers (or implies) the motivation for those who will be involved in and possibly instrumental in bringing about the subsequent 'official' persecution of Lindy. Firstly, there is, at the point in which the coroner is making a criticism of the forensic evidence presented by Doctor Brown and in general by the Northern territory police, a series of reaction shots or scenes which suggest that the coroner's words are having an effect—an effect that will produce a reaction which in turn leads to the persecution of the

Chamberlains as a consequence of bruised egos, damaged reputations and/or petty revenge for slights.

The ways in which these subtle hints are taken up and translated into actions—scenes in which the film advances the narrative—are almost as equally as subtle. It is difficult not to feel that the film's makers are attempting to be deliberately obscure—whether this is for fear of legal action against them or an unwillingness to advance a clear argument of their own about the cause of the miscarriage of justice (because they don't have one or are not convinced by the ones they imply) is hard to determine. The film relies upon events or incidents to do double duty. Firstly, to show what happened, when and to whom—to whom are inevitably the Chamberlains. Secondly, to imply a motivation for those actions. In this second, the film in singularly unsuccessful. Or rather, the film is so determined to argue that Lindy Chamberlain was the victim of inchoate but arguably universal (in the sense of trans-Australian) cultural perceptions or prejudices—by mechanisms which the film is unable to articulate—which in turn translate into a set of pressures upon certain social institutions—the politics, the police, the judiciary—that then respond as much from that felt pressure as from motivations inherent to the institutions own systems.

In all this, there is the place and role of the media. The media are omnipresent and linked throughout by the montage with both the popular (mis)conceptions and the institutions engaged in enacting the miscarriage of justice. Here again, ambiguity reigns. In some instances the media are placed into the same category as many of the anonymous citizens—ignorant, bigoted, vulgar. In other moments, they are seen to be the 'vultures of the press', swooping (literally from the skies in helicopters) on the Chamberlains. On other occasions, it is implied (but crucially not demonstrated) that the media distort the material they have obtained with the willing if naive compliance of the Chamberlains. And yet there are also times in which the film shows singled-out but unnamed individual journalists to be supportive and sympathetic to the Chamberlains (but not 'bright' enough to figure out what is going on below the surface).

Nonetheless, the montage frequently insists that press and television drives public opinion, although it is only occasionally clear that the public derives its bigoted opinion directly from the media reports. In some, quite cleverly constructed montage-sequences, dialogue carries over a single idea, often from the police to the press to the public. But on other times, it is by no means apparent from the media material shown (a television interview, a newspaper headline) just how the precise tenor of a negative response is aroused.

Another obvious way *Evil Angels* sets out to defend Lindy Chamberlain is by denigrating—ruthlessly denigrating—her detractors, and by showing the way in which the media is implicated in creating public opinion. One of the mechanisms by which the film redeems Lindy Chamberlain is by demonstrating that her critics in the broadest Australian social context are ill-informed, bigoted, crass, vulgar, easily swayed by media distortion, and barely redeemable themselves. Given that the film provides a cross-section of Australian society, by class, by gender and by location (urban and rural), it is fairly certain that all Australians are deserving of this judgement and censure. (The irony of enacting the same type of judgement and censure on all Australians as the film accuses all Australians of doing to the Chamberlains seems to have escaped the film maker's notice.)

Throughout the narrative trajectory is punctuated by scenes (usually but not inevitably of one shot) of anonymous but stereotypical or phenotypical identifiable Australian types (mise-en-scene is also used to locate these otherwise un-individuated individuals in terms of class, status, ethnic origin, etc). Each of these individuals, who are almost inevitably grouped and equally as inevitably occupied in eating and/or drinking, is in some way or another responding not to unmediated Chamberlains (with one or two exceptions—a woman who spits at Lindy, people outside the courtroom as she and Michael arrive) but to a media report of some sort. In many cases, these anonymous individuals are in the acting of looking at a television set in which a journalist or newsreader is presenting 'information' or on which Michael and, less often, Lindy are speaking through edited versions of interviews. In other of these interpolated *vox populi* scenes, individuals are associated with newspapers, by either having one in their possession or by the editing in which newspaper headlines are immediately followed by a *vox populi* scene. In some of these scenes the link is implied rather than present: an issue raised in court for example is then seen to be being discussed by 'ordinary' people, the implication being they have learnt of this from the media without the link being filmically spelled out. Throughout, there is also the frequent use of diegetic voice-overs—the voice of various media, presumably radio and television.

This inevitable linking of media coverage and/or distortion would seem to operate to justify or at least excuse and explain why the great Australian public are 'wrong' in their opinions by presenting the source of their mistaken perceptions. It is achieved within the formal structure of the film by what I call the Chain of Complicity. For example, matters damaging to Lindy are originated by the 'impartial' forensic expert (his impartiality will be questioned later by the film even more closely when he is revealed to and thus blamed for setting the legal prosecution of Lindy in chain). This passes to the police (via juxtapositional editing and the continuity suggested by the dialogue). And then by a less demonstrable process (that is juxtaposition but not temporal or spatial continuity across the edits) from the police to the press. And from there to rapidly inserted newspaper headlines (which again one must assume summarise a story which repeats and distorts the information which began with the forensic scientist) and the cover of the *Woman's Day* (whose presence in this sequence can only be understood by hindsight when Lindy later accuses the *Woman's Day* of being the most distorted press article of them all, thus subliminally suggesting within the pages not seen distortion is taking place). And finally to two anonymous males on a Melbourne tram, one holding another newspaper with a similar but different headline: 'Dingo Not Baby Killer'. Again the putative spectator is left to assume this individual has read the newspaper report before offering his opinion that 'these bloody Chamberlains. They wouldn't know the bloody truth if it got up and bit them on the arse'. At several points then the threads of scientific investigation, police investigation, press and public are drawn together in this manner quite explicitly (as distinct from the implied connection in other places). These have the effect of claiming that public opinion was very deliberately orchestrated by the unholy alliance of officialdom and journalism. Thus, in this particular sequence a piece of false/mistaken evidence is filtered/mediated along a clear chain that links the information but which explains the mediating process not by stating clearly the intent behind the process but by *post hoc, ergo propter hoc* (after this, therefore an account of this, or that a thing which follows another is therefore caused by it).

But the film does not let the Australian public off that easily. The film insists that ordinary Australians—or perhaps the ocker end of the spectrum, seemingly a very large proportion at that—is already predisposed to accepting the distortions about the Chamberlains themselves in the first instance and then the incident itself. Even before the disappearance of Azaria takes place, the first of these anonymous ordinary Australians appears in the form of a suitably blue-singlet-attired Mt Isa truck driver who states emphatically across the CB radio to, presumably, another truck driver: 'Jesus. Have a look at those fucking adventists. Talk about up yourself. More money than you can poke a stick at.'

This serves to set the base and the parameters of the *vox populi*: the use of profanity ('Jesus'), the use of swear words ('fucking'), an irrational prejudice against Seven Day Adventists ('up [them] selves') and factually incorrect ('more money than you can shake a stick at'). The film provides no explanation whatsoever for where this anonymous individual (whose anonymity argues that he must be understood as typical) arrives at his complex of prejudices. Certainly there is no diegetic media involvement to provide these specific accusations.

In a slightly more complex way, one of the earliest responses to initial media reporting of this incident provides another inexplicable expression of attitude. A young mother (mise-en-scene derived definition) watching Michael explaining about dingoes, turns to another and says 'There is more to this than meets the eye'. The film does provide what may be interpreted as a rationale for this scene inasmuch as previously it has shown two shots within separate television editing suites in which anonymous television personnel are shown to be editing a previously seen interview (part of which is showing when the remark is made). The juxtapositions and the brevity of the scenes suggest that they are to be interpreted by the putative spectator as examples of media (or media practices) bringing about distortion (although they both demonstrate routine television journalistic practice and not specific use of editing and sound dubbing to incriminate the Chamberlains). On one hand then the editing and the content of these brief shots would seem to be classical Eisensteinian montage effect. A: media arranging material to suit themselves + B: a media consumer responding to this material, = C: media distortion has caused the negative suspicious response. This sequence does not present any reason why the media should wish to distort the material, nor does it do anything which implies to the layperson that this is routine media practice.

There are some thirty-seven of these *vox populi* interpolations (or more if one includes non-attributed voices on the sound track in crowd scenes). Of them only six could be reasonably said to be positive comments about the Chamberlains. The rest are derogatory or, at best, concern disbelief in the Chamberlain's innocence or 'their story'. Quite a number involve the expression of opinion in strident, vulgar and often profane, or at least colloquially 'bad' language (fucking, bloody, bastards, wank[er], 'doesn't know shit from clay', 'bitch', 'cunning as a shithouse rat' 'bloody Chamberlains …wouldn't know the bloody truth if it got up and bit them in the arse' and so on. The effect, immediate and cumulative is to undermine the speakers, individually and collectively, by making them foul-mouthed as well as bigoted and, at the same time seemingly incapable of making up their own mind but being reliant totally on the media or other hearsay and rumour. Combined with this, and undermining the credibility of these ordinary Australians in the first instance, is that the putative audience *knows the truth*—knows what actually happened, knows the media distorts (if not how and why), knows that Lindy is not a bitch, that Seventh day Adventists are not some weird, child-sacrificing cult, etc. Lindy is redeemed because her ordinary Australian critics are irredeemable themselves.

The film does present a few moments which invite obvious interpretation as example of chicanery or underhand methods to incriminate the Chamberlains or to collect evidence, no matter how spurious or dubious, that can be used to implicate them. There is a scene, for example, where the senior investigating police officer, Charlwood, attempts to 'verbal' Lindy and a couple of times he is seen to use or attempt to use a hidden tape recorder when talking off the record to her. None of the 'evidence' collected in this manner shows up in the film, mainly because the film completely eschews the second inquest at which it was, presumably, presented.

There are implications of political expedience and further chicanery of a different order here and there, inserted or interpolated like the *vox populi* scenes but far less numerous. They add up to an impression of some sort of political interest, at least at the level of finding the incident politically 'inconvenient' In this regard, Everingham (not named as such within the diegesis) and his remark on first hearing the news (via the inevitable television set in his office) 'They could have picked somewhere else'. (Before this is also uses the expletive 'Christ'.) There is also a hint that the incident is economically threatening in some political sense. Everingham again—when the first coroner suggests that the powers-that-be may need to take some sort of position on the conflicting claims of wild life and tourists—'Cheeky bastard!'. (This use of profane language places Everingham within the ranks of the ordinary Australians seen and heard elsewhere.) This same politician and later others are shown making announcements—of new (false) evidence and simultaneously side-stepping the question of a second inquest (which the takes place via an ellipsis), and of announcing new (genuine) evidence which leads to Lindy's release. Beyond oblique references to Darwin—Charlwood to the detective he is replacing: 'I've been instructed. I'm in charge of the Chamberlain investigation now.' Replaced detective: 'Oh. Darwin. Politics.'—there is little to support any claims that film states that political motives drove the trial and the verdict. There is also nothing to suggest why it is that the replaced officer so easily assumes that politics are behind his replacement. Why should he think that he is politically unsound and that Charlwood is equally politically sound? He just does.

Other than the implications within that the 'cheeky bastard' remark and the immediately following (in editing terms) 'He doesn't know shit from clay that fellow' made by an anonymous uniformed Northern Territory police officer, the film offers as possible motivation other bruised egos, notably the challenged reputation of Dr Brown, the chief forensic witness at the first inquest. Shown reacting with dissatisfaction to the coroner's remarks about the unreliability of his forensic evidence, he also shares a sideways glance (or complicity) with Charlwood. Following the delivery of the coroner's finding, Brown with Charlwood is seen to be the first leaving the court house, pushing through the press throng without reacting to the question (from an unidentifiable female journalist on the soundtrack): 'Mr Brown, what is your reaction to...?'. Almost immediately, he is seen to be on the telephone to, presumably, a bureaucrat within the government, suggesting he can obtain the expert opinion of a London-based scientist and requesting 'the minister's' permission to take evidentiary material out of the country 'at his own expense'. The extent to which Brown's bruised ego motivates his further involvement is then not developed by the film: he does not reappear as a forensic witness nor even an observer at the trial (and the second inquest is absent). He does not appear after the guilty verdict to savour his revenge. (The actor's name does not even appear in the credits in *Australian Film 1978-1994*.[6]) If it is Brown's bruised ego that is the cause of providing an excuse for others—police and politicians—whose collective institutional egos have also been bruised to pursue the Chamberlains, the film does little to confirm what it initiates in the short scenes I have mentioned, and nothing to show that this bruised ego is massaged by the consequences. In defending Lindy, the bruised ego hypothesis is as equally underdeveloped as any other. If it is even noticed by spectators, it may well only serve as a further contribution to the unstable and difficult to quantify propositions the film offers or hints at to why Lindy was hounded into gaol.

Even so, articulated as I am doing it here makes it sound as if, contrary to my assertions, there *is* a clear if fractured statement of a hypothesis of why the train of events which culminated in Lindy being convicted of murder and incarcerated was activated and pursued. I assert, however, that the cues I am elucidating from the text have only been arrived at by and through a particularly close textual analysis which involved going backwards and forwards through the video release version of *Evil Angels*, of freeze framing, of transcribing dialogue and voice-over narration and so on, simultaneously deconstructing and reconstructing the film. The structure of the film mitigates against this interpretation when watched in sequence and in real time. Even without this proviso, however, too many threads are left dangling for there to be a coherent sense in which the defence of Lindy is subsumed by an explanation of the reasons behind the events to which the film offers witness.

As I stated much earlier but feel called upon to reiterate here, the film for the defence, ironically, takes the very position which the actual prosecution took in regards the motivation for Lindy's alleged murder of Azaria. Neither the film nor the prosecution are willing to offer a coherent motivation for the actions and therefore the film itself sidesteps presenting anything but a hint or two.

NOTES

1.   John Bryson, *Evil Angels*, Viking, 1986.

2. For example, James Simmonds, *Azaria: Wednesday's Child* (TPNL Books, 1982); Richard Shears, *Azaria* (Sphere Books, 1982), Norman H. Young, *Innocence Regained: The Fight to Free Lindy Chamberlain* (The Federation Press, 1989).

3. *Through My Eyes: An Autobiography* (William Heinnemann, 1991). It may be of some interest that, much later, Michael Chamberlain wrote his own version of events: *Heart of Stone: My Quest for Justice for Azaria* (New Holland, 2012). Both of these appear after (in the latter case, well after) the production and release of the film.

4. *Cinema Papers*, no.71, May 1989,

5. *Images of Australia: 100 Films of the New Australian Cinema* (SMU Press, 1991).

6. Scott Murray, ed., *Australian Film 1978-1994*, Oxford University Press, Melbourne, 1995, p.250.

DOES DAN DIE? THE NED KELLY FILMS AND THE QUESTION OF THE FATE OF DAN KELLY AND STEVE HART AT GLENROWAN.

In his article, 'Ghosts of Glenrowan', in this issue[1], Rodney Noonan draws attention to the 1951 film, *The Glenrowan Affair* and its suggestion that Dan Kelly had escaped from the shoot-out at Glenrowan. But what of the other Kelly films? (Table 1.) I propose examine these, and the one major television incursion into the area, in terms of what their narratives (and their expression of those narratives) may indicate about the issue of whether Dan Kelly (in particular) and Steve Hart survived Glenrowan.[2]

Table 1.Kelly films and television

Date	Film	Director	Comment
1906	*The Story of the Kelly Gang*	Charles Tait	
1910	*The Story of the Kelly Gang*	Charles Tait (?).	Remake or re-release with new footage of 1906 film.
1920	*The Kelly Gang*	Harry Southwell	
1923	*When the Kellys Were Out*	Harry Southwell	
1934	*When the Kellys Rode.*	Harry Southwell	
1951	*The Glenrowan Affair*	Rupert Kathner	
1970	*Ned Kelly*	Tony Richardson	
1977	*The Trial of Ned Kelly (TV)*	John Gauci	ABC TV production
1980	*The Last Outlaw (TV)*	George Miller, Kevin Dobson	Seven Network mini-series
1993	*Reckless Kelly*	Yahoo Serious	Spoof/parody using aspects of Kelly legend
2003	*Ned*	Abe Forsyth.	Spoof/parody using aspects of Kelly legend
2003	*Ned Kelly*	Gregor Jordan	

THE STORY OF THE KELLY GANG (CHARLES TAIT 1906)

There is no doubt engendered in this, the first and arguably most famous Ned Kelly film, that Dan Kelly, along with Steve Hart and Joe Bryne, did not survive the battle with the police at the Glenrowan Hotel. Little remains of this film and, despite assiduous archival and historical research by other scholars, it is not clear quite what this film actually consisted of in terms of the narrative of Ned Kelly and of his activities. By pure chance, what footage has survived includes the mutual murder-suicide of Dan Kelly and Steve Hart.

This particular scene, in the Glenrowan battle sequence, is headed by an intertitle (one which may or may not have been in the original release print), describing (in the way of many intertitles in early silent films) what is about to be enacted as 'STEVE AND DAN SHOOT EACH OTHER'. This is followed by a single take from a camera which has framed, as if via a proscenium arch, part of the barroom of the Glenrowan Hotel, the bar with rows of bottles behind it in the back (of the set) extending out of frame on the left, and with a door leading out the back on the right.

As the scene commences, Steve and Dan stand on the extreme right of frame (in the DVD version released by the National Film and Sound Archive) with Dan almost out of frame[3] They are in the act of shaking hands. Steve then turns and takes several paces to the left. Both men transfer their pistols to their right hands. Steve turns and faces Dan, who raises, lowers and then raises his pistol towards Steve. Steve raises and aims his pistol at Dan. Despite the waving about of their pistols, each man does seem to fire simultaneously. Steve reacts first, throwing back his arms and arching his body before collapsing. Dan is almost entirely out of frame and only his outstretched arm and his left boot are seen until he half enters the frame as he lurches back and onto his right side. Steve collapses on his back and lies, after several twitches, in the bottom centre of the frame, his left leg bent with the knee upwards.

Table 2. Death of Dan and Steve

Shoot each other	Shoot themselves	Unknown means	Unseen/Dan survives
The Story of the Kelly Gang (1906 and 1910?) *Ned Kelly* (1970)	*Ned Kelly* (2003)	*The Last Outlaw*	*The Glenrowan Affair*

An intertitle appears, 'Gallant Rescue of the Wounded Platelayer by Father Gibney'[4] and, in essentially the same framing, Father Gibney, hatted and in a frock coat, walks in through the door at the back. The 'wounded platelayer', who has lain still against the bar in the centre of the frame throughout Dan and Steve's actions, is now leaning upright and forwards, grasping his chest. Gibney checks first Dan (almost leaving the frame right to do so) and then Joe (whose body has lain between Steve and Dan throughout) and, finally, Steve before helping the platelayer to his feet and supporting him out through the door at the back. Swift as his examination of Dan, Joe and Steve is, the implications of Gibney's actions are clearly that each of these men is dead.

It is obvious that the film offers no possibility of the survival of Dan Kelly nor of Steve Hart (nor of Joe Bryne as his corpse lies on the floor throughout these scenes). They are shown to shoot each other[5], they collapse, and their bodies are checked (for signs of life) by Father Gibney. In the interests of keeping the action going, he does no more than place his hands upon each in turn, but, again, the implications are clear: each is dead. Newspaper reviews of the film (a representative sample are reproduced in Bertrand and Routt[6]) mention the death of Dan and Steve, so it would seem circumstantially as if their reviewers saw what the film presents in these terms—or at least did not see anything that could be interpreted (no matter how perversely) as the possibility that Dan and Steve lived (even if, as Noonan notes, 'rumours of Dan's survival existed as early as 1890', sixteen years before this film was produced).

THE GLENROWAN AFFAIR (Rupert Kathner[7] 1951)

As Noonan points out in his article, *The Glenrowan Affair* rather more than implies that Dan Kelly escapes from the siege at Glenrowan. The film further insists he lives long enough to tell a passing painter 'the' story of the Kelly gang sixty years later. (He does so, presumably, in the same area he lived in as a boy—the film implies he lives in the historical Kelly homestead). This claim is made relatively unambiguously, and so is out of keeping with the otherwise near incoherence of the film's narrative. The evidence is provided through a double-narration. The opening of the film is narrated (off-screen) by an (on-screen) unnamed young artist painting scenes in 'Kelly Country' in rural Victoria in (presumably) the 1940s. But his narration becomes then that of another character, Old Dinny[8], who tells the painter the story of the Kelly gang; the painter and thus the film (by visualisation) tells the audience. As the painter says via voice-over narration: 'I dared not interrupt Dinny. His story was too real. It was as if he was living it all over again. Yes, really living it again.' At which point a fade takes the action from Old Dinny and the painter in the vicinity of where Ned Kelly was captured to the outside of what a title asserts is 'Mrs Jones Hotel Glenrowan 1887'[9]. From this point onwards, it must be assumed that what is seen and heard is the filmic equivalent of Old Dinny's story although there are occasional interpellations of the painter's voice, in which he seems to have knowledge either outside Dinny/Dan's or is couched in terms which are unlikely to be those of Dinny/Dan.

The point of providing an 'eye-witness' account and of making that eye witness Dan Kelly (presumably aged around eighty years) is unclear. It may be an attempt, not uncommon in Kelly narratives on film, to argue for the historical accuracy of the events and characters portrayed. Almost instantly (and, it must be granted, not unusually for films), the authority of the narrator is undermined by having him describe (i.e. the film dramatises and visualises) events at which he was not present. Indeed, most of the film's actions take place in the specific absence of Dan Kelly. While it might be argued that those actions which involved Ned but not Dan—as with this first confrontation with the police at Mrs Jones' hotel—were later told to Dan, this case cannot be made for the innumerable scenes that take place in the office of Commissioner Nicolson (presumably in Melbourne) and include at various times Aaron Sherrett, Superintendent Standish and Superintendent O'Hare. Nor indeed is there during the conversation between the bank clerks at Jerilderie prior to Joe Byrne and Ned's appearance there. Dan is absent from the lengthy scene at the bank because, presumably, he and Steve are guarding the townsfolk who have been seen to be rounded up and lock in a barn.

The film establishes Dan Kelly's escape and survival in two ways. Firstly, via the clear implication that Old Dinny is Dan Kelly. The narrator introduces the character as 'Old Dinny. Some say his real name was Dan, but few would go into details about it'. (Dinny is a not uncommon Irish diminutive of Daniel.) Dinny, an apparent fount of knowledge of the past of the area, is particularly well informed about 'the legend of Ned Kelly and his gang'. Since what follows for the rest—the greater part—of the film is, ostensibly, Dinny's story, the (presumed) accuracy of detail lends credence to the implication he *is* Dan Kelly. Despite the teasing hints in the early, present-day narration, with lack of subtlety the film also hedges its bets by showing that Old Dinny has an identical scar on the back of his hand to one on the back of Dan's hand.

The first revelation of this scar occurs slightly before an incident in which Dan and Steve rescue Ned and Joe from the police. A totally unmotivated edit to a close up of a hand with a distinctive 'V'-shaped scar is made in between two shots of Dan and Steve watching from the bush as Ned and Joe are captured. The close-up is of a left hand gripping a tree trunk or branch (but neither man in the longer shot/s seems to be doing so). The only reason for this tight close-up is to show the scar. And the reason for this is to show the scar again at the very end of the film to confirm Dan's survival and that he and Old Dinny are the same man. Whether this 'revelation' is intended to merely confirm what most audience members would have figured out for themselves or as an attempt at a (pretty clumsy) surprise remains uncertain.

Considerably less clear than the scar is what presumably is Dan's escape. In the early stages of the siege, Ned tells Joe to 'try and get Dan away. He's still a kid'. Joe replies, 'I'll do my best.' Even so, there is no action in which Joe is seen to be insisting that or helping Dan to get away. What does happen is that in the midst of a series of shots of Ned, in full armour, exchanging gunfire with uniformed police outside the hotel, there is a shot of a man running through the bush.[10] Is this Dan escaping?[11] If so, this, frankly, looks a bit cowardly as the fight inside and outside the hotel is continuing. Indeed, the next shot seems to show Dan still inside the hotel with Joe and Steve. Is there a continuity error here or has somehow the footage become rearranged for the DVD release by the National Film and Sound Archive?

Admittedly, at one stage earlier, before Ned appears outside in his armour, there are four men inside the hotel shooting out, but one of these is (or seems to be) Ned as Joe is in the act of handing him the iron helmet. The actor does not seem to be Bob Chitty, who has played Ned to this point, and seems to be dressed in a darker shirt than previously. So, after Ned goes out in the armour (not seen until he appears some distance away from the hotel) and after Dan escapes (if this is who this fleeing horseman is), then only Joe Byrne and Steve Hart should still be inside the hotel.

The capture of Ned is then interrupted at the end by an image of the gutted but still burning remains of the hotel, with the sounds of shots in the background, before returning to Ned lying wounded and a trooper galloping up and standing over him. The next shot is of an exhausted and ash-grimed Father Gibney walking up hill, then a closer shot of the burning hotel, then a mid-shot of Gibney facing a police officer and saying 'They're all dead'. Gibney admits to seeing Joe Bryne and Steve Hart, meaning their corpses. The officer asks Gibney several times if he 'saw Dan' and eventually Gibney replies, 'No. I didn't see Dan.' The whole sequence, and to all intents, the film's narrative, ends with another close-up of the burning hotel. Whether with conscious irony or not, a fade returns the film to the present day and the painter lighting a cigarette while still listening to Old Dinny in the same place as the Ned Kelly story commenced. There follows, first, a mid shot of Old Dinny nodding (and speaking, his words are not heard) and, secondly, a close-up of the back of a hand, presumably Dinny's, with an identical (if suitably aged) 'V'-shaped scar. There is a return to the mid-shot of Old Dinny and a fade to a title 'The End' over a drawing of a revolver.

Dan, in a film hardly noteworthy for its characterisation, is a singularly non-individuated character. Joe Bryne is, in fact, the most developed character as his actions and utterances give to him a (slight) complexity of personality that none of the others, including Ned, possess. It is odd then that Dan is so central to the telling and the film so determined to hint so strongly at Old Dinny being Dan and yet he is as peripheral to the Kelly story as told. There is as well the fact that most of that story is of actions, places and characters which Dan could not have witnessed. But that may written off as simply a clumsy but hardly unusual filmic conceit (after all it even happens in a much greater cinematic masterpiece *Citizen Kane*, made only ten years earlier).

So, with only the minor hiccup caused by Dan being seen to escape and then being seen afterwards still inside the hotel, the film certainly asserts his survival. A question which the film alone cannot answer is why the writer/

director Rupert Kathner bothered with this romantic folk tale. Perhaps he felt that, at the time, it was sufficiently familiar that it could be used dramatically but not sensationally. Or that the story being 'by' Dan gave it a spurious authenticity.

NED KELLY (TONY RICHARDSON, 1970)

Unlike the 1906 film, this version does not actually show Dan's and Steve's deaths, and nor their corpses. It does imply their deaths (and by extension, refutes or refuses any suggestion of their survival) in two ways. Firstly, and with intentional if tragic irony, the film shows Dan and Steve shoot one another in an instinctive suicide pact, driven by Dan's assumption that Ned is already dead, which he is not an indication of this (his final gun fight with the police) erupts simultaneously with the shots from Dan's and Steve's guns. The cut away from Dan and Steve inside the Glenrowan Hotel to Ned shooting at the police who surround him (seen initially through the visor of his helmet) perhaps obviates absolute certainty about Dan's death. That is, Dan and Steve are not seen reacting to the shots—there is no bodily mutilation, no falling bodies, no corpses. But given that the film has them stand face-to-face, inches apart, and with each placing his pistol in the other's mouth before firing on their alternating count to ten, it seems almost perverse to conclude they have not killed each other at the same moment. In tight close-up, their respective fingers are seen to tighten on the trigger of their pistols. Still, it must be noted that the (expected) sound of the shots is dissolved, overlapped, or replaced by the sounds of gunshots in the next image (from inside his helmet) of Ned from firing on and being fired upon by the police. I do not think the ambiguity is deliberate—the sound bridging is a dramatic effect via editing. The rather obvious Freudian interpretation of the image of two young men, each with his pistol barrel placed in the open mouth of the other, should be neither exaggerated nor perhaps ignored.

Secondly, further circumstantial evidence is provided by a brief scene following Ned's capture. He is lying wounded and bloody in a railway carriage. He attempts to raise his head and (in close-up) says, 'If they're alive, they'll fight'. This line is (as result of elliptical editing) comes as if in response to Standish saying to Ned, as he lies wounded at the conclusion of the gunfight, 'Ask the boys to surrender'. A further elliptical edit takes the action to the setting fire to the Glenrowan Hotel. A zoom into the flames catching hold is followed by two progressively distant shots of the hotel fully ablaze, the last of which dissolves to the end of Ned's trial and his speech to the judge (presumably following being found guilty). Again, the implication is surely that Dan and Steve are dead— since they do not fight on, they are not seen alive—and that their bodies are consumed in the flames that are seen to totally engulf the building.

No Father Gibney, nor anyone else, is seen to enter, or crucially exit, the Glenrowan Hotel following Dan and Steve shooting each other. (Table 3) The surviving hostages have, as in *The Story of the Kelly Gang*, left the hotel prior to Dan and Steve's actions.

Table 3. Father Gibney as Witness

Sees Dan and Steve's bodies	Denies seeing Dan's Body	Not present
The Story of the Kelly Gang *The Last Outlaw*	*The Glenrowan Affair*	*Ned Kelly* (1970) *Ned Kelly* (2003)

The film concludes with Ned's sentencing—the final image is a freeze frame of Ned predicting he will meet the judge who has sentenced him 'there', his downward pointing finger implied 'in hell'. There is nothing that in anyway indicates or could be taken to imply that Dan and/or Steve have survived. Such possible ambiguity as I have indicated is not deliberate, at least in this matter. It arises rather more from the simple fact that to see Dan and Steve's death throes, their corpses and their charred remains is dramatically and narratively unnecessary. The element of tragic pity, raised by Bertrand in relation to the conclusion of *The Story of the Kelly Gang,* is present but muted; the film's emphasis is on Ned as class-rebel not as wasted life (his or those of Dan and the others).

NED KELLY (GREGOR JORDAN 2003)

This, the latest cinematic retelling of the Kelly story, modifies Dan's and Steve's deaths slightly but without offering anything more substantial in the way of suggesting either of both survives. Their deaths occur, as with *The Story of the Kelly Gang* but unlike the 1970 film, after the Glenrowan Hotel has been set alight. The two men, or more appropriately boys, sit slumped against the front of the bar, Joe Bryne's body on the floor in front of them (as with *The Story of the Kelly Gang*). Previous shots have shown the hotel to be well ablaze although only smoke but no flames are apparent in their immediate vicinity. Steve checks his revolver at Dan's request and points out that he has only two bullets left. 'I guess that's all we need then,' Dan says. In a tighter shot, Steve turns to look at Dan, who seems to say 'yes' before adding, 'We never stood a chance, did we?' Dan shakes his head; both boys are crying. Dan takes Steve's pistol with his right hand, grasps Steve's right hand in his left and raises the pistol to his right temple. The shot is heard over a cutaway to an image of intense flames and spiralling ash and debris through which can be just seen a window of the hotel. The next cut is to Steve cradling Dan's head in his arms, taking the pistol in his right hand and (in tighter close-up) raising it to his right temple. Again, the sound of the pistol shot is heard, more distantly this time, over an edit to Ned, outside, slowly getting to his feet from behind a log where he had collapsed during the night. Although only seen in profile, in dim light and in a loose close-up, the implication seems to be that Ned hears the shot and understand what it means. This is enhanced by the fact the police have stopped shooting at the hotel some time previously (silence on the soundtrack save for the music—soft and slow strings—and faint sounds of Ned's movements; prior to the deaths an image, possibly from Ned's point-of-view, has the police surrounding the burning hotel, watching but not shooting). The last scenes are of the final shoot-out, of the wounded Ned in the train and the train departing from Glenrowan.

Neither Dan nor Steve is seen again after the close-up of Steve with the pistol to the side of his head. There is no Father Gibney nor his equivalent to enter the hotel. Like the 1970 film, no-one is seen to enter or exit the hotel following the deaths of Dan and Steve. Unlike that film, no enquiry or request that Dan and Steve be called on to surrender is made. They are not mentioned again. The clear implication is that they are dead, that the shot (or shots) Ned hears informs him of that fact, and that the police believe this to be so as well. The difference is that, contrary to previous films, Dan and Steve kill themselves not each other. There is (thankfully) no gruesome graphic depiction of the fatal shots. It is true that only Dan is shown as a (presumed) corpse with Steve holding his body and taking the pistol from his (presumed) dead hand. Steve's corpse is not seen because, as noted above, the interior of the hotel is not revealed again. (The exterior of the burning building is seen in the wide shot at the beginning of Ned's final shoot-out with police.)

The finality of Dan's and Steve's deaths is actually dramatically important, the tragedy of these two young and naive young men is meant to be felt as such, the final line, 'We never stood a chance, did we?' is clearly intended to register both their heroics and the futility of them. Any implication of their survival would undermine this dramatic and emotional (not to say, thematic) intensity.

THE LAST OUTLAW (KEVIN DOBSON, GEORGE MILLER 1980)
The Last Outlaw is not a feature film but a television mini-series. At slightly more than six hours in length (four episodes of a little over 95 minutes each), it has much more time to use the story of Ned Kelly—historically, imaginatively and extrapolated upon—than any of the cinematic versions. This enables it includes events either shared out between the various films (with no one film containing the full range) or to include events, characters and actions (and it must be said interpretations) ignored in those films and spend more of its

narrative exploring (or imagining again) the psychology and personality of many of the characters central and more peripheral to the narrative.

What is relevant here is, however, what the series indicates about the death (or possible survival) of Dan Kelly. Understandably, the siege at Glenrowan comes towards the end of the fourth episode (the whole series concludes with Ned's trial and execution). The deaths of Dan and Steve occur during the relatively long conclusion to the Glenrowan sequence. Both are still alive at the moment (noted by a caption as '7.15 am') that Ned appears out of the bush behind the encircling (but silent) police and commences to exchange shots with them. After this has gone on for some minutes, Dan and Steve run around the side of the hotel and also commence firing on the police from outside. Ned is eventually downed by Sergeant Steele—the shooting (presumably by Dan and Steve and other police) continues in the background. Dan (in a big close-up) fires (at the police struggling to disarm the wounded Ned), then after Dan fires several more shots, Steve grabs his arm and pulls him back (out of frame, into the hotel).

A scene follows with Superintendent Sadlier and then Father Gibney talking to the wounded Ned at Glenrowan Railway station before Dan and Steve are seen again. Inside the hotel, with shooting ceased, Dan stands near the window, Steve nearby who calls on him to move away from the window. After a brief discussion, Steve says 'I'd hate to die alone'. The two are face-to-face, inches apart. Dan's reaction to Steve's words—to look directly into Steve's eyes—and Steve's returned gaze and slight (wry?) smile implies a mutual thought. Dan places his arm around Steve's shoulder and they both walk towards a door at the back of the room (almost as if saying 'let's go in the back room and kill ourselves'). As they leave, Steve glances down and the camera tilts to Joe Bryne's body on the floor. A commercial break follows and the action resumes with a high angle shot of the hotel and then various shots of watchers, including Sadlier. The hotel is then set alight, Kate Kelly is restrained, and Father Gibney rushes into the burning building. Inside, Gibney sees Joe's body on the bar room floor, checks his pulse and makes a sign of the cross. He leaves to go into the back room as two unidentified men burst in and lift Joe's body.

Gibney enters the back room and sees Steve and Dan's bodies lying on the floor on their backs, next to each other, touching. Dan's dog lies dead at their feet. Gibney approaches, places Steve's hand across his body so it touches/grasps his left (as Dan's already do). A close-up shows both men, their heads inclined towards each other, resting on bags (or some sort of pillow) and their eyes open but staring lifelessly. Gibney makes the sign of the cross above each in turn and then staggers out. As he looks back, a low-angle shot from the floor across the bodies tilts up to the burning ceiling which begins to collapse. A second shot of falling, burning ceiling and then a close-up of Gibney leaving. Outside, the blazing building is watched by police and on-lookers. In the railway station, Steele observes, 'Well, that's the end of it'; the camera pans to the supine Ned, presumably listening (or at least hearing) Steele's words.

Several more shots are provided of the burning hotel until it collapses completely. The scene changes to the arrival of Commissioner Standish at the station. Sadlier tells him he has allowed the remains ('burned beyond all recognition') to be taken by the families. Standish appears about to object but does not. The implication is that the police have seen and recovered the remains of Dan and Steve—and are satisfied that is who they are.

A high angle shot of two objects—presumably the remains of Dan and Steve—covered in blankets on the tray of a cart is followed by three shots of a horse and cart followed by a number of people, including Kate Kelly) moving through the countryside like a funeral procession. This is the last (presumed) appearance of Dan and Steve in narrative.

It seems conclusive that Dan and Steve have died and not escaped. The manner of their deaths is not shown; it is implied that they either killed themselves or, somehow, killed each other. The manner of their deaths is obscure; no weapons are in their hands nor lie near the bodies although their discarded armour does. Their bodies seem arranged on the floor, their shoulders touching, heads inclined towards each other. Did they lie down and kill themselves or each other? How did the dead dog come to be arranged at their feet?— its hindquarters are across Dan's lower leg, so it may be that he placed it there before lying back himself. There are no discernible wounds to either body, nor, particularly, to either head removing any suggestion of shooting themselves in the head (as with both the 1970 and 2003 films).[12] The bodies (or whatever remains of them) are not seen when removed (which takes place off screen) and are implied to be what are two separate objects, each smaller than an intact body, covered by blankets, immediately subsequent to Sadlier stating he has allowed the bodies to be taken by the families. Unless one assumes an unsupportable improbability that Dan and Steve were feigning death to fool Gibney (or someone else foolish enough to penetrate the burning building looking for them) and they then crept out of the hotel unseen—the narrative makes no hint of this—then this mini-series argues conclusively for Dan's and Steve's death in the hotel at Glenrowan. (Table 4)

Table 4. Dan and Steve's corpses (as shown in film/seen by audience)

Both corpses seen	Neither corpse seen	Ambiguous
The Story of the Kelly Gang *The Last Outlaw*	*The Glenrowan Affair* *Ned Kelly* (1970)	*Ned Kelly* (2003) Dan but not Steve.

Unlike the other films (save of course for *The Glenrowan Affair*), this version does not have Dan and Steve die by shooting either each other or themselves. The idea that they did die by gunshot may have originated with *The Story of the Kelly Gang* or with earlier folk tales. It seems to be maintained in later films, possibly because it is more dramatic, more in keeping with the gun violence or 'heroic' behaviour, or because the inexplicability of Dan and Steve somehow having poison and taking it seems narratively implausible. *The Last Outlaw*, with its assertion (at the beginning of each episode) that 'All characters, events, names, events, and places in this series are drawn directly from fact', may have eschewed dramatic license and speculative explanation for what is ostensibly known about the deaths of Dan and Steve. In other words, what is known is that their cause of death is unknown but the fact of their death is.

CONCLUSION

In summary, the filmic (and televisual) versions, or those of them that survive and/or can be viewed, with one exception, state with only narrow margins for ambiguity that Dan Kelly and Steve Hart both died at Glenrowan. Only one, *The Glenrowan Affair*, has Dan escape—and live on. The films show slight variation in mode of death—suicide, murder-suicide, unexplained—and vary as to the presence of a witness (Father Gibney) to their corpses. Father Gibney is shown (on screen) to see the bodies of both in *The Story of the Kelly Gang* and *The Last Outlaw*; he reports seeing Steve but not Dan in *The Glenrowan Affair*, is absent in both the 1970 *Ned Kelly* and 2003 *Ned Kelly*. In the 1970 *Ned Kelly*, Dan and Steve's bodies are not shown at all, in the 2003 *Ned Kelly*, Dan's body is shown before Steve shoots himself (or seems to). Other than for *The Glenrowan Affair*, it is only the 1970 *Ned Kelly* that sustains the remote improbability that Dan and/or Steve may have survived, but this is only credible if it is accepted the shots heard are *not* the shots of them shooting each other. It must be concluded that, for whatever reasons, *The Glenrowan Affair* purposefully takes cognisance of folk tales of Dan's escape (unless Kathner invented this himself unknowingly), but other versions do not know of these stories, or do not accept them as either factual or relevant, or do not care. Unless Dan's escape is of narrative significance, (again as with *The Glenrowan Affair*), it is much more dramatically satisfactory, effective and poignant that Dan and Steve die in these narratives irrespective of what is or is not factual.

NOTES

1. *Australian Folklore*, No.23, 2008, 131-147.
2. Three of the Kelly films, each directed by Harry Southwell, are not considered here; two exist today only as fragments and the third. *When the Kellys Rode Out* (1934), has not been viewed (it is only accessible as a preservation copy at the National Film and Sound Archive in Canberra). Nothing of what can be learned of these films outside of viewing them indicates their narratives state or nor do they imply that Dan Kelly or Steve Hart had survived. Harry Southwell, a pioneer of Australian cinema, seems to have had something of an obsession with the Kelly legend. He produced three (see Filmography) and attempted a fourth. This last production seems to have involved Rupe Kathner in some capacity who then proceeded to produced his own film (*The Glenrowan Affair*) when (or causing) Southwell's production was abandoned. It is not known whether Southwell's abandoned film had Dan's survival as a key element.
3. I am assuming the identity of the characters from the way in which they are dressed. Although continuity seems often to have been ignored in terms of different actors playing the same role and in the costuming, I will follow the description provided by Routt in Bertrand and Routt, 2007, pp 64 &5, and assume Steve is wearing a white hat and white kerchief, and Dan a dark hat and dark kerchief. Neither man has a beard.
4. Although each of the intertitles contain the trademark 'J & G' (Johnson and Gibson—the film's producers), the fact that the first intertitle is all in capitals and the second in mixed capitals and lowercase suggests they were not made and/or inserted into this extant footage at the same time.
5. While clearly this is the first cinematic version of this event, it is not known where or when the idea that Dan and Steve killed each other (in a murder-suicide pact) arose and whether it is a common element in folk takes around the Kelly gang.
6. Ina Bertrand and William D. Routt, *The Story of the Kelly Gang*, The Moving Image, no. 8, 2007.
7. Rupert Kathner (better known it seems as 'Rupe') is a strangely idiosyncratic figure even within an industry fairly replete with eccentrics. Seemingly as much a conman as a showman (the two may be synonymous), his talents as a film maker seem to have been well below his ability to be one. *Hunt Angels*, a quasi-documentary of his life as a film maker was made in 2006 and, by a delicious irony, is probably a much better film than he could have made of himself as a subject. The inadequacies of *The Glenrowan Affair* cannot be simply attributed to the financial stringencies under which it was produced.
8. In the opening credits, the character is simply referred to as 'The Old Man'.
9. The title over this shot also includes (in small print) the information that 'Glenrowan is a small Township in Nor. E. Victoria near the border of New South Wales...'
10. This sequence consists of the following shots:

    1 Mid shot of Ned in armour, pistol in his right hand, firing out of frame to the left

    2 Two troopers, partly behind a tree stump and ant hill, running forward and to the right, one leaps the ant hill.

3 In a matching action, a man (Dan?) runs through the bush from left to right, the camera panning with him.

4 A wide shot of a downhill slope of bush with a horse tethered (or standing) behind a tree, centre. A man, initially obscured by the tree, mounts the horse and rides off out of frame to the left.

5 A man (the same?) rides out of trees that lie across the low ridge in the background into an area of long grass, at first into the camera then turns to the right and the camera pans to follow his movement, which is in a shallow semi-circle to the right and away from the camera again.

6 Interior of the hotel. Joe leans a rifle out of a partly opened window and fires out. Steve is hunched on the floor below the window but starts to get up, holding one hand to his head. A third man, who resembles Dan, enters from the left in a crouched position and goes, seemingly to help Steve. This man is carrying a rifle (which suggests that he is part of the gang, but who is he if not Dan?)

7 A long shot of Ned, walking out from behind a small tree or bush towards the camera, firing a pistol in his right hand and, momentarily, raises his left hand to his breast plate as if responding to a hit.

11. It looks a bit like Dan, but the figure is never seen clearly enough and at the point where the horse and rider come closest to the camera, the rider is leaning low *behind* the horse's neck and is obscured. Is this because it was a different actor? Or as part of the 'is Old Dinny Dan or isn't he' game the film is playing? Given that the give-away scar on Old Dinny is not revealed until the second last shot of the film and after Father Gibney admits he did not see Dan's body, the director may be simply attempting to maintain the enigma a bit longer.

12. This seems in keeping with various factual accounts. See, for example, Frank Clune, *The Kelly Hunters*, (Angus and Robertson, 1954), p.312. This books is subtitled 'The Authentic, Impartial History of the Life and Times of Edward Kelly, the Ironclad Outlaw'. Clune attributes this to 'Father Gibney [seeing] them both dead, lying peacefully with their armour off and no sign of blood' (p.357) but offers no precise source for saying what Gibney saw but it may be assumed it is part of the evidence 'Dean' Gibney gave to the Royal Commission and contained in pp. 442-5 and pp.461-5 of the *Minutes of Evidence* cited by Clune.

BIBLIOGRAPHY

Bertrand, Ina and Routt, William D. 2007. *The Story of the Kelly Gang*. The Moving Image, no.8. Australian Teachers of Media (ATOM),

Clune, Frank. 1954. *The Kelly Hunters*. Angus and Robertson, Melbourne.

McFarlane, Brian. Mayer, Geoff and Bertrand, Ina, eds. 1999. *The Oxford Companion to Australian Film*. Oxford University Press, Melbourne.

Pike, Andrew and Cooper, Ross. 1981. *Australian Film 1900-1977*. Oxford University Press, Melbourne.

Seal, Graham. 1996. *The Outlaw Legend*. Cambridge University Press, Melbourne.

Shirley, Graham and Adams, Brian. 1983. *Australian Cinema: the First Eighty Years*. Angus and Robertson/Currency Press, Sydney.

SHOOTING NEW ENGLAND: A CINEMATIC HISTORY OF THE REGION.

BEGINNINGS

It is a testimonial to the power of the appeal of cinema that in less than twelve months of the first public screenings of 'moving pictures'—in Paris in December 1985 (the Lumière brother's Cinématographé)—moving pictures were being both shot and exhibited in Australia. Film production (if it can really be granted the epithet) was quickly taken up by would-be entrepreneurs, 'chancers' and by the Salvation Army (which realised the potential of the new medium to assist in its evangelical activities and set up its own film production arm in 1899). Story films, rather than *actualities* (short films recording daily life, the precursors of travelogues and documentaries), quickly developed. Producers less religiously minded than the Salvation Army ignored its obsession with re-enacting Christian martyrdom on Melbourne tennis courts[1] and took to the attractive narrative possibilities of bushrangers, real or imagined. *The Story of the Kelly Gang* (1906) was followed by the first film version of *Robbery Under Arms* (1907)[2] and in short order by films on other bushrangers including New England's own Thunderbolt, and others real and fictional.

Although bush or outback settings appear in the narratives of many of the early films made in Australia (and not all were bushranger stories), the locations for shooting these productions seldom strayed far beyond the immediate confines of Sydney or Melbourne. There was no need for them to do so. Irrespective of purported setting (which, in most cases, was generic bush rather than regionally specific), bush locales close to Sydney (especially) and Melbourne usually proved accessible and sufficiently 'authentic' even when dealing with historical figures or events known to have specific locations. The 1907 version of the Captain Thunderbolt story, *Thunderbolt*, was shot around Lithgow and the Blue Mountains and certainly not in the vicinity of the real 'Thunderbolt'/Fred Ward's actual bushranging activities. For the first twenty or thirty years of film-making in New South Wales, then, bush-located narratives were shot in places like Windsor, Camden, Gosford, French's Forest and the Blue Mountains but only rarely further afield than these. New England locations do not figure until 1921 (Guyra: *The Guyra Ghost Mystery* of which much more below), or 1920 (*The Man from Kangaroo*) if the region is considered to stretch as far as Gunnedah.

•

128

The cinema industry, locally and worldwide, has basically a tripartite formation: production-distribution-exhibition, and is highly centralised in the first two aspects. Exhibition is, perforce, the most decentralised aspect of the business, although in terms of regional Australia there has been a large-scale reduction in exhibition since the 1950s with most country towns losing their cinemas. In New England as elsewhere, exhibition has been the point of contact with the film industry for close on one hundred years, and remains so for at least the major centres and the occasional small town survivor.

At the beginning of the cinema-as-industry equation is production: actually making films. There may be any number of variables that influence where (and how) a film is produced (or at least where it is shot). These range from banal (but often crucial) economic reasons to aesthetic reasons. In between these polarities, and of some importance to films in general but especially to these films I am daring to call 'New England' films, are concerns with authenticity and verisimilitude. Authenticity may extend to considerations that are geographical, or to concerns that are historical, or even in the case of films which have been adapted from literary originals, to faithfulness to what is already, paradoxically, fictional.

These factors (and others too, some of which are pragmatic matters such as accessibility, availability, or simply technology) can blend in odd and intriguing ways. In the case of *The Chant of Jimmie Blacksmith* (1978[3]), profilmic aspects include the complication that the *story* material of the film is a novel, based upon historically verifiable facts. Thus, for example, locations for some scenes and sequences for the film were chosen because of a desire—a need even—for a level of authenticity to a 'history' as well as a faithfulness to the fictionalisation of that very history. Yet, despite the quite extraordinary use of a considerable number of wide-spread locations (not all in New England), *The Chant of Jimmie Blacksmith* does not use many of the 'actual' places that are part of the history (of Jimmy Governor upon whom the eponymous 'hero' is based) or even part of the fictional account from Thomas Keneally's novel.

Put simply, New England films may be placed into three categories.

(1) Films 'about' New England subjects, and which have been shot in whole or in part in New England. That is, those based directly or clearly connected at some close remove to verifiable events, individuals or histories.

(2) Films which, for some reason, have been shot (in whole or in part) in New England locations even though there may be little or nothing that links their narratives with those locations.

(3) Films fictionally about New England and shot in whole or in part in New England. That is, those films based in original or adapted fictions whose stories (or parts of them) are located in identified or identifiable New England locations (such as *The Chant of Jimmie Blacksmith*).

NEW ENGLAND SUBJECTS, 'NEW ENGLAND' FILMS

The Guyra Ghost Mystery

It is best to start at the beginning, or at least with the first film shot in the New England region for the express purpose of commercial exhibition. As far as is known at present, this seems to have been an eccentric production called *The Guyra Ghost Mystery*, shot in Guyra in May 1921, and based on some curious and widely reported events of the previous month in that very same town, alleged to be visitations from the spirit world or the activities of poltergeists.[4]

The film, produced, directed and acted in by John Cosgrove, a reasonably well-known stage actor, has long since disappeared. That the film was made, completed and exhibited is beyond doubt. The Bowen family, whose 'story' (which may well have been an elaborate practical joke that got out-of-hand) is the source, appeared as themselves, and Cosgrove took the role of 'Sherlock Doyle', which suggests that he (at least) was not taking the whole thing very seriously. The whole film was shot in three days according to the Sydney paper, *Smith's Weekly*[5], and even allowing for the uncomplicated nature of film production at the time, this sounds very rushed indeed. The length of the finished film is unknown.

The presence of Cosgrove and his film 'crew' (if any beyond a camera operator) does not seem to have excited as much newspaper attention as the 'mystery' itself. His arrival is noted in the *Armidale Express* of 12 May 1921 in a short item (among others from Guyra) in the 'Inter-district News' section. The *Guyra Argus* of the dates (those which are available) makes no mention of this[6]. The same item concludes that film (or as it is described: 'series of humorous pictures') 'will probably be shown here in a couple of weeks time'. There is no evidence that any screenings did take place in Guyra.

Captain Thunderbolt

It was another thirty years, almost to the day, before another feature film on a New England subject was shot in the region. In those years from 1921 to 1951, cinema had become a vastly influential and international medium, films had passed from being just mass entertainment to a thing called 'Show Biz' (their production was in many ways as enthralling as the films themselves); actors had become 'stars', the nexus of glamour and celebrity had become firmly established in popular consciousness throughout the world. The people of New England were hardly immune from the allure associated with motion pictures. And so the reaction to a production crew arriving in Armidale in March 1951 to begin the location shooting for *Captain Thunderbolt* was not the passing interest that seemed to be the case with Cosgrove and his shooting of The *Guyra Ghost Mystery* three decades previously. *Armidale Express*, no doubt encouraged and fed by the production's public relations section, followed events with more than casual attention.

Of course, the film was based on the region's favourite scallywag, the gentleman bushranger, Fred Ward, known as 'Thunderbolt' or 'Captain Thunderbolt'. No Ned Kelly he, his legendary chivalry was more than matched by the fact he does not seem to have shot anyone at all, not even the odd policeman.

The film was directed by Cecil Holmes, more noted before and since as a socially committed documentary film maker. He only directed two fictional feature films in a relatively long career. Given Holmes' socialist concerns, it is not surprising that he used the Thunderbolt story to explore aspects of class and class conflict in nineteenth-century Australia. In this he may have been influenced by reading Jack Bradshaw's 1930 book *The True History of the Australian Bushrangers*, where Bradshaw takes a strongly pro-bushranger and anti-authoritarian stance to bushrangers in general. Whether *Captain Thunderbolt* plays fast and loose with the legend is not especially important, although one disgruntled individual wrote to The *Armidale Express* following the film's premiere in Armidale on 20 June 1955: 'The falsities are so many that it's far easier to enumerate the few points in which the film infringes upon truth'. The writer was an 'R.B. Walker' and it may only be a coincidence that Walker was also the surname of the police constable who killed Thunderbolt near Uralla in 1970.[6]

The production itself used locations within Armidale itself—the Sheriff's House, the Armidale Court House—and locations at Kelly's Plains and Kentucky. It also, as is almost *de rigeur* for such film productions, used locals as extras including local children as friends of Fred Ward as a child and local men riding horses in some action scenes. Locals were helpful in other ways, supplying horses and in one case a genuine stage coach of the period. Shooting took place between 5 March and 22 March 1951.

The production was actually intended for television (but not in Australia as television had not arrived here at the time). The Australian release was intended to be a cinematic one. For some reason, the film was not released in Australia until 1955. It did have its world cinema premiere at the Armidale Capitol Theatre on 20 June of that year. Not surprisingly, it proved immensely popular to audiences from Armidale and Uralla, attracting even such a redoubtable local identity as 95-year-old Mrs I.S. Gordon, who 'had not previously seen a talking film' but who could 'recall incidents relating to Thunderbolt's activities.'[7]

Another quarter of a century passed before New England provided both the site and the source of material for another feature film production, barring a couple of oddities to be mentioned below. This was a period in which the production arm of the Australian film industry seldom roused itself from a coma-like state, in which cinema attendance plummeted in face of the implacable advance of television, and in which as a consequence, cinemas closed *en masse*. In the early 1970s, a dramatic turn-around occurred. Enthusiasm grew for revitalising Australian film production, encouraged by the success of films made in the first flood of that enthusiasm. Of these, *Picnic at Hanging Rock*, and *Sunday Too Far Away* revealed the cinematic potential of both history and the bush.

The first of a mini-flood of films to choose historical New England subjects and to shoot them, more or less, in their historical locations was *The Picture Show Man*. This was based, with a mixture of historical truth and cinematic licence, on the activities of that unique business, the travelling cinema exhibitionist of the 1920s and 1930s, and specifically on the biography of one Lyle 'Pop' Penn (in the film, Pop Pym), as recalled by his son.[8] The Penn exhibition circuit had been centred for a long time on Tamworth and had involved the towns along the Peel Valley towards and including Nundle and at other stages, west as far as Gunnedah. At one point, Penn had operated a circuit that went as far north as Glen Innes. His last circuit was one based on the northern rivers area.

The film's producers used only limited number of locations from within these areas, although it is far from clear why they felt obliged to obey any some sort of geographical imperative in the name of 'authenticity' (the film could have been easily shot elsewhere without detracting from its rural and period feel). At no time within the narrative are any of the locations identified by their actual names, so any knowledge that this story takes place in parts of New England is extra-filmic, from the book rather than from the film. It was thus a little premature for the *Northern Daily Leader* (Tamworth) of 20 October 1976 to offer, via a front page headline, the prediction: 'Film Seen as Tourist Drawcard', and to go on to assert that 'audiences will see all the beauty spots in glorious colour [*sic*]'. A certain degree of latitude must be allowed for film publicity puffery, and it's true that one of the film's clear attractions is the cinematic rendering of landscape and location.

As is usual for films made on location—at least for those which are remote from the normal centres of production—*The Picture Show Man* called for and made use of locals as extras. The first call for interested individuals, made via the *Northern Daily Leader* on 6 October 1976, resulted in the producers being overwhelmed: as many as 800 would-be actors turned up for interview. The majority were used in a picnic race sequence, shot at the Somerton Racecourse a few weeks later. Small groups of local people, suitably dressed and made-up to look like country folk of the 1920s were also used in the several sequences that involve an actual screening. The interiors for these scenes were shot in Tamworth, although a couple were shot in Sydney, *sans* the local extras. (Unlike the shooting of *Danny Deckchair* in 2002—to be discussed below—where many local Bellingen people travelled at their own expense to Sydney to take part in a similar crowd-in-a-hall scene.)

The first scenes were shot at Murrurundi, but this was to be the furthest from Tamworth the production was to travel. It is unclear why Murrurundi was used as the production's small budget seems to have prevented the frequent relocation of cast, crew and equipment. Several rural properties were used: 'Lalogooli' at Breeza and, notably for its use of the exteriors of house and garden, Bective Station, this latter being the site of shooting when the production was visited by the then Premier of New South Wales, Neville Wran. The latter stage of the location shooting took place in late November and early December 1976, on the banks of the Clarence River, at Woodford Leigh and actually, *in* the Clarence River at one point when a scene calls for a vehicle to be pushed into the water. Again, locals were called upon as extras including a small number of local girls who acted as pupils in a modern dance class held on the suitably picturesque surrounds of the hall at Woodford Leigh. The *Daily Examiner* (Grafton) took a rather more prosaic view of the presence of the production, as much impressed by the 'Revenue Pay-off' (part of a headline 30 November, 1976) as the presence of 'stars.'

Overall, *The Picture Show Man*, in accordance with the prevailing ethic of Australian cinema then and since, does considerable cinematographic justice to the photogenic qualities of the Australian landscape. It offers little by the way of insight of the actual operations of a travelling film exhibition business, although the producers went to some trouble to locate genuine cinema machinery from the time. The central dramatic conflict, if it can be so-called, come from the presence of a rival picture-show man, Palmer the American (played by Rod Taylor), a situation which did not actually occur. The film offers some 'typical' incidents (on the road, actual picture shows) and borrows a couple of odd ones from Penn's memoirs. It tends to paint the New England life of the time in a nostalgic light: quaintly rustic, vaguely idyllic, unsophisticated or, at least, 'unspoilt' and clearly class-structured.

Unlike *Captain Thunderbolt* and, as will be noted below, *Little Boy Lost* and *The Chant of Jimmie Blacksmith*, *The Picture Show Man* was not given a premiere screening in Tamworth or Grafton upon release in May 1977.

Scarcely had the cameras ceased rolling on *The Picture Show Man*, or more accurately, scarcely had the projectors started revealing the finished film to audiences in the metropolitan areas, than the next feature film production to be shot in the region and based, more or less, on New England history began.

The usual harbinger of a film being shot in the locality, the call for locals interested in being cast as extras, took place in Armidale, Walcha and Uralla in July 1977. The film was *The Chant of Jimmie Blacksmith,* based on the Thomas Keneally novel, itself based upon the historical events surrounding Jimmy Governor and his brother Joe in 1900. The film itself was shot in a wide number of locations, not all within New England, but not as far afield as the places actually traversed by the historical Jimmy Governor, nor by the novelised Jimmy Blacksmith. The choice of locations in and around Armidale and Dorrigo was determined (as is usually the case with feature film production) by budget, suitability (will pass for the genuine article) and availability. There is, of course, no reason why a fictional account (in this case the adaptation of a fictional account) should be shot in historically actual locations, nor even those locations mentioned in the source material. If anything, the finished film is rather unclear as to the precise location of much of the action. For example, the trial of Uncle Tabiigi in the novel takes place in Dubbo, in the film the court house is Armidale but neither is mentioned by name or sign. Like *The Picture Show Man*, this lack of specifying precise locations inhibits any chance of the film becoming a tourist advertisement for the New England—although the subject matter could hardly be conducive either.

Key scenes were, nonetheless, shot in New England. The extras were required for those scenes concerned for the most part with the beginning of the manhunt, the murderous actions preceding which were shot on a property near Uralla. Brief shearing scenes were shot in a shearing shed at Ebor and 'Woodpark Cottage' near Armidale stood in for a clergyman's residence near Gilgandra. A granite peak in the Dorrigo National Park served as an Aboriginal scared site, and later scenes were shot in the vicinity of Kempsey.

Slightly less than a year later, on 21 June 1977, *The Chant of Jimmie Blacksmith* was premiered at the Capital Theatre in Armidale, simultaneously with its being released in Melbourne. Understandably the premiere itself was popular event; local opinion of the film itself is harder to gauge.

It would be pleasant to be able to record that film was both an artistic and a popular success. Certainly it was one of the earliest Australian films to be screened at the prestigious Cannes film festival but it did not garner any awards. Response overall tended to be mixed, and this may well be less a reaction to the subject matter, or even to the considerable violence that is the centrepiece of the narrative, than to the didactic, even preachy tone taken by director-writer Fred Schepisi. In keeping with many Australian films of the time (including *The Picture Show Man*) this one shows the Australian landscape (varied here between rugged mountains, deep rain forest, and undulating rural land) to splendid advantage. But it does not avoid the stereotyped assertions of Aboriginal affinity with the land and it falls back on too many clichés regarding white racism and oppression of the Aborigines. At the risk of facile summary, it is worthy but too earnest and far too angry.

Little Boy Lost

Hot on the heels of crew of *The Chant of Jimmie Blacksmith* came the third and final production in this late-70s mini-flood of New England located film projects, *Little Boy Lost*. This film was based on much more recent events: the four day search in the Guyra district for a small boy, Stephen Walls, lost in rugged bush country near his family's property in November 1960. Perhaps because it made sense to shoot the film where the events took place, the actual locations were used for the most part. Ironically, however, these locations— bush country, farm houses, a tiny bush church—are as much generic of their type as particular to the actuality, and no greater sense of authenticity it is achieved by using them.

Shooting commenced in April 1978 and in addition to 'imported' actors— John Hargreaves, Don Crosby (who had also been seen in *The Picture Show Man*), John Jarrett, Tony Barry and a young boy Nathan Dawes (all the way from Rockhampton, Queensland, to play the four-year-old Stephen Walls)— the film called for and used hundreds of locals from as far as Glen Innes and Armidale as well as from the Guyra district itself. The recreation of the search, which originally had involved about two thousand people, utilised perhaps three or four hundred extras. Shooting finished a month later, on May 3, 1978.

With considerable fanfare, *Little Boy Lost* was premiered at the Capital Theatre, Armidale, on 14 November 1978 and premiere was attended by Sir John Gorton, ex-prime minister of Australia, to whom considerable credit has been given for his role in encouraging the rebirth of the Australian film industry in the late 1960s. *Armidale Express*[9] reported Gorton claiming that 'The [Australian] film industry is aiming at producing better films than those acclaimed in America, the United Kingdom and Italy'. It can only be presumed that he made these remarks before seeing the film. Although the same issue carried the headline: ''Lost' film applauded' and published a review headed 'Film deserves its success' but perhaps most of the local enthusiasm came from the audience seeing themselves, and people and places they knew on 'the big screen'.

This is not the place to analyse the shortcomings of *Little Boy Lost* as a film, its banal and ill-conceived dialogue, spurious attempts at dramatic conflict, lack of convincing characterisations, and seemingly endless repetition of the stunningly obvious. There was no story, simply an historical incident (and a hit song), not the substance for a narrative.

•

NEW ENGLAND ORIGINALS, NOT NEW ENGLAND.

Almost a decade of quietude then descended on New England, at least as far as film production activity was concerned. During the 1980s, the Australian film industry underwent a number of significant changes, not the least of which was a loss of interest in period films based on a traditional sense of national identity. Nevertheless when after a long break, further films were shot in the region, they were period films yet again. Dealing with contemporary life in the Bush seems to have had little immediate appeal for film makers. Also, they were not particularly 'New England' films. They used New England locations but were not specifically New England stories. The locations were 'generic' or else, as, in the case of *The Winds of Jarrah*, a New England location stood in for one geographically remote to city life.

The Winds of Jarrah

In early 1983, the Film Corporation of Western Australia, ignoring what one would have thought was a prime imperative—to promote film production in Western Australia—chose to shoot a film in and around Dorrigo. The reasons were, presumably, economic. It was cheaper and easier to shoot the film in New South Wales than in Western Australia. The choice of Dorrigo is also explained by its proximity to 'tall timber' and existing logging businesses— with the addition of a bullock team or two and the temporary removal of more recent timber working technology for authenticity. Nonetheless, the title suggests a Western Australian location: Jarrah (*Eucalyptus marginata*) dominates the hardwood forests of the south-west of that state and is hardly found naturally occurring elsewhere. As the film's narrative resolutely declines to identify its location, other than 'Australia, 1946' as an early caption states, and the town in the story is never named, the implication can easily be that this is Western Australia.

Not in the true sense an 'original' film, it was adapted from a Harlequin/ Mills and Boon novel (*The House in Timberwoods* by Joyce Dingwell). Filming began in January 1983 and seems to have taken place almost entirely in and around the Dorrigo. This particular production is unique to the extent that the house within which most of the action is centred was purpose-built near Gangara. Great use is made throughout the film of the picturesque scenery of the area: timbered hillsides, creeks, lush pastures, panoramic views of mountains and so forth. *The Winds of Jarrah* does not, however, integrate this landscape into the film's thematic. Little exists even by way of the most subtle implication, to suggest that the landscape, its properties or qualities, make or shape the people who live in and through it. Personalities are forged for the usual clichéd Mills and Boon reasons, especially repressed sexual urges, sublimated passions, and the common panoply of 'romantic' longings, rather than (as with many other Australian films and fictions) as a result of interaction with the Australian bush, let alone the New England bush.

The Winds of Jarrah does manage to include several heavily determined Australian images beyond the frequent emphasis on landscape itself: a bush fire and an Anzac Day service—one narratively on top of the other for maximum melodramatic effect. For the latter, the Anzac Memorial in Dorrigo's main street was used, and (as always) locals made up the several hundred extras for the scene. Local extras were also used in a log-chopping contest scene and for a dance scene. The Anzac ceremony also serves the narrative purpose, otherwise unexplained, for the remote, taciturn, saturnine 'hero' to realise and declare his love for the long-suffering 'heroine'. Nothing else seems to be the cause of his finally recognising and embracing both the inevitable and the heroine simultaneously.

Principal photography was completed on 2 March 1983. The film itself was not released until 1985, and then only in New South Wales country towns before going to video hire. The reasons for its failure to find exhibition in cinemas in metropolitan areas are obscure. They may be related to a shift away from interest in period, bush-located films. If such a shift was actually felt by producers and funding bodies, it did not prevent a very similar bush-based period romance (of a slightly darker tone) from being shot not far away two years later. That film was *The Umbrella Woman*.

The Umbrella Woman

Unlike most of the films that preceded it, *The Umbrella Woman* was an original film, the screenplay being written for the film and not based upon existing material, historical or fictional. The writer was Peter Kenna, well-known as an author for the stage—so much so that the film's title credit actually reads 'Peter Kenna's The Umbrella Woman'.

The Umbrella Woman was shot in and around Bowraville in 1986, a place made to look like a country town in 1939.[10] Particular buildings are singled out for narrative action—the hotel, the railway station—and streets, especially the main street, are viewed in passing. As per usual, locals make up crowd scenes, especially several shot in the pub, but most of the action concerns a limited number of characters, played by Bryan Brown, Rachel Ward, Sam Neill and Steve Vidler.

The film is basically a sexual melodrama concerning a young married woman's unconsummated obsession with a womanising barman. While the film goes some way to suggestion that the 'umbrella woman's' neurotic behaviour is partly the consequence of the stultifying boredom of living in (or near) a small country town and partly the consequence of unmet sexual needs it does not really satisfactorily answer the central question of her behaviour.

The town itself is not identified as Bowraville. A sign at the railway station indicated it is 'Corrimandel'. And other than some activities associated with Bowraville and the area—logging, dairy farming—the town and the countryside is intended to be generically Australian rather than regionally specific. Once again, much of the incidental scenery is attractive although not spectacular, and one or two sequences, a picnic scene in particular, are designed to suggest almost an idyllic existence through nature, albeit one in which sexual tensions cannot readily be deflected.

A Little Bit of Soul

A Little Bit of Soul was shot in the vicinity of Glen Innes, and briefly at the town's railway station and the court house. Any other connection with New England is tenuous. The decision of the writer-director Peter Duncan to shoot the film at a property at Furracabad, 'Nant Lodge', was due to it being owned by a personal friend of Duncan. The main actor, Geoffrey Rush, also had an historical family connection with Glen Innes. Duncan told the *Glen Innes Examiner* that the shooting would not add to the economy, would take place on a closed set (so curious locals could not even watch), and would not offer any, even passing employment opportunities. He suggested that, nonetheless, the production would 'add a vibe to the town' (although he did not say how) and at the same time considered it 'unlikely the movie would have its world premiere at Glen Innes'.

•

WHERE IT IS, WHERE IT ISN'T

Two further films took advantage of the possibilities of different areas of the region to shoot part of their films. Both were partially set in New England itself but, ironically, the locations chosen involved almost a direct transposition. That is, where they fictionally took place was exchanged for where they were actually shot.

Oscar and Lucinda

The first was an adaptation of Peter Carey's novel, *Oscar and Lucinda*. An epic and sprawling narrative, the novel's final scenes are played out on the Bellinger River, to which the protagonist, Oscar Hopkins, although monumentally unsuited for the task, has travelled first overland to and then up, bringing with him a fantastic glass church. In the novel, he drags the church to a place called Boat Harbour (a real one is on the Clarence River further north); in the film the barely established settlement is clearly designated 'Bellingen'. The novel commences with the present-day narrator (Oscar's great-grandson) and his recollection of growing up in Gleniffer, near Bellingen. This location, and indeed the idea of moving a church, is not mere coincidence but is drawn from Carey's own short time living in the same area.

When the film came to be produced in 1996, the Bellinger River, not surprisingly, no longer resembled the untouched wilderness of the 1860s (as imagined by Carey). Another river was required and the producers decided to use the Mann River, near Jacadgery not far from Grafton. On 16 November The *Daily Examiner* reported the production's interest in looking for old machinery for use as props in the scenes to be shot at Jackadgery, where Bellingen of 1866 had been constructed. Shooting commenced a few days later.

As ever, local people, about one hundred this time, were employed as extras. And later, The *Daily Examiner* was able to report that the production had 'poured' 'more than $700,000 into the local economy'. The final scenes, as the glass church is boated majestically, up the Bellinger/Mann River probably justify the expense. The film's (and the novel's) anti-climax is, of course, that the church sinks during the night, taking Oscar with it.

Danny Deckchair

If *Oscar and Lucinda* had to move from Bellingen to the Clarence Valley for its conclusion, a film originally written to take place in the Clarence Valley had to move to Bellingen for its cinematic location. The towns of the Clarence Valley did not provide, it seems, images or settings that sufficiently resembled what a contemporary but idyllic Australian country town would (or should, according to writer/director Jeff Balsmeyer) look like. So, Bellingen became the location for *Danny Deckchair*. In the film the town into which the hero Danny literally descends from the skies is known as 'Clarence', a remnant of the original fictional setting. But Bellingen/Clarence is, unlike some earlier films, not simply a generic, 'quaint' Australian country town. Its New England setting is fairly clearly presented. Danny is thought to be a visiting academic from 'up north', from the 'Lismore University'.

Although the story begins and (nearly) ends in Sydney, most of the action takes place in and around Bellingen, and the film uses a number of Bellingen locations including the main street several times, the hotel, a car park behind the main street, the court house, various roads in the vicinity, a 'quaint' local weatherboard house, and the several parts of the Bellinger River, including the old Pacific Highway bridge.

The resulting film is something of a rarity in the Australian cinema, as it presents a positive view of life in a small country town. It does maintain the inevitable view that such rural folk are simple souls—Danny, who is in real-life the driver of a concrete truck, easily fools them into believing he is a university professor and is able, rather like a character from a Frank Capra film of the 1930s, to effect changes in nearly all their lives. Nonetheless, it is a charming comedy, and does much to make Bellingen seem an equally charming place.

CONCLUSION

Film-making in the New England region has tended to be clustered around three sub-areas: the vicinity of Tamworth; Armidale-Uralla-Guyra; and eastern edge of the Ranges (Dorrigo-Bellingen-Bowra;) with occasional visits to the Clarence Valley and, once, to Glen Innes. The times when these productions took place have tended to be more scattered, although there is a central cluster in the late 1970s. No consistent representation of New England has emerged from these films, but then they were made across a period of eighty years, and many social, cultural and, to some extent, environmental changes must be expected in that time frame. Even so, the predominance of period narratives does suggest that towns and farms in New England region lend themselves easily to period reconstruction, a suggestion perhaps that the region is a little 'out of time'. Of life in the area, the nostalgic tone of the period films, and even of the contemporary film *Danny Deckchair*, serves to provide an impression of a society that is simple perhaps even backward, unspoilt (by modern, city ways). While many of the representations are flattering, there are negative images as well: racism in *The Chant of Jimmie Blacksmith* in particular, and sexism in most other films, and a negative view of bush behaviour in *Little Boy Lost*. Balancing these human images are visual images of often great beauty, showing the landscape in its various forms: mountain ranges, forests, open grasslands, rivers and streams. The absence in most instances, however, of specific narrative reference to actual places diminishes the capacity of these films to serve, inadvertently or otherwise, as 'advertisements' for the region. As with most Australian cinema, audiences are offered the typical and generic Australian bush and rural towns rather than anything specific to New England.

NOTES

1. The Salvation Army film, *Soldiers of the Cross* (1900) consisted of thirteen short films of episodes from the Bible. Most were shot in the grounds of the Salvation Army's girls' home at Murrumbeena.

2. Despite the limited connection of the author of *Robbery Under Arms,* Rolf Boldrewood (Thomas Alexander Browne), to Armidale, there is really nothing in the films or the novel to suggest a New England inspiration, especially as the novel appeared in serialisation prior to Browne taking up a magistrate's post in Armidale. The claim by *The Oxford Companion to Australian Literature* that 'Terrible Hollow... is probably based on Horse-stealer's Gully in the Gwyder District near Inverell' has some scholastic support but remains uncertain and irrelevant to the story and to the cinematic locations of the film versions.

3. Following film scholarship practice, the dates given for film titles herein are those of the first release of the film in question, and not the dates in which shooting may have taken place in New England (or elsewhere if applicable).

4. Eerily, the issues of *The Guyra Argus* for April 1921, in which details of the events were reported (or may have reasonably been expected to be reported) are absent (explained as 'being unavailable') from the microfilm archive of the newspaper held in Dixson Library at the University of New England. It is tempting to muse upon supernatural or conspiratorial explanations for the absence of the copies in question. The affair was widely reported in other newspapers around Australia and gains an entry, albeit an inaccurate one, as 'the Guyra Poltergeist' in W. Fearn-Wannan [Bill Wannan], *Australian Folklore: A Dictionary of Lore, Legends and Popular Allusions* (Lansdowne, 1970).

5. As noted in Andrew Pike and Ross Cooper's invaluable survey of Australian films from 1900-1977 (Oxford University Press, 1978).

6. It has been suggested to me that 'R.B. Walker' was a member of the History Department at the University of New England.

7. *Armidale Express*, 24 June 1955.

8. As published in the memoir by Lyle Penn, *The Picture Show Man,* (Nelson, 1977), which prior to film's production was an unpublished manuscript, 'Penn's Pictures on Tour'.

9. November 17, 1978.

10. This date comes from David Stratton, *The Avocado Plantation* (Macmillan, 1990).

AMERICANIZATION AND AUSTRALIA: FILMS

From the first murmurings associated with the rebirth of Australian cinema in the early 1970s, the question of Australian films' relationship to America has been raised, debated, embraced, denigrated but never resolved. How do Australian feature films *represent* Americans? Why are Americans in Australian film narratives? Are Americans in Australian films always American, and does it matter whether they are or not? The very need to ask these questions arises from the extra-diegetic (commercial and cultural) significance of American actors as well as their diegetic presence (in the filmed, 'story world' or fictional reality) of Australian films. The two are not always synonymous. In various ways, in multifarious forums, Australian have been told for thirty years how important America is to the Australian film industry, but on the external evidence of numbers of films alone, they hardly rate at all. My filmography lists some 49 films, but there have been approximately 600 feature films made in Australia since 1970. If anything, since the mid-1980s and *Crocodile Dundee,* Americans in Australian filmic narratives have become less significant rather than more. Even so, the presence of Americans in those 49 films ought not to be ignored.

Prior to the resurgence of Australian films in the mid-1990s, the importance, felt differentially, of America as the fountain of eternal success led to the oft-derided situation of American actors being imported to play characters which the logic of the narratives and the diegesis argued need not be American. The most 'notorious' was the importation of Hollywood star Kirk Douglas for *The Man from Snowy River,* in which he played not one but two characters. Other examples, among many, are child actor Henry Thomas (fresh from success in *E. T. The Extra-Terrestrial* (USA, 1982)) for *Frog Dreaming,* Richard Chamberlain for *The Last Wave,* Rosanna Arquette in *Wendy Cracked a Walnut,* and Tina Turner for *Mad Max Beyond Thunderdome.* The use of imported actors is complicated according to whether or not they are American within the diegesis.

MID-PACIFIC BLUES

The category of films which can be dealt with most easily is those films which, while by most criteria are Australian,[1] contain American actors who seem to make no conscious attempt to disguise their 'Americanness', but which are also films that make no particular attempt within their dieges es to assert that their location is Australia despite the occasional obviousness of landscape, Australian accents and/or familiar Australian actors. The most common explanation for American actors (and/or characters) in these Australian films is that an American actor in a main (i.e. promotable) role enhances the prospect for the film to find American distribution and concomitant box-office appeal. While this calculated (if in most instances futile) reason may be true for some films, it is difficult to see how, say, Broderick Crawford in *Harlequin,* Joseph Cotton in *The Survivor* or Tom Skerritt in *A Dangerous Summer* might conceivably have been thought to serve such a function. This seems equally true even in films which do register Australian narrative locations and concerns. For example, the same question may be asked of Piper Laurie in *Tim,* John Savage in *Hunting* or Peter Coyote in *That Eye, The Sky.*

These Mid-Pacific films, making no particular mileage from their Australian location, seem almost totally dependent upon this marketing explanation for the presence of American actors. Their non-specific locales, indeterminate time periods, and non-existent social references make it irrelevant whether their characters are recognisably of one nationality or another. That these films are yearning for an American audience is often confirmed by the over-dubbing of Australian actors with American accents, even for Australian release.

AMERICAN ACTOR, NON-AMERICAN CHARACTER

There are a handful of Australian films in which American actors have played roles which quite specifically are not American characters. It is possible that in some cases, these actors were used because of artistic reasons, because of their ability as actors or a particular quality in performance or (diegetic) presence they could bring. For example, the presence of Meryl Streep as Lindy Chamberlain in *Evil Angels* or Dennis Hopper as the eponymous hero of *Mad Dog Morgan.* Even so, these characters do not bring an American presence into the diegesis, although the extra-diegetic effect may be of some interest in a study devoted to audience response and interpretation.

IS YOU IS? OR IS YOU AIN'T?

Hollywood films, and to a greater extent American television with its historical evolution towards greater realism in style and content, have ensured that screen Americans (and all that they might stereotypically represent) are not alien to Australians. Thus, the presence of Americans in Australian narratives works on the levels of both familiarity and otherness. Familiarity, perhaps self-evidently, allows Americans to be placed in my formulation of cousins. It may well be argued that this familiarity is what enables films such as *Wendy Cracked a Walnut,* *'Norman Loves Rose'* and *Now and Forever* to use American actors who make no attempt to disguise their Americanness (mainly their accents) but whose self-same Americanness is never commented upon or raised as an issue within the diegesis. Otherness, on the other hand, is quite deliberate in a number of films, particularly those that fall into my category of 'Colonisers'.

Americanism is thus a flexible commodity which can be emphasised or ignored depending upon the specific needs of particular narratives. Since the obvious American origins or status of certain characters is not an internal issue with films such as those mentioned above and others, then Americanness (as distinct from or as complementary to Australianness) is equally not an issue nor at issue. These films, while they might say something about certain practices, certain commercial inclinations within the film-production industry at particular times, do not aid in explaining the American presence in Australian films at the level of effect upon narratives, issues or themes. But these films cannot be simply abandoned as belonging to a sub-category of the Mid-Pacific films. There remains the possibility that by being diegetically non-specific but extra-diegetically American allows these characters certain traits, behaviours, reactions, or attitudes that would not be considered to be 'appropriate' for an individual of Australian identity. Thus the measure of American Bible Belt evangelism in the enigmatic personality of Henry Warburton (played b American actor, Peter Coyote) in *That Eye, the Sky* would risk seeming even more inexplicable with an Australian actor/character.

Of these films, it can only be assumed that these characters are what I call not-Americans[2] because nobody comments upon the fact that they may be American. In a number of them there are others who also designate themselves as not of Australian origin, usually by accent, occasionally by behaviour, and they too are not subject to comment by others, nor routinely comment themselves upon their status as Australians of other origin. *'Norman Loves Rose*[3] provides confirmation of this. The American actress Carol Kane plays Rose, a recently married, possibly Australian-Jewish wife. The film's milieu is, for the most part, a Jewish subculture in Sydney and nearly everyone speaks with some sort of Jewish-accented English. Kane/Rose's Americanness is lost within a plethora of ethnicity that surrounds her. Only one, Rose's father-in-law, specifically locates his non-Australian origins—in Poland.

One of the more bizarre examples of the not-American is found in *The Earthing*. Here a very well-known Hollywood actor, William Holden, plays the not-American. The American child actor, Ricky Schroder (reasonably well-known at the time) plays an American, and his parents are played by well known Australian actors, Jack Thompson and Olivia Hamnett, with (in the video release version) over-dubbed American voices. Not-Australians? Whereas my next category deals with films in which American characters admit they are American (but not much else), Patrick Foley (the character played by William Holden) in *The Earthling* clearly claims to be Australian but one who has spent many years, most of his adult life, abroad and has returned home to die. Sean Daley[3] (the character played by Ricky Schroder) is plainly American, a fact that is 'explained' by his parents having American accents and probably being tourists. The slight extra-diegetic dissonance created by an American child having parents played by very familiar Australian actors is quickly dissipated when the latter plunge terminally over a cliff early in the film. After which, no matter to what extent Foley makes it clear his returning to his birthplace and reminisces about growing up in the bush, these two characters are Americans in the Australian bush.

While a number of films in this category make so little of their Australian context that their narratives might as well be taking place anywhere, others notably use the Australian landscape in ways which impose an often clichéd locational identity. *The Earthling* goes further than this. It Americanises the Australian bush. This Americanisation of the Australian landscape occurs in a number of ways including providing all Australian fauna with homicidal tendencies (with the exception of 'cute' kangaroos), and the selective use of 'atypical' scenery that emphasises lushness, water, shade and trees and shrubs that are not obviously eucalypts. Unlike the fatal effects of the landscape itself in *Burke and, Wills,* unlike the supernatural power of the bush in *Picnic at Hanging Rock,* both of which represent quintessential Australian views of the Australian environment, this film makes of the Australian bush a surrogate Hollywood jungle or American backwoods. It is here that *The Earthling* slips into the category of American presence as colonisers in Australian film. An Australian landscape colonised both within and outside the diegesis.

YES, I'M AN AMERICAN—SO WHAT?

The not-Americans function to suggest an Americanisation of the Australian cultural consciousness has taken place, rendering Americans 'invisible'. Even in the most obvious of Australian locations or situations, their Americanness causes no comment. Nobody meeting or recognising Foley after thirty years says anything about his having developed a flawless American accent. Nor are not-Americans granted any special status beyond that which the contingencies of the narrative may require. To what extent the various films' makers expect the diegetic invisibility to transpose itself to audiences is impossible to judge. In the films within this next category, however, the Americanness of the characters is explicitly acknowledged. But often it is no more than a passing acknowledgment. In *Tim,* Mary Horton mentions that she was born in America but nothing further is made from this. Her Americanness is not a source of curiosity to the simple-minded Tim, nor commented upon by Tim's jealous/envious sister, nor by Tim's working-class parents. The only reason for its passing reference seems to be because the film's makers felt it had to be acknowledged, in order then to be dismissed as irrelevant. Unlike those films with not-Americans, here it was felt the film's audience would notice. In other words, the makers of this film do not feel that the Americanisation of Australia was not a *fait accompli*. The same is true for most films in this category. In *The Delinquents,* Brownie (played by an inescapably American Charlie Schatter) explains his Americanness by claiming to have been born in Australia but taken to the United States as a baby. There is nothing in Brownie's behaviour, attitudes or in reactions of others to him which serves to suggest that he is shaped by being American (other than the way he pronounces English).

Roadgames has not one but two clearly American characters, played by relatively well-known American actors, Stacy Keach and Jamie Lee. Neither denies their American origins, although Quid (played by Keach) has little to say about his, and Hitch (played by Curtis) is specifically identified only by reference to her American diplomat father in Canberra. Their Americanness goes largely unnoticed by any of the Australians they have contact with, and there is quite a number of these, many of whom might have good reason for drawing attention to Quid being an American. These two characters (and the film) find nothing remarkable in being Americans in Australia, not even the extraordinary coincidence of one American, hitch-hiking across the Nullarbor, being given a lift by another American, driving a truck. It is all so taken for granted that it is again curious that the film makers felt it necessary even to mention it at all.

Frog Dreaming continues this pattern of explaining the presence of an American in an Australian context by one or two lines of exposition. In this case, Cody (a suitably American name, reminiscent of Buffalo Bill Cody) is the ward of an Australian, having become so after the death of his parents. (Cinematic Australia seems surprisingly fatal for parents of pre-pubescent American boys.) As in *The Earthling,* the location is the Australian bush and, like *The Earthling,* the bush plays a significant part in the drama. Here, however, it is not simply the Australian landscape as it is imagined in white Australian culture that is colonised, but also an Aboriginal perception of it. Cody, a white American boy, becomes an 'initiate' into Aboriginal mysteries. After the identity of the 'bunyip' in a flooded quarry is finally, through Cody's persistent curiosity and intellectual precocity, revealed to be an old engine, abandoned and subsequently subjected to explicable if unexpected natural forces, it is to Cody alone that an Aboriginal kadaicha reveals that the place is, in fact, a sacred site, a place of 'frog dreaming' (which presumably whites had defiled with their mining). This is taking Wim Wenders' oft quoted line 'the Americans have colonised our subconsciousness' to another level—an American colonising 'our' Aboriginal dreaming as well. This is also the case in a confused way in *The Last Wave,* where the appropriation of (alleged) Aboriginal mythology by a (not?) American is even more absolute.

Gross Misconduct is an exceptional case of 'So what?'. The protagonist, Justin Thorne, is played by American Jimmy Smits (presumably well known from the television series *L.A. Law*, and more recently *NYPD Blue*). The fact that Thorne is an American is not relegated to a throwaway line as in *Tim*, or the marginally longer biographical expositions in *The Delinquents, Roadgames* and *Frog Dreaming*. The very opening scene of the film makes overt reference to the Americanness of Thorne and his family—a totally incongruous Fourth of July picnic on the banks of the Yarra. A later discussion emphasises the fact that Thorne is a recently arrived American academic. Thorne is later falsely accused of raping a student, but nothing of this seems to be specifically related to his national and cultural origins. The sexual attraction from Jenny, the student, does not seem to have any basis in his Americanness; it is explained as her neurotic obsessions and the effect of her traumatic relations with her father. Nonetheless, masculine sexual attractiveness is a regular aspect of the construction of Americanness in Australian films, and *Gross Misconduct* uses this as a part of Thorne's character to maintain suspense. He *is* sexually attractive (in the diegesis); the film maintains the probability that Jenny's obsession with him *may* be because of this, until the revelatory denouement.

There is an important 'twist' to the tail in *Gross Misconduct* when it is revealed that Thorne had previously contracted a 'Green Card' marriage in the United States, and that he will not or cannot reveal in his defence the status of his previous marriage because of its illegality in the United States, and the possible consequences for his previous wife. This is obviously an intrusion of matters that are intrinsically American (and make it less likely that this character could have been Australian without damaging the narrative). This serves, however, only a narrative convenience, providing a dramatic irony that enhances both the innocence of Thorne and his moral stature, while his silence helps ensure his (wrongful) conviction.

JUST A COUSIN OF MINE: YOU'RE LIABLE FOR TO SEE HIM HERE ANY OLD TIME[5]

Americans as 'cousins' in Australian films depend upon a simultaneous familiarity—a 'family resemblance'—and a difference which makes them sufficiently interesting to warrant inclusion as protagonists or main characters. Most importantly, as cousins, these Americans do not represent a threat to Australia, Australians (except those who for narrative purposes 'deserve' it) or to the 'Australian way of life'. Some become 'adopted' Australians or, in one way or another, are established on a journey towards being 'Australianised', a distinct reversal of the usual perceptions of Australian-American relations.

The best known of these films are the two *Crocodile Dundee* films, yet in relation to the American presence in Australian film, these are atypical. *Crocodile Dundee,* looking simultaneously to a local audience and an American one, takes for granted a pre-existing Americanisation of Australian culture. This is not an Americanisation that insists Australian culture has been 'colonised', has been modified (from whatever it was) in ways which have worked to make it more 'American'. That perception would have been fatal for the film as it relies on a clear sense of cultural difference between Australian and American identity. The film 'loads' this difference by making the main signifier of difference a 'throwback' Australian, a bushman of an earlier cultural tradition. This image remains a powerful signifier of Australian myths of identity and national character, while still allowing Dundee some attributes of the later twentieth-century version of the larrikin. At the same time, *Crocodile Dundee* is dependent upon the unstated assumption that Americanisation of Australia has produced in Australians a familiarity with America and Americans. The adventures which Dundee undergoes in New York are explicable only because unfamiliarity with American culture and social existence is restricted to Dundee and not, by implication, to a putative Australian audience. Indeed, the amount of time the film spends 'explaining' Dundee—the first third of the film, which is in narrative terms almost pointless—may be as much for the benefit of an Australian audience as it is for an American one. Americans in America are as familiar as family members, occupying a range of stereotypes 'known' from Hollywood films and American television programs.

Americans are also cousins in *Crocodile Dundee* because they so readily recognise the essential attractiveness of the all-Australian Dundee. Jealous boyfriends and the odd pimp notwithstanding, Americans in this narrative are all won over by Dundee's charms, and allow him to take liberties that it is difficult to imagine they would allow their fellow citizens. Crocodile Dundee is a reverse colonial. Super-Ocker Mick Dundee travels to the United States to win the hearts and minds of the local inhabitants, and succeeds. Americans fall willing, mesmerised victims to this atavistic, anachronistic cousin, this reminder of what they once were. The 'cousin' from Down Under is able to achieve that which the cousins from Over There can seldom do—win over the 'other'.

Leaving *Crocodile Dundee* aside and noting the exception of the Vietnam War film, *The Odd Angry Shot,* the American cousins in all these Australian films achieve sexual relationships with such relative ease that this characteristic becomes a fundamental way of defining Americanness in Australian film. In *High Rolling* the sexual confidence of the American Tex is pointedly contrasted with the more 'normal' Australian male diffidence of Albie. Essentially a road move, *High Rolling* proceeds with Tex as a successful sexual predator and Albie the more reluctant, easily embarrassed sidekick. Throughout, Tex's character, his Americanness, is consistently underlined by his sexual aggression, accompanied by the other consistent American trait, abrasive extroversion. Tex's caricatured Americanness does differentiate this film from others where the presence of an American in the plot also serves no clear narrative purpose. But this difference is simply one of the *quantity* of Americanness given the character rather than that Americanness contributing to or influencing the narrative.

The same might be said of *One Night Stand*. This disjointed narrative of four young people 'trapped' in the Sydney Opera House on the night that global nuclear war commences does not seem to require that one of these is an American. That Sam is an American is never in doubt, nor do the others ignore it. Arguably, for dramatic purposes it is 'easier' to create four distinct characters by making one of them 'foreign'.[6] All the same, there is no narrative reason for Sam to be an American beyond the irony that he is a deserter from the armed forces of one of the nations responsible for the nuclear war raging outside. In a reversal of the roles of the two men in *High Rolling* here it is Sam who is the more introverted, more sexually repressed while the Australian (Brendan) is the more active. Sam's status as a cousin is not so much that his Americanness has narrative function but that he quite clearly and equally shares the experiences of the three Australians. His thoughtfulness, sensitivity and intelligence are a deliberate contrast to Brendan (who, despite the approach of Armageddon, seems concerned with little more than sex) but none of these qualities is asserted because he is an American. There is in *One Night Stand* a curious inversion of Bob Ellis's aphorism to the effect that 'Americans act as if they believe that they are Superman on furlough, while Australians act like crims on parole'.[7]

In *Rebel,* the eponymous American protagonist does both. Rebel, like Sam, is a deserter from the American armed forces on some rather inchoate conscientious grounds. Rebel, in keeping with the general perception of Americans in Australian films, is sexually attractive, active and successful; he courts and beds Kathy, the older, married Australian woman. His American charms, sexual and otherwise, are such that he has the effect of arousing sympathy even from the dogged Australian cop helping the American military police capture him, and the amoral black marketeer, Tiger Kelly. Nonetheless, Rebel is less a rebel (if his desertion can be categorised as such) than he is a victim.

Being an 'ordinary' American does not itself make the American in question a cousin. At some level, nearly all American cousins are victims. Even as cousins, their Americanness sets them apart, defines them and sets the parameters for the variety of relations they have with Australians. Almost, inevitably, one of these relations is a sexual one. Others involve differing levels of victimisation or exploitation by Australians—as blatant as Tiger Kelly's attempts to exploit Rebel, homicidal in intent (as the Baker brothers in *Razorback),* or class-based snobbery towards Davis in *Phar Lap.* All four characters in *One Night Stand* are victims, of course, but whereas the three Australians are victims of forces over which they have no control, Sam, ironically, brings on his own victimisation. Nearly all the Americans in the *Crocodile Dundee* films are victims of Dundee in his role as a trickster, or if victim is a little harsh, then perhaps they are simply comical dupes.

Some victim-cousins manage to change their status, to reverse their situation. Alma Harris, in *Over the Hill,* is seemingly a lifelong victim of familial demands and patriarchal oppression. But her victimisation is, moreover, in America and related to American cultural circumstances. She requires the liberating experience of the Australian bush to release her. In other films, Australia is the source and site of victimisation. In *Razorback,* Carl Winters is doubly a victim of Australia inasmuch as the Outback in the combined form of the psychotic Baker brothers and a giant boar cause the death of his wife and unborn child. He too becomes a victim, albeit not terminally, of the brothers, through them of the environment itself, and finally of course of the eponymous razorback. Carl, however, goes from victim to avenging warrior in the space of the narrative. Rebel is a victim of war and in a more direct sense than Sam in *One Night Stand.* To an extent, he triumphs over military and local police, and the exploitative Tiger Kelly, although his victory is as hard won as is Carl's over a rampaging giant pig. Victimising Americans in these ways reduces their capacity to act as if they are 'Superman on furlough'. An *actual* Superman on furlough (or retirement really) occurs in *The Return of Captain Invincible* in which a super-hero, victimised by the McCarthy era in America, has found his way to Australia and drunken obscurity. A 'deserter' from the fight for 'truth, justice and the American way', he is brought back to the fray by the love of an Australian policewoman. As victims, however, few of these Americans are alone. There are Australians who take their side, share their battles, even in the case of *One Night Stand,* share their fate. Thus common ground is often found, and not always and only on the basis of sexual attraction. Jake Cullen, whose grandson is the first victim of the boar in *Razorback,* has a family loss in common with Carl. Tex and Albie, in the formulaic requirements of the road movie, are buddies or mates who share adventures. Rebel is supported by other Australians and his own fellow servicemen. In all these films, outsider status is thus mitigated. In *The Odd Angry Shot,* this similarity is carried to the level of making Americans largely indistinguishable from Australians in their interest in boozing, gambling, whoring and brawling.

CAPTIVATING CAPITALISTIC COLONIALISTS

Historically, World War II is a key moment in at least the cinematic version of the Americanisation of Australia. Several films explicitly recognise this: *Blood Oath, Death of a Soldier* and *Rebel*. The first two also implicitly demonstrate that this Americanisation was accompanied by a measure of political colonisation, which America in various ways interfered, directly and indirectly, in Australian affairs. These two films argue that in asking 'Big Cousin' for succour, Australian had surrendered some of its sovereignty.

Blood Oath is concerned with what are exclusively Australian matters, the trial of Japanese soldiers on the Indonesian island of Ambon for war crimes against Australian prisoners-of-war. The Americans are literally present only through an apparent 'observer' whose purpose is to ensure an acquittal for a high ranking Japanese officer. However, America itself is a constantly referred to absent-presence. Americanisation here is political and interferes with and (mis)directs Australian legal proceedings. This Americanisation—an implied imposition of a 'New World Order'—extends to Australia, and 'explains' why the Australian Judge-Advocate is determined subtly to obstruct or direct the proceedings to favour the Japanese and to avoid satisfying any Australian 'desire' for revenge. (The film ensures an Australian viewpoint by casting the quintessential Australian Brian Brown in the main role of indefatigable but frustrated investigator/prosecutor.) By use of graphic flashbacks of ill-treatment and execution of POWs, this excessively legalistic even-handedness is subverted by the film and the need for explanations for the obstructive actions of the Judge-Advocate heightened. The explanation offered is that of the ongoing Americanisation of the Post-war Western World, including Australia. *Blood Oath* takes an anti-American stance, touching a deeply embedded historical thread in Australian attitudes to America and, like *Death of a Soldier*, does so by selecting an historically sensitive moment when particular aspects of this anti-Americanism coalesced. The representation of Americans here is that they are duplicitous, self-serving and 'corrupt' to the extent of interfering with the Australian legal system to achieve their own ends.

The Australian legal system is also subverted to American ends in *Death of a Soldier*. The film begins with the arrival in Australia of General Douglas MacArthur along with tens of thousands of American soldiers. Actual newsreel footage and reconstructions recreate the public acclaim accorded MacArthur but this is instantly contrasted to footage which emphasises the Australians fighting alone in New Guinea. This deliberate dichotomy remains a thread within the film, which is actually concerned with the murder of three Australian women by a Private Eddie Leonski and his subsequent court-martial and execution by the American Army. In a telling scene, MacArthur is shown to be seated in a place of honour in the Australian parliament, listening to Prime Minister Curtin respond to hostile questioning about the right of the American army to prosecute an American soldier/citizen for 'crimes committed in Australia, against Australian citizens'. The clear implication is that MacArthur is controlling events, including the Australian government.

Leonski is, however, another American victim, although this time he is a victim of his own nation, not of Australia or Australians. He is a murderer but he is also clearly insane. The American army, for reasons of 'public relations' is determined to hang him. His status as a victim attracts the sympathy of Australians, represented here by a duo of Australian detectives whose investigations of the crimes are often hampered by the Americans. This sympathy is similar to that accorded Rebel by the Australian policeman and is based solidly in the Australian tradition of the 'fair go'. They, and, by extension, Australia itself are powerless to prevent the Americans doing what they want. The same powerlessness is evident in *Blood Oath,* where a less important Japanese junior officer is also sentenced to death in the name of American expediency, although this time it is by an Australian court. Both these films demonstrate American colonialism within the very fabric of Australian social institutions—the legal system and the government. Individual Americans, in *Death of a Soldier* at least, are given some redeeming features although certain basic characteristics are present, especially the sexual attractiveness of Americans. This is, however, a sustained representation of Americans as invaders, so much so that the film retells and even exaggerates what are known to be fallacious incidents of conflict between Australian and American servicemen. More accurate in *Rebel* is the resentment which Australian men, servicemen or otherwise, felt towards the willingness of American MPs to wield batons, and Rebel himself is rescued by waterside workers who object to his being beaten by 'dog wallopers'—a recognition of common cause at a key moment and a reason for Rebel's last minute refusal to take the ship to safety. In *Death of A Soldier* and particularly in *Rebel,* due to the latter's idiosyncratic style, there are parts of Sydney and Melbourne that become indistinguishable from (less desirable) parts of American cities (or Hollywood images of these), especially in the way in which the streets are patrolled and policed only by American MPs. Like the colonisation of the landscape in *The Earthling,* there is a colonisation of the Australian cityscape in *Death of a Soldier* and *Rebel.*

In films without wartime narrative locations, American colonisation is usually less institutional and less political, more individualistic and, most importantly, economic. Colonisation by Americans in Australian films is more often an extension of capitalism, or at least its practice by individuals. This is in keeping with the common perception, true of most of the films that have been discussed above in different categories, that Americans and Americanism are defined by wealth and materialism. In short, Americans are rich, or even if cousins, much better off than Australians.

Out-and-out capitalist Americans are found in *The Man From Snowy River* and *The Man From Snowy River 2*, *The Picture Show Man*, *Hunting* and in *Exchange Lifeguards*, with a lesser version in the character of Dave Davis in *Phar Lap*. Agents and spokesmen (they are always male) for American capitalism, American 'colonists' are found in *The Coca-Cola Kid* and *Undercover*.

Ownership of bits of Australia is clearly fundamental to the capitalist/ colonist and in the case of Harrison in *The Man From Snowy River* films, his ownership has presumably been accomplished in the same way as any white colonist of the nineteenth century: 'I carved this place out of the bush'. But Harrison is more than a normal squatter. Clancy, even he of the Overflow and spokesman for a more traditional, pre-capitalist Australia, accuses Harrison of being far more greedy and ruthless than the old time squatters. Yet the reasons for Harrison being an American in this most Australian of all legends are far from clear. One reason is the inevitable extra-diegetic commercial one, and for once the producers did attract an American actor of sufficient reputation to justify this strategy. But Harrison is also an American precisely because of his ruthless attitude towards owning property and making money. It is easier to locate these traits in an American than in an Australian, who as a credible dramatic character would have to 'work' to overcome the residual cultural traits of 'fair go', egalitarianism, and mateship—even as an employer and landowner— and who would face greater condemnation on these grounds alone.[9] Even so, the film is careful to soften the image of Americans it creates via Harrison by the expediency of introducing his more acceptable brother, who despite being as American (the same actor after all) has all the qualities of a genuine Australian bush-man: mateship, egalitarianism, humour in adversity, a touch of larrikinism. He is, however, also an exploiter of Australian resources through his gold-mining activities. What makes him more Australian than American is his singular lack of success at it.

By the time of *The Man From Snowy River 2*, Harrison's out-and-out capitalist status has been modified. The 'colonist' American is himself 'colonised' or 'out-colonised' by the English and particularly the Bunyip aristocracy. Harrison's functioning as a capitalist is reduced by the plot device that he needs the financial support of the banks (or the Bunyip aristocracy who run them), which in turn makes him into something of an 'Aussie battler' who rejects the banks' form of capitalism and thus his own expansionist plans, and aligns himself with the 'ideology' of Jim Craig, the 'Man' himself. Here, Americans have shifted slightly towards the cousin-end of the spectrum and away from the traditional class view of the ordinary Australian, the upper-class English and, especially, who would emulate them in Australia, the Bunyip aristocracy.

This colonising shift (from American to English) is continued in *Quigley*. The film is basically a Hollywood western in an Australian location,[10] in which the eponymous hero, an American gunfighter brought to Outback Australian as a 'vermin controller' soon finds himself at war with the 'English' station owner, Marston (when he discovers Aborigines are the 'vermin' to be controlled). Of the dozen or so white men Quigley kills along the way, not one speaks with an Australian accent. They are purportedly Scots or Irish convicts who resent Quigley because he is American—rather than turning against their 'master' for whom they are actually prepared to die. In Quigley, as in quite a number of these films (for example, *Over the Hill* and *The Last Wave)*, an American has an instant affinity with Aborigines. To what extent this is a by-product of their Americanness is far from clear.

In *Phar Lap,* the American part-owner of the horse, Davis, is a capitalist both in the sense that he has the money to buy the horse and is a wealthy businessman. He is contrasted to Harry Telford, the trainer, who is consistently on the verge of bankruptcy—a real little Aussie battler. Davis is, however, also a victim of the Bunyip aristocracy, this time in the form of the upper-class rulers of the racing industry. He is described by one as a 'pushy little Jew' (but significantly not disparaged as an American) and his horse (another Aussie battier even if he did originate in New Zealand) is victimised by the handicappers at the behest of the threatened upper-classes.

It is rare but not unknown in these films for the American capitalist to get his comeuppance. Across the two *Man From Snowy River* films the colonising American is brought down from his capitalist place of power to a more Australian level of equality by events in the second half of the story. In *Exchange Lifeguards,* a trivial film as interested in tits-and-bums as anything else, the same process is at work. Exposure to the simple, 'she'll be right' pleasures of Australian littoral living alerts a colonising American, this time a developer threatening the Australianness of a beach location, to the joys of Australianness. This re-culturalisation causes him to use his Yankee know-how against the agents of rampant capitalism. Interestingly, his father, who owns the company, has predicted this and wants it to happen.

Palmer, the piratical rival in *The Picture Show Man* is defeated (deflected, actually) by Australian larrikinism; the truck with his projecting equipment 'accidentally' runs into a river. Some American capitalists are more resistant to the Australianising process. Rapacious and clearly crooked, Michael Bergman, the capitalist in *Hunting,* functions at some 'rarefied' level of capitalist activity that minimises his connections with ordinary, everyday Australians to barely existent. The exception is the Australian woman whom he seduces and rapes. He receives his comeuppance in the form of bullet from this excessively wronged Australian mistress. In filmic terms, this is an Americanisation—shooting the villain to provide resolution and narrative closure is the *sine qua non* of Hollywood cinema, as is amply demonstrated when bullets remove Marston in *Quigley*, but then he is not an American villain but something (in Australian eyes) much worse, an upper-class English villain.

Agents of American capitalism also undergo a unique form of Australianisation whereby their exploitative tendencies are eroded by a slow but effective absorption. This is not always achieved without the agents' colonising activities first having sometimes dire effects. In *The Coca-Cola Kid,* the piratical capitalistic techniques of Becker, the representative of Coca-Cola's territorial expansionism, and thus of America itself, destroys the last holdout of Australian enterprise (of Australianness) against Cocoa-Cola/American imperialism. In doing, and with the help of sexual attraction to an Australian woman, Becker comes to realise the consequences of his own actions and abandon the trappings of capitalism (signified by his discarded wallet of credit cards) and embrace a 'she'll be right' approach to life. Ironically, this decision is made easier by a tangential Americanisation of Australia—American dollars provided by a local 'subversive' group who believe him to be with the CIA. In *Undercover,* Max, the American marketing expert imported by an Australian undergarment manufacturer Fred Burley, is also won over from his abrasive Americanness by the charms of Liz, a young Australian woman, but not before he, rather like his counterpart in *Exchange Lifeguards,* and with the active cooperation of the Australian manufacturer, Americanises the business. With no apparent sense of irony, Burley thanks Max for helping Australian industry to be *more* Australian. Max completes his Australianisation when in response to Burley's claim, 'It isn't even your country'. He replies, 'But it's my future'.

Max, as with Becker and Bobby (*Exchange Lifeguards*) maintains the Australian filmic convention that American men are sexually irresistible, even if their Americanness sometimes takes a while to be broken down. Max has the full cultural stereotyping of abrasiveness, extroversion and vociferous over-assertiveness, but he also has shiny white teeth (which he shows constantly) and brilliantined, patent-leather hair, all of which combine to give him an American-sized male ego that insists upon the recognition of his own irresistibility. (The others have their own versions of American male beauty and matching egos.) The all-Australian country girl, of course, resists his charms—at first. Becker, on the other hand, is the instant focus for sexual desire for Terri, the Australian woman. Yet there is a strong measure of sexual ambiguity about Becker, his resistance to the obvious advances, display of certain 'feminine' traits (crying when upset, over-concern with appearance), and when he finally renounces capitalism and sheds the uniform (his three-piece suit), his new appearance (white shirt, open to the navel, tight blue jeans) gives him a more-than-vaguely gay appearance. A similar sexual ambiguity attaches itself to Bergman in *Hunting*, implicitly signified in an early sequence, a party Bergman is holding where the guests are all beautiful young men. He also has an ambiguous relationship with a young, saturnine (and presumably Australian) male personal assistant. In all other instances, rampant heterosexuality is twinned with the colonising impulse in the representation of Americans. True love (or old fashioned sex) finally deflects the colonising imperative. Americanisation is successful at both the level of capitalistic enterprise and sexual conquest but the two actually prove to be incompatible. To put it abruptly, Americanising impulse succumbs to Australianness not through resolving the cultural incompatibility or even by being 'absorbed' by Australianness, but by sex—with an Australian.

While these films place Americanness and Americanisation as sources of conflict with Australianness and shape their narratives to greater or lesser extents around the confrontation of the two cultures, they are also engaged in demonstrating the power of Australianness to resist such colonisation. While some films (*The Man From Snowy River 2* and *Exchange Lifeguards*) may suggest that compromise is the best resolution, others effectively reject Americanisation and insist that Australianness will win through. The only true case of the 'triumph' of Americanisation is to be found in *Quigley*, with its OK Corral shootout (i.e., its fundamentally American) resolution. Even here, though, the true winners are the Aborigines; Quigley returns whence he came without being Australianised.

In numerical terms alone, it is hard not to conclude that Americans and America are of no great importance to Australian filmmakers, at least in the sense of their being important components in narratives, or as a source of characters of significance because of their nationality or accepted national/ cultural characteristics. The less easily detected influence of American *culture* on Australian films, leaving aside the matter of aesthetic and production practices, is perhaps more pervasive, as it is in Australian culture more generally, but equally difficult to quantify. It exists in the occasional use of Hollywood genres and in the films designated 'Mid-Pacific' in which national identity is deliberately eschewed. Despite the wide variation in the content and styles of Australian film, over the nearly 30 years since the rebirth of the Australian cinema, the majority of films has been concerned with Australian matters, and are in fact profoundly introspective. This introspection then confirms that America, Americans and Americanisation are not matters of overwhelming concern, and that they do not constitute a powerful cultural force requiring representation and reproduction in any more than a relative handful of films. This may be because Americanisation has become *naturalised* in Australia to the extent that it is invisible. But film is often concerned with making discernible the overlooked (the taken-as-*natural*) with allegorically and metaphorically raising matters from below the surface of the cultural subconscious. The limited number and limited modes of representations of Americans in Australian films do imply that whatever may be on the Australian cultural agenda, or whatever is lurking below its surface, it does not seem to have much to do in any direct sense with a concern over Americanisation.

NOTES

1. Definitions of what is an 'Australian' film are difficult. Scott Murray attempts this before recognising that 'there is no foolproof way of determining what constitutes an Australian film. Common sense must be applied, with all its attendant flaws'. *Australian Film, 1978-1992,* Oxford University Press, Melbourne, 1993, p. 6.

2. My idea of the 'not-American' has an echo in a film mentioned in this papa, *Frog Dreaming,* where a husband attempts to deflect his wife from interrupting him further by telling her of the existence of the not-wind (a wind that can be heard when there is no wind to be heard) and the not-light. 'The not-light,' she says, 'oh, you mean the dark.' 'Exactly,' he replies. A not-American is an Australian for purposes of the diegesis, but retains a ghostly, extra-diegetic image as an American.

3. Why both have expressly Irish names is beyond my wit to explain.

4. Written, as was *Roadgames* and *Razorback,* by ex-patriate American Everett De Roche.

5. Line from a popular Tin Pan Alley song of the 1920s.

6. In fact, two, as Eva is a Czechoslovakian born immigrant.

7. Cited in S. Dermody and E. Jacka, *The Screening of Australia,* vol. 1. Currency Press, Sydney, 1987, p. 43.

8. The mysterious loss of the baby and the subsequent trial of Jake, together with the public disbelief that an animal took the child and personal vilification, give *Razorback* a more than passing resemblance to the Azaria Chamberlain incident.

9. In a twist of the same scenario, the greedy (and in this case, crooked) land-owning capitalist in *Minnamurra,* (a sort of *The Man From Snowy River 3*) is an upper-class Englishman.

10. And not the first of these. For example, *Rangel River* (1936), *The Kangaroo Kid* (1950), and *The Shadow of the Boomerang* (1960).

FILMS DISCUSSED

Attack Force Z, 1982, Tim Burstall.

Babe, 1996, Chris Noonan.

Blood Oath, 1990, Stephen Wallace.

The Coca-Cola Kid, 1985, Dusan Makavejev.

Crocodile Dundee, 1986, Peter Farman.

Crocodile Dundee II, 1988, John Cornell.

A Dangerous Summer, 1982, Quentin Masters.

Dead Calm, 1989, Philip Noyce.

Death of a, Soldier, 1986, Philippe Mora.

The Delinquents, 1989, Chris Thompson.

The Earthling, 1980, Peter Collinson.

Evil Angels, 1988, Fred Schepisi.

Exchange Life Guards, 1993, Maurice Murphy.

Frog Dreaming, 1985, Brian Trenchard- Smith.

Gross Misconduct, 1993, George Miller.

Harlequin, 1980, Simon Wincer.

High Rolling, 1977, Igor Auzins.

Hunting, 1991, Frank Howson.

The Last Wave, 1977, Peter Weir.

Mad Dog Morgan, 1976, Philippe Mora.

Mad Max Beyond Thunderdome, 1985, George Miller and George Ogilvie.

The Man From Snowy River, 1982, George Miller.

The Man From Snowy River 2, 1988, Geoff Burrows.

Minnamurra, 1989, Ian Barry.

Newsfront, 1979, Philip Noyce.

"Norman Loves Rose', 1982, Henri Safran.

Now and Forever, 1983, Adrian Carr.

The Odd Angry Shot, 1979, Tom Jeffrey.

One Night Stand, 1984, John Duigan.

Over the Hill, 1992, George Miller.

Phar Lap, 1983, Simon Wincer.

The Picture Show Man, 1977, John Power.

The Pirate Movie, 1982, Ken Annakin.

Quigley, 1991, Simon Wincer.

Race for the Yankee Zephyr, 1981, David Hemmings.

Razorback, 1984, Russell Mulcahy.

Rebel, 1985, Michael Jenkins.

The Return of Captain Invincible, 1983, Philippe Mora.

Roadgames, 1981, Richard Franklin.
Star Struck, 1982, Gillian Armstrong.
The Survivor, 1981, David Hemmings.
That Eye, The Sky, 1993, John Ruane.
Thirst, 1979, Rod Hardy.
Tim, 1979, Michael Pate.
The Time Guardian, 1987, Brian Hannant.
Turkey Shoot, 1982, Brian Trenchard-Smith.
Undercover, 1984, David Stevens.
Wendy Cracked a Walnut, 1990, Michael Pattinson.
The Year of Living Dangerously, 1982, Peter Weir.

BARRY, MICK AND KENNY: BLOKE-HEROES IN AUSTRALIAN CINEMA

If feature films are to be believed—not necessarily literally, of course, although this may occasionally be the case—then they often can be valuable indicators of aspects of the *zeitgeist*. It is in this spirit, that I would like to suggest that the image of the Australian 'bloke' has changed in the broad folk context over the past several decades and that those changes can be charted by reference to the Australian cinema of the period. In particular, I would like to reference three major films (major in the sense of my present thesis rather than in and of themselves although that argument might be made in a more appropriately cinematic forum). They are *The Adventures of Barry McKenzie* (Bruce Beresford, 1972), *Crocodile Dundee* (Peter Faiman, 1986) and *Kenny* (Clayton Jacobson, 2006).

Before considering these films specifically, it should be noted that the Australian cinema's interests in the Australian male as bloke is almost conterminous with the development of cinema in Australia. One of the first narrative films produced in Australia[1] concerned itself with Australian pre-eminent bloke-hero, Ned Kelly: *The Story of the Kelly Gang* (1906). The plethora of bushrangers films that followed—with or without historical figures at the core of their narratives—tended to emphasis, unsurprisingly, the contrary image of the bloke as heroic (or at least bold and daring) and criminal, more or less a refined version of the larrikin (a folk figure which contributed much to the attributes of the bloke[2]). With the official suppression of the cinematic bushranger, the next and potent representation of the bloke was the eponymous one: the first film version of C.J. Dennis's *The Songs of a Sentimental Bloke*, released as *The Sentimental Bloke* in 1919 (and again, in a sound version in 1932). Here, the larrikin aspects of the Australian bloke are firmly established and giving an air of respectability and 'normality' through the Bloke's conversion to or acceptance of community morality via romance and domesticity.

While an interesting study could be made of the fluctuating cinematic fortunes of the bloke (as a standard Australian folk image) throughout the 1930s, 1940s and (to a limited extent) in the 1950s Australian cinema, it is not my intention to do so here. But it is my contention that the bloke by no means dominated Australia films of these decades and is noticeable more through his rare appearances than through his persistence. These appearances were sustained on one hand by the comedian George Wallace (1894-1960, a crucial figure in the cinematic evolution of the bloke through his consistence portrayal of the Australian bloke as a working-class, good-hearted if dim-witted näif[3], and on the other by emblematic Australian actor Chips Rafferty (1909-

160

1971), who reinstated some of the heroic qualities of the bloke while (often but not inevitably) confirming the simple or at least unsophisticated nature of the bloke.[4] The mention of these two actors is deliberate because aspects of both the characters they played and something at least of the narratives of their films were to have considerable influence in the films I wish to consider here. Or if that implies too direct a connection then a subconscious effect through the very folk-image of the bloke they and their films had respectively tapped into and shaped.

At the start of the 1970s, the moribund Australian film industry, rather unexpectedly[5], burst into life and with that sudden vitality the bloke returned with a vengeance. This was mainly due to *The Adventures of Barry McKenzie* although it should be noted that *Wake in Fright* (mentioned in footnote 4 below), a particularly vicious demonstration of the 'horrors' of 'blokedom[6] and *Stork* (Tim Burstall, 1971) both predate *McKenzie* by about one year (in terms of release). *Stork* is significant in that it is the first appearance of the 1970s version of the bloke: the ocker. Barry McKenzie, however, predates Stork by a good half-decade through his comic-strip version, created by Barry Humphries for the British satirical magazine, *Private Eye*, in 1964. Whatever either of these earlier films may have said about the bloke, it was *The Adventures of Barry McKenzie,* it was 'Bazza' (the use of the distinctive diminutive is a strong indicator of bloke status) who captured the cultural condition of the bloke and indeed cemented it, cinematically at least, for at least a decade and a half and, as I shall argue with *Kenny*, even longer.

Because of the satirical intent, taken from the comic-strip origins, the bloke in this film is fairly clear placed in the sub-category of the ocker, a particular cultural category only then coming into common parlance and nearly always as a pejorative. This is amply reflected by the uncertainties in definition and usage offered by *The Macquarie Dictionary*:

1. The archetypal uncultivated Australian working man.
2. A boorish, uncouth chauvinistic Australian.
3. An Australian male displaying qualities considered to be typically Australian, as good humour, helpfulness and resourceful.

The first two of these may well have been largely formed by the characteristics attributed to Barry McKenzie by the film, especially as the first edition of *The Macquarie Dictionary* did not appear until 1981 by which time the attitudes and behaviours of Barry McKenzie had either permeated the cultural mainstream or, if they pre-existed the film's (and Barry Humphries') exposure of them, been elevated out of the cultural background. Inescapably, Bazza fits the first two definitions, with some ambiguity about his being a 'working man'. Assuming a socio-economic sense to that term (the old distinction between wage and salary earners not that between those in paid employment and *rentiers*), then it is unclear where Bazza fits. The only indicator is a fleeting image of his home which looks solidly middle-class. For the rest of 1 and 2, this is Bazza to a T. The only part of 3 which applies to him is 'good humour'; 'helpfulness' is slightly present in his character, perhaps, but the film is resolute in his representation of a complete lack of resourcefulness—expect perhaps for his organisation of a hose-gang of urinating Australians (ockers to a man) to put out a fire (they started, of course) in a BBC television studio.

No doubt intended to be caricature, if not full-blown satire, the representation of the bloke in *Barry McKenzie* emphasizes a catalogue of undesirable characteristics—undesirable that is from a *haut bourgeois* point of view, the one largely taken by the film's first reviewers. Bazza's two (indeed only) concerns in life are to guzzle as much beer (in the Australian icy-cold lager form not the British room-temperature ale variety), at which he is singularly successful, and 'featuring with a sheila' (having sex), at which he is singularly unsuccessful. The first of these leads inevitably to the need to urinate and regurgitate and it is these two functions that provide Bazza with the endlessly expressive euphemisms that, offered as poetically original, give an impression of the bloke (although perhaps not Bazza himself who does not seem to be coining them as much as drawing them from an well-used vocabulary) as an earthy wit. The sense of the Australian bloke being 'uncultivated' has shifted here beyond the possible sense of unsophisticated or even naive to simple-minded. For the purposes of comedy no doubt, Bazza is simple-minded almost to the point of being moronic (in both its literal and its colloquial senses). This serves the narrative purpose, of course, of allowing situations to be created in which fun can be had by sending up 'the poms' far more than sending up Australians (although no doubt this was intended as well) with the (no doubt unintended) consequence that Barry McKenzie—bloke-as-ocker—became the acceptable, even acclaimed, face of Australian masculinity. As Sandra Hall astutely noted at the time of the film's release, 'the sentiments are closer to an updated Dad 'n' Dave. Bazza has lost his [comic strip] awfulness, with time and the transfer, and become over-fond folklore'.[7] A significant narrative aspect of the cinematic renditions of the bloke was established with *The Adventures of Barry McKenzie*, that of the journey overseas the undertaking of which provides a key arena in which the qualities of the bloke (positive and negative) can be displayed.

Cinematic representations of the bloke were confirmed as the renaissance of Australian cinema continued throughout the 1970 and into the 1980s, often despite the cultural cringe his existence (cinematically and socially) may have caused. Not all or even a predominant number of these were of the bloke-as-ocker, or bloke-as-clown since the ocker was usually presented as a figure of fun and ridicule; it seems that audiences were intended or expected to laugh *at* Barry McKenzie rather than *with* him. Bloke-as-folkhero—despite or because of the example of Barry McKenzie—followed in films such as *Sunday Too Far Away* (1975), *Newsfront* (1978) both of which have the ordinary Australian working man as bloke-hero, and *Breaker Morant* (1980)[8] and, of course, *Gallipoli* (1981)[9] wherein the Anzac/digger image serves to enhance the bloke image and vice versa. In both these latter films, it should be noted, the narrative structure of overseas travel (historically necessary of course) is dominant. There are too many other renditions of the bloke in Australian cinema of the period to enumerate here but they and Australian culture were all leading to what remains perhaps as his finest cinematic flowering as the eponymous hero of *Crocodile Dundee* in 1986.

In Mick Dundee the ocker and hero version of the bloke met and melded. Of course, no small percentage of Dundee's status as a cultural (and, let's face it, fairy-tale) hero was due to his bushman qualities but his ocker characteristics are established from his first tumultuous appearance in the pub at Walkabout Creek. His bushman knowledge and skills are, seemingly paradoxically, what enable him to be an ocker when in New York.[10] Dundee is a much tamer version of the bloke-as-ocker than McKenzie—for instance, he certainly does not have McKenzie's obsession with beer drinking and its physiological consequences. What he does share with McKenzie is the narrative need to travel to and immerse himself in another culture. This time the United States of America rather than Britain, a choice which reflects both changes in Australian society and economic cinema reasons. New York serves much the same purpose in *Crocodile Dundee* as London does in *The Adventures of Barry McKenzie*. It is a foreign (for Dundee) but familiar (for the audience) location in which his essential bloke/ocker characteristics can be clearly delineated—and, in the case, of Dundee valorised. Although Dundee's ocker credentials are displayed in the first few minutes (before heading into the Outback) and then, expressly, in New York, they begin to be modified when he returns to Australia. (McKenzie is barely seen to operate on his native turf.) Whereas McKenzie demonstrated and exaggerated the first two *The Macquarie Dictionary* definitions cited above, Dundee epitomises the third. And in so doing, captured and even caused a shift away from the ocker aspects of the bloke, a lessening of his more objectionable qualities, or caused what might be argued to be a separation between the ocker and the bloke. The ocker-as-hero never was a stable image and perhaps could not be in the Australian cinema nor in the broader Australian culture. Mick Dundee was a single and important moment of stasis for the ocker but also he represented the ocker's incipient demise: if the ocker could be a hero (fairy-tale hero in this case) then he could not be an ocker.[11]

The bloke was thus primed for a continued, even renewed, place of prominence in the Australian cinema. But this did not happen or at least not immediately. Oddly enough, the very financial success of *Crocodile Dundee* was a contributing cause to a downturn in Australian film production. It is sometimes argued that, amongst other factors, that as *Crocodile Dundee* was produced and then made such huge profits under an extremely favourable tax concession regime, the taxation office was led to the end those very concessions. It may have also been that Mick Dundee set the bar too high for other cinematic blokes to follow. Certainly it is hard to see much blokedom in, say, Scott Hastings, the hero of *Strictly Ballroom* (1992) or in Carl, the ineffectual, mother-dominated protagonist of *Death in Brunswick* (1991)[12]. (It may be argued the Muriel of *Muriel's Wedding* [1994] had most of the characteristics of the bloke save, obviously, for the gender.)

The normalization of the bloke is accomplished in large part in *Kenny* by the use of the stylistics of the documentary, by being what is now known as a 'mockumentary'. This, by appearing to be an television-style observational documentary of the life and occupation of an ordinary Australian bloke, and not a dramatized narrative, has the effect of taking the aspects of the bloke as limned in *The Adventures of Barry McKenzie* and *Crocodile Dundee* and giving them—or confirming them—as those of the everyday, ordinary Australian bloke. The film is, of course, not a documentary but a carefully crafted fiction masquerading, for the most part successfully, as reality.

The game is given away (if it was ever intended to be deceptive) by the fact that the film is really an elaborate and extended scatological joke. Kenny, the eponymous hero, frequently asserts he is a plumber and while that is true to an extent, his occupation is to supply and service portable lavatories. This provides (if the pun may be pardoned) an endless stream of scatological humour. In this, *Kenny* outdoes *Barry McKenzie* by several degrees of magnitude, and *Dundee* is left floundering in his wake. (There really is only once example of lavatory humour in *Dundee*: an obvious, even antiquated, joke involving a bidet.) Scatological humour is the *raison d'etre* of *Kenny* but, while often both obvious and ingenious, does mean the film's sense of being a documentary in undermined; Kenny is given very little interest in life (other than an interest in his family—something resolutely absent from Bazza and, until, the later additional films, from Dundee) beyond the specifics of his job and the type of plumbing it involves. Even so, and not only because of its mockumentary aesthetics, *Kenny* thoroughly humanises the bloke (or embeds him in the folklore). If McKenzie is the epitome of *Ockeri extremus* and Dundee of the fairy tale bloke-hero, Kenny is the unalloyed bloke; in British culture he would be the working-class hero. He is that popular if mythical creature, the bloke, trying to make a living within a peculiarly Australian notion of integrity and the fair go. He is the bloke as family man—or at least as a father and as a son (like many Australian males in recent films, he is divorced from his wife who makes his life a misery). And what makes him even more quintessential is that he is a victim. Not a tragic victim as with the males of *Gallipoli* or *Breaker Morant*, nor even of his own Australian brand of stupidity as with Barry McKenzie (although the film does flirt dangerously with aspects of this characterisation) but, paradoxically, of his job and of his family. In other words, of being an Australian male and, in this case, of being a bloke: it goes with the territory.

In *Kenny*, the trope of travelling overseas established in *The Adventures of Barry McKenzie* and *Crocodile Dundee* also occurs and for much the same purpose and effect. As with Dundee, Kenny travels unexpectedly and not entirely of his own volition to the United States. Here he repeats many of Dundee's experiences and responses all of which serve to underline his bloke credentials while also, as with both his precursors, having his lack of worldliness seem like at best child-like simplicity, at worst as dimwittedness. Unlike McKenzie but like Dundee, Kenny befriends strangers without reservation or even consideration of their 'difference'; both indeed overcome difference by being blind to it. Both Kenny and Dundee like Americans (and they like them) and America (even if confused by a lot of it) but retain their blokeness in the face of it. McKenzie retains his blokeness of course but dislikes the English (and they dislike him) and England up until, possibly, the last moment (after he has left).

Both McKenzie and Dundee are extreme examples—exaggerations and caricatures of the bloke. Kenny is a normalisation of and an indication of the acceptance and integration of the 'qualities' of Barry and Mick into the cultural mainstream definition and celebration of the bloke.

Kenny is a 'hero', all the more so when compared with the contemporary trend of depicting in the cinema the Australian male as feeble, ineffectual, even emasculated (save for a few truly criminal ones). The crisis of masculinity arrived late in Australia or in the Australian cinema at least. *Kenny* is an attempt, perhaps, to head the crisis off, to restore the confidence in the bloke, or in the folk image of the bloke, once sounded so stridently by *Barry McKenzie* and *Crocodile Dundee*.

165

NOTES

1. And, it is often argued, one of the first feature length (i.e. 60 minutes or more) narrative fictional films produced in the world, not a claim easy to validate although certainly there seem to be no American or British contenders for the title.

2. Bloke is, of course, not a term of Australian origin or exclusively Australia. But, as Sidney J. Barker points out in *The Australian language*: 'sometimes we find that... words acquire greater currency in Australia —are used among more varied classes and more continually—than they had in the their country of origin. *Bloke* and *cove* are cases in point'. (Macmillan, South Melbourne, 1970, 397) Cove, I would suggest, has largely disappeared from contemporary Australian speech; bloke is still there.

3. Wallace's films are *His Royal Highness* (1932), *Harmony Row* (1933), *A Ticket in Tatts* (1934), *Let George Do It* (1938), *Gone to the Dogs* (1939), with lesser roles in *The Rats of Tobruk* (1944) and *Wherever She Goes* (1951). The influence of Wallace on providing some images or behaviours for a generation of Australian males—or perhaps the other way around—is a subject that deserves some study.

4. Rafferty's (or John William Pilbeam Goffage—his actual name) film career was more extensive and more varied than Wallace's. Nonetheless, he provided through a variety of roles, an image of the bloke as variously quintessentially Australian, heroic in those terms, with more than a touch of the Anzac about him. It is no coincidence then that Rafferty played the-bloke-as-soldier/larrikin in two formative films produced during the Second World War: *Forty Thousand Horsemen* (1940) and *The Rats of Tobruk* (1944) and confirmed that image (although not a serviceman) in *The Overlanders* (1946). Fittingly, Rafferty's last feature film role was to play the police sergeant in *Wake in Fright* (1970), so in uniform again albeit a police uniform he had also worn in the two *Smiley* films, although a rather less avuncular bloke in the final manifestation.

5. Perhaps not all *that* unexpectedly as efforts to bring about a revival in Australian film production had been taking place during the 1960s in parallel with a general thrust towards a 'cultural renaissance' in Australia that included literature, theatre and the arts more generally. What was unexpected, although intensely lobbied for, was the degree of government—federal and state—involvement and support, even initiative.

6. *Wake in Fright* was 'rediscovered' in 2007 (the alleged last remaining print was found in 2002), re-realised in cinemas in 2009 and was acclaimed as a lost masterpiece— or in the terms of the popular cinema magazine *Empire*, a 'long-lost cinematic touchstone' and 'a certified Australian classic' (no.100, July 2009, p.36)

7. Sandra Hall, 1985, *Critical Business: The New Australian Cinema in Review*, Adelaide: Rigby. P.10.

8. The bloke in *Breaker Morant* is not the eponymous tragic hero, who was after all an educated English remittance man, but Lieutenant Peter Handcock, the larrikin victim of English duplicity.

9. As with *Breaker Morant*, the bloke is the larrikin-inspired character, Frank Dunne rather than the sacrificial hero, Archie Hamilton, a pure hero 'untainted' by most of the characteristics of the bloke.

10. My fuller discussion of the importance of Mick Dundee as an Australian folk hero may be found in Neil Rattigan, 1988, '*Crocodile Dundee*: Apotheosis of the Ocker', *Journal of Popular Film and Television*, Vol.15, no.4. 148-155.

11. In the broader social context, the ocker did fade from cultural prominence or, at least, transmuted into the 'hoon' and the 'bogan', re-emphasising thereby his (and increasingly, her) place at the periphery of social acceptability albeit maintaining a strong presence in Australian folklore.

12. I am tempted to encapsulate these films (and others like them in their representations of the Australian male) as depicting the bloke-as-wimp—the subject perhaps of another analysis.

SPOOL BRITANNIA

THE DEMI-PARADISE AND IMAGES OF CLASS IN BRITISH WARTIME FILMS

Even if the film itself did not make it manifest, it would be clear that *The Demi-Paradise*[1] was intended to be propaganda. It was made in a Britain fully engaged for some three years in total war and under conditions whereby all British films were, to some degree, official inasmuch as the Ministry of Information (MoI) had a whole network of statutory and bureaucratic controls that amounted to approval, direction, and supervision of all filmmaking activity. The film is determined to present an all-encompassing and unarguable perception of British national identity (assumed apparently unproblematically to be *English* national identity), and this is what it does without relaxing for its nearly two hours running time.[2] Given the time and the context of its production, the overkill in which the film indulges is explicable and forgivable, especially when one considers that as propaganda it was aimed at both a domestic audience and an American audience. For the American audience, the film hoped to create a positive image of Britain/England to encourage Americans to accept the importance and urgency of becoming engaged in the theatre of operations and, subsequently, to maintain a positive image in the face of that engagement and the disruptive presence of millions of American servicemen in Britain.

It was a conscious determination of the ruling class, functioning through the MoI and other cultural institutions and structures not necessarily directly government or state, that the theme of a people's war be the dominant one during the war. Examining the reasons for doing so may bring us close to the political unconscious[3] and to the concept that the ruling class could not anticipate the subordinate classes' willingness to fight for Britain/England. This position was informed by the ruling-class belief that Britain/England belonged to them. In this sense, the ruling class definition of England *was* the real England. Thus, the ideology that functioned as an unconscious structuring principle in these films was one that defined England within terms that were (1) inherited from a set of perceptions of a mythical pre-industrial England, (2) thoroughly imbued with the natural class order, (3) certain of the power of English civilization (an amalgam of 1 and 2) to which the existence of an Empire gave concrete evidence, and (4) equally certain that the true exponents and the living evidence of these principles was embodied in the upper and upper-middle classes as classes and in the individual members of those classes.

There is no doubt that *The Demi-Paradise* has little to say about and only slightly more to display of the working class. As in other films of the war such as *The First of the Few* (1942), such members of the working class as do exist within the diegetic world of the film exist only to enthusiastically carry out the policies of the enlightened owners of, in this case, the Barchester shipyards. One working-class character in the film, Tom, the attempting-to-be-upwardly mobile young assistant, dreams of a better social system along Russian lines. It is significant that Tom is marginalized representative of the working class. He is seemingly moving up the social ladder and expresses his chagrin that he is forced by economic circumstance to stay put in his social milieu. If anything, Tom is an intermediary figure. He is mediator between the workers (he asks Ann Tisdall, the shipyard owners granddaughter, to give out the prizes as the workers dance) and the employers (Ton also is the one who initially encourages the workers to even greater efforts to complete a ship being built for the Soviet government *after* the employers have given up. But the film does not endorse this attempt by a member of the working class a move out of his class position. Tom's valorization of the allegedly more egalitarian Russian society is made to look implicitly ridiculous. When he is introduced to the audience for the first time, Tom tells a working-class brat who is fiddling with Ann Tisdall's car to get out of it, while Ann responds that it is quite all right and take the kids for a ride. Tom's naive and possibly misinformed enthusiasm for Russia is both premature and, of course, wrong. Tom feels that things are unsatisfactory in England and he also feels that the existing political system cannot remedy the current situation. We do see later that the workers are enthused to express solidarity with 'our Russian allies', but only after the lead is given first by Churchill and then by the Runalow/Tisdall family, who own the shipyard.

The film revealingly but incidentally shows some of the conditions of the working class—living in crowded, slum dwellings right next to the shipyard kids playing in the streets—but it seems to accept this environment as natural and beyond comment. It also is silent some time later when bombs are falling o the shipyards during an air raid. Given the proximity of the workers dwellings 1 the shipyards, surely some of the workers homes have been hit. Everybody, workers included, are concerned only about the damage to the yards and the ship therein. Meanwhile at the semi palatial country home of the Runalows, somebody is playing the cello to the nightingales. Indeed, during the raid of the shipyards, a feigned sense of egalitarianism is produced when Runalow, despite his age and position, runs off to take part in the fire fighting. Runalow is slightly but genuinely injured by a bomb, while a nearby worker is injured by having one of his corns trodden on by a fellow worker.

From the very opening scenes of *The Demi-Paradise,* the working class is portrayed within the stereotyped roles and narrative and thematic functions inherited from pre-war British cinema: as comic relief or comic sounding boards for the dominant ideology. Indeed, the two sailors limping into the Russian port quarters might have stepped out of the working-class community much admired by Richard Hoggart (1957), with their encapsulated working-class catchphrases—'Never mind', 'Makes a nice change any old 'ow'—having arrived by way of the West End theatre. One might argue that these two working-class and/or regional characters serve to permit the comic exposure of English xenophobia, which for propaganda purposes the film is intending to reverse and deny without implicating the middle class in such a limited outlook. Even so, the film does later repeat this comic discovery of English xenophobia, seen now as understandable ethnocentricity rather than as racial superiority, through the character of Miss Winnie, a maiden aunt within the Tisdall family. 'Russians spread things', says Miss Winnie with alarm when she learns that Ivan Kouznetsoff, an engineer sent to help with the construction of an icebreaker, is Russian. She hides in her room rather than eat at the same table.

The film is constructed around narrative doubling: nearly everything happens twice. There are two visits by Ivan to England, two pageants, two visits to the same theatre, two workers dances, and so forth. The conversion of the working-class sailors to an understanding and appreciation of aliens who understand and appreciate *them* is doubled with Miss Winnie's conversion. Hers is, however, the more significant one. It leads to actual positive action: the adopting of Ivan's home town, Ninjni-Petrovsk, by the charity committee of the annual Barchester pageant. This annual pageant is of particular importance to the narrative. Although treated humorously, its particular view of England's glorious history is a direct representation of the upper-class interpretation the film itself is promoting. Miss Winnie's conversion is also given much more narrative space and thereby thematic or propagandistic importance.

It is not only the actual labouring classes that are given limited narrative space as comic relief. *The Demi-Paradise* is presumably intended to be a comedy, and audiences were expected to be amused as much by the representatives of the upper classes as by those of the lower classes, but in rather different ways. The working-class characters seldom have recourse within the diegesis to reinterpretations of their actions in the way in which the upper-class characters do. Representatives of the lower-middle class, fleetingly presented as they may be, are still important to the film's ideology and to its need to show all classes working together for the ideology of a people's war to be confirmed. Yet, although the workers seem to have a sense of a self-supporting community that exists parallel to the community that is the true focus of the film (specifically the irresistibly middle-class community of Barchester and the Runalow family as its admirable and admired metonymic symbol), the lower-middle class represents the meeting or touching point of the governing and the governed classes. To this extent, the lower-middle class is shown to be far more dependent upon the upper classes, not only economically but also in terms of authority and function. Two are especially important here: Jordan, the fussy, elderly clerk in the shipyard's London office, and Toomes, the Runalow's butler. Neither, significantly, seems to have a first name or, at least, is never referred to by one. Jordan is seen to be totally unable to cope with the arrival of Ivan, unable to make a simple decision, and then completely at the beck-and-call of Ann. Moreover, he describes Ann as 'a nicer person you couldn't meet', although she has rudely ignored Ivan throughout—when she isn't insulting Russians generally. Jordan is rendered even more pathetic when he speaks at Hyde Park Corner: he is heckled by the crowd and has to be rescued by Ann and Ivan. Toomes is even less effective. On the night of the air-raid, when the nightingales are being broadcast from Runalow's garden, he directs an enquiry to his employer as to whether the participants should sleep under the stairs or the billiard table (only to be told to figure it out for himself, so to speak) and later has to be told by Runalow to turn out the lights before opening the curtains in the middle of an air raid. He also had no idea what a pageant is for—despite a working lifetime in which the Barchester pageant has taken place virtually under his nose in the grounds of the Runalow mansion.

While it is not true that the working class and the lower-middle class are unimportant to the ideology of the film, they are marginalized by its narrative. They are seen to be dependent to a greater or lesser extent upon the upper classes—for employment, for instruction in their duties, and importantly for leadership. But they have little part in the community that the film is intent upon presenting as a metaphor for and image of the living reality of England. There are no discernible members of the working class in the audience of the pageant nor, indeed, as participants in the re-enactments that make it up. Indeed, it is noticeable that in the crowd scenes, such as ones depicting the audience at the pageant or the workers at the address by a Russian delegate, their dance, and at the launching, the narrative/camera point of view changes to express differing points of view. The crowds at the launching, assembly, and ball are nearly always shot from a high vantage point; at the launching this is the visual equivalent of the point of view of the serried ranks of the upper class on the platform. However, the crowds at the pageant are shot from an eye-level position. Although there is a slightly more flexible set of viewpoints at the Hyde Park Corner sequence, throughout the film the lower classes tend to be literally rendered as being beneath the gaze of the camera in terms of the resultant cinematic image.

The film's dominant focus for its representation of the ideology of Englishness is on the upper classes. Surprisingly, given the uniformly patriotic tone of the film, there is not a little ambivalence expressed about this Englishness and, more specifically, about those whom the film equates with cultural centrality, those who represent the true English national identity—namely, the upper and/or upper-middle classes, the British bourgeoisie. There are no easily determined representatives of the aristocracy, and the gentry are, of course, represented by Runalow, who is a self-made member of the gentry. While making a determined effort to construct a unified and unifying monolithic image of the nation, *The Demi-Paradise* actually builds a few cracks into that very image as it does so. George Orwell described Britain in the 1940s:

> as [resembling] a family, a rather stuffy Victorian family ... It has rich relations who have to be kow-towed to and poor relations who are horribly sat upon, and there is a deep conspiracy of silence about the sources of the family income. It is a family in which the young are generally thwarted and most of the power is in the hands of irresponsible uncles and bed-ridden aunts. Still, it is a family. It has its private language and its common memories and at the approach of an enemy it closes ranks. A family with the wrong members in control. (1968, 68)

Orwell's metaphor of the image of England as it reappears in *The Demi-Paradise* (devoid of the implication that 'the wrong members [are] in control') was probably close to the way in which the upper class perceived Britain. The previous discussion of the representations of the working class in this film should perhaps give some sense of where they would fit into Orwell's Victorian family. What of the others?

Runalow is the patriarch of the family in both senses of family: his immediate relatives and the closed community—middle-class rural village and dockyard slums. This familial structure is metonymically England within the films diegesis—and the film's construction of his character places Runalow almost above reproach. Thus this paragon of capitalist virtue is able to deflect and defend himself from most of the reproaches that Ivan, in his function as outsider, throws at him. It is interesting that he never really gives a positive answer to the questions that Ivan asks him on why he is a big businessman. Runalow rather disingenuously denies obsession with wealth as being at the bottom of his actions, claiming in some strange logic by way of mitigation that the firm's motto of Duty and Service exempts him from interrogating the employer/employee structure he is at the pinnacle of. What is unspoken in this scene is the assumption that Runalow is fit to occupy the authorative position he does and that it is therefore proper that he does so. Thus, within the text of the film, Runalow represents the ideology of the proper or natural function of the upper classes, especially the upper-middle class since the Industrial Revolution.

The character of Runalow is constructed by and through the image of his being a paragon of everything that is good and fine about being English. Yet or perhaps because of this, his character is subject to interrogation by Ivan Kouznetsoff. Thus in the scene just referred to, Ivan, in his forthright, foreign way, challenges Runalow to justify his status and position as a capitalist. Each of Runalow's equivocal rationalizations leads only to a further undermining of his position by Ivan. The scene declines to carry itself through to what seems to be another possible, if externally determined, conclusion, that Runalow is an unrepentant if benevolent capitalist/autocrat. This is prevented by the convenient expedient of the arrival of tea ('at once a beverage and a poem'). Given the film's ideology, it is unlikely to arrive at a conclusion that is critical of Runalow's societal position. Nonetheless, a fissure is present in the seemingly immutable ideology being provided in *The Demi-Paradise*.

Ann Tisdall, by her actions and her persona, comes much closer to the unacceptable face of the ruling class. She lacks this kindly feudalism of Runalow, and her possibly unconscious contempt for the working class, or indeed of anyone not of her class or circle, is revealed frequently. The way she treats both Jordan the clerk and Percy the office boy almost as pets is revealing, and it makes Jordan's praise of her even more pathetic. Her attitude is revealed particularly when she unfeelingly and unthinkingly dismisses her promise, or feudal duty, to present prizes at the workers Benevolent Fund Dance, preferring to have a night out in London at the theatre with Ivan. This reflects just as badly on the workers as Jordan's sycophantic 'a nicer person you couldn't meet', in suggesting that the workers are pathetically dependent upon the guvnor's daughter to grace their communal rituals.

The narrative is at some pains to distance itself from Ann's heartless behaviour. Ivan criticizes Ann's callousness and suggests she apologize for it. Her response is to fall back into the sarcasm with which she has shown particular facility from her very first scene. Ivan's criticism is particularly fixed upon the claim that her Lady Bountiful act is just that—an act; her apparent kindness is nothing beyond mere condescension. It is possible to interpret this as meaning that Ann has not, unlike Runalow, fully absorbed the tenets of noblesse, or bourgeois oblige. The Runalow/Tisdall family are after all, by Runalow's own account, parvenus, so it cannot come as total surprise that some members do not have the appropriate behaviour patterns of the governing classes fully in the genes as yet. As a result of Ivan's lesson, she is able thereafter to display the proper upper-class behaviour and attitudes in this regard—including presenting the prizes at the workers dance at which she also intervenes (allied with Tom) to bring the situation of the need to put in extra efforts to complete the Russian icebreaker to the workers' attention and enthuse them to high achievement. Following the commencement of the war, Ann seems much more socially responsible. Ann works at the canteens at the shipyards, and it seems that she is responsible for taking in the two working-class evacuees. Mrs. Tisdall describes them to Ivan as Ann's evacuees—the possessive being rather disturbing. When Ann later joins the Wrens, she just leaves her evacuees with the family.

One might profitably consider the images of evacuees in this film and at least one other, *Went the Day Well?* (1942, Dir. Alberto Cavalcanti). The evacuation of hundreds of thousands of children, an overwhelming proportion of whom were working class, from the cities at the beginning of the war and again with the commencement of the blitz in the autumn of 1940 had considerable social repercussions, the effects of which are still a matter of debate among historians. These debates are not particularly pertinent here. What is relevant is that on the basis of the evidence of this film and *Went the Day Well?* it might be assumed that the upper classes took the greater part of the responsibility for housing and caring for the lower-class evacuees. Certainly no one else in Barchester or in Bramley Green (the village in *Went the Day Well?*) seems to have any evacuees other than the wealthy Tisdalls and the lady of the manor in Bramley Green, Mrs. Frazer.

The truth seems to be rather the opposite: lower-class families, in fact, took most of the burden of additional children into their already limited facilities, and there is considerable evidence to suggest that those who were better off and thus the more socially influential managed to avoid any responsibility in the matter (Turner 1961, 75-98; Calder 1972, 40-58; Marwick 1980, 217-19). What is important, then, is that most wartime films ignored the matter of evacuees and that those that did not fostered, deliberately as far as can be judged, a false image, one in which the upper classes comforted and succoured the lower classes. There is more than an air of feudalism about this; a harking back to the Middle Ages when baron's serfs would fly into the safety and security of the barons fortified castle upon the approach of an enemy. It is intriguing that while nearly all wartime films scrupulously avoid any unnecessary fraternization between the classes, in these two films domestic or familial fraternization—of a carefully prescribed type—is shown favourably and in contradistinction to the observed facts, in the interests of showing the upper classes leading the way by example in the propaganda call for communal action.

In regard to the changes undergone by Ann Tisdall, *The Demi-Paradise* is rather ambivalent: are they the result of Ivan's critique? Or are they part and parcel of the hidden qualities of English culture brought to the surface by the advent of war? Ann and Ivan are the only characters to change significantly, to develop through the course of the narrative. Ivan's critique of Ann is not an objection to the upper class as such; his questioning of Runalow's position as a capitalist employer is much more apposite in this regard. In the narrative doubling when Ivan repeats his visit to England, although the social structures are still intact, his criticisms have evaporated. Ann's failure to understand that higher or upper social position carries social responsibility to the lower orders does not challenge the basis of that social order: class distinction. The failure on Ann's part (as seen by the film) is to fully realize her allotted duties in and to the social order she inhabits.

This then points to the fact that Ivan is, as a fictional character in a fiction film (an actant, or function of the narrative), an English creation. That is to say, his characterization within the narrative is not that of a real Russian and/or a real socialist.[4] The film is not concerned with propaganda on behalf of Russia or with promoting the official sleight of hand over Russia that had been adopted. Ivan is in fact a stalking-horse for the film's true perspective and its ideology. If he was constructed as a socialist and a Russian, he would be consistent and presumably feel the workers were much better off without the presence of the upper classes at their communal rituals. Ivan is set up as a socialist only in order to prove that the English social system is superior to foreign socialism. Ivan is therefore shown favouring Ann fulfilling her role as caring and concerned ruler/owner rather than rejoicing that she has revealed the true face of the class enemy. He is set up as a foreigner for a much more direct propaganda purpose as well: to indicate, as the last speech he makes so eloquently makes clear, that foreigners (i.e., Americans) do not understand the English, not because of what the English *are*, but because of what they *appear to be*. This was an important propaganda point for Britain in light of images of England—quite accurate ones—as class-bound and undemocratic, images that were widely accepted during this period the USA.

The character of Ivan is thus seemingly schizophrenic but is in fact consistent in terms of the ideology of the film. Even so, his criticisms of England, which are intended to provide an agenda by which the English national identity will be (re)constructed within the film, often have a resonance that cannot be adequately explained away as being the miscomprehensions of an outsider, a representative, in other words, of another and alien culture whose narrative function is to motivate the demonstrations of mythic Englishness the film is obsessed with. There are clear structural contradictions in this. Nearly all of Ivan's articulated objections or interrogations of the nature of Englishness, in both concept and practice, go unanswered by the film. The redressing of these criticisms late in the film—the climatic ship-launching sequence during which Ivan makes a speech in which he claims to now understand that the surface of Englishness is deliberately duplicitous (and in which the deeper layers of English culture are affirmed and confirmed)—does not effectively remove

177

some of the validity of the original critique. This is the consequence of the narrative structure of doubling to which I have already referred. In essence, the film consists of two acts, the second of which is a mirror image of the first, with one significant difference. In the first act, the very Englishness of the situation and the characters was a constant irritant to Ivan and a source of his investigation on behalf of the audience into the nature and condition of Englishness. In the second act, these selfsame conditions of Englishness are embraced by Ivan as essential and sustaining. The war, off screen, serves as the only possible lens that has altered Ivan's perspective.

The Demi-Paradise seems, on occasion, to not fully believe in the strength of its own apparent convictions. Occasionally, it is surprisingly strident to the point of jingoism in ways that suggest satire. I cannot be the only one, surely, to find it difficult to fully comprehend the amazing scene of dinner at the Tisdall's home when Ivan's insistent questioning prompts some claims that can be explained only by reference to the need for this film to function as propaganda in America.

In this scene, heated objections are raised to Ivan's claim that England has conquered half the world. It is difficult to accept or really believe a serious intent when Mrs. Tisdall replies, 'Conquered? We never conquered anybody. We just happened to get there first'. Here, it seems to me, the film is perhaps insufficiently aware of its own ideological position, confirming, perhaps, the unconscious nature of ideology. The film *does* know, in the final analysis, which side of the fence it stands on. It is the side of the fence that understands England to equal Britain and to equal a perception formed of an imagined, pre-industrial past, which persists in some fashion into the present of the film. Inasmuch as industrialism intrudes into this cultural image of identity, it takes the form of enlightened paternalism that sees the new upper classes as the natural inheritors of the top of the pre-existing social order.

The working-class ritual, the benefit dance, which Ann first blights by her absence but then the second time around, enhances by her presence, is, significantly, seen only once. The middle or upper-class ritual, the historical pageant, is a central component of the narrative doubling of the film. While on the one hand it is clearly meant to be comic, and is successful at that level, it also has considerable significance in the presentation of an image of England that is at once old-fashioned and quaint but also pertinent and firmly embedded in the English character. Thus Runalow, although he disparages it quite openly on both occasions, also attends it as its most prominent patron and provides the location for it to take place. Ridiculous ritual as it seems to be, the pageant is given enormous prominence in the narrative. It is at the first pageant that Ivan's accumulated distaste for English culture finally breaks out: he denounces it as 'all piffles' and something done only because it has always been done. The film answers this challenge, not directly, but through the narrative doubling of another pageant, which Ivan again attends. This time he applauds tableaux that are no less ludicrous this second time around. He also takes part by accepting the money raised on behalf of Ninjni-Petrovsk.

To a spectator viewing the film nearly half a century after it was made, the two pageants seem high comedy. It is likely that contemporary audiences did not see them as quite so ludicrously unreal. Indeed, rather than some quaint custom of sleepy rural villages still somewhat lost in the past, it seems that pageants were considered vital and relevant aspects of British culture even during the war. Ronald Howard (1981), in his biography of his father, Leslie Howard, describes in detail a national pageant of almost epic proportions staged on the steps of St. Paul's Cathedral, London, in 1942 in which his father, along with a veritable Who's Who of the British stage of the time, took part. It is difficult not to equate almost exactly the Barchester pageants of *The Demi-Paradise* with his description of the historical pageant of 1942 and to conclude that, sent-up though they may have been, the pageants in the film were intended to serve something of the same propaganda-patriotic purpose as the real one on the steps of St. Paul's.

The Demi-Paradise is about a people's war without being about the people, at least to the extent that, using knowledge external to the diegesis of the film, the people of England were not the upper-middle class. It is about the people to the extent that it is convinced, or it is trying to convince its audience, that the cultural and national identity of England is not merely implicated in but synonymous with upper-middle-class ideology. In any construction of the films message as being, in part, *we* are all in this together the *we* is narrowly defined. Those whom the film cannot disguise, even if it tries, as other, are thus encouraged to accept this *we* construction of British identity.

Ivan Kouznetsoff is the surrogate for those others, be they foreigners or other classes in British society. The reason he is cheered at the end, as the recipient of a rousing chorus of 'For He's a Jolly Good Fellow', is not because he is Russian or because he has solved the engineering problem of the propeller (the external narratives nominal Macguffin) but because he has fully internalized the understanding of England in the film's ideological construction of it. Thus, the governing and governed, those who have the image, and those outside this image but exhorted to adopt it, cheer Kouznetsoff as one of the we the film so fervently embraces.

NOTES

1. *The Demi-Paradise.* 1943. Two Cities Films. Produced by Anatole de Grunwald. Directed by Anthony Asquith.
2. The extent to which there may have been a secondary propaganda purpose in presenting a sympathetic image of Russia and reversing the pre-war negative image of the Soviet Union is confused by the selective and fairly inaccurate view provided. That the Soviet Union is referred to throughout as Russia and its inhabitants as the Russian people suggests deliberate attempts to activate the images of prerevolutionary Russia rather than the communist Soviet Union.
3. A term borrowed from Marxist literary/cultural critic Fredric Jameson (1981) that seems particularly apposite in this context.
4. The government and many of its ministries, including the MoI, were placed in an awkward position when the Soviet Union was invaded by Germany in 1941 because, while wishing to embrace the Soviet Union as an ally rather along the lines of the politically expedient adage, The enemy of my enemy is my friend, they were almost paranoid about the possibility that support for the Soviet Union might mean an embracing by the greater British public of communism. Another example of the ruling class failure to understand the lower orders and another example of the fear that the ruling class had of the lower classes. The solution the government adopted and the MoI put into effect was the rather schizophrenic concept that Russian and Communism were not the same thing, that the Soviet Union was engaged in a nationalistic rather than an ideological struggle, and that British support was thus from one country engaged in such a struggle to another similarly engaged (McLaine 1979, 186-216).

WORKS CITED

Calder, Angus. *The Peoples War: Britain 1939-1945.* New York: Pantheon, 1969. New York: Ace, 1972.

Hoggart, Richard. *The Uses of Literacy: Aspects of Working-Class Life with Special Reference to Publications and Entertainment.* London: Chatto and Windus, 1957; New York: Oxford UP, 1957.

Howard, Ronald. *In Search of My Father: A Portrait of Leslie Howard.* London: William Kimber, 1981.

Jameson, Fredric. *The Political Unconscious: Narrative as a Socially Symbolic Act.* Ithaca: Cornell UP, 1981.

Marwick, Arthur. *Class: Image and Reality in Britain, France, and the USA since 1930.* New York: Oxford UP, 1980.

McLaine, Ian. *Ministry of Morale: Home Front Morale and the Ministry of Information in World War II.* London: Random House, 1979.

Orwell, George. *The Collected Essays, Journalism and Letters of George Orwell.* Vol. 2. Ed. Sonia Orwell and Ian Angus. London: Secker and Warburg, 1968.

Turner, E. S. *The Phoney War on the Home Front.* London: Quality Book Club, 1961.

THE LAST GASP OF THE MIDDLE CLASS: BRITISH WAR FILMS OF THE 1950S

The late 1940s and 1950s in Britain is seldom seen by film historians as a distinctive period in its own right. Most British cinema histories see the importance of the period not in the films produced but in terms of the disruptions caused to production by the various and mostly ill-advised interventions into the overall industry by the Labour government (1945-1951), and in relation to the monopolistic practices of the Rank organization and the problems this caused as well as the problems caused to Rank by the government (Perry 1985, 104-144; Betts 1973, 209-225; Armes 1978, 156-173). In terms of the films, for the most part the late 1940s is a period that tends to be categorized as harbinger of the 1950s, and the 1950s themselves as little more than a hiatus before the flowering of British social realism in the 1960s. The rare exceptions are the justly praised (if critically overworked) Ealing Comedies, which bud and flower in the late 1940s and come to mellow fruitfulness in the 1950s, and which are often felt to be the most substantive form of British cinema in the first decade or so after the war. The period 1946-1959 deserves more attention than it has received, notably for the very way in which it is *precisely* a bridge between wartime films and those of the socially realist 1960s.

As the Second World War ended, British society, not surprisingly, began to take stock of the many changes which had, or which appeared to have, taken place during and because of the demands of six years of hostilities. The British Council for example undertook a series of appraisals of the state of British art and culture, and one such appraisal of British film was written by the prominent film critic Dilys Powell. Powell's summation of the radical changes undergone by British films as a consequence of the demands of the war became the accepted view of the state of British cinema of the time, and remains largely unchallenged:

> The British no longer demand pure fantasy in their films; they can be receptive also to the imaginative interpretation of everyday life. The serious British film has thus found an audience as well as a subject. If it preserves its newly-found standards of conception and technique, it will find not merely a national, but an international audience (1947, 40).

This analysis was repeated almost verbatim by Dennis Forman five years later:

> During the war a school of young film makers had triumphantly struck a mould of story-documentary production [in] which...all show[ed] a

mastery of film technique which before the war had been apparent only in
the work of a handful of leading (and well established) directors (1952, 7).

A selective history of the wartime production was already being cemented
into place within a year or two of the end of the war. Like most national
film histories, this one argued that the British wartime film was defined by
the qualities of a carefully selected group of particular films—the cream of
the films—rather than from an overview which took the good with bad, the
mediocre with the best.

Whether or not the aesthetic and social promises of wartime British films
were later met, post-war British cinema did not take either Britain or the
world by storm—at least not for another ten years or so. Today the 1950s is
an almost entirely critically forgotten period of British Cinema. It does not
rank in attention to anything like the degree of the two critically identified
periods which precede and follow it: the war period (1939-1946) and the
period of the new realism (1959-early 1970s). The future which both Powell
and Forman predicted from their assessment of the wartime cinema seems not
to have occurred—at least, that is the conclusion the critical silence over 1950s
British cinema would lead one to make. In fact, immediate post-war British
films *did* continue trends and directions that had been encouraged during the
war, without making any abrupt alterations to themes, concerns, ideologies or
aesthetics of wartime films other than a shift in the social class focus.

The concern of this essay is with British films made during the 1950s that
deal with the British involvement in the Second World War, films that are almost
totally ignored within this area of critical under-attention.[1] It may be that the
1950s war films have been ignored by recent British film scholars because
they have been intent on re-writing British film history—rewriting which has
been concerned to rediscover the repressed (i.e., social realism) within British
film production, a repressed totally at odds to these 1950s war films and their
unabashed middle-class and nostalgic ideology. And yet, the 1950s war films
were direct descendants of the critically valorized wartime films.

British wartime propaganda promoted the notion of a people's war by
showing what looked like the old, class-bound Victorian Britain as being, in
fact, the new democratic twentieth-century Britain. Even before the war had
been fought to a conclusion, the single-minded thrust of British propaganda
towards the notion of a people's war through images of Britain that successfully
managed the prestidigitational skill of showing what looked like the old, class-
bound Victorian British society was in fact the new, democratic twentieth
century Britain, was being attacked because it was felt in some quarters that
the illusion was in danger of becoming the reality. That is to say, the images of

Britain which the propagandists were attempting to promulgate at home and abroad were seen by some to be not enhancing or valorising the best of Britain but to be denying or subverting it. These notions are useful as an indicator of the often unspoken beliefs which came to inform the 1950s war films: the attempts to bring about a return of the repressed middle class. There underlies these claims that British propaganda films of the war were offering false or distorted views of British society that very concern which I detect in the 1950s British war films: the fear that the middle class had lost social and cultural centrality within British society during the war because of the demands of a peoples war. The very characteristic English institutions,[2] which were judged to be threatened by the images of Britain (past and future) put forward in British wartime films, depended for their existence and their structures upon a fundamentally class-divided society in which the middle class took the formative role as to the meaning, function and continuance of those institutions. These notions about British propaganda do find some support in British films of the war period inasmuch as they occasionally show that the previously governed classes can and do demonstrate capacities and abilities to think, organize and act for themselves.[3] What seems to me is at work in the objections to wartime propaganda images is a specifically middle-class sensitivity to changes already abroad in the culture (maybe as yet unconsciously), and that could be detected within the films as well. The middle class were beginning to feel left out, taken for granted, and what they stood for diminished thereby. My interpretation of British war films made in the 1950s is that while many attempt to partially re-write history most are rather more engaged in attempts to re-write the wartime films themselves.

Immediately following the end of hostilities, with less than a handful of exceptions, the war *as a topic* did disappear from British films. This may well be understood a simple commercial prudence. No doubt few producers saw many pounds to be made from harping on about that which the audiences for their films would rather put behind them. A few socially aware films were made which dealt with issues arising from the war (*Frieda* [1947] for example), but others used the war as a source of comedy (*Whisky Galore* [1949]) or romance (*Piccadilly Incident* [1946]). This seems perfectly understandable, even logical. But what seems to have been overlooked at the time was the developing strength of the myth of wartime England, a myth the wartime films themselves had helped to foster, a myth which said in part that it was *then* that the British were at their best, when if Britannia did not rule the waves unchallenged, she certainly did not allow anyone else that privilege, that Britain and the British could and did take it. This myth took root initially during the war but it was not until the

1950s in a renewed cycle of production of war films that the myth came to have particular cinematic attraction.

As the wartime austerity which remained and even deepened in the late 1940s continued into the new decade of the 1950s, and as British international prestige faded with the waning of the Empire, and as the bureaucracy of the welfare state became part of the new way of life of the British, two impulses served to make the war film an attractive proposition for British film makers and British audiences.

First, it was a way to instantly hark back to that mythic time when (it was believed) the British people stood alone but together, bravely faced adversity of the most fearsome type and bested it. The corollary to this, to the benefit of film makers, was that where during the war films had been determined to show the British not losing the war, now there was an opportunity, even a demand, to show the British actually winning it.

Second, the undercurrents of a surge of class conflict, a demand by the working class not simply for more of the nation's resources but also for more of the nation's attention was beginning to be felt. Historians accept that overall the war strengthened the solidarity and self-awareness of the working class and that the material conditions of life of the working class improved because there was a new upper-class and middle-class concern that, having played so crucial a role in the war effort, the workers should not be plunged back into the economic depression of the inter-war years (Marwick 1982, 42). These combined with the election of a Labour government and the implementation of a vast array of welfare programs to change in substantial ways the parameters of working-class culture. The working class, it might thus be said, came to share more equally in the overall image of the nation. But this was not immediately reflected in popular culture, and certainly not on the cinema screens. Here the working class were *initially* rewarded for their crucial role in the war effort by narratives about them and sympathetic characterizations, as in, for example, *Hue and Cry* and *It Always Rains On Sunday* (both 1947). But this soon faded. The paternalism which Marwick suggests motivated the upper and middle classes after the war is reflected in these films—and its limits as well. Eventually, the working class would demand its own voice, or failing that, demand accurate representations of its actual conditions of existence in the cinema (and in other popular culture forms: theatre, novels and finally pop music). This would manifest itself in the so-called revolution in British cinema dating from about 1959. There is a corollary to this second condition, another explanation, related to changes being felt—consciously and unconsciously—within British society, as to why 1950s war films seem to reflect desperate attempts to hold the wartime community spirit:

> ... it does seem that 1951 can be seen as a pivotal year for British society, marking a shift from a period of post-war austerity...to the consumer boom of the 50s....The shift can also be characterised in terms of changing national values, *community spirit giving way to individualism* and an increasing emphasis on the private domain of home and family. (Barr 1986, 355) (My italics.)

These factors combined to bring about a return in some concentration (although never to the stage of that of wartime production) of war films by British film makers. The types of films which they made during the fifties (and the cycle did peter out with the coming of the social realist films of the sixties) were both alike and unlike those of the war period. Some looked as if they could have been made at anytime during the war (e.g., *The Gift Horse* [1952], *The Cruel Sea* [1953] *The Sea Shall Not Have Them* [1954]); some were concerned to replace the upper classes in the forefront of winning the war (e.g. *The Battle of the River Plate* [1956]). Others, picking on a minor trend of wartime films, revelled in the upper-middle class intellectuals playing cunning games (e.g. *The Man Who Never Was* [1956] or *I Was Monty's Double* [1958]). And there were those few films that dared voice a certain amount of reservation about the glory of war and the particular way the British fought it (e.g., *The Bridge on the River Kwai* [1957]). Some differences in content are noticeable. It is obvious that certain types of stories could not have been made during the war in any case. For example, prisoner-of-war stories—since the actualities of conditions and activities within prisoner-of-war camps can only have been vaguely surmised, and such stories can hardly have been conducive to a positive war effort.[4] There is in the 1950s a mini-cycle of such films (e.g., *The Wooden Horse* [1950], *The Colditz Story* [1954]). Or again, authentic stories about real secret operations, counter-espionage, secret weapons and so on (e.g., *Odette* [1950], *Carve Her Name with Pride* [1958], and others mentioned above). Nearly all such films, except those like *The Bridge on the River Kwai*, are replete with self-congratulatory tones in keeping with an overall theme of how we won the war. There is another mini-cycle of films whose narratives are concerned with the disillusionments of post-war civilian life experienced by ex-servicemen who had a good war and which emphasize nostalgia for the myth of the war (e.g., *The Intruder* [1953] and *The Ship that Died of Shame* [1955]).

Two issues paramount in any understanding of British wartime films—the question of class, and propaganda/ ideology—instead of disappearing with the conclusion of the war, return in something like full force (but with greater subtlety) in 1950s war films. T.S Eliot, writing while the war was still on but with more than one eye to the post-war future, made an observation which turns out to be surprisingly pertinent to the question of the relations between wartime films and post-war British films dealing with the war:

> Of the advantages of administrative and sentimentalist unity we hardly need to be reminded, after the experience of war, but it is often assumed that the unity of wartime should be preserved in time of peace. Amongst any people engaged in warfare, especially when the war appears, or can be made to appear, purely defensive, we may expect a spontaneous unity of sentiment which is genuine, an affectation of it on the part of those who merely wish to escape odium, and, from all, submission to the commands of the constituted authority. We should hope to find the same harmony and docility among the survivors of a shipwreck adrift in a lifeboat. People often express regret that the same unity, self-sacrifice and fraternity which prevail in an emergency, cannot survive the emergency itself (1968, 124).

There are other notable differences between the films of the wartime and the war films of the 1950s. At the most general level, the latter are more often than not (although not exclusively) concerned with showing the British *winning* the war as opposed to *not losing it*. This is typically through small-scale, imaginatively conceived and boldly carried-out actions by small groups (e.g. in *The Gift Horse, The Dam Busters, They Who Dare* [both 1953] *Above Us the Waves, The Cockleshell Heroes* [both 1955] and *Sea of Sand* [1958]). The metaphor is obvious. Then again, the wartime need for examining (or burying) the question of class and the promoting of a certain ideology of social relationships, is changed in the 1950s—although not all that changed: it is still rooted in the British class system. In the 1950s, however, it is not necessary to try and foster notions (credible or not) of social and cultural solidarity in order to unite the country to the demands of a peoples war. Arguably, 1950s war films are concerned with putting the people back into their place (where, presumably, T.S.Eliot for one would like to see them put.) So while the films *are* involved with notions of national identity—bolstering the failing image of Britain as a power both at home and abroad—they are also concerned with a revisionist history of the war—showing the British winning the war without the need to also propagandize the lower classes into helping. The lower classes, inasmuch as they are present, are naturalized to an extent that goes beyond that of wartime films such as *In Which We Serve* (1942) which clearly asserts the unquestioned naturalness of the division of society into discrete classes hierarchically organized. Any doubts on the unimportance of the lower classes in 1950s war films can be quickly dismissed by comparing *In Which We Serve* with *The Bridge on the River Kwai*, two films which invite such comparison on the level of the haughtiness of their respective commanding officer main

186

characters and the blind obedience and loyalty of the lower ranks. Yet, unlike *In Which We Serve*, there is no need in *Bridge on the River Kwai* to humanize the men beyond that of ordinary British Tommies. They are what they are. Is it their war? Hardly so. The post-war films are as much as exercise in papering the gaps of social inequality as the war time films; indeed, even more so. By the 1950s, the gaps are wider, spreading and in different places. And by the 1960s, such remedial patch-working becomes, and is seen to become, futile. With the social realist films of the 1960s, the gaps become the decor.

A glance at the number of war films made in the 1940s and 1950s clearly implies that, in relation to other sorts of films, the 1950s is not statistically remarkable for its war films. But then, it is also apparent that during the war itself, there was a considerable weighting of war-film production in the first three to four years and a recognizable dropping off in the last two years. What is significant is that the downwards trend began even before the war was over and that the peak of production of war films was in 1942. From 1943 onwards the war provided a subject for fewer and fewer films. So while the dearth of films after hostilities ceased can be explained by straightforward war-weariness, the waning from the middle of the war (not known as such at the time of course) needs further explanation.

One explanation for the decrease in the production of war films during the hostilities can be related to the claim that the propaganda task of converting the people of Britain to the task of responding to the fact of a people's war had been accomplished by 1942. But another explanation suggests itself. The films of the first three or four years of the war, in addition to whatever else they had to say about the notions of a people's war and, advertently or inadvertently, about the class structure of Britain, also tended to concentrate on the theme of not losing the war rather than winning the war. With the increasing involvement of the U.S.S.R. and the United States it became clear that any winning of the war which might take place would not be exclusively or even primarily British. It may then be a question of the blow to British self-generated prestige that caused them to be less concerned with making films about winning the war. But it may also be that the myth of the British at war which had become quickly and firmly entrenched, and which emphasized the Britain-Can-Take-It syndrome and a certain masochistic satisfaction in hardship was too powerful to give up. Britannia with her back to the wall but refusing to give in is, to British eyes and minds, a much more appealing national image than Britannia out in the middle of the ring beating the living daylights out of a reeling opponent with the help of several larger allies.

In light of this latter situation, it makes many of the films of the 1950s rather more interesting. Some show a very real continuity with the realist dramas of the war. *The Dam Busters*, for example, is a linear descendent of *Target for Tonight* (1941) and *The First of the Few* (1942). These, and others of a more Hollywood-ish tone, are simultaneously concerned with reversing the pattern just described and with showing Britain not simply fighting back but winning on its own terms.

Other aspects drawn from the history of the 1950s suggest themselves as possible motives for a revitalization of the myth of Britain at War, with the new emphasis of winning: the return to conservative government after the post-war Labour Government; the disintegration of the British Empire, the fiasco of Suez.

It would seem then that the films which preceded the revitalization of a newly social-realistic British cinema in the 1960s represented a reflection of and a contribution to a last ditch effort by the dominant culture to keep the lid on the British social revolution, complicated by a middle-class backlash against the way in which the images of a peoples war had given emphasis to the working class and taken the middle class for granted in wartime propaganda. Even so, one reason why the war as a narrative subject returned in significant quantity to the British film in the 1950s is an attempt to try and revive the myth of the war as a time (the last time?) in which the British stood together *in their various social positions*, united in common goals and communality. The war films of the 1950s then wished to re-energize and re-activate that magic moment when all the class and social contradictions of British culture evaporated (Britton 1989, 39) with these essential differences: this time Britain would not be winning-by-not-losing but simply winning; and without the awkward (from the dominant ideological point-of-view) need to draw attention to the contribution required and attained by the working class.

Thus, the war films of the 1950s drew heavily upon war nostalgia, the British myth of the war as a golden age (Britton 1989, 39) but at the same time revised that myth, that history, by subtracting from it the very thing that had formed the basis of the myth-creating films of the 1940s: the notion of a people's war. Now the dominant classes of Britain could fight the war (or could be seen to fight the war) the way they had wanted to (and believed they had) from the first, without making concessions to the sensitivity of the lower orders simply to ensure that they would turn out for the match. The powerful myth of the war could be used as the very tool by which it was simultaneously and fundamentally re-written. The need to do so was, then, a consequence of the perception that the concessions wrung out of the dominant classes by the lower classes for going to war (for the second time in twenty years) were not only put into place (by the Labour government of 1945-1951) but that the changes in the class system which the lower classes expected (and the upper and especially the middle classes feared) were actually coming about. The war films of the 1950s are ironically prophetic of the social-realist films of the 1960s not through being a voice crying in the wilderness but by being the reflection of the last ditch effort by the dominant class to maintain its hegemony by re-writing the history of the celluloid war in its own favour and offering this as a remembrance of the way things were.

There is, however, a complicating and contradictory spirit at work in the war films of the 1950s. One of the effects of the deliberate fostering of the notions of a peoples war by and through the wartime films was to imply an alliance of interest and identity of all social classes and all sub-national regions in Britain. Since the aim was to bring the working class around to sharing the dominant classes view of the need to fight Germany and Nazism, founded in an arrogant belief that the working class would need to be cajoled into this, there was inevitably set up the notion that the working class and the ruling class not only had much in common but that they could form a natural alliance through that. Less a hatred of tyranny—since that may well raise awkward questions about the social relationship of ruling and ruled in Britain—the emphasis was on a mutually shared love of Britain (defined within the dominant mythos of Englishness). The prevalence of upper-class leaders in wartime films is one of its particular but not surprising features, as is the way in which the working class representatives in those films, no matter how poorly or inadequately characterized (in terms of authenticity and understanding), shared the perceptions and goals of those upper class leaders. The middle of the middle class, it could be or was safely assumed (by the ruling class), would understand the dominant perceptions of the war. Their screen presence in wartime films is generally unremarkable, and usually takes the form of individual representatives who concur with the dominant ideology but showless aptitude that the upper class representatives to conduct the war properly—to lead men, organize, and so on.

There are exceptions, and these will turn out important in relation to the direction taken by some post-war war films. The exception which proves the rule of the quiescence of the middle classes is *The Way Ahead* (1943). In the 1950s, however, more important are those films in which the middle class (almost inevitably upper rather than lower-middle class) are shown to be taking a leading role in *supporting* and *promoting* the cause of Britain. Here, in the sphere of the combined attributes of intellect and practicality, is the place for the middle class to lead. They are, of course, dependent upon the ruling classes to permit them this role. Their intellect is also of the severely technological kind, not the lofty realms of disinterested philosophy. They are the boffins, or in another especially telling term, the back room boys. The exemplar in the post-war war films is Barnes Wallis in *The Dam Busters*. This trend may be perceived at the very end of the war in *The Way to the Stars* (1945), a film not concerned with a technical meritocracy it is true, but very much cantered on the way in which the middle class are able to rise to the occasion and lead and serves as well as the upper class (both in matters military and of the heart).

There is then a sort of tug-of-war in the 1950s war films. On one hand there are those films which show the upper class winning the war almost single-handed, thus, revising the myth. On the other, there are those which emphasize the role of the middle classes. These, rather more numerous, arise partly from the perception (shared with the upper class) that in post-war Britain, and as a consequence of the Labour Government (while it lasted) and the introduction of the Welfare State, the working class were getting too uppity: they wanted not only to be looked after (a continuance of paternalism) but also to be seen and heard. But equally as important, the middle-class emphasis of these films was driven by the fear the middle class had of an alliance between upper class and working class. That great Victorian era invention, the middle class, had always affected to despise both these other classes, although remaining ready to allow the upper class to rule and the working class to work as long as their own class position as the backbone of England remained undisturbed. The promises made or implied by a peoples war seemed to offer consolidation of that position and to have improved it along with improving the conditions of the working class. But the results, in retrospect, were rather more disturbing to the middle class. The speed with which Conservative governments were elected after the initial flirtation with Labour suggests the degree to which the implications of social change became apparent to the middle class.

Post-war British cinema in general rather quickly fell into the mode of attacking the upper class. (The most devastating example is Ealing Studios' *Kind Hearts and Coronets* [1949]). Awaking to the 'danger' of the working class rather later, the British cinema was slower but eventually more determined to attack the working class through films such as *The Man in the White Suit* (1951) and *I'm All Right, Jack* (1959). These films, not being concerned with recreating the war are outside the scope of this discussion but they do add indirect support to the claim that, by and large, the post-war British war films are middle-class films. There is at least one war film that matches the cynical middle-class attitude toward the alliance of the working class and upper-class that figures *The Man in the White Suit*. This film is *Privates on Parade* (1956). The films view of the venality of both upper and lower classes is less surprising when it is recognized the extent to which this film is simply a variation on a theme found in a number of the films made by the Boulting brothers——*I'm All Right, Jack*, and *Heavens Above* (1960) rehearse this same theme.

An even obvious example of the way in which these films, or some of them, re-wrote history as it was understood from the wartime films can be found in *The Bridge on the River Kwai*, where the working class (the ordinary soldiers) are led totally astray by blind affection for their officer-leaders, and where the object of the stupidity of the officer class, the bridge itself, and the misguided, even treacherous, British colonel are both destroyed by a middle-class Englishman and an American working together. The reversal of the ideology of the wartime films can hardly be more complete. But to get to this point, the shape and structure of those wartime films had to be rehearsed then modified in the films of the 1950s. It was, however, a doomed attempt. The bursting on to the British cinema scene of the social realist films of the 1960s drove British war films from that point away from any attempts to re-write history in terms of realist aesthetics and the use of selected actuality (most of the war films of the 1950s are based on actual events and individuals).

The eulogy to the short-lived revisionist cinematic history of the middle class at war is found in a film which is not about the war at all but about the post-war military. *Tunes of Glory* (1960) has as a central character, a good, honest upper-middle class colonel who is, quite literally, destroyed by a considerably less gentlemanly lower-class, up-from-the-ranks subordinate. The film is a bitter lament over the shift in social relations which by 1960 (when the film was released) had been firmly established. The Thatcher years in Britain embodied the triumphant return of the middle class. The 1950s war films, for all their celebration of the middle class, are seen in hindsight as the swan song (for two decades at least) of that class.

NOTES

1. My concern will be with the social aspects of these films, especially related to social class; the ways in which the transformation in the aesthetics of British film practice that took place during the war were continued and modified in post-war cinema deserve extended, but separate, discussion.

2. A phrase used by the economist F.A. Hayek in 1944 in an amazing attack on the notions of a planned society, which he further equated with both fascism and communism.

3. My reading of the wartime films I have analysed elsewhere would not bring me to the conclusions Hayek indicates about the left-wing propaganda affectivity of those films. Quite the contrary: these films seem, in one way or another, supportive of the status quo at least as far as British class structure is concerned.

4. There is an interesting exception to this. *2,000 women* (1944) which is not only an exception because it is a wartime film about prison camp life but also because it deals with women internees rather than male P.O.W.s.

WORKS CITED

Armes, Roy. 1978. *A Critical History of British Cinema*. New York: Oxford.

Barr, Charles. ed. 1986. *All Our Yesterdays: 90 Years of British Film*. London: BFI Publishing.

Betts, Ernest. 1973. *The Film Business: A History of British Cinema 1986-1972*. New York: Pitman.

Britton, Andrew. 1989. Their Finest Hour: Humphrey Jennings and the British Imperial Myth of World War II. *CineAction!*. No.18. Fall 1989.

Eliot, T.S. 1968. *Christianity and Culture*. New York: Harcourt Brace Johanovich.

Forman, Dennis. 1952. *Film 1945-1950*. London: British Council/Longmans, Green and Co.

Marwick, Arthur. 1982. *British Society Since 1945*. Hardmondsworth: Penguin.

Medhurst, Andy. 1984. 1950s War Films. *National Fictions: World War Two in British Film and Television*. Ed. Geoff Hurd. London: BFI Publishing.

Perry, George. 1985. *The Great British Picture Show: From the Nineties to the Seventies*. 2nd edn. London: Pavilion/Michael Joseph.

Powell, Dilys. 1947. *Films Since 1939*. London: British Council/Longman Green.

SOAPS & SITS

THE ORDINARY AS TELEVISION SPECTACLE: NOTES ON OZ SOAP OPERA IN THE 80S

INTRODUCTION

In a country of limited resources for production of indigenous television drama, the quantity and quality of soap opera production in Australia for over a decade is remarkable. Three commercial networks and two national (State operated) networks compete for a total national audience of just over 16 million people. The three commercial networks also compete for the limited advertising dollars in the Australian economy. While Australian content (drama and non-drama) is regulated by the Australian Broadcasting Tribunal, the commitment of the commercial networks to soap opera production generally exceeds regulatory requirements (which do not specify genres anyway). The experience of soap opera production in Australia has resulted in soaps[1] which have a distinctive local inflection. (The term 'soap opera' will be used throughout this paper to refer to the genre of soap opera; the term 'soaps' will refer to the individual productions which fall within this genre.) It is some of the parameters of this local inflection I wish to outline here. Full discussion of the causes of this inflection will have to await another opportunity.

ORDINARINESS

Ordinariness is the single-most defining aspect of Australian soaps. Ordinariness in terms of the way in which the drama and the *mise-en-scene* are rooted in representations of the 'realities' of suburban existence in Australia. Ordinariness in terms of the absence of many of the dramatic conventions of soap opera (as genre is understood from the American model) which moves them away from reality— e.g., the comparative rarity of disease (physical and mental) except as part of the medical practice of some of the characters, the lack of interconnected families by marriage, divorce, paternity, etc., the low-key presentation of emotional relationships, the relative evenness of economic status and the absence of extremes of wealth and poverty. An even flow of life as opposed to the constant tremors and turmoil of American soaps is another factor of the ordinariness which Australian soaps celebrate.

If ordinariness is an essential part of the ideology of soap opera production in Australia, it is also an essential part of the ideology of Australia. The dominant cultural belief is that Australians are all 'ordinary folks,' all equal, all sharing the same common perceptions of what it means to be an Australian and what it means to live in Australia. The class-stricken decay of the 'Old World' and the avaricious individualism of the 'New World' are held, and thankfully held, to be absences from Australian culture, a new country and a new 'improved' culture.

POSITIVE UNORIGINALITY

Positive unoriginality means using genres, formulas and codes of cultural production already established and practiced in other cultures but in ways which produce distinctly culturally specific products. Soap opera production can be, and almost inevitably is, conventional and formulaic and culturally specific *at the same time.* The models provided by American daytime soaps and by American prime-time soaps, especially when viewed within the larger hegemony of American television production practice, seem to be the points of origin, and departure, for most local, indigenous, and/or national soap opera production.

The way in which Australian soap opera typically demonstrates rejection of the two dominant cultural perceptions of those other cultures to which Australia might seem to be indebted (or even overwhelmed by, from a cultural imperialist point of view) is through the production of soaps which are clearly different from the soaps produced in Britain and the soaps produced in America-different in terms of the defining formal and thematic characteristics of soap opera from either of those cultures of origin.

Class is consciously denied through absence in the first instance and through demonstrations (not always totally convincing) of egalitarianism in practice and social interaction in the different fictional communities of the various soaps. Greed, avariciousness and sexual peripateticism are consciously rejected as motivators for narratives in Australian soaps. Australian soaps are concerned with saying 'we're not like them.' The need to distinguish Australia and Australians from their historical and cultural origins in Europe has been an Australian obsession most of its 200 years of European settlement. Since the 1970's this obsession has taken the additional dimension of not only placing 'Australian-ness' in popular culture (particularly films and television) but also in implicitly rejecting (a qualified rejection at the best of times) the powerful cultural influences of the United States and of Britain. Australian soaps reveal both these processes at work—albeit in different ways: *Neighbours,* for example, through its especial emphasis on suburban normality as source of television spectacle; *A Country Practice* through a self-conscious attempt to present Australia in microcosm.

On occasion Australian soaps have followed the format of traditional American soaps: *The Young Doctors, Sons and Daughters,* or *The Power and The*

Passion are easily comparable in format, in construction of micro-narratives, with American soaps. Others show a comparison with the community/street soaps of British television. Some, like *Cop Shop* or *Prisoner* in the past and the continuing and highly successful *A Country Practice* seem to owe little in terms of form to other soap opera models and, drawing at least some inspiration from other television genres (the police show, the medical show), have evolved a particular inflection of the soap opera genre within the sphere of television production and broadcast practice within Australia.

LOCATION OF AUSTRALIAN SOAPS' FICTIONAL WORLDS

The locations of the narratives of Australian soaps emphasize the ordinariness of those soaps through the 'typicality' of the locations. No location is used in an Australian soap in a way which exaggerates or 'fantasies' about some aspect of it. Nearly all Australian soaps demonstrate, emphasize and reiterate the ordinary reality of their locations through their carefully constructed opening tide sequences.

A Country Practice is located in a 'typical' small country town, Wandin Valley. It is isolated but not remote: Sydney is implied to be accessible, and a fictional larger town, Burrigan, is close by.

Neighbours is locationally metonymous for any Australian suburb. The location is Erinsborough, a suburb of a large metropolis, possibly Melbourne but never specifically designated as such.

Richmond Hill, which takes its title from its fictional location, suggests that its location is somewhere between Wandin Valley (a reasonably remote and isolated town in its own right) and Erinsborough (a suburb). Richmond Hill seems to be a semi-rural, outer suburb, a type of community well understood in the Australian demography.

Home and Away is closer to *A Country Practice* than the other present Australian soaps. Its community, Summer Bay, is a beachside town/village sufficiently isolated from bigger urban and suburban centres to be a self-contained yet not so remote as to inhibit reasonably free movement of characters to and from that urban center. The beach or the ocean-edge of Australia occupies a somewhat ambiguous place in Australian cultural perceptions. Other than the city beaches, such places are neither the Bush nor, clearly, the suburbs. Narratives may take advantage of the mythic perceptions of either.

E Street declares its geographic (and its socio-economic) setting more openly than is usual in recent Australian soaps: Eden Street is located in the fictional working class suburb of Westside. But the 'actual' location is clearly (and possibly deliberately) identifiable as Sydney.

Despite the variety of these settings. Australian soaps do not have the option of placing themselves in the anonymous small towns which (until recently) have been the favoured fictional locations of American daytime soaps. The reality of Australian demography is that nearly 80% of the population live in the five big cities (and nearly 80% of *that* percentage live in Sydney or Melbourne). Australia does not have a spread of larger and smaller towns across the continent like the United States, nor large regional populations like Great Britain. The conventional small towns/all towns location of American daytime soaps tends to make them more regionally-free—'Anywhere, USA'—Australian soaps can only be city (the few Australian cities are basically the same) or suburban (of which the same is even more true) or the Bush.

NARRATIVE STRUCTURES

Soap opera typically organizes its narratives dramaturgically around the problems and conditions of everyday life. These problems and conflicts, the sources of drama, are nearly always couched in personal terms and take little direct account of a wider social or economic context. But this seemingly hermetically sealed world of soap opera, or this world extracted from a fragment of the real world, is not devoid of 'relevance' to that real world of which it seems such a minuscule part. Ideologically, soaps are closely allied to the culture which allows and sometimes encourages their production.

In comparison with American soap opera (the master-model for the genre) Australian soap opera conventionally structures micro-narratives which are short-lived and engage only a few characters directly, some of whom are 'outside' characters only brought into the diegesis for the purpose of a particular micro-narrative. These micro-narratives have fairly clear resolutions which do not always lead to further problems or conflicts (another immediate micro-narrative). Australian soaps also seem overall to be less concerned with some of the themes seen as being conventional soap opera themes. For example, suffering seems more muted in Australian soap or put another way, happiness is typically more available to Australian soap opera characters; pregnancy, birth, and death less omnipresent. Complicated and ever-changing sets of legal/familial relations (convoluted by and through marriage, divorce, uncertain paternity and so on) are also less present in Australian soap opera.

HAPPINESS AND OPTIMISM

Beyond what differences in stylistic practice and production practice exist between Australian soap opera and that of the dominant models for comparison (American and British), there is a question of a fundamental difference of 'attitude' which may well be informed by distinct cultural difference. This degree of difference can be succinctly generalized as: Australian soaps are overall optimistic, the all-encompassing air of unhappiness of American soaps has been noted on many occasions and does not need to be explained here. Little seems to have been said about the prevailing pessimism of British soaps. It is worth noting that Australian and British soaps are generally constructed around the same (or conventionally similar) narratives that involve disruptions of the 'flow of life' of a set of individuals which lead to pain, confusion, emotionality, failure to communicate, and so on. In Australian soaps hope is always around the comer, the equilibrium to which Australian soaps attempt to return their various micro-narratives is generally a happy one. The micro-narrative are usually resolved happily or at least in ways which cause *minimal* unhappiness at worst, and in those soaps which have one-off narrative resolutions, those resolutions are almost always happily satisfactory (in terms of the dominant social values and ruling ideology) and are seldom tragic.

Again, it is worth noting that the opening title sequences of Australian soaps inevitable introduce the main characters in happy situations and with smiling or laughing faces. The contrast with American soaps credit sequences is striking. (British soaps credit sequences tend to ignore characters and emphasize environment).

LACK OF HOSTILITY

Personal relationships in Australian soaps, although often stormy, are not built inevitably upon hostility. To Australians most British soaps seem irredeemably pessimistic; the worst is constantly expected and inevitably arrives, happiness seems at best fleeting and for the most part illusory. Hostility, intra- and inter-family, seems to be distinguishing features of British soaps. Australian soaps are less dissatisfied with the conditions of the modem family. Families in Australian soaps are not the sure and certain source of conflict of British soaps nor arenas of constant power struggles of American soaps.

REALISM

Very few soaps anywhere regularly (or successfully) postulate a fantasy world distanced from reality. Australian soaps seem even more than the rule concerned with verisimilitude and this reveals itself in material realism. That is to say, there is a strong correlation in much of the *mise-en-scene* of Australian soaps to the actual physical appearances of the reality of Australian environment, architecture, and decor. A great many of the interiors of many soaps are shot in studio-constructed sets. But there is considerable location shooting as well;

it is quite practical to do so given the geographic and climatic conditions that pertain in Australia.

The frequent presentation of the obviously 'real' Australia via location scenes, whether they are suburban landscapes of *Neighbours*, the rural setting *of A Country Practice,* the beach setting of *Home and Away,* or the semi-rural/outer suburb setting of *Richmond Hills,* has much to do with the material realism of Australian soap operas. This carries over into the construction and decorating of sets. It is often unclear which sets and which are real locations in many of these productions. The fact that, for the most part, the characters of Australian soap opera narratives are 'everyday' Australians permits (or demands) a reality of the spaces which they occupy and inhabit. Australian soaps are not peopled by the rich (and/or famous) who infiltrate even the American daytime soaps, and what is more, as the characters are 'intended' to be understood as ordinary and typical, so their dwelling and working spaces are constructed (or chosen) and dressed to be ordinary and typical (and, of course, functional to the demands of shooting scenes within them).

REALISM AND HAPPINESS

While it may be no more accurate to say that Australian soaps are unrelievedly happy than to say British soaps are unrelievedly gloomy, it does seem a fair comment to state that overall Australian soaps have a greater quotient of happiness, of good cheer, of bonhomie, and indeed of happy (partial) endings than is true of either British or American soaps. This is partly the consequence of there being typically more humor, more comedy as such than in British and American soaps. It is partly the consequence too of the fact that gloominess and pessimism is not an integral part of their ambiance. Happiness is part of the Australian cultural mythos: Australians seem themselves as, or believe themselves to be, a happy people. (This despite the deeply set streak of fatalism within the Australian character).

It is easy to point out that not merely does every cloud have a silver lining in Australian soaps but that the clouds are never very dark, seldom threatening for more than a moment, and scud across the skies of soap narratives very rapidly. Temporary unhappiness in Australian soaps is just that: temporary. A lack of seriousness is another facet of the Australian character, mythical or otherwise, and so it is that Australians soaps do not take themselves as seriously as do American and British soaps. There appears to be an inability (or a reluctance at least) on the part of Australian soap opera producers to be anywhere near as serious (in *what* they produce not *how* they produce it) as American and British equivalents. And this translates to the narrative situations and characterizations of Australian soaps. This can be demonstrated by the number of comic and semi-comic characters in Australian soaps. It is conventional of Australian soap opera that characters can be both comic and serious (or be involved in both comic and serious micro-narratives) without confusing their characterization.

There is also the overall lightness of tone of most Australian soaps. This is perhaps most obvious in *Neighbours* (which may be because nothing *really* serious ever happens in *Neighbours*—or rarely anyway). *A Country Practice* deliberately maintains a balance between drama (and melodrama) based on topical medical issues and light-hearted humor. A balance between seriousness and humor with the consequence of an overall lightness of tone not typical of American or British soaps is true of most Australian soaps. The speed with which micro-narratives are resolved in Australian soaps adds to this happiness/ lightness. Situations of conflict, emotional conflict especially, do not drag on unresolved and endlessly complicated for (seemingly) ever, causing an ever-widening circle of misery, as is often the case in American soaps—and British soaps too.

There is lack of the 'essential ingredients' of American soaps: Sexual desire, sexual infidelity (or fears of it), complicated marriage relationships, ubiquity of divorce and separation, frequency of illness or injury, rape and abduction. Australian soaps are by contrast far more *ordinary*. An unhappy situation seldom segues into yet another unhappy situation but usually resolves itself (or is resolved) quite quickly and quite happily.

ECONOMIC CONDITIONS

Few Australian soaps make much of the economic 'realities' of Australian society (imagined or otherwise). This is not to say that the 'economic facts of life' are somehow irrelevant to Australian soap opera narratives but for the greater part, economics do not impinge beyond specific micro-narratives from time to time. The pressures of 'making a living' or 'making ends meet' although mentioned occasionally are *seldom particular* concern. Australian soaps (with rare exceptions) do not concern themselves with the doings, the problems, machinations, and worries of the rich. There are very seldom individual characters of conspicuously wealthy status in individual Australian soaps. In Australian soap opera the old adage need, perhaps, to be reversed to 'happiness doesn't buy you money'. By Australian standards, the characters of Australian soaps are, by and large, not especially well off but most are comfortable. The lack of money, the need to obtain it, or to obtain more of it, do not provide micro-narratives that assume social importance; and do not generate the macro-narrative for any Australian soaps. (An exception which proves this rule is *The Power and the Passion,* a short-lived attempt at a daytime soap which was born and died in 1989) As part of this the jobs people do are ordinary, unspectacular, and mostly, unglamorous.

UBIQUITY OF CHILDREN

Ordinariness (the verisimilitude of family situations) is also partly explained by and explanatory of the proportionally greater presence of children and especially adolescents in Australian soaps than is conventional for the genre. Thus the presence of micro-narratives cantered upon schools and the situations of adolescent characters at school (used especially in *Home and Away, Neighbours,* and in the past in *A Country Practice)* tend to emphasize the ordinary over the exotic.

CONCLUSION: WHAT ARE AUSTRALIAN SOAPS 'ABOUT'?

It is difficult to specify what Australian soaps are about if they are not what soaps are *supposed* to be about. Australian soaps are less committed to soap opera stereotype although they *do* draw upon stereotyping with peripheral and/or comic characters. Equally they are less concerned with a broad spectrum of representative types drawn from the reality of Australian society. This then adds both to the apparent closeness of Australian soap opera to ideas of the real and to the ordinariness which is fundamental to Australian soap opera as a genre, a culturally inflected genre in its own right, but which varies somewhat, as would be expected, from soap to individual soap. The proper province of soap opera narrative in Australia soaps seems to be the domestic, but the domestic in these constructions is different from the domestic in U.S. daytime soaps.

The domestic in Australian soaps is defined by reference to a perceived realism of domesticity drawn from within the norms and confines of actual lived experience in Australia *and* to a set of culturally determined images of what Australian familial domesticity is: suburban, cantered on the nuclear family, shaped by bourgeois moral values and ethical behaviour, unaffected by economic extremes and strongly expressed viewpoint, with sexual behaviour regulated within a set of understood parameters of permissibility.
Australian soaps are everyday Australia, every day.

FROM NORMALITY TO CHAOS BUT NOT NECESSARILY BACK AGAIN: SITUATION COMEDY NARRATIVE

Situation comedy and soap opera[1] are the two oldest and thus most enduring television narrative fiction genres. Both these genres originated on television in the United States in the late 1940s and early 1950s[2]. Soap opera has clear origins in broadcast radio in the United States in the 1930s.[3] Situation comedy's origins are less clear-cut, or at least its mutation from prototypes on radio to its television form is more extreme. Both genres are, in their televisual forms, distinguished by the way in which they take particular narrative structures that are distinct from each other and from traditional narrative form, both televisual and extra-televisual.

Although it is seldom recognised, situation comedy's narrative structure is a greater departure from the traditional than is soap opera. Soap opera is, however, the television genre that is more typically defined by its alleged narrative uniqueness. That is it is almost routine for soap opera to be described and defined as having *no* narrative structure, to consist of an endless 'middle' without beginning or end. This is not only simplistic but it overlooks or denies the fact that soap opera, in its many hybrid forms, *does* consist of two co-existent and mutually dependent narrative structures: the *macro-narrative* which encompasses the entire individual soap's diegesis and which might be said (for purposes of practical criticism) to have begun and (when an individual soap ceases production or broadcast) to end *in media res*; and the many *micro-narratives* which make up the macro-narrative and which are organised and capable of being analysed according to their structures of equilibrium —> disruption —> development (complications and consequences)—> resolution —> new equilibrium, even or especially when incidents and action that are part of any of these aspects of the narrative structure may also serve as disruptions that trigger another micro-narrative.[4]

Situation comedy does routinely structure narrative in a way which disrupts this traditional linear narrative chain. Put simply, situation comedy removes the last two aspects in the linear narrative chain: resolution, and new equilibrium. Unlike soap opera, with which situation comedy shares a greater sense of diegetic continuity beyond the terminal point of any individual episode than is usual for television series, in situation comedy it is paramount that the equilibrium does not change as a consequence of narrative development. The initial equilibrium is, of course, the very *situation*, the existence of which defines the genre and the individual sitcoms that make up its corpus. As there is seldom a sense in which situation comedy characters exist in a world that has history, there is no equivalent of the macro-narrative of the soap opera, only a *macro-situation* that functions rather differently. History here also means a personal history, a biography, of the characters in which experience and time combine to produce a personality that develops and that has memory.[5] Hyacinth Bucket, in *Keeping Up Appearances*, is a prime example of this. She never learns from experience the inappropriateness of her hyperbolic snobbery. At the beginning of each new episode, Hyacinth is still at *ground zero* and her exaggerated sense of bourgeois mores will yet again lead to the comic complications and consequences that the narrative of each episode is structured around. The same is true, *mutatis mutandis*, of Maggie Beare (*Mother and Son*), or Betty (*Hey Dad*), or Alf Garnet (*Till Death Us Do Part*) or his transatlantic equivalent, Archie Bunker (*All in the Family*). The list is of course as great as there are sitcoms and sitcom characters.[6]

The truncated narratives of situation comedy owe something to the exigencies of television programming, although it is by no means clear that situation comedy has to be no more than the thirty minutes of television time (with or without commercials) it routinely occupies. At the same time, the half-hour timing is crucial to any definition of situation comedy and the placing of any sitcom within the corpus of the genre. Longer fictional comedies on television, even when they take the series format, almost inevitably present themselves through structures which follow the linear trajectory from equilibrium to (new) equilibrium. At the same time, the series nature of both comedy and non-comedy fictional programs does tend to create a sense in which the lack of development of character, their lack of their own sense of their own history, is evident. The establishment of a new equilibrium at the conclusion of each narrative does have an effect on the overall series. It is also the case that longer fictional programs tend also to de-centralise the main characters, that the protagonists react to events around them that originate in others rather than being the prime causers of the events. It is not necessarily disruption to the protagonist's personal or immediate equilibrium that triggers the narrative.

Arguably then, the shorter format 'suits' situation comedy and, inversely, situation comedy 'demands' the shorter format in order to do precisely what its most single defining feature 'demands': avoid closure. Situation comedy avoids closure because of an inherent internal defining contradiction. For what binds the corpus of situation comedy together is the inescapable attraction of *normality*. Normality can, for the purposes of this argument, be a combination of what Terry Lovell has described as 'the social order which sitcom references... the normative order (roughly, what people think ought to be the case) and the typical social order (what they think is usually the case).' (1982, 22) Situation comedy is based in the normative and the typical; normality is the centre of gravity which holds the solar system of situation comedy—all the individual sitcom 'planets' that whirl around, for different lifetimes, burning brightly, and eventually burning out —in place. A 'map' of situation comedy, if such a thing were possible, could resemble a extensive solar system, a galaxy perhaps, with 'normality' at the centre, and each and every sitcom ranged from near to far orbits depending on the extent to which the gravitational pull of that normality is manifest in the content and the approach of each sitcom.[7]

Normality is of course a concept which is culturally and historically determined and thus, to some extent, changeable. However, to take what is a common approach to the study of situation comedy, the chronological approach[8], it is clear that for each 'period' of situation comedy, no matter what boundaries are determined to such periods (usually decades), the prevailing *ground zero* of situation comedy is located in notions of social, domestic or personal normality of the place and period in question. This is as equally true of the suburban sitcoms of 1950s USA (*Father Knows Best, Leave it to Beaver*, etc) as it is of the so-called 'magicoms' of the next decade (*Bewitched, I Dream of Jeannie, Mr Ed*, etc). In the latter, the presence of a supernaturally endowed characters does not obviate the setting of normality (white-collar, suburban, family-based America) nor the supra-normality of the characters with whom they interact (and upon whose normality of personality, position and values the situation depends for its comedy). All sitcoms do not, of course, occupy the same orbit in the situation comedy galaxy but all are held in place by the centripetal force of normality which counterbalances their centrifugal force of chaos.

The contradiction to the basis of normality which defines situation comedy is that it is equally and simultaneously defined by being concerned with the representation and the exploration of chaos; situation comedy is 'the safe space from which to witness social transgression' (Curtis 1982, 11). Situation comedy is uniquely equipped to explore the delights and the possibilities of social chaos, of the deliberate flouting of social behaviour and social norms precisely because it is grounded in normality and precisely because it is not required to provide, in fact prohibited by conventions of the genre, from providing resolution to the problems and contradictions inherent in a clash of the socially acceptable and controllable with the socially unacceptable and anarchic. The chaos is structured not through the 'development' stage of the narrative trajectory leading, as is routine, to a gradually diminishing set of possible then probable conclusions until only one *logical* conclusion 'resolves' the conflict and thereby inserts a new equilibrium that represents a satisfactory (from some ideological position or another) restored if modified status quo. Situation comedy chaos is contained, if it is contained at all, through the return *at the commencement of the next episode* to the original equilibrium, the unalterable status quo. Thus, in a social sense, situation comedy is remarkably free to examine chaos because, ultimately chaos has no effect. The chaos—the 'social transgressions'—is not 'rewarded' by bringing about change (new equilibrium). But, importantly, the chaos or rather the chaos-causers are not punished—other than to be modern Sisyphuses and to be returned (in between episodes) to the bottom of the hill to start all over again with the next episode. But unlike Sisyphus, the Lucys (*I Love Lucy*), the Hyacinths, the Bettys, the Fletchers (*Porridge*), the Captain Mainwarings and Corporal Jones (*Dad's Army*) and the innumerable others don't *know* they are starting again.

Situation comedy narrative is conventionally structured as a spiral: a Spiral of Chaos. Situation comedy chaos in formal terms is reflected in the measure of an individual sitcom's farcicality and degree of exaggeration, the major sources of its comedy. That is, the formal conventions of situation and character within situation comedy can be measured for any individual sitcom along two lines, which are parallel and function formally in the same way for each. Put simply, this may be expressed as a figure thus:

```
                         <-----------farcicality--------------->
COMIC SITUATION    ordinary_____extraordinary
                   (credible)                        (bizarre)


COMIC CHARACTER  ordinary_____eccentric
                 (credible)                        (weird, magical)
                   <----------exaggeration---------------->
```

Chaos is present as the structuring device irrespective of where along these imagined lines any individual sitcom is placed. The *type* of chaos (how chaotic in relative terms, how disruptive in social terms) varies in accordance to the relative degree of farcicality inherent in the *macro-situation* (the one which is the ground zero of the sitcom), the relative degree of farcicality in the *micro-situation* (the episode-specific narrative) and the amount of exaggeration inherent in the characterisation of the major character/s and, sometimes, those around her/him/them. Thus, the macro-situation provides the base or initial equilibrium which will be disrupted each episode (by the commencement of the micro-situation). This, with rare exceptions, is always the same.[9] The base of the macro situation is then the closest most sitcoms come to normality (which is in turn defined both by the individual sitcom's own terms of reference and in an ideological sense by prevailing cultural perceptions of normality, which includes the television industry's perceptions of normality).

In keeping with traditional narrative form, situation comedy micro-situations are *triggered* by an event or action, usually quite early in the episode.

The longer running a sitcom, the earlier the trigger can come, as there is an assumption that the macro-situation and the characteristics of the main characters have been established in earlier episodes and are familiar. From this trigger, the narrative progresses as a spiral, each consequence becoming both a further complication and more chaotic (farcical, anarchic, crazy) than the previous one, the spiralling being fuelled by the fixed or established character traits of the central character/s. As this narrative progression is a spiral, it does not have a fixed point of closure; nor does it imply it will lead to one. This is not to say that the micro-narratives do not end—the limited time available in the broadcast schedule provides a crude finality, of course. But formally, situation comedy narrative concludes at a point of maximum chaos and before a resolution can be achieved, even if the possibility of resolution of the disruption the chaos has both caused and which it represents is even mooted. Certainly, no new equilibrium, the result of a *negotiation* between normality and chaos, happens.

I Love Lucy (commencing in 1951), though not necessarily historically the first American television production which can be placed in the situation comedy corpus, is frequently credited with establishing the popularity (with audiences and with producers and broadcasters) of the genre, not only in the USA but in other countries as well. It also reveals the conventional narrative structure of situation comedy extremely clearly, and points to how early in the history of television the basic conventions of the genre were established. The macro situation was, as Brooks and Marsh, point out 'not that much different from that of other family situation comedies on television and radio' (1988, 365). The fact that it was, or could be easily encapsulated as a 'family situation comedy' indicates the basis in normality—sociological surveys notwithstanding, the family is a keystone of normality in Western twentieth-century culture. The macro-situation in *I Love Lucy* is, moreover, complicated slightly by the particular situation and the particular characters who make up this family. At the time of the episode to be discussed, the family in *I Love Lucy* consists only of a married couple, Lucy, an American of Scottish or Irish ancestry and Ricky, a Cuban band leader. Cross-cultural coupling was not unknown in American television (and earlier, on radio) but it was unusual. The macro-situation had an extra dimension beyond the basic family/domestic situation: Lucy consistently tried to get into show business; Ricky wanted her to be only a simple 1950s housewife.

As has been often noted, television programming requirements have an effect on the structures of fictional narratives, these effects being those caused by the need to allow for the placement of commercials into the scheduled time, thereby interrupting the diegetic continuity. Although this disruption is of some significance in the way in which a narrative develops, at least to the extent of 'directing' that development towards particular points of 'climax' (cliff-hangers) before a commercial break (ostensibly to keep the putative spectator interested enough to want to return to the narrative after the commercials[10]), little analysis seems to have taken place as to the way in which narratives so created differ from tradition narratives. Truncation (in situation comedy) is not the only effect of television production and scheduling practices.

'Lucy Does a TV Commercial' is an early *I Love Lucy* episode in which the series' macro-situation equilibrium has Ricky and Lucy Ricardo living as a married couple. (This episode precedes their having children and moving to a more suburban, middle-class locale in later series.) The normality of the situation—married couple, house(bound)wife, breadwinner husband—is confirmed as Lucy is darning a sock while Ricky prepares to go to work. This being a comedy based in the 'crazy' antics of Lucy, there is a joke here as Lucy actually sews up the foot hole to the sock. The plot of this episode concerns Lucy attempting to get (underhandedly) and inevitably messing up a job of doing a commercial spot on a TV show Ricky is hosting. (This is in the days of live commercials.)

The spiral of chaos begins at home (macro-situation) and moves eventually to the TV studio via various accumulating gags and comic business (micro-situation). The commercial presentation involves the promotion of a tonic, containing a high percentage of alcohol, which Lucy has to consume in rehearsal. Lucy is rehearsed by the director, with each rehearsal causing Lucy to consume more of the tonic. Each time through Lucy becomes more intoxicated and her presentation more exaggerated. (A good old vaudeville standby, this gag.)

The spiral of chaos to comes to its culmination with Lucy, drunk, 'invading' the diegetic set, her behaviour becoming more 'outrageous' until Ricky finally resorts to lifting her bodily and carrying her off the set. The episode ends here, at the point of maximum chaos. There is no resolution and no new equilibrium.

Overall, the defining narrative structure of situation comedy proves to be remarkable resilient across national/cultural boundaries. Genre conventions are not immutable. Indeed, each new addition to the corpus contains the possibility of modifying the taxonomy of conventions. Different sites of production, that is, different cultural loci of sitcoms, will also produce modifications determined by the particular cultural concerns, perceptions and background working on and through the conventional formulae. British sitcoms, as a general rule, tend to cluster towards the outer extremities of the situation comedy galaxy, with a greater emphasis on farcicality and on exaggeration of comic character. (This may well be a legacy of the music hall tradition, but it may also be a reflection of the endemic class structure of Britain whereby 'addressing' class prompts a greater sense of antagonism within sitcoms, this antagonism being simultaneously demonstrated and deflected through comedy.) American sitcoms, as has been noted many times and in many places, tend to include as part of the formula a sense of conveying a moral message (often as a coda, somewhat like Aesop's Fables) and this gives to routine American sitcoms an *appearance* of resolutions to their individual episode-narratives. These apparent resolutions do not establish a new equilibrium; if anything they more firmly confirm the existing and original equilibrium. But, of course, they are not resolutions in the macro-situational sense. If, for example, the disruptions are caused in *Family Ties* by Alex Keaton and his behaviour as a adolescent Reaganite and exemplar of the 1980s 'me generation', then no matter to what extent the moral message of any individual episode demonstrates the 'inappropriateness' of such a philosophy and the behaviour it licences, by the next episode Alex will again be demonstrating the same behaviour. There are innumerable sitcoms of this type which, despite the apparent defence provided by the moral lesson of each episode, are *celebrations* of the breaking of moral and social conventions and codes; that is why the characters keep doing it, and why situation comedy history is a history of consistent representations of the denial *not* the confirming of social conventions and the social order. Situation comedy is, to this extent at least, *carnivalesque*.

Australian sitcoms owe something to both British and American formulae. At the same time, indigenous situation comedy production has been distinguished neither by its quantity nor its quality. Only some fifty series of individual sitcoms have been produced in Australia since the earliest, *Barley Charlie* in 1964.[11] Of these, very few managed more than one season, (usually 13 episodes; series on the ABC are generally shorter, 6 or 7 episodes), some not even broadcasting their full quota before being pulled off in American network fashion. The most popular, in terms of number of episodes and, presumably, with viewers, was *Hey Dad*, which represents in episodes about one-third of all sitcom episodes ever broadcast in Australia. Originality has hardly figured Australian situation comedy and attempts at cultural specificity have been no guarantee of success in production, critical or audience terms. Sitcoms such as *My Names McGooley, What's Yours?* and *Kingswood Country*, for all that the locations and the characters had an authentic flavour of Australian-ness to them were little different in the essentials of their macro-situations from British family/generation based sitcoms such as *Until Death Us Do Part*. And it is hard not to perceive in *Mother and Son* more than a few echoes of *Steptoe and Son*.

Hey Dad reveals this same sense of unoriginality. The macro-situation of a single parent, bringing up children and working from home, is found in various permutations in American sitcoms such as *My Three Sons, Silver Spoons, The*

Courtship of Eddie's Father, The Lucy Show, (single parents), *Growing Pains, The Brady Bunch* (father working from home), *Blossom* (single parent, father working from home), *The Partridge Family* (single parent and the whole family 'working' from home) and so on. The family in *Hey Dad* has been over time more of an 'extended family' inasmuch as various individuals not directly related or not related at all have been included—and the actors who play same members of the family have changed. By and large, however, *Hey Dad* has followed the formula of the family-based situation comedy as defined, modified and seemingly endless produced by American television since the late 1940s.

The spiral of chaos in *Hey Dad* is, routinely, narratively *doubled.* There are two spirals of chaos in each episode. One inevitably involves Betty, the bimbo employee. The other is related to the actions of one (or more) of the children. Whereas in sitcoms from other places, and indeed with most sitcoms from Australia, the actions and events which make up and confirm the spiral of chaos are represented visual and dramatically; in *Hey Dad* they are, routinely, *reported.* That is, the physical, slapstick absurdity of Betty's actions are in essence (probably) rather like those of Frank Spencer in *Some Mothers Do Have 'Em,* but Frank's physical disasters are enacted, Betty's are reported on by her or another member of the family. Thus, in one particular episode in which the spiral of chaos is centred around Betty's having to go to defensive driving school in order to learn to drive her motor scooter with due care and attention, the various ways in which this leads to spiralling chaos are 'narrated' by her or by Martin Kelly (the Dad/employer). He describes the event which led up to Betty having to take the course in the first place (Betty avoiding a bus, swerving onto the footpath, sending an old lady catapulting upside-down into a privet hedge). From here on, a greater part of the chaotic events are narrated in the same way, usually by Betty, concluding with her recounting her driving test in which the instructor leapt off the motorbike while it was still being driven. An earlier spiral, which has Ben (the surrogate son) and Betty 'hotting up' Betty's motor scooter in the living room, leads to the bike literally exploding. The explosion, however, takes place outdoors and off-screen, with the event and the immediate consequences being sound-effect explosion, smoke, and the two characters coming inside, made-up with the comic-cliché effects of an explosion (blackened faces, torn clothes, hair sticking up on end) and Betty holding the detached handlebars of the motor scooter.

Nonetheless, the spiral of chaos is still firmly in place. It runs from:

–>Betty asking for time off to go to defensive driving school (*seen*)
–>Martin describing the event that lead to this 'disruption' (*unseen*)
–>Betty complaining that she is embarrassed because of her little scooter

comparing unfavourably with the powerful motorbikes of the others in the class

–>Betty and Ben 'hotting up' Betty's motor scooter (*seen*)

–> the motor scooter blowing up (*unseen*)

–>Betty borrowing Ben's motorcycle (*unseen*)

–>Betty obtaining an 'armoured' motocross racing costume (*seen*)

–> Betty taking her lesson including the instructor leaping off the moving motorcycle (*unseen*).

The spiral 'concludes' at this point, albeit that this last spiral is reported after the event.

The narrative doubling is present via a 'seen' parallel spiral of chaos, a fully 'internal' family one (albeit that a prime causer is a small child who is, presumably a neighbour) concerns problems involving the use of razors. It commences with:

–> Martin complaining his razor is blunt because one of his daughters used it to shave her legs

–> mistaken identity of which daughter

–> revelation the accused daughter has in fact used Ben's razor, when he appears with similarly damaged face

–> Arthur (prepubescent boy from next door) prevails on Ben to show him how to shave

–> Martin buys different coloured disposal razors for whole family

–>both daughters complain that their razors are now blunt and reveal nicked legs

–> Arthur confesses he has been 'practising' with their razors, on the toilet brush.

In this second spiral, most events are seen save that of the actual shaving in all instances (no slapstick gags here) and Arthur 'shaving' the toilet brush. This last is kept 'secret' for purposes of the success of the gag, and is another 'narrated' gag at the end. But again, the spiral reaches its maximum point and the narrative stops. There is no resolution beyond revelation (of the cause).

The two spirals of chaos have no narrative connection to each other, they do not intersect, complement or complicate each other, and other than sharing some *dramatis personae*, might as easily belong in two distinct episodes of the series. Indeed, it is difficult not to feel that had both been 'expanded' to include dramatic and graphic presentation of the incidents which are simply reported; there is enough material for two episodes.

Acropolis Now (1989-1992), according to Moran is 'the first series on commercial television to deal with an ethnic minority' (1993, 39). Its basis is thus in an alternative normality to that of previous Australian sitcoms. In short, it accepts the normality of multicultural Australia (appropriate for the late 1980s) rather than the normality of a mythical monocultural Australia. That said, in the situation comedy galaxy, *Hey Dad*, is closer to normality than *Acropolis Now* but the normality of the former is almost cultureless; it is not a specifically Australian normality at all, and without the accents and Betty's references to her origins in rural Walgett, it could as easily take place in suburban USA or even suburban Britain. *Acropolis Now* is dependent, perhaps even over-dependent, upon a set of stereotyped assumptions about ethnic/ Greek-Australian subculture.

Given its emphasis on verbal humour, mainly based in exaggerated accents, puns, malapropisms, and use of apparent Greek idiomatic expressions for comic effect, *Acropolis Now*'s spiral of chaos is sometimes obscured or at least interrupted by set-piece verbal exchanges between the principals. These occasionally take on some of the aspects of reported-but-not-seen comedy as with *Hey Dad*. *Acropolis Now* does additionally on occasion have the doubled narrative structure of *Hey Dad* as well. The episode, 'From Russia with Love' reveals this binary structure but it also brings the two spirals together. One 'buds off' the other and both culminate together.

The episode commences in the status quo macro-situation of the restaurant of the title. The first spiral commences almost immediately but it is almost unnoticed as its effect will not be felt for some time.

Nemo needs money so he can take a 'spiritual journey' to Graceland –> (ellipsis)

The main spiral commences with:

Alfredo mentioning Liz is picking up a Russian exchange student from the airport
–>Jim assumes the Russian is a spy
–>Liz arrives with Yuri, and Jim, Nemo and Alfredo act as if he is a spy but they pretend not to know it
–>Jim dresses and acts like James Bond
–>In discussing what Australia has to offer, Greek 'plate smashing' is mentioned

The first spiral is now reactivated:

–>Nemo decides to start a 'Dial-a-Plate' delivery service for Greek restaurants

The main spiral continues:

–>Yuri wants to meet a 'typical Australian woman'

–>Jim sets up a tape recorder to eavesdrop on Yuri

–>Jim convinces his cousin Effie to wear a blonde wig and pretend to be
a typical Australian woman

–>Jim listens while Effie attempts to find out about Yuri

–>Yuri enthuses over blondes and denigrates Mediterranean women

–>Effie abuses Yuri and, taking off her wig, storms out

First spiral returns:

–>Nemo discovers the tape recorder and assumes it has been planted by a
rival Greek businessman

–>Nemo calls the rival to ask for a delivery at midnight

The two spirals converge:

–>Jim overhears the call and assumes it is Yuri arranging an espionage
meeting

–>Nemo and then Jim and Alfredo arrive, disguised, at the restaurant at
midnight

–>a cross-purposes 'negotiation' takes place

–>the three reveal themselves

–>Yuri does arrive

–>a fight starts

–>Liz arrives

–>a remarkable ellipsis, and all drink vodka together and commence to
dance 'like' Elvis.

There is no closure to either spiral. Nemo's 'Dial-a-Plate' business is just forgotten (as too, presumably, is his urgent need to travel to America to see Elvis). There is no resolution to the Yuri-the-spy spiral inasmuch as it is never explained to Jim that Yuri is not a spy. At the point of maximum chaos, with Jim, Nemo and Alfredo locked together, thinking they are 'capturing' Yuri, with Yuri looking on and Liz fresh from calling the police (who never arrive), there is an ellipsis. If any 'resolution' has taken place, it has been in the ellipsed period. Closure takes the form of bacchanalian celebration. It is not even a restoration of the status quo as Jim, Nemo and Alfredo are still wearing their disguises and Yuri (who will not appear in the series again) is still there. This 'coda' is superfluous and the episode logically concludes at the point in which Liz appears. Although Yuri claims to have learnt (to smash plates, to appreciate Ethnic-Australian women— although when he did this is hard to know, especially since Liz is blonde—and to revere the King, Elvis) there is no suggestion that the regular characters have leant anything. *Acropolis Now* is not concerned with reconfirming or reinstating social norms and codes of behaviour. It is a celebration of transgression. Once Jim has decided on no evidence whatsoever that Yuri is a Russian spy, once Nemo decides to overcome his financial problems with a take-away plate service, lunacy takes over, the chaos spirals. In each of these given examples, chaos has commenced from a trigger-point within the macro-situation and

212

has spiralled out of control as the micro-situation develops to simply conclude at a point of maximum chaos (maximum being defined by the maximum the amount of television time available allows rather than in some relative or abstract sense.)

Far from being a genre conventionally, historically, and routinely one of containment, situation comedy is a genre of transgression. The transgressors and the sites of transgression are far from limited. Family and home may statistically dominate but men, women and children are, at different times, in different places, within different sitcoms, all transgressors. And a huge range of occupations—from insurance salesmen to hotel owners, from restaurateurs to architects, from civil servants to convicted criminals—all provide transgressors. Transgressing social codes, gender conventions, generational roles, etiquette, and even the law, are endemic in situation comedy—and it is confirmed rather than denied, resolved or deflected by the truncated narrative and the resolute avoidance of resolution and closure.

NOTES

1. Throughout this essay, I shall distinguish the genre from the individual manifestations by referring to the genre as 'situation comedy' and individual programs or series as 'sitcoms'. The same rule applies to 'soap opera' (which is the genre) and 'soaps' (which are the individual examples).

2. Staying within the English-speaking world, British situation comedy is reliably considered to have begun with *Hancock's Half-Hour* in 1956 (Goddard 1991), and Australian situation comedy with *Barley Charley* in 1964. Soap opera production in these two countries shows similar starting dates. Of course, television broadcasting did not start at all in Australia until 1956.

3. The term itself seems to have come into use in the late 1930s (Allen 1985).

4. This simplified narrative linear chain does not mean that soap opera cannot or does not alter the order of the items in the chain (as may any narrative). However, flashbacks or flash forwards or other disruptions to the temporal order are rare in soap opera, although time may well be extended or truncated, especially the former in American daytime soap opera.

5. There are exceptions to this general rule. Sitcoms which have been based in families with children have, if they run long enough, had to perforce deal with the obvious physical and mental maturing of the actors who play the children. This sometimes gives a spurious sense of a macro-narrative. It is also arguable that long-running sitcoms tend to become in many ways like soaps, both in terms of losing some of their comic emphases in favour of sentimentality, and through characters

developing personalities that have histories and an awareness of those histories. It is highly likely that a loyal audience for such a sitcom, as for soaps, 'constructs' its own history.

6. Sometimes, when sitcoms spin-off sequels, there may seem to be a spurious sense of 'growth' as with some of the later manifestations of Alf and Archy, but more likely the spin-offs and sequels endeavour to reproduce the same characters only more so, for example, George and Mildred Roper as they move from *Man About the House* to *George and Mildred*.

7. By this metaphor, some programs which are called, uncritically, sitcoms may be better understood as comets whose paths randomly intersect with the more orderly solar system of 'real' sitcoms. I am thinking, for example, of the various *Black Adder* series.

8. See, for example, David Marc, 1989, Gerard Jones, 1992.

9. These exceptions are often within sitcom series which are more clearly character based than situation based. For example, *Hancock's Half-Hour*, particularly as the series continued over a number of years constructed its micro-narratives around the eponymous 'hero' whose characteristics remained the same but whose situation (physical, social) changed as the micro-narratives demanded. True character-based sitcoms are rare, at least to the extent that the characters are not also simultaneously *actants* within a fixed macro-situation.

10. It is far from clear how this 'received wisdom' functions in relation to motion pictures not made for television or in relation to television programs made originally for non-commercial broadcasters wherein commercial breaks are usually imposed according to some logic (e.g., that of the clock) other than locating or waiting for a 'natural' climactic moment at which to insert the commercial break.

11. I am indebted to Albert Moran (1993) *Moran's Guide to Australian TV Series* for providing much otherwise difficult to locate information on the many short-lived and soon forgotten sitcom series.

REFERENCES

Allen, Robert C. 1985. *Speaking of Soap Operas*. Chapel Hill, NC: University of North Carolina.

Brooks, Tim & Marsh, Earle. 1988. *The Complete Directory of Prime Time Network TV Shows*. New York: Ballantine.

Goddard, Peter. 1991. ''Hancock's Half-Hour': A Watershed in British Situation Comedy', in John Corner, ed, *Popular Television in Britain*. Studies in Cultural History. London: British Film Institute. 75-87.

Lovell, Terry. 1982. 'A Genre of Social Disruption?', in Jim Cook, ed, *Television Sitcom*. BFI Dossier 17. London: British Film Institute. 19-31.

Marc, David. 1989. *Comic Visions: Television Comedy and American Culture*. Boston: Unwin Hyman.

Moran, Albert. 1993. *Moran's Guide to Australian TV Series*. Sydney: Australian Film Television & Radio School.

AMERICAN PATRIARCHY

FATHERS, SONS AND BROTHERS: PATRIARCHY AND GUILT IN 1980S AMERICAN CINEMA.

AN AMERICAN OBSESSION

From *Kramer vs. Kramer* (1979) to *Indiana Jones and the Last Crusade* (1989) American motion pictures in the 1980s have demonstrated a virtual obsession with father-son relations. So much so that we have been able to identify over 170 titles that could be said to make up a 'Father/Son' cycle. This obsession continues into the 1990s through films as diverse as *Boyz 'N the Hood* and *My Heroes Have Always Been Cowboys*. This single theme has provided a number of different narrative structures and a number of subthemes through which multifarious aspects of this apparently vital cultural concern are explored. Somewhat surprisingly, practically all these variations of narrative structure can be discerned initially in just five motion pictures, all of which were released about the same time—in 1979 and 1980—and seemingly coincidentally.

These motion pictures were *Kramer vs. Kramer* (1979), *Ordinary People* (1980), *The Great Santini* (1979), *Tribute* (1980) and *Breaking Away* (1979). Three of these films garnered between them fifteen Academy Award nominations and won ten Oscars.[1] The different narratives of each of these films all explore changes in and challenges to the shifting perceptions of masculinity and patriarchy in American culture, changes and challenges which were to become more pronounced during the 1980s.

What makes these films stand out in retrospect is that throughout the 1980s more and more films were made which directly or indirectly addressed this theme, used a father-son relationship as the central narrative framework or provided motivation for other narratives by reference to some aspect of such a relationship. The significant number of such films, together with the particular ways in which this theme has been explored leads us to hypothesize that there is some, possibly deep rooted, contemporary cultural perception being addressed or responded to through these films.

There are two broad, linked notions that underpin the reiteration of this theme. They are related to the changing role and perception of, first, patriarchy (specifically growing uncertainties about the social place and function of 'the father'), and, second, masculinity itself. This latter notion is especially complicated by the growing social awareness of the acceptability, even the need, for the 'sensitive male,' which then dovetails into the growing cultural acceptance of expressions of male-to-male emotions.

STRUCTURES OF GUILT

Further complexity to the problematic of father-son relations that these films variously address is provided by other contemporary social and cultural concerns that find simultaneous articulation through the same narrative structures. Of particular relevance here is an inchoate undercurrent of guilt; a feeling that a gulf exists between the two generations (represented by this fundamental structural opposition, father/son) which is, in turn, the result of some unspecified wrong committed by either or both. This subtheme of guilt finds its expression not through examinations of this guilt itself (which remains vague) but by providing narrative variations on the two broadly based themes we have just delineated: patriarchy and masculinity.

In one particular category of films within the group we have identified, this unclear notion of guilt finds specific narrative shape. This small but significant number of films explores the general theme of father-son relations through narratives structured around two distinct but parallel and complementary relations. That is, these narratives postulate a central relationship between the son (who is the protagonist of the narrative) and his father as being determined by a second, similar relationship: that of the father to his other son, the protagonist's brother. In nearly all cases the brother is dead or dies in the course of the narrative.[2] The surviving son assumes, or is made to assume, a burden of guilt irrespective of whether or not he is responsible for his brother's death. This guilt then functions as the barrier that blocks his efforts to reach out to his father. *Ordinary People* is both the prototype and the most profound example of this narrative and thematic structure at work. It is also found in *The Stone Boy* (1984), *Tank* (1984), *Stand By Me* (1986), *Dakota* (1988), *Rain Man* (1988), *Split Decisions* (1988), *Gleaming the Cube* (1989), *The Wizard* (1989), and *The Rookie* (1990).

The narratives of these films are predicated upon a conflict between the father and the son, or an impediment to the 'proper' degree of attachment between them, which in turn originates in or is magnified by the death of the brother. In a notable number of these narratives, the brother is the elder son: *Gleaming the Cube* (an adopted brother), *Ordinary People*, *Rain Man*, *Split Decision*, *Stand By Me*, *The Stone Boy*, *Tank*, *Dakota* and *The Wizard* are the exceptions.

Irrespective of whether he rationally can be held in any way accountable for the death of his brother, there is the equally important narrative emphasis that the surviving son is, in any case, less worthy, less *lovable*. This question of whether the surviving son *deserves* the love of his father, which he so desperately craves, transcends any guilt: the various narratives do not suggest that the surviving son connived in his brother's death from sibling jealousy.

219

Indeed, the younger brother in all instances adored the older brother as much if not more than the father did. In some cases, the death of the brother serves as the narrative motivation for the surviving son to try harder to earn his father's approbation and love. In several of the narratives, the son has suppressed his desire for the father's approval as a consequence of the clearly perceived greater love the father had for the older brother.

I deliberately choose not to utilize any notion of Oedipal conflict as shorthand for the concept of a 'natural' conflictual relationship between a father and his son. Because of psychoanalysis, especially the use feminist criticism has made of Freudian/Lacanian psychoanalysis, the Oedipal complex/conflict/

crisis has come to bear a plethora of meanings which, while usually related in some way to notions of patriarchy (the Law of the Father, the castrating father, etc.), seem to have little to do with any discussion of 'authentic' father-son relations. Nonetheless, the Myth of Oedipus (if not the over-worked Freudian metaphor) does provide a useful analogy, especially when it is noted that it is Laius, the father, who wishes his infant son Oedipus dead, and it is Laius who initiates the fight that leads to his death at Oedipus's hands. Nothing Oedipus does causes his father's 'hatred.'[3] There are elements of what then ought to be called the Laius 'complex' in some of these narratives, particularly *Stand By Me* which also does not resolve itself with any sense of reconciliation with the father (unlike most of the others). Although in several films, the death of the brother provides the father with a reason to hate the surviving son (whether that reason is rational) there is still the underlying idea that fathers can and do hate their sons *as a matter of course*; and that as a corollary, it is sons who are required, through their actions, to reverse this 'natural' condition. Fathers in these narratives are nearly always 'unreasonable' creatures; they carry with them something of the arbitrariness of the gods whose actions may be explicable but not necessarily rational.

Thus sons are made to feel guilty in *Stand By Me* and *Ordinary People*, and are made to bear a greater burden of guilt than is truly fair in *Dakota* and *The Stone Boy*. In *Gleaming the Cube* and to a lesser extent in *Tank*, the surviving son is not so much implicated in the death of his brother, as guilty of not measuring up to the qualities that allow a father to love his sons (whatever these may be, usually socially valuable qualities like academic excellence and acceptable personal appearance).

It is important to note, however, that fathers are far from avoiding culpability in these narratives. Sometimes they do have some responsibility by contributing indirectly to the death of the brother, and this may then manifest itself in hostility toward the surviving son. But occasionally the fathers are blind to the needs of the surviving son, unaware that the son's conspicuous difference from his brother may be deliberate, not as a sign of rejection of the father but as an appeal for love and acceptance on his own, personal terms. Fathers, then, often represent a particular set of social norms that may get in the way of a true relationship between a father and his son. The films vary by claiming either that these norms must be overridden or ignored in order for the (far more important) relationship between father and son to flourish, or that the son must move more towards the social mainstream in order to meet his father at least halfway. *Gleaming the Cube* seems to offer this latter solution, but it is ambivalent as to the extent to which it is requires the son sacrifice the freedom of his skateboarding sub-cultural lifestyle in order to achieve full integration with his father.[4]

The burden of guilt that each son carries in the narratives of these 'brother films' is not actually the guilt of fratricide. Only Arnold in *The Stone Boy* can be said to have contributed directly to the death of his brother in a shooting accident. As far as can be ascertained, the most that can be said of several of the others (Conrad in *Ordinary People*, David in *The Rookie*, Dakota in *Dakota*) is perhaps that they did not do enough to prevent the death of their respective brothers. Just how they might have acted to save their brothers is unclear: the incidents routinely are told only in scrambled flashback or dream sequences. Through these disjointed recapitulations (offered as suppressed memories or nightmares), we can glean some idea of just why the surviving sons may, in each case, consider themselves to some extent responsible. But all this is simply supplying a logic which, while inherent in the actions (as we can discern them) in these various films, is not the logic advanced by the films themselves.

THE GUILT OF INADEQUACY

The narratives are shaped by the guilt which is placed upon or felt by their different protagonists. If this guilt cannot be said (by external observation) to be the guilt of fratricide (or something associated with it: negligence, culpability), then what is it? It is actually the guilt of inadequacy. These sons carry the burden of being, or believing themselves to be, inadequate sons, of not measuring up to their respective father's requirements. Mingled with this is the feeling, often confirmed by their fathers' actions and attitudes, that the dead brother was more beloved because he was closer to what the father desired in and of a son. The clearest sustained example of this is *Stand By Me* but it surfaces in nearly all these films.

This guilt of inadequacy is particularly noticeable in *Gleaming the Cube*. It cannot be argued that Brian, the surviving son, is guilty, by commission or omission of the death of his brother, or even implicated in it. But Brian, nonetheless, does feel guilty: as he says at one point, 'I can't help feeling that I failed Vinhe.' And it is this that motivates Brian to carry out his own investigation of Vinhe's death after his parents and the police have all been satisfied that Vinhe's death was suicide. This is, of course, a device of the narrative, a motivation for Brian's actions and the plot which follows. But it is still interesting that it is the consequences of Vinhe's death, coupled with the intrafamily relationships prior to this, that provide the motivation for the plot. In other words, while the film is not 'about' father-son relationships (and thus is not especially concerned to explore them), it clearly bases much of its context and motivations within them. Thus, a father-son relationship becomes a powerful subtext within a formula film which does not necessarily have to contain such a subtext.

In a brief moment from near the end of *Stand By Me* several important subthemes of the Father/Son cycle of films are encapsulated. Here, just after the four boys who are the central characters of the narrative locate a body they have set out to find, Gordie, the protagonist (and narrator), breaks down and is consoled by Chris, his best friend. The sight of a corpse (of a boy about their own age) is the catalyst that causes Gordie's barely coherent emotional declaration that his father hates him and wishes it was he and not his brother who had died—a idea that Gordie has internalized, providing the burden of guilt. Chris, for all the abuse he suffers from his own father, will not accept the notion that fathers can hate their sons. He insists that Gordie's father does not hate him, only that he does not know him.

These subthemes are, first, the idea of guilt, undeserved and often self-generated, over the death of a beloved brother which in turn is an impediment to the true relationship between the son and his father.[5] Second, the idea, in a more general way, that relationships between fathers and sons must be, or ought to be loving ones, and that without this there are enormous emotional consequences for the son. (The idea that Gordie's father hates him prompts the very tears Gordie claimed he did not shed at Denny's funeral.) And third, and unexpectedly in this film but a frequent theme in many others, that the real impediment between fathers and sons is often a lack of knowledge of each other, of each other's true personalities, feelings and qualities.

ABSENCE OF ATONEMENT

The narratives of these films generally require some form of expiation by the sons of the guilt, not of fratricide, but of not being the son their father expects. They are less certain, however, about arriving at a sense of complete atonement with the father. To take *Dakota* as an example, the narrative stops short of Dakota actually accomplishing atonement with his father. The film concludes with him setting out after his father and, by implication at least, offers the likelihood of reconciliation and forgiveness. In so doing, *Dakota* rehearses the constant theme of father-son films: sons must seek atonement with fathers.[6]

Although it may be possible from film to film to impute varying degrees of blame on fathers for creating barriers between themselves and their sons, in most cases such blame is the result of the fathers' inability to 'forgive' their sons. This inability to forgive is rather biblical in nature because it is not so much that fathers cannot or will not ever forgive their erring sons (except in rare instances), but that the sons have to *earn* that forgiveness. The point is made boldly within most of these narratives. In *Dakota*, following an act that saves rather than costs a life (acting *responsibly* in other words), Dakota leaves to seek his father only after asserting that 'for the first time I really felt that I could be forgiven, and maybe forgive myself.' A similar transformation takes place in *Gleaming the Cube* where Brian must change himself (appearance, attitude) at least to the point of providing external evidence that he conforms to his father's image of what a son should be. In *The Stone Boy*—far more biblical in its implications—Arnold must come to the realization of his guilt, suffer for it through separation from his father, and then seek his father's forgiveness. (Dakota too suffers a form of exile from his father, and during that exile he learns how to be a responsible son.)

There are, of course, ogre-fathers in some of these narratives; fathers who cannot or will not forgive their sons. But as the God of the Old Testament was still considered a 'Loving God' even though capable of demanding, for instance, that Abraham sacrifice his son Isaac, so most of these fathers are still considered to be Loving Fathers even though capable of driving their sons away from them (which is taken for granted as being a terrible punishment). Biblically god-like fathers such as this are found most obviously in *The Stone Boy* and *Rain Man*, but there is something of this quality to the father in *Dakota* and *Stand By Me*.

This analysis so far suggests that these 'brother films' (and by implication many others within our designated broader category Father/Son films) are all examinations and, in most cases, affirmations of patriarchy, of in fact that very 'Law of the Father' with which I expressed some uneasiness earlier. It is difficult to deny that many of these films invite this very interpretation. At the same time, in apparent contradiction, it must not be overlooked that many of these films are also concerned with demonstrating the acceptability of expressions of masculine emotionality. Arguably the very essence of *Ordinary People*, the whole thrust of its trajectory, is towards its final few seconds when father and son are, at last, able to say directly that they love each other and to embrace. Scenes such as this, admittedly, are more prevalent in films other than those with the theme of fraternal guilt but these brother films do provide other images of male *sensitivity*. (Especially noticeable in this regard is the tenderness and intimacy displayed between the two main male characters of *Stand By Me*.)

A UBIQUITOUS THEME

The Rookie, a late addition to this cycle, eloquently makes for us an argument we have not so far emphasized: that many Hollywood films of this period while about something—anything—else, take as unproblematically relevant in providing either character motivation or a minor subplot (or, of course, both) a conflict between a father and son. *The Rookie* is simply another cop-buddy formula film, and like most films of its type, is far more concerned with (1) a maximum of action via car chases, destruction of property, and gunfights; and (2) with describing a gradually developing rapport between two, initially antagonistic policemen. It is precisely because *The Rookie* is just one example of a relatively popular formula film that the inclusion of a subplot around a conflict between a father and son is so interesting. This inclusion emphasizes the degree to which this concern is embedded in contemporary American culture. *The Rookie* takes it for granted that this particular conflict will find a ready acceptance, a cultural point of contact and familiarity (which does not arise from its own formula). One that will not need to be expanded or necessarily explained within the diegesis.

The Rookie has an added relevance here because it also uses, in much the same way, the very theme we have been discussing, guilt over the death of a brother. It takes for granted that the audience will understand at some level the implications for one of the protagonists that, as a child, he was involved in the accidental death of his brother. In addition and more importantly, that he will carry a burden of guilt as a consequence, which has effected and continues to affect his relationship with his father. This additional subtheme is to some degree narratively unnecessary. It could have been enough, surely, that a source of conflict between son and father was simply along the lines of the son's rebellion against both his father and what his father's wealth represents (a common enough narrative motivation in other films).[7]

MANIFESTATIONS OF GUILT

This then raises the question which we are exploring: why should the idea of relations between fathers and sons be so clearly of such concern to contemporary America that it occurs as a theme both in films which explicitly construct their narratives around it and those which are, much more clearly, 'about' something other than this theme. It also raises a corollary pertinent to this paper: why should a number of films seem to willing to dwell, to greater or lesser extent, on the narrative device of the death of a sibling and its seemingly inevitable consequence of guilt? It is tempting to take these narratives literally; as manifestations of a submerged guilt within American culture, guilt over the failure of one part of society towards another one--a failure to prevent death, or injury, or to render vital assistance. Even so, it is less a sense of guilt over failure in a direct physical sense than of social integration at some level.

It seems, then, that this may well be a metaphoric delineation of that complicated, tangled guilt which American culture has taken on over Vietnam. Yet this particular explanation can only be valid if it is assumed that the guilt felt by the sons is legitimate. But these films nearly always postulate that it is not. The question of guilt thus comes to be not guilt over what was done (i.e., old men sending young men to wage war and find death in an unjust cause) but a guilt over the fact that those who actually were 'blameless' were held to be culpable. These films suggest an apparently irreconcilable contradiction that *is*, nonetheless, reconciled through their metaphoric narratives. The younger generation--who stand for the Vietnam generation in this construction--is made to feel guilty for that which was not, directly, of its own doing. Thus, the emphasis in these films on the sons adopting a burden of guilt not legitimately (or wholly) theirs. This theme is worked through and a sort of social catharsis achieved. At the same time the power of the father is re-established rather than challenged (as rationally should follow the lifting of the guilt from those to whom it does not belong). It does not matter whether the guilt is based in any empirical reality, rather that the guilt is culturally real; it is 'believed' rather than 'articulated', except through the mythic function of popular culture.

There may be other reasons why American culture contains an unarticulated undercurrent of guilt (which can only find partial expression through the metaphors of popular culture). For instance, the obvious social differences and equalities which exist and are seemingly endemic in a society and a culture ideologically and mythologically committed to a notion of 'freedom and equality for all.' Or, in a less metaphoric sense, the breakdown of the family as exemplified by the (alleged) loss of role/function of the father. Here we move, however, rather deeply into murky grounds of conjecture. The metaphorical nature of the way in which popular culture so often addresses matters of cultural concern makes positive interpretation of those concerns difficult. And it is doubly difficult when instances of these concerns appear briefly in films which have no seeming interest in exploring them. But it is here, perhaps, that any notion of popular culture texts 'reflecting' the culture which gives them life has some validity. To extend the argument by analogy, it is impossible to conceive that a mirror chooses what it reflects; and so it may well be argued that films such as *The Rookie* do not 'choose' those aspects of the contemporary cultural milieu which are reflected within them and which are simultaneously not fundamentally germane to their narrative structures or formulaic codes. The reason for the character David Ackerman in the film *The Rookie* being guilt-ridden over the childhood death of his brother may not be—clearly is not—'accidental': the makers chose to put this in. But the reason why this devise, this motivation, this 'history', as opposed to any other or none at all, was included may well be located within the cultural unconscious.

To use another analogy then, the presence of an iceberg is made manifest by that small percentage of it that is visible above the surface of the water; it may be safely concluded that there is much more of it below the surface and invisible. Thus the notions of guilt are what are seen above the surface of these movies; the causes and the extent of that cultural 'guilt' remain hidden but capable of being estimated by what is discernible. Both analogies sustain many of the analyses which inform this discussion, and the evidence for our position and our methodology, the iceberg in this instance, is *The Rookie*. There is no shortage of icebergs in the ocean of American motion pictures of the 1980s. For the most part we are more interested in those films which are, to extend the metaphor, more like *terra firma*, islands in the ocean which can be landed on and explored. From time to time, however, we need to draw attention to the icebergs.

NOTES

1. *Ordinary People* and *Kramer vs. Kramer* won Best Picture Academy Awards; *Kramer vs. Kramer* took five Oscars in all, and *Ordinary People* four. *Breaking Away* received a Best Screenplay Oscar.

2. The exceptions, *Rain Man* (1988) and *The Wizard* (1989) provide interesting variations that support our analyses.

3. The other important aspect of the myth, the son's desire for his mother, is totally absent from the films we discuss here. Indeed, within the broad category of Father/ Son films as a whole, it is noticeable that on many occasions fathers and sons unite against the mother, who is viewed as an impediment to the proper father-son relationship. (The prototype is *Ordinary People*.)

4. The question of the importance of social norms arises in other Father/Son films which do not have the narrative framework of fraternal guilt. In *Distant Thunder* (1988), for example, the question is whether the father can be brought back into 'normal' society through the love of his son.

5. In this particular instance, the film strongly suggests no affection from the father, even lesser affection, existed before the brother's death. Even so, the son, Gordie, has taken on the burden of guilt over the failure for there to be a loving relationship between his father and himself.

6. *Stand By Me*, however, shows no such seeking after atonement but does suggest it in another way: that the grown-up Gordie has a loving relationship with his own son.
7. It should be noted that the film is rather confused in most story aspects other than the most formulaic bits or those bits more concerned with action than with plot.

The writing of this article was greatly aided by research by and advice from Thomas P. McManus (who located and identified all of the 170-plus titles made during the period in question). This assistance was invaluable and is greatly appreciated.

DYING FATHERS

The five American films discussed in this essay are all concerned with examining the ways in which the barriers between men, between fathers and sons specifically, can be broken down. Each argues for reconciliation between fathers and sons, although none make a case for the need for propitiation and atonement with the obviousness of the films analyzed in my essay, 'Fathers, Brothers & Sons'. With one exception the narrative of these films postulate a father who is dying, who in fact learns he is dying at some point in the narrative. Three of the fathers do indeed die within the narrative. Only one father is seriously but not terminally ill. The narratives do not, however, use the fathers' illness to set the scene for the reconciliations that follow, at least not initially. But the illness does provide a strong, even irresistible incentive for the reconciliation to take place.

In two of these films—*Dad* (1989, Gary David Goldberg) and *Family Business* (1989, Sidney Lumet)—the father is also a grandfather and so within these films the relationship between fathers and sons is complicated by being doubled. Actually, the relationship between *men* is trebled: (grand)father and son, father and (grand)son, grandfather and grandson. This allows these films to offer three conflicting definitions or styles of masculinity, three types of man. The conflicts which have to be resolved in these various narratives are, as is nearly always the case within this cycle of films, not between male and female, masculinity and femininity, but between different conceptions of masculinity, between the old, traditional masculinity and the new, 'developing' definition. Here again, popular culture serves the function of alerting those to whom and of whom it speaks to changes taking place within the social and cultural structure. And as always, the messages it 'sends' are not unambiguous. Nevertheless, these five films present a relatively harmonious voice in *their* particular view of father/son relationships.

The clearest task which most of these films have set out to accomplish is to engage with changing notions, ideologies and discourses of masculinity. Not always has this been with the intention of celebrating these changes but surprisingly often films *do* note 'the new man' with approval, often concerning themselves with chronicling in some way his development or transformation (for example, both Jake and John in *Dad* in different ways exemplify this) in ways which are supportive. The ever-present question of whether films (and other popular culture texts) *present* or *represent* viable cultural images and frames of reference is pertinent here. It is possible to argue that some films within this category are indeed sufficiently ahead of 'trends' to be presenting a set of images of masculinity that are new. It remains central to our thesis that this may well be unconscious on the part of the film makers in most situations, is drawn, in other words, from the cultural unconsciousness. That is, the discourse of masculinity may encompass the structural changes we note but they are more likely to be hidden—at least at first—and film makers 'pick up' on them (as do members of the cultural at large) often without realizing quite why and where these notions come from. It is for this reason, of course, much of what we argue is present in these films remains sub-textual. But there are times when it becomes more openly manifest in the text, indeed *is* the text. This aspect can be seen in *Ordinary People* (1980, Robert Redford) where the father/son relationship and the 'load' of the definition of masculinity remains largely subtextual (until the very end); and in *Dad* where the discourse of masculinity is arguably the text, the whole text, and nothing but the text.

The first of these films, the prototype or 'founding' film which 'creates' the category and in a way delimits it is *Tribute* (1980, Bob Clark).

TRIBUTE (1980)

Tribute is a rather confusing film, or more specifically, its narrative is figured by a degree of repetition which slows rather than hastens its narrative development. This may well be because the origin of the story was a theatrical play and thus heavily reliant upon dialogue rather than action. But it may also be because of the early place of *Tribute* in this cycle. The film knows that there are problems with contemporary relations between fathers and sons but it is not quite sure what they are, or how to express them. Even so, it wants to explore father/son relations, and indeed that is what it does. (It is not a film in which the father/son relationship has somehow seeped into the narrative and then taken over as with, for example, *Indiana Jones and the Last Crusade* [1989, Steven Spielberg].) Later films are able to address the concept with greater degrees of clarity, possibly because American culture itself began to form the previously inchoate 'feelings' into more concrete notions as the eighties progressed—and as more films (and other popular culture forms) work on and through it.

The main thrust of *Tribute* is towards the bringing together in a spiritual rather than a physical bond of a father and his son. It provides as a starting point that the father and son are estranged. This is so for two reasons. First, a physical separation because of a previous divorce which has resulted in the son living for the most part with his mother. An important corollary to this is that the film concerns itself with the son moving from the 'world of his mother' to the 'world of his father', a journey not undertaken in any of the later films in this particular category. Second, a psychic separation, manifest in the completely different personalities of father and son. Change, or rather, transformation is the key to *Tribute*'s exploration of this father/son relationship, but change only in order to bring about the dissolution of the barriers between father and son, most especially the psychic barrier. Unlike the other films in this category, however, *Tribute* is not especially concerned with redefining masculinity. This may well be because of its early place in the whole cycle, that concerns with father/son relationships had as yet not crystallized fully into concerns with or over masculinity. Perhaps more accurately the film had not found common ground upon which to explore or interrogate each simultaneously, let alone 'realized' that the two were intimately connected.

In *Tribute*, the father, Scotty Templeton, is the more attractive man. This does not necessarily mean more physically attractive—although the son, Judd, does on several occasions deprecate his own looks (although not by comparison with his father but with John Travolta and Robert Redford). Scotty is an extreme extrovert, a 'people person', as Judd later describes him (without meaning it as a compliment) 'a crowd pleaser'. Scotty is amusing, a public and private clown. More than this, he is a 'real' man to the extent that a real man is, by definition, sexually driven. Within minutes of the narrative beginning, and despite the fact that he is in a hospital, Scotty is flirting with a young woman. He even takes her home with him but does not have sex with her. The point being made is that Scotty is both sexually attractive as a result of his wise-cracking, charming personality, and that he is (to some extent at least) a sexual predator. His masculinity is not in question, except to the point that he did not seduce the girl. The chink in his armor (as his public persona will prove to be) is revealed here. His 'failure' as a man and as a father is his inability to make an emotional commitment. This would not matter, perhaps, except that it applies to his son as much as to other people. Or so it appears from the surface. There is in this an immediate comparison with Abe Polin in *Memories of Me* (1989, Henry Winkler).

Judd is the complete opposite. (Perhaps too much the complete opposite for the film to be satisfactory in the filmic story sense rather than the thematic sense.) He is introvert, repressed, serious and by his own admission, 'not good at making contact'. It is not clear why he is this way—other than for the need to motivate the incompatibility between his father and himself around which most of the narrative is structured. Judd's rigidity is not an alternative form of masculinity; he does not represent an alternative to Scotty (as is often the case between fathers and sons in later films) but represents instead an *under*developed masculinity as opposed to Scotty's *over*developed masculinity. Judd is, in short, a Mamma's Boy, at least to the extent that he fails to manifest the public expressions of masculinity that Scotty represents. Arguably, Judd's 'feminine' side is as equally repressed as his masculine side. That is, he cannot express his true emotions any more easily than Scotty. Both 'hide' their femininity: Scotty through excessive public display; Judd through introversion. It is no accident that their names suggest a 'reversal': Scotty is a name more fitting for a child, Judd for a mature adult.

There are two ways in which the film indicates simultaneously the barriers between Judd and Scotty *and* the manner in which each inadequately reach out to one another. Each uses a 'device' by which he can deny his emotions an expression. Or in fact to *allow a public* expression which at the same time is sufficiently displaced or metaphorical to avoid open commitment to those feelings. Scotty uses a chicken costume, once brought home when Judd was a child. Used when Judd was still a kid, Scotty dons it again to try and break down the barrier largely of his own erecting as a result of Judd learning that the girl he 'picked up' was planted by Scotty. The chicken outfit serves both as a real 'mask' of his emotions and as a metaphor for the way in which Scotty uses his outward, public persona to avoid expressing directly his emotions. His clown persona is literally present in his clown (chicken) costume.

The importance of the chicken outfit is further indicated by the fact that both Scotty and Judd have photographs (taken by Judd) of Scotty in the outfit with Judd (as a child) and Maggie. Photography is the manner in which Judd distances himself from emotional commitment or at least emotional display. The importance of the photographs as both distancing device and conduit is emphasized on several occasions in the film. In the very opening credit sequence, a series of shots of photographs of Judd and/or Scotty is intercut with Scotty leaving to go the hospital and arriving at the same. The two sequences are worth noting:

Sequence one.
1. Photo in dish in darkroom. It is of Scotty and Judd as a small child. This photo is taken out of the dish by a pair of hands and the camera follows it and tilts up to
2. Photo of Scotty in chicken costume with Maggie and Judd. The camera lingers on this photograph. (It is the same photograph we are to see on two more key occasions). The camera pans to
3. Photo of Judd aged 10, clasping a football. The pan continues to
4. Judd (at 15) and Scotty (46), dressed formally and smiling at the camera.

Sequence two
1. Maggie in a formal portrait. Pan to
2. Two photos, both candid shots, of, firstly a quite young Maggie and, secondly, a young Scott with a dog. Pan to

231

3 Scotty, middle-aged, at the piano. This photo is taken down from the line it is clipped to (like all the others) by a pair of hands. A pan reveals Judd holding the photograph. He stares at it intently for a long moment before clipping it back up. The camera moves into close-up on the photograph.

It is important that these photos, taken in the past, are being printed in the present, just before Judd meets his father after a two year absence. Photographs of his father taken by Judd serve to indicate the connection between them, not simply in terms of shared memories of childhood (although that is important) but in terms of emotions which Judd cannot express, for a love for his father than he is perhaps not even prepared to consciously admit—until the point that he actually destroys the chicken-outfit photograph.

This photograph (and the chicken outfit) represents then the degree of love which *does* exist between father and son while at the same time being the measure of their inability to express that love. Thus it is the same photograph which Judd finds by his bedside when he arrives to stay with Scotty. A note on the photograph asks Judd if he remembers this incident. It is clear that he does as this is one of the photographs he has been developing prior to arriving in New York. He stares at it for some time, the length of time being because of the memories or emotions it arouses rather than unfamiliarity with the subject of the photograph. Ironically, a few moments before Scotty has expressed his regret that he will not be able to leave Judd any childhood memories. It is while looking at the photograph that Judd's mother comes into to ask him to stay longer than he intends. She knows that Scotty is dying but she does not mention this. She rationalizes her request by suggesting Judd and Scotty could 'make a fresh start'. Judd glances back at the photograph before agreeing to stay. While this scene indicates the power his mother still exercises over him (a power she seems quite determined to relinquish), it also implies that the photograph/chicken outfit is recognized as the symbolic attempt to express feelings between father and son.

This particular photograph and what it symbolically represents resurfaces with narrative force following the scene in which Judd returns to Scotty's apartment after leaving upon discovering Scotty has just had sex with his mother. Judd demands to be let into Scotty's emotional life, a request Scotty refuses, and Judd subsequently smashes the chicken-outfit photograph. This action serves to pinpoint the moment when Judd ceases to be the child who Scotty has insisted he remain and which Judd himself has adopted or retained (thus the ease which he reverts to a pre-oedipal condition on discovering his mother at Scotty's apartment). Judd becomes more truly Scotty's son rather than his male-child at that point and, shortly thereafter, successfully insists that Scotty go to hospital for treatment.

Photographs remain, however, the main way in which Judd attempts to get close to his father. Following Scotty's successful medical treatment, Judd arranges a testimonial for Scotty. (It is not entirely clear as to why Judd is still disturbed by the fact that Scotty is only able to operate behind the mask of the public crowd-pleaser. In strictly narrative structural terms, this testimonial matches the one Scotty has arranged much earlier for a favorite call-girl.) Judd intends to include projected photographs of Scotty taken by himself. Here, at least, he recognizes what the narrative has recognized in the credit sequence (and which Judd may well have 'known' even then), that as he puts it, 'I had this idea. That by objectively studying the photographs I took of him, I'd be able to bring him into focus.' This is however a remnant of Judd's child-persona which he must discard in order to get close enough for Scotty to be 'in focus' and even closer than that, to actually physically touch rather than simply visually 'touch' him—the kiss on the lips. It is significant then that these photographs are not shown during the testimonial sequence. If, as Judd claims, his father is a 'master of disguise' then photographs will not penetrate that disguise. Ultimately he recognizes this, and finally Scotty 'bares' himself to Judd, dispensing with the chicken suit.

There is something about the way in which *Tribute* constructs its characters and the framework of the narrative into which it places them that invites (despite my misgivings) psychoanalytical explanations. Other films in this category seem less easily interpreted in this way. Thus, there is a strong sense that part of the initial conflict, or part of the initial trajectory of Judd's 'journey' is concerned with his move away from his mother and to his father, to become the object of his father's love. There is not, however, the concomitant need for Judd to replace his mother in his father's affections: Scotty has been divorced from Judd's mother for quite a number of years. Nonetheless, this desire to be the center of and the focus of his father's love seems to be the only explanation for the hysterical way in which Judd reacts when he discovers his father and mother sleeping together. It is less that his mother has betrayed him than that his father has. The situation which might have been a classical Oedipal situation—competition with the father for the mother—does not develop that way. Judd's anger seems to be because his father has 'betrayed' him although it is not clear quite how. Because Scotty has been physically intimate with someone else? Or because Scotty has been sexually intimate with his mother? It remains that Judd expresses little or no anger toward his mother.

Whatever has occurred, it has the effect of causing Judd to revert to a more childlike state. The stuttering he had as a child returns, an affliction which, it is implied, was the consequence of the overpowering effects of Scotty as a father. An 'Oedipal' reading is possible but it does not fit easily with the rest of the narrative. Judd does not seem particularly concerned with trying to retain possession of his mother. Arguably, he already possesses her in the sense that Scotty and she divorced when he was eight (he is twenty-three at the time of the story). She is absent from the narrative from this until the final sequence. His stepfather does not appear in the narrative and is referred to twice in ways which establish nothing about his relationship with Judd. If anything, the film encourages us to see Judd as being possessed by his mother and, importantly, that it is she who is anxious to push him in the direction of his father. The mise-en-scene places the mother literally above both men throughout, in an implied position of control even omnipotence. She has the 'godlike' position of looking down upon and perhaps even directing the actions of these mortals. The most obvious explanation of this scene is that it exists as a further narrative hurdle designed to delay the final reconciliation between father and son. It allows one further difference between father and son to be brought out into the opened, aired, and ultimately, to be overcome.

Despite packing his bags and storming out, Judd does return to Scotty's apartment after this incident. The magnetic pull of the Father is too strong. And Judd *is* seeking the Father not his father. His motive for returning is, so he claims, to see if there is 'anything about the son-of-a-bitch I can admire'. Judd is not prepared to permit his father to fail as a Father for all his shortcomings as a man.

The fact of Scotty's terminal illness is only partly a contributing factor in Judd's decision to return. It adds urgency to the need to learn whether or not he can admire his father because it reduces the amount of time which he has to come to terms with Scotty. It also provides a way for Judd to demonstrate to Scotty and to himself that his father is important to him inasmuch as Scotty initially refuses to undergo the treatment that may cause his symptoms to go into remission. Scotty, however, refuses Judd's requests that he take the medical treatments. By this time, Scotty has given up attempting to come to an understanding of his son. He has failed with Judd (to this point) because he has been attempting to mould Judd into his own image (or facsimile at least). He tells Judd that if he (Scotty) is not the father Judd always wanted then, equally, Judd is not the son he wanted either. Why then does Scotty change his mind and undergo the long and painful treatment? The change of heart is, in fact, accomplished by Judd demanding he stay alive because he 'is not ready to cry over you yet'. Judd, then, is not yet sufficiently in touch with his feminine side and he needs Scotty in order to be able to become so. Here, as elsewhere, the film is unclear about the motivations of its characters (other than to 'motivate' a furthering of the narrative development). It is as if the film-makers are touching the buttons without quite knowing which floor they want to get off at or even why they are in the elevator at all.

The final sequence, however, does seem to be on the right floor. In this scene Scotty has been brought to an auditorium for a 'testimonial' from the many friends he has made over the years. His public persona is brought face-to-face, as it were, with his previously repressed private one. While others eulogize him, he sits and recalls the private, if often conflictual, moments with Judd. Finally Scotty takes the stage. Here in public he speaks privately to his son (whom he is not even sure is in the auditorium—even though it is Judd who has set up the whole occasion, again it is not clear why). In a direct metaphor of his own life, Scott finds himself dying (in show business terminology) on the stage. His 'life' has no punch-line, no finish; he does not know how to get off the stage, how to in fact get 'off' life *without his son*. Judd is present, and in a neat (for this film) indication of how the lessons of fatherhood have been learnt, Judd literally becomes his father. That is, for the first time, Judd provides the punch-lines to Scotty's straightman. And as a consequence, Scotty is able to kiss Judd fully upon the mouth, and Judd is able to let him. There is more genuine passion (which Scotty has wished for his son in his speech moments ago) in that one kiss than in the several that Scotty has obtained by the same 'trick' (offering his cheek and then turning his face) earlier in the film.

Certainly, Judd has by the conclusion made the journey from the realm of his mother to that of his father. His mother is present to watch the embrace approvingly. In this at least the film suggests that the importance of fathers is to provide that guidance into the masculine realm. And arguably it has also presented 'a case' for the need to make that realm more attractive to the coming generation of men by showing that men need to reveal their capacity for emotion. That it does so in a rather awkward fashion may be, as we have indicated, because this is an early film that was still struggling with what were as yet inchoate and indistinct cultural perceptions. Later films built upon the foundations, pursued the lines which were not quite as obvious to makers of *Tribute*. Taking *Memories of Me* as an example, it is possible to argue that it is almost a direct descendant of *Tribute*—*Son of Tribute* perhaps? Certainly there are remarkable similarities in both characterization and narrative structure and incident. But there is also a greater sense of clarity of idea, approach and theme. *Tribute* points to the way these later films will go.

Finally, it is worth noting that it is in *Tribute* that is first heard an expression that runs like a *leit motif* through the many films that fit this Father/Son cycle. Scotty in his address to Judd in the public forum of the testimonial (where appropriately the private man is at last able to be revealed) tells Judd that he wishes him but one legacy, to discover passion and 'to go the distance'. Inability to go the distance is in many ways the hallmark of the fathers in the films which make up this chapter (and in some others, most notably this command is essential to the narrative trajectory of the son in another if differently themed father–son film, *Field of Dreams*[1989, Philip Alden]). The distance to be traversed in this and other films is actually the quite narrow gap between the love that fathers and sons feel for each other and the capacity to adequately express that love. Yet narrow as that gap may be, it often seems insurmountable. The different films in this chapter offer slightly different images of that gap (or barrier) although nearly all state, directly or indirectly, that it is somehow created by definitions of masculinity. *Tribute* is less clear about this than later films. It posits the gap and shows the barriers symbolically through the 'mask' of the chicken outfit and the distancing effect of the camera lens. It also suggests that overtly public expression of masculinity (exaggerated but still evident in the personality of Scotty) and its complete opposite, clinging to the security of the realm of the child and the mother, are two untenable poles.

Less clearly, it is true, than later films, *Tribute* insists that men must release their femininity but *Tribute* is somewhat shy of in fact equating emotional expression with femininity or is somewhat equivocal about it. Its somewhat disturbing emphasis on 'rampant' heterosexuality (Scotty does, to all intents and purposes, 'pimp' for Judd) tends to suggest that the repressed emotions both father and son feel for each other are hidden aspects of masculinity. Judd seems no more capable of expressing his feelings when he is with his mother (with whom he has presumably spent much more time) than with his 'girlfriend' or, initially his father. Scotty may be more publicly at ease with women but he does not seem any more able to be open in his feelings with them. Where *Tribute* tends to depart company with the later films (films with which it has considerable continuity nonetheless) is that the journey the son makes is out of the realm of the mother and into the realm of the father. Later films tended to make this journey one out of the realm of one definition of masculinity into another, more 'appropriate' definition of masculinity. As stated previously, *Tribute* was responding to as yet barely felt tremors in the cultural fabric. It 'knows' as do all the films discussed in this study, that father/son relations are important. It is not quite sure why. Of course, there is no one answer to that question anyway. The films discussed in this essay reveal one possible set of answers.

DAD (1989)

Dad represents the integration of a number of the key themes which have woven through the tapestry of father/son films in the 1980s. It is concerned—

arguably over-concerned—with providing the image of and the rationale for the 'new man', demonstrating this changed image of masculinity across three generations. That is to say demonstrating three historically produced male-images, and 'allowing' each to undergo the necessary degree of change sufficient to bring them each into line with the prevailing cultural representation of masculinity as a lived experience. The least amount of change is required of the youngest generation, present day sons, now known as 'Generation X'—those who have not yet achieved that status of fathers. The most change is in fact required of the baby-boomer generation, the present-day fathers. This runs against the implied socio-historical logic that the older the male the more likely he is to be represented as a 'traditional' male/father. Using this logic, the older generation, the grandfathers, would seem to need to undergo the greater degree of change and/or to be the most in need of change. Yet in this instance at least the change by the grandfather is both more easily accomplished than his son (the baby-boomer) and is to a large extent self-generated.

In this self-generation lie the seeds of the integration of two themes. One is quite clearly the accepting of the capacity of men for expressing emotion and of becoming (or allowing themselves to be) caring and nurturing. In other words, to break down the fundamental dichotomy that (it is often claimed) patriarchy creates and maintains: the distinction between the public world (male or at least masculine) and the private world (female or at least feminine). *Dad* and many of the other father/son films are concerned to bring men into the private world, the world of emotion, sentiment and personal relationships. At the extreme it may be argued that patriarchy is thus claiming even more cultural or social 'territory' for itself; the extent to which this is a response to the increased colonization of the public world by women is open to debate. A strong case can be made for patriarchy not breaking down but extending its hegemony by altering its structure to include characteristics that were previously defined as exclusively feminine. *Dad* is a key text in this argument.

Thus the second theme: the notion that women get between men (fathers and sons) and prevent them demonstrating their emotions towards each other. Thus the idea which runs through many of these father/sons films that women are in fact destructive of this capacity for caring in men. In other words that it is not patriarchal or phallocentric notions of masculinity that have, in the past, ordered that men are defined by a lack of emotion or a lack of expression of emotion but rather that it is women who have created and fostered this order.

The first and still the most clearly stated example of this latter theme is found in *Ordinary People*. Coming as it did at the very beginning of the period which I have identified, it does not offer a substantial examination of the notion of the nurturing father or the caring male in general. While its determination to show the destructive capacity of the female (wife/mother) demands that the focus be more upon that aspect, it is nonetheless quite clearly demonstrated that the father does have a capacity for caring, for emotional identification with his son, and that this capacity is not allowed full exercise because of the conflicting demands of the wife *and* because it is *expected* that a mother will provide and demonstrate the greater emotional bond. *Ordinary People*'s narrative trajectory is simply towards the very point at which it becomes clear that this cultural gender stereotyping is problematic. That the film is not a feminist tract (arguing for example that a woman should have the right to choose to grant or withhold her affections) is clear from the way in which it positions the wife-mother as being in the wrong. Equally it does not strongly make the point that what is inappropriate are the *expectations* of what a mother should be.

Ordinary People is much more concerned with offering tentative new definitions of masculinity, of leading to the point where a father can be physically intimate with his son, can embrace him, and where a father and a son can tell each other than they love each other. This occurs at the climax of *Ordinary People*; it is the tension around when or even whether the two men can make these emotional statements to each other which drives the narrative. (The cause of Conrad's psychological state is, to this extent, a macguffin.[1])

Nearly a decade later, this delaying of a moment of intense emotional and physical bonding between two men, that is between a father and his son, is no longer sufficient to support a whole narrative. *Dad*, although it is concerned with demonstrating that new definitions of masculinity are viable, even desirable, through a similar narrative progression cannot attenuate the narrative to the extent *Ordinary People* does. Indeed, it must and does go much further in terms of demonstrations of the physicality of emotional attachment than the mere first, tentative hug which concludes *Ordinary People*.

One of the most striking aspects of *Dad* is the degree to which bodily contact between Jake Tremont and his son John occurs—after the initial breaking down of the barrier (taboo?). Even so, the film avoids any misunderstandings about this contact by contextualising them within the narrative by having them occur when Jake is in the hospital. The first, which is highly determined occasion, is when Jake is facing an operation and as John leaves the side of his hospital bed, Jake says, 'I see men hugging these days. We never hugged much.' John, after a moment, replies, 'Would you like to give it a try?' Jake's answer is highly significant; he says 'I do.' The familiar ritual response of the marriage ceremony can hardly be accidental. They then hug.

From this point on, intimate physical contact between the two men increases. It reaches the point when, after Jake has gone into a near catatonic state on learning he has cancer, John carries him from the hospital in his arms,

238

and later cradles him in his arms in the car while Betty (Jake's wife, John's mother) is removed from the house prior to John attempting to nurse his father at home. It also noteworthy that at this same time John quite aggressively refuses the assistance of his own son, Billy, in looking after Jake.

Finally, after Jake recovers from his coma (largely because of John's refusal to leave his side after he is readmitted to hospital) and has a brief spell of renewed vigour and life, he returns to hospital this time to die. He dies (it is implied) with John not simply hugging him this time but lying with him on the bed, in a posture that suggests submission as well as love; a pictorial representation of atonement more complete than in any other film. Before doing so, Jake again invites physical contact with John when he says 'I wish I'd kissed you more as a kid. I wish I'd held you more.'

In learning to allow physical contact with his father to express emotions previously denied or suppressed, John also learns to express himself in the same way to his own son. It is apparent that Billy does not have the same problem with physical acts of emotion, at least with his grandfather as he hugs and kisses him without invitation after his first admission to hospital. This re-emphasizes that the film is still concerned with relations between fathers and sons and not just with presenting a case for the 'new man' by showing men being intimate with each other, demonstrating capacity for emotional display and so forth. Billy's relationship with his grandfather at this level implies that, firstly, Billy being of the post-baby-boomer generation (what has become known in the 1990s as 'Generation X') is able to be more open in his demonstration of affection and, secondly, that he instinctively recognizes Jake's readiness to accept such intimacy. Within the general theme of representing the new(er) definition of masculinity, *Dad* is still concerned with the barrier between fathers and sons in contemporary American society.

Dad is clearly not only concerned with demonstrating that masculinity is no longer defined by avoidance of physical contact between men—other than violent contact of course. It is concerned also with arguing for the failure of previous social and cultural definitions of masculinity to provide emotional outlets for men, implying thereby that men need emotional channels and have the capacity for such emotions. Indeed going as far as to suggest that men have a greater capacity for emotion, caring and nurturing than women. Thus, the narrative is complicated by a 'sub-plot' of Jake's fantasy life as a farmer with a demonstrative and idyllically happy family. He is, in fact, a retired manual worker living in suburban Los Angeles. These dream sequences are presented in quite realistic fashion within the mise-en-scene, and the film actually commences with this fantasy without any indication that it is a dream. The explanation offered for this fantasy is that a lack of an emotional dimension to his real existence has led Jake to create an alternative fantasy life that becomes (after the cancer incident) more real than his actual life.

Much of the conflict between John and his mother in this latter part of the narrative is centered around the fact that John can readily accept the manner in which Jake has created his more emotionally satisfying (it could be said more *natural*) fantasy life. More importantly, John understands the reasons that Jake has done so—reasons concerned with the culturally-acceptable but restricting role for men/fathers that society designated for men of Jake's generation but reasons also, and more importantly, related to the place and function of Betty as wife-mother.

The explanation for Jake being what he is (seemingly emotionally sterile and remote, a 'classic' patriarch) is given by John to his sister. (Again implying that women have, contrary to phallocentric ideology, a diminished capacity for understanding the emotions.) The responsibility is placed squarely at the door of the social norms of Jake's generation:

> JOHN: That man got up every day of his life and went to a job he didn't like. We didn't ask him to. He did it because he was the father and that was the deal he made. He didn't ask himself if he was satisfied, or happy, or .... Didn't even know he had the right.

And this is reiterated later when John attempts to justify his 'absence' from his own son's life.

> JOHN: That's what I thought a man was. What I thought a father was. Some guy who wore a suit and made a lot of money.

But John immediately modifies this: 'That's too easy.' He further demonstrates that he is 'the new man'—the changed baby-boomer—when he says: 'I've missed you, Billy. And you may not need me or even want me around but I'd like to stay in your life. I'm your father.'

This scene which has been presented in conventional shot/reverse shot style, moving closer to John and Billy with each cut, ends without them touching, which seems to be contrary to the emotional trajectory of the scene. This is somewhat strange given the manner in which physical intimacy between Jake and John has signaled the degree of change that has come about in John's masculine self-definition.

Something seemingly curious is happening in many of these father/son films which is exemplified in *Dad*. In the mid-1970s, Joan Mellen surveyed masculinity as it had been historically presented by Hollywood. She comments: 'Were masculinity not confused with the suppression of feeling, women would

240

not, in this curious inversion of the masculine ethos, be a threat to male sufficiency' (1978, 44). No sooner (or so it seems) had Mellen written these words than definitions of masculinity (within Hollywood films and within the culture generally) began to change. Masculinity began no longer to be defined by 'suppression of feeling' (many of these films are determined to demonstrate just this very point) and indeed the 'true' man was able to, even encouraged to, let his feelings show through. Women did not, however, stop being a threat to 'male sufficiency'. As films such as *Dad*, *Ordinary People*, and *Kramer verses Kramer* show only too well, men must now compete with women in the private sphere of feelings—and almost inevitably win where the stakes are emotional relationships with other males or, as it is typically couched in these films, between fathers and sons.

This is clearly shown in *Dad*. At first, the narrative seems to be concerned with patriarchy in decline. Jake Tremont is shown to be pathetically dependent upon his wife, Betty. She sugars his coffee, butters his sweet roll, and even puts the toothpaste on his brush for him. She tells him when to get up and what to wear and she lays out his clothes for him. These actions are presented in a fashion which implies they are carried out neither because Jake is incapable nor from affection. This sequence is clearly presented as an unacceptable representation of female dominance, despite it taking place in the domestic situation, traditionally considered the female domain. Moreover, when she suffers a heart attack, it is to be with his mother rather than his father, that their son John interrupts his work as a high-powered broker.

John's concern, however, quickly turns from his mother to his father; he is in more need of John's attention and care. Why? The answer is, because he is manifestly not the patriarch he *ought* to be (if in fact he ever was). John's concern, then, is to restore Jake as patriarch and father. Jake has been 'emasculated' not by age but by a woman, his wife; he must learn to be a man again. Ironically, but in keeping with the determination of this film to show how ideologically sound it is, Jake first becomes a functioning man again (i.e. learns to do things for himself) by doing routine housework. In other words Jake starts back on the trail to recovering his masculinity by doing housework, which has been traditionally considered 'women's work'. If men are to enter into the private sphere of the emotions then they are also going to enter into the domestic sphere of household labor, and by so doing confirm rather than deny or distort their masculinity. This foundation is built upon when Jake and John start doing other things together. Again these are initially things that Jake and Betty did together such as going to bingo, but even here what had previously been something a man and a woman did together is given an extra dimension through its being done by two men (John: 'We were awesome tonight'). Bingo becomes a more meaningful experience when the masculine qualities of competition, drive and ambition to win are brought into the arena. (The film has not vouchsafed a scene in which Jake and Betty play bingo but it may be assumed from the earlier sequences that here too she would have made all the moves for him and so on.) And then doing possibly feminine things changes to activities that traditionally only men do together. There is a brief but significant scene in which John and Jake toss a baseball back and forth in the front yard of the house.

As a consequence, a female (John's sister) is able to proclaim to John, 'I can't believe how good Dad looks. You've been terrific for him.' The implication being that Betty, despite or because of thirty-five years of marriage, has not been 'terrific for him'. More than this, John is able to reply, 'He's been good for me, too.' This mutually beneficial relationship provides a rationale for John staying longer than the expected two or three days. Since John has been shown in introductory scenes as a socialized man in the pre-1980s sense (confident and powerful in a business context), this decision to spend more time with his father doubly emphasizes the power of male-to-male relationships. It also serves the narrative purpose of allowing the gradual 'breaking down' of traditional male behaviors and thus leading to greater expressions of feeling, including importantly the physical affection discussed previously. Thus a man who has ceased to be 'male' (Jake) and man who is too much implicated in tradition and inappropriate masculinity (John) are brought into juxtaposition and the trajectory of the narrative will be to redefine or rather to 'free' each. In the process patriarchy will actually be reconfirmed while being redefined, and women will be marginalized, or continue to be marginalized.

It should be noted that *Dad* does not speak with an unambivalent voice of misogyny. John's initial concern is, after all, for his mother. Throughout, Jake is expressly concerned for Betty and his initial drive to do things around the house is ostensibly to make life easier for her. Even so, there is no escaping that the impetus to start and to continue is because he is learning these things and doing these things with his son. Like Cal in *Ordinary People*, Jake attempts to balance his love for his wife and his son—two people who are in conflict over him. This conflict resolves itself narratively by simply showing that Jake's needs are more important than Betty's; that he needs and must have the equivalence of the emotional happiness of his dream world in his actual world. John recognizes this, Betty does not. It is she who is seen as being selfish. Patriarchy is served but this service is rationalized by the claim that as a father, Jake has previously sacrificed his right for happiness (self-fulfillment) by exactly conforming to the cultural and social demands of being a father/patriarch (going off to a job he didn't like, etc). Here it is appropriate that women be a focus for men's emotions; Jake often expresses his love for Betty and indeed wins (seduces) her

242

to his new found expression of self in a quite tender love scene. But beneath or rather parallel to this is the more important focus of emotion between men, between fathers and sons. It is, after all, in a mutual embrace with John that Jake dies. This is a reiteration of the earlier scene when John holds Jake in his arms in the car, except this time both men are at peace: atonement has been achieved. A more complete atonement (since the whole narrative has been in fact driving towards this very resolution) than when Jake and Betty dance in an embrace in the greenhouse at the point when he wins her to his point of view about his being able to live a more complete emotional life.

Misogynist or not, *Dad* does clearly place women at the periphery of the emotional core of the narrative. Not only is Betty shown to be incapable of comprehending the depth of Jake's emotional needs and not only is she shown to be incapable of providing for them but actually to be stifling of them, but Annie, Jake's daughter (and thus John's sister) is also denied any opportunity to show the capacity of emotional connection that John displays. There is a fleeting criticism of the 'new woman' when Annie indicates that she cannot take time off from *her* job to look after Jake whereas John (who is shown to have a very important job) can and does do so. By and large, Annie is little more than a peripheral figure, in the background throughout. She is shown to be less sensitive than her husband Mario who makes frequent attempts to show concern for Betty and the notion of family—all of which are rebuffed by Betty who in so doing reveals a lack of capacity for expressing or accepting emotions that is more like that associated with tradition masculine images. There are no other women in the narrative. John's ex-wife is referred to in passing but she is not in the frame so to speak.

It is, therefore, of no little significance that John has no-one of the opposite sex as focus for his suppressed emotional capacity. In this, *Dad* is rather different from other comparable films (e.g., *Nothing in Common*, *Memories of Me*). This places a different emphasis on the male-to-male relationships in *Dad*; it focuses them more completely. Other films suggest that by men learning to express their emotions, to reveal their capacity for feeling so their relations with women are improved: they can express their feelings *for women* without losing their masculinity. *Dad* quite plainly does not do this. Rather, through getting in touch with his sublimated feelings by the intensity of his experience with his dying father, John is able to revitalize his relationship with *his* son (rather than a girlfriend as is the experience of the protagonists of *Memories of Me* and *Nothing in Common*. (*Ordinary People*, as noted stops short at the climactic moment that the two men can express physically and vocally their love for each other. Whether this will 'allow' either of them a greater capacity for expressing emotions in any heterosexual relation is not canvassed. Perhaps neither needs to:

it is the women in their respective lives who have been incapable of receiving or more particularly responding to the emotions offered them by both Cal and Conrad.)

It seems in the almost total absence of a heterosexual relationship for the protagonist (although John has a history of such a relationship) that *Dad* offers some support for our hypothesis that some of these father/son films are metaphors for discussing homosexuality. Jake, of course, does have a heterosexual relationship, and it is suggested more than once he has had a very active physical sex life, which is revived once he recovers his abdicated masculinity. But it is inescapable that, despite thirty five years of married life, that heterosexual relationship is not as fulfilling as the few weeks of (homosexual) relationship with his son. Like John, Billy too is denied any on-screen heterosexual relationship. He does mention that two of the five 'guys' who share a house in Mexico are girls, but it does not follow (nor does he indicate) that he has a heterosexual relationship with either of these two girls. This may be clutching at straws a little and the film itself does not make any overt suggestions of homosexuality. Nonetheless, the most intense scenes of physicality *do* occur between men. More than this, the three men are shown, in a montage type sequence, indulging in a session of frenetic dressing up, which does not quite reach the stage of 'drag' but there is more than a slight suggestion of feminization in the clothes adopted, as well as an element of display not far removed from the 'traditional' perception of how women display themselves for men. It may be that this sequence can be interpreted as a demonstration of another way in which the discourse of masculinity is changing; sexual implications are muted although the three men are seen (fleetingly) in poses or postures which involve a considerable amount of intertwining of bodies.

The question remains unanswered however: why is this film about fathers and sons? Put another way, what is specific within the thematic framework to the relationship between a father and a son? All too obviously the narrative is 'about' a father and a son (or rather a father and a son and *his* son). But the analysis we have made hardly finds any actual details which are dependent upon that relationship—beyond the fact that the condition of being father-and-son legitimates the intensity of feelings and in turn the expressing of those feelings by men.

There is a degree in which *Dad* does operate mythically (through patriarchy) to reiterate the culturally-valued act of the passing on of wisdom from father to son. There is not any real sense in which Jake can be seen as being a 'law giver' with his function as patriarch, and this must mute this mythological dimension. If John learns to be 'a new man' from Jake, then this learning is in fact a two-way process. Jake is the catalyst ('I have seen men hugging') but he is not the exemplar, let alone the teacher. The mythological resonances of the dying king are far less apparent in *Dad* than in, say, *Memories of Me*. Indeed, Jake's 'crown', an old baseball cap which Betty had previously forbidden him to wear around the house but which he (re)adopts in her absence, passes not to John but to Betty herself. In this it may amount to a symbol of the degree to which she too has learnt to accept her emotions, but it confuses any notion of the dying king passing on his symbols of wisdom, power, knowledge and, in this case, capacity for feeling, to the 'new' king. Further, John leaves the family setting after Jake's death. The narrative satisfaction of this leaving comes from the knowledge that John returns to the public, masculine world as a truly reborn new man. (The notion of 'rebirth' is confirmed by the last image of Jake and John together where John lies cradles in Jake's arms in a foetal position and posture.) Is this also a resurrection for John? This is difficult to say. Like *Ordinary People*, *Dad* finishes before the consequences of the changes are seen to flow on. But narrative pleasure comes from the changes themselves. The changes are those of the definition of masculinity; but not in the ideology and social hegemony of patriarchy.

Dad has thus played it safe. John returns to the 'real' world (the public world of men: Wall Street) now in touch with his feelings and able to express them openly, without fear, with confidence. But by restricting the arena of the changes, and learning to 'use' them has been in the private world where the 'new man' may safely exercise his capacity for emotional expression of many levels—without raising the insinuation of homosexuality. Hollywood, as has been seen in the films in the cycle of '80s Father/Son films (and in general), has not been able or willing to come to terms with homosexuality even in periods of both increasingly liberal attitudes and 'gay militancy'. But Hollywood, and popular culture in general, often (more often than is usually credited) speaks of 'the (culturally) unspeakable' with the voice of allegory, metaphor and the unconscious. (Equating movies with dreams may not be entirely insupportable.) There is nothing new in claiming that male relationships in American film (be they antagonistic, distanced, unexpressed, or whatever) are based in homosexuality and/or homoeroticism (see Mellen, 1977 for a book-length claim along these lines), nor that American cinema has shown a more than usual interest in representations of male bonding in the past twenty or so years. The emphasis on father/son relationships we detect during the 1980s seems to have taken this notion both a bit further and, frankly, added a degree of credibility to what was often rather far-fetched claims made of earlier films. Not all films in the father/son cycle seem to be concerned (whether consciously or unconsciously) with presenting, exploring, flirting with male homosexuality. And within the group of films dealt with in this chapter, *Dad* seems far more implicated than *Memories of Me* or *Nothing in Common. Dad* seems to go beyond stating that a man's true emotional interest is (or should) be in the males of his own flesh but it does not, however, go as far as the logical extension of that notion. But neither does it deflect this implication (as does *Nothing in Common, Memories of Me, Welcome Home*, etc) onto a heightened awareness of the place of emotionality in a heterosexual relationship. Overall, it is hard to conclude that, ironically enough, *Dad* is not actually 'about' father/son relationships. Ironic in that the narrative *is* concerned with little other than a father/son relationship, while its thematic is totally concerned with a male/male relationship.

The significant father/son relationship is that of Jake and John but is not the only one in the narrative. John's own son Billy is present and places a part in the focus on male-to-male relationships through John's relationship with him. As the film places its emphasis on the 'education' of the baby-boomer generation, again it is John who must reach out to his son rather than vice-versa. Billy, the representative of the newer masculinity is already more in touch with his emotions, or at least more able to express them more easily. His remoteness from his father is, somewhat against the usual theme of these films, attributed to John's emotional (masculine) sterility, and it is up to John therefore to make the moves which will break down the barriers between them. John is able to do this *because* he has been able to get in touch with the previously suppressed or sublimated emotional side of his 'nature' through his revived relationship with his father. Billy: 'He [Jake] looks really good. What's been going on?' John: 'We've been spending time together.' Billy is at first ironic about the need for family to spend 'quality time' together but as John 'matures', so he is able to confront Billy in a genuinely caring way and the emotion barriers are dissolved. The three generations come together (perform, literally, for the women) and are united even in death when John and Billy offer a personal eulogy and farewell to Jake in the inner sanctum of Jake's private world, the greenhouse.

MEMORIES OF ME (1989)

Dad might more appropriately be called *Men*, although it does seem to deal, at a superficial level, with notions of contemporary family—in a similar way to *Ordinary People*. And in so doing, its title is perhaps not all that inappropriate given its emphasis on (re)placing the father at the head of the American family. It chooses to do so by emphasizing the changes that have (or need to be) made in definitions of masculinity; changes which will result in men being able to express their love for each other in physical and verbal ways to such an extent that it becomes, as we have argued, a film about male love rather than a film about fathers and sons.

This is not the case with *Memories of Me* (and many other films within this cycle). That is to say, while *Memories of Me* (again like *Ordinary People*) is concerned with and directs its narrative towards the moment when a father can say to his son 'I love you', it is not as expressly concerned with demonstrating the masculine capacity for expressing feelings in a general sense. It is concerned, far more typically of the cycle, with reconciling estranged fathers and sons. It is the old definitions of masculinity that have caused the estrangement. *Memories of Me* has, of course, its own narratively specific causes of the estrangement of its two main characters but in keeping with other films such as *Nothing in Common* and *Family Business* the implications are that this gulf between fathers and sons in the 1980s is located in the cultural ideology of masculinity and/or fatherhood.

What is being criticized in many of these films (with considerable ambivalence) is the success syndrome in American society. It may well be that those aspects of American culture which encouraged the notion of success in the public sphere (education, business, profession, politics) were, in the 1980s, beginning to be questioned because they seemed to have gone too far (or that men—and perhaps women as well—had taken them too much to heart) at the cost of a deeper-felt cultural ideology, that of family. In each of the films *Dad*, *Memories of Me*, *Nothing in Common* and *Family Business*, the sons have been more successful in social terms than their fathers. They are respectively: *Dad*, father a (retired) manual worker, son a high executive financier; *Memories of Me*, father a Hollywood extra, son a specialist heart surgeon; *Nothing in Common*, father a (fired) clothes salesman, son a successful advertising executive; *Family Business*, father a unrepentant thief, son an owner of a meat packing company. In each case (and other examples may be found in other films, for example *Wall Street*) it would seem that the American Dream is being shown to be demonstrably true. But each film is concerned to suggest that there has been a cost involved.

That cost has been the construction and/or retention of a particular ideology of masculinity. Thus John Tremont (*Dad*), Abbie Polin (*Memories of Me*), David Bazner (*Nothing in Common*) and Vito McMullen (*Family Business*) have each demonstrated their capacity as men through their success in the public world of ambition and success but, by the *new* definition of masculinity, have simultaneously failed as *new* men. It is not their fault, but the films differ in the extent to which they suggest that this failure is in whole or in part the fault of their fathers. *Dad* makes no such claim; *Memories of Me* and *Nothing in Common* are less certain.

Memories of Me is then concerned with the breaking down of the traditional male requirement to be masculine through not showing emotion, to be seeming

247

to be incapable of showing emotion, but it does so in a circumscribed way. Its protagonist is a successful heart specialist Doctor Abbie Polin. (His complete success in the 'public' sphere in shown in a quite short, fast-paced sequence which begins the film.) Abbie has a heart attack while in fact operating, the implications, as his girlfriend points out, being that it is because he 'works like a maniac' and 'is too busy being a doctor'. In other words (if in another context) 'doing what a man's gotta do'—being successful in the public, masculine arena even if it nearly kills him. (That it is dangerous, even fatal to 'be a man' is, of course, a perception to be found in genres even more intimately concerned with images of machismo, especially the Western.)

The narrative is triggered, the equilibrium disturbed, not by Abbie's heart attack itself but by a dream he has while in recovery. The dream is of his father reciting to Abbie (as a child) a speech made by Paul Muni in the film *Inherit the Wind*—this speech is to recur as a *leitmotif* throughout the narrative and to serve as an indicator of the existence of a brain aneurism that will kill Abbie's father. Thus it is not that Abbie has had a heart attack (while in his thirties) that is important (except as a narrative motivation for much of what follows) but that he is made aware (by the dream and later, more importantly, by his girlfriend) of the extent of his estrangement from his father. This estrangement seems at first to be the result of his father's capacity for embarrassing Abbie while a child and, perhaps, because of the fact that his father and mother were divorced while Abbie was still young.

But it is additionally implied that the estrangement is also and even primarily the consequence of Abbie's emotional sterility. It is not immediately apparent what causes this but given Abbie's obvious involvement in the work ethic and the need for success it seems that emotional sterility is tied up with his (self) definition as a man. That is, his emotional lack is explicable because it is not aberrant behaviour *for a man*. Even so, Abbie is enough of a man to attract a woman; another doctor Lisa McConnel comes to his bedside following his heart attack and returns with him to his apartment after his discharge. She had previously broken off a previous relationship with Abbie because of his inability to reveal himself emotionally to her. After Abbie's dream of his father, he looks at old movie footage of himself as a child taken by his father, and Lisa is surprised to learn that Abbie's father, Abe, is still alive. She assumed that Abbie's refusal to talk about him was tacit admission to his being deceased. Abbie's refusal to discuss him is interpreted by Lisa as 'the turtle going back into his shell'. Somewhat out of the blue she asks Abbie, 'Have you ever thought you might love him?' to which Abbie replies succinctly 'No.' The notion that a man should automatically love his father comes from a woman and is designated thereby a specifically 'feminine' one. Moreover, lack of love for a father, or lack of ability to admit to love for a father, is interpreted as part of an overall lack of ability to express emotion. Lisa tells Abbie 'You're great in bed...but then you don't know how to hold my hand.'

It is not enough (for women) for men to be physically attractive and sexually competent, they must be capable of showing their feelings as well. This is a measure of how definitions of masculinity have changed. Previous films (if Mellen 1977 is correct) would have found physically attractiveness and sexual ability sufficient for defining masculinity, and have dismissed women's 'need' for expressions of tenderness as threatening to that very masculinity. Hollywood in the 1980s held onto the first two factors and expended energy upon demonstrating that the third was also an essential element of masculinity; that a combination of all three added up to the 'new man' of the 1980s and 1990s.

It is immediately following Lisa's assertion that he lacks the ability to express his emotions (she seems not to doubt that he has them) that Abbie flies from New York to L.A. to visit his father. This is accomplished by narrative ellipsis, and emphasizes thereby that a man's true emotional focus is his father (or another, specific male). After all, why should Abbie pursue his father rather than attempt to patch up his relationship with Lisa?

The rest of the narrative is concerned with charting the bumpy path Abbie follows in coming to terms with his father (and to a lesser extent, his father with him). Abe is very much a public man: extroverted, popular, funny, capable and sexually attractive to women (rather like David—the son—in *Nothing in Common*). From the outset, it is clear that Abe and Abbie cannot communicate, or rather that their communication is conducted through a series of 'filters'— the most obvious of which is the telephone which Abe uses immediately upon Abbie telling him of his heart attack. Abe goes to the phone in the bar he they are in and calls Abbie on another phone in the same bar. This leads immediately to Abbie leaving the bar and threatening to leave L.A.

But another, less obviously physical 'filter' is that Abe expresses his feelings for Abbie through criticism. After Abbie has intervened in the aftermath of a car crash and given medical attention to an injured man, Abe criticizes him by claiming he could get sued for malpractice. Abbie is looking for overt expressions of concern, even praise for his skills. In this he is reminiscent of Indiana Jones looking for parental approval for his actions and not getting it in *Indiana Jones and the Last Crusade*. This perceived criticism in place of approval prompts a confrontational scene in which Abbie accuses Abe of never saying he (Abe) loves him, and that he (Abbie) had made the trip 'to get Abe either in or out of his life.' He further accuses Abe of being a fraud as a father. Clearly then Abbie's definition of a father includes being 'there' (an earlier anecdote expresses the bitterness of Abe's absence during Abbie's childhood) and expressing feelings of love openly. (The film seems less than fully aware of the irony of Abbie's demands for Abe to show feelings when he himself cannot.) The implication is that fathers are—or ought to be—part of and in the life of their sons. It follows then that there are problems consequent upon fathers *not* being in the life of their sons: if Abbie cannot express his feelings (to Lisa, to his father, and thus generally) it is because of the previous and continuing absence (physical and emotional) of his father: Abe is neither in nor out of Abbie's life.

Although it appears, following this confrontation scene in which the two nearly come to blows (or make gestures as if they would like to), that Abbie has decided to get Abe out of his life, the narrative trajectory and narrative expectations demand that he will not. In a rather unsatisfactory narrative 'twist', Abbie stays rather than leaves and as a consequence becomes aware of symptomatic behaviour in Abe. He conducts medical tests and Abe's terminal condition is diagnosed. As with *Dad*, the immediate prospect of the father dying jolts the son into facing his feelings, recognizing his need to be reconciled with his father, and taking steps to ensure this. In the case of *Memories of Me*, this includes not simply refusing to leave ('We've know each other for thirty-five years and we've just found each other') but also in undertaking a scheme whereby Abe will get a speaking part in a movie for the first time. Abe does get the part but dies before shooting begins; it is the act not the consequences which are important. The son has done something significant for the father; he has earned his forgiveness. Like so many other films, however, it is not clear what the son has done to need to seek atonement, what action needs to be expiated save for the act of not properly seeking to keep (or allow) his father in his life. Given the number of times this occurs, it is reasonable to assume that not keeping one's father in one's life is the sin which must be expiated.

Being less concerned with, or less willing to emphasize emotionality or sentimentality than *Dad*, *Memories of Me* is less clear in structuring the process of reconciliation, expiation and atonement but the process is there nonetheless. The early scenes in which Abbie is accused by Lisa of being unable to express his emotions and of being completely open in any emotional relationship can now be seen to be less a matter of providing a critique of masculinity as it is epitomized by the yuppie/baby-boomer generation than in establishing Abbie's 'guilt', the reason why he must seek not simply reconciliation to be at-one with his father but expiation. Like *Dad* and *Nothing in Common*, *Memories of Me* states (although far from unambiguously) that whatever cultural insecurities and uncertainties are manifest in contemporary American society, they are (in part) attributable to the actual successful implementation of the American Dream. Success, ambition, achievement have been attained, it seems, at the cost of separating younger men (sons) from older men (fathers). The echoes of Robert Bly are quite distinct here.

In *Memories of Me* at least, it is not asserted that Abe has deliberately and consciously driven Abbie to seek success in the public/professional sphere. Indeed, if anything, Abe is a contrary example, having chosen to remain throughout his career a 'mere' extra rather than seek more success (or at least public notice) as a 'real' actor. Arguably, it is the absence of Abe from Abbie's life which has prevented him from serving as a modifying influence rather than his presence providing a spur to striving for success. Thus, whatever blame for the barriers between them the narrative may attribute to Abe, these are seen as being rather more idiosyncratically personal than the consequence of cultural perceptions of fatherhood and/or manhood. Abe is a 'public' person in a different way from Abbie: he is extroverted, friendly, and popular but not a success in the sense of ambition, power and prestige. He is, in fact, a caring person. So too is Abbie, the difference being that Abbie, as a doctor, is a professional carer. If Abe has a flaw it is that he cannot express his caring to his son as easily as he can to his fellow extras. The notion that Abe is a father (king?) to the community of Hollywood extras, that they are a family, is not seriously challenged, and is indeed confirmed at the conclusion when they turn out en masse for his funeral—which Abe had predicted they would *not* do because of the demands of work.

In *Dad* and *Memories of Me*, the respective fathers are able to pass away, having been reconciled with their sons. More than this, of course: the sons have also become 'new' men, able to express themselves fully in the private as well as the public sphere. They have not been taught to do so by their fathers (or at least only partially in the case of *Dad*) but have learnt to be so as a consequence of discovering their love of their fathers—and/or earning the love of the their fathers. It remains, furthermore, that the fathers do not have to earn the love of their sons. This remains in these films as a rigid principle: fathers are deserving of their sons' love whether or not either can express this openly. This point is made even more clearly in *Nothing in Common*.

NOTHING IN COMMON (1986)

On the scale of 'lovability', I find that the fathers in three of these films are characterized as more lovable the more recent the film. That is, Jake Tremont in *Dad* is the most instantly lovable (and becomes more so as the narrative unfolds), Abe Polin is lovable but also irritating, but Max Bazner (in this film) is hardly lovable at all even at the end of the film. The chronological exception is *Family Business*, and this film is complicated by the dual focus of the father/son

251

relationship, being as much between Vito and his father, Jesse as between Vito and his son, Adam. As films based openly in narratives which have fathers and sons 'finding' each other and simultaneously finding the ability to express their love for each other have become more common, and the themes more familiar (and thus, presumably, commercially acceptable), the fathers have become more 'mild', less like traditional patriarchs (remote, irascible, dictatorial).

Nothing in Common raises the question even more firmly than either *Dad* or *Memories of Me*: what is it about fathers that can demand and get the love of sons? Max Bazner is a grumpy, demanding, brusque, and by most definitions a thoroughly unlikable person—as an individual and as a father. In the course of the film he drives away his wife of thirty-six years (this is indeed the narrative device that motivates the plot), and it is revealed that he has already driven away his son (his only son, as is the case with *Dad*, *Memories of Me* and *Family Business*). There is little about him that can be reasonably said to arouse sympathy (from characters within the diegesis, or from any audience for the film) even when the extent of his illness is revealed. His humanity, such as he has, is not revealed until the very end—and then rather ambiguously.

And yet David, his estranged son, responds to his father's demands instantly and without question. The status of 'father' is apparently sufficient. As Max says, shortly after he is fired from his position as a clothing salesman, 'I know you hate me but you have to help me.' And David neither denies the charge nor the request. There is then seemingly an obligation upon a son to his father, an obligation that does not need to be explained. This apparently inescapable obligation, this promethean bond ties a son to his father in a way that very few of these films in the entire cycle question. Most indeed take it entirely for granted, even when or especially when they are not specifically exploring that relationship in any meaningful way. *Nothing in Common* is exploring the relationship not by bringing to the surface the very nature of the relationship but by (again) taking it for granted.

Nothing in Common differs from *Dad* and *Memories of Me* in that the antagonism between father and son is much more open, hostility is much more clearly expressed. *Memories of Me* admits to a degree of hostility between father and son but modifies it by revealing it to be the consequence of the inability of Abe and Abbie to express their feelings: a failing of masculinity. *Family Business* also shapes its narrative around hostility between, in this case, two sets of fathers and sons but the hostility is tempered by, in one case, the social dimensions of the role of father that is being explored and, in the other, by the fact that the father cannot adequately or appropriately express his love for his son. This is to an extent true of *Nothing in Common* as well, but the hostility goes deeper, the aggression is more openly articulated. In addition to an unexplained bond between father and son which cannot be easily (if ever) broken, it appears that there is also an inevitable hatred between them. In this, *Nothing in Common* is similar to *Stand By Me* and Gordie's heart-breaking revelation that fathers can and do hate their sons. This love/hate relationship is the central tension of *Nothing in Common* and unlike *Dad* (in which hate does not exist) and *Memories of Me* (in which mutual love overpowers whatever antipathy exists between father and son), in *Nothing in Common* the father never does say 'I love you' nor indeed makes more than the most ambivalent of moves towards any articulation of affection for his son. The inability of the father to say 'I love you' to his son is also a narrative factor in *Family Business*, but in this latter film physical gestures 'say' what cannot be verbalized.

Curiously then *Nothing in Common* does not interrogate in any direct sense nor criticize beyond the unsympathetic characterization of Max Bazner the older notions of masculinity which Max embodies. As unattractive as Max is (because of his masculine definition) he has not changed at the end of the narrative. The greatest change is in his son; this change is towards becoming the 'new man', the burgeoning definition of which has become familiar through this quartet of films (and not a few others), and yet the change is caused in large part because of his father. The film therefore suggests that what David was is *not* the consequence of his father, but it does this by sleight of hand, by ignoring this proposition (even though in the usual cultural perception it is fathers that 'create' their sons.)

There exists then a contradiction at the heart of *Nothing in Common*. It postulates two types of man, two definitions of masculinity: that of Max Bazner's generation, the traditional or old-fashioned man; and that of David Bazner's generation, the baby-boomer or yuppie-era man. ('Fifties man', discussed below in relation to *Family Business*, is somewhere in between these two.) The film finds little or nothing admirable about Max. It works hard, however, to make David appear a thoroughly attractive representative of yuppie-era masculinity. He is extremely successful at what he does (advertising), he is self-sufficient and self-controlled, sexy and (hetero-)sexually active, witty, popular, dominating. In other words, he is overwhelmingly masculine by most contemporary cultural criteria. And yet it would seem that both these representatives of different, competing masculinities lack a common element: the ability to express their feelings. The characterization of Max is so overwhelmingly patriarchal it is hard to consider that he has any feelings to express. Unlike *Memories of Me*, here only one man will (must) learn to express his feelings: the son. It remains somewhat mysterious as to why he should bother.

At the same time, the more old-fashioned masculinity is revealed to be inadequate, to be crumbling. Max is the dying king—he is referred to as 'the king of the salesmen' shortly before he is seen as being unable to sell anything; his strength is failing him. It is worth noting that Abe in *Memories of Me* is also referred to as 'the king of the extras'. These mythical allusions are strengthened by the death of Abe and the physical incapacity of Max, although Max is not 'dethroned'. In the latter case, he is actually wheeled away in a throne (wheelchair) pushed by David, in the film's final shot.

Like Jake Tremont, Max Bazner is incapable of fending for himself. He calls for David every time something goes wrong: his wife leaves him, he has a minor car accident, he gets fired, he does not even know how to shop for groceries. So complete is Max's failing masculinity that while shopping with David he admits to impotency. The film is not so much critical of the old-fashioned definition of masculinity that Max represents as it is dismissing of it, showing through Max the total irrelevance and failure of his male position. All it retains of whatever the power of patriarchy that Max represented is the power of fatherhood, this mysterious power that must be recognized, to which acquiescence must be made.

Nothing in Common is still in love with the eighties-man. So too are *Memories of Me* and *Dad*, but they are not as concerned to scream it from the rooftops, so to speak. *Nothing in Common* finds it difficult if not impossible to register just how attractive the eighties-man is; it is not really prepared to interrogate the cultural definition of masculinity he represents, nor to find that definition as problematic--beyond the absence of the eighties-man's father. This absence, according to *Nothing in Common*, is a minor flaw in what it means to be a man; failure to recognize the need for (and the love for) *the* father does not invalidate the reigning definition of masculinity, only, it seems, to render it partial.

In none of these four films do the sons, each of whom epitomizes the American male (which for at least three of them is the white, middle-class baby-boom American male), renounce those aspects of their existence which define them as characters and as males, namely their public sphere activities—their careers. In all except *Family Business*, each son seems as if he is ready to make such a renunciation in order to maintain a newly forged relationship with his father. In *Dad* and *Memories of Me* the possibility of doing so is effectively negated by the death of the father, leaving the son 'free' to pursue the American/masculine success story with renewed vigour because they are now more 'complete'. They have incorporated into their self-concept the essential 'feminine' characteristic they have previously denied or have been unable to articulate. But this has not been at the cost of other aspects of their masculinity—except that part which previously denied them the liberty to express their innermost emotions.

This is also true of *Nothing in Common*. The climactic moment here is specifically when David puts all he stands for (or seems to stand for)—

professional success, ambition, opportunity in the public sphere, even sexual relations with a highly desirable women—on the line in order to be with his father. It does seem, for a moment, that there is a real conflict between the demands of the public aspects of the definition of masculinity and those of the private (feminine) aspects of the new man. The narrative tension is quite palpable at this point, and it seems that it demands that David's stand in favour of father (private) over profession (public) be understood as the stand that is 'right'. The dialogue is significant. The head of the company for whom David is creating an advertising campaign demands he come to New York: 'You don't have to stay here with your father'. David replies, 'No, I don't, but I'm going to.'

We are also encouraged to see it as right that John Tremont and Abbie Polin take time from their public careers to be with their fathers; neither is really faced with having to make a choice between the two. And neither, finally, is David; his boss turns out to be thoroughly understanding and even relates a little anecdote about his failure to be reconciled with his own father before the latter's death. In *Nothing in Common* this seems something of a cop-out but from the outset the film has been particularly concerned to present an entirely attractive picture of David's public existence. Indeed, frequently the spectator is quite clearly positioned to 'share' David's annoyance at being interrupted by incursions into his public life by his father (and, it must be noted, his mother).

Nothing in Common and *Memories of Me* are linked by the fact that their protagonists are involved with heterosexual relationships, albeit at different levels of intensity. *Dad*, as noted, seems quite concerned to dismiss females as irrelevant to men. Inasmuch as one 'type' of irrelevant women is the mother, all three films are in agreement. *Memories of Me* takes the easy way out and does not even allow the mother narrative space beyond one or two disparaging references. *Family Business* is, again, more complicated in that one mother is absent (dead) but one is present, although peripheral. But even here, there is a commonality with the two previously discussed films: all suggest and/or demonstrate that women (or at least the mothers, thus 'traditional' women) are lacking in the very emotionality that the men manifest. Of course, the films are concerned to show that men do have very high levels of emotionality and that it needs only to be tapped to gush forth—without damaging their status as *men*. Each of the mothers is characterized in part or whole by absence of 'feeling', which it is implied makes them less than women (because it is a feminine characteristic to have feeling) or alternatively which makes them less human than men (because men have feelings in addition to all their other 'superior' attributes). Once again, it is difficult not to note a high level of misogyny.

Yet it must be equally recognized that this misogyny—if it is truly such—extends only to the mother-generation, at least in *Nothing in Common* and

255

Memories of Me. Both Abbie Polin and David Bazner have females in their lives who direct them, one way or another, along the pathways leading to contact with their emotions--and thus in turn to focus those emotions on their fathers. It is females *but not mothers* who start the process of these men discovering their 'femininity'. Thus the conflict is not between masculinity and femininity. The 'good' aspects of femininity are also present in masculinity; they simply need to be realized, recognized and incorporated into contemporary cultural perceptions of masculinity. The conflict is between the opposing claims of fatherhood and motherhood, of patriarchy (in the private rather than public sense) and matriarchy. Thus one way or another each of these films dismisses the mother: by ignoring her existence in *Memories of Me*; by quite cruelly demonstrating her failure to provide true emotional support and understanding in *Dad*; and by revealing the demands she makes upon her son are less important (to him) in *Nothing in Common*. In *Nothing in Common* the absence of the mother, her voluntary removing of herself, creates a vacuum of love. If the mother cannot love the father or is not there to do so, then the son must fill the void. More generally in these films the mother must be pushed aside in order to allow the relationship between a father and son to flower into full expression, the point made precisely by *Ordinary People* at the beginning of this cycle of father/son films.

Women as (but not simply as) bed-partners are shown to be important in *Nothing in Common* and *Memories of Me*, and not only important in providing a complete definition of the respective protagonists as men in the old sense. Becoming in touch with the 'feminine' side of their natures makes the men more attractive than less—or at least the narratives of both *Memories of Me* and *Nothing in Common* seem to stipulate. Indeed, David's 'claims' upon his onetime girlfriend and 'pal', Donna, are resisted until the very point at which his own resistance to his sublimated love for his father is overcome.

Two aspects of relationships between men and/or between fathers and sons are important in these films. As with *Dad*, physicality is of considerable consequence. In *Nothing in Common*, physicality is limited but is of key significance in tracing the development or liberation of David's feelings, while at the same time providing a signpost of old-fashioned masculinity. Towards the end of the narrative, as Max faces surgery, David makes a gesture towards embracing him—a gesture which is resisted. Later, as Max recovers from the operation David, thinking him to be still unconscious, embraces him and sobs on his chest. Max opens his eyes but does not reject the gesture: it is the moment of forgiveness. And in being so it is a very biblical moment inasmuch as Max has been throughout and remains throughout a stern (if seemingly weak) patriarch who accepts David's devotion as his proper due. He has done little if anything to deserve this love, other than to be David's father. Unlike the other films discussed here, Max never comes to say 'I love you' to David. The closest he can manage is to say, as David wheels him away from the hospital (to a new life together?) is 'You're the last person I ever thought would come through for me.' This may be a recognition of his own failures or inadequacies as a father but the film suggests (by a close up on the look of happiness which passes over David face) that this is tantamount to a declaration of love.

FAMILY BUSINESS (1989)

Family Business, like *Dad*, concerns itself with three generations of men, and again places the second generation male in conflict with both his father and his son. As with all the films analysed in this chapter, each generation consists of only one male. That is, none of the males, whether they are grandfather, son or grandson, has any male siblings. Indeed, only in *Dad* are there any siblings at all. This allows, of course, for a more single-minded narrative focus while at the same denying the possibility that any one son's reaction to his father is simply idiosyncratic and not located within the general perception of relations between fathers and sons. Unlike *Dad*, *Family Business* focuses more upon the grandson than upon the father, and explores the relationship between the second and third generation more deeply than the relationship between the first and second generation. Even so, there is still the sense that the grandfather and the grandson are more attuned to each other and at times form an alliance against the father.

Family Business does not immediately appear to be a film 'about' father/son relations because it has some of the features of a genre film, and as such is concerned with the demands of that formula. Superficially *Family Business* is a Caper film. That is, a film whose narrative is concerned with the planning, execution and (sometimes) aftermath of an elaborate robbery of some sort. Here the 'twist' is that the robbery is planned and carried out by three men who are, in fact, grandfather, father and son. They are the McMullens, a family 'complicated' by a curious ethnic diversity: Jesse McMullen, the grandfather is originally Scots; his son, Vito, had an Italian mother, and *his* son, Adam, a Jewish mother. The latter situation serves to, at least, provide an alternative and presumably 'normal' set of (Jewish) grandparents whose sentimental and loving passivity stands in contrast to the energetic and aggressive personal relations between each of the men on the McMullen side of the family.

As with all of the films dealt with here, the generations are distinguished by the manner in which each represents a furthering of the American dream, of advancement from generation to generation. Jesse is a 'successful' immigrant, albeit successful in terms of being a lifelong criminal. He still lives in New York's Hell's Kitchen district.Vito owns and operates a wholesale meat business, and lives in an apartment overlooking Central Park. Adam is a brilliant student, attending MIT on a scholarship. An initial motivation for contention between Vito and Adam is that Adam has recently dropped out of the masters' program at MIT. Here is a familiar situation of the traditional or 'Fifties' father endeavouring to push his son in a direction dictated by education and the resultant social position without, seemingly, to consider the son's feelings in the matter. Examples may be found in *Dead Poets Society*, *The Flamingo Kid* (1984) and *Grandview USA* (1984). Certainly, this aspect of the narrative has its direct counterpart in *Dad* where Billy has dropped out of college, to John's dismay and incomprehension. And in that film as in this, the measure of the change that has been wrought in the father (John, Vito) is their acceptance at the end that the son (Billy, Adam) has the right to choose his own path. The barriers that exist between father and son at the beginning of the story can only be explained through Adam's seeming 'rebellion' against the dictates of his father.

It has become commonplace to find the post-war generation of American males described as lost. Not lost in the physical sense, but lost in the sense of personal definition as men. Robert Bly describes this particular version of the American male as

> 'the Fifties male' who got to work early, labored responsibly, supported his wife and children, and admired discipline....Many of his qualities were strong and positive, but underneath the charm and bluff there was, and there remains, much isolation, deprivation, and passivity....receptive space or intimate space was missing in this image of a man. (1990, 1-2)

This definition of the father seems to me to hold true much later than the fifties. With only small variations, it remains true for the seventies and eighties, while parallel to it are other types of male pertinent to particular cultural demands of the sixties and seventies: the baby-boomer father; the yuppie-era father. Each of these films explores this 'lost man'. In *Dad*, in a scene already referred to, John Tremont explains to his son, Billy, the extent to which his acceptance of this definition led to the disintegration of his family: 'Something had to give and it was my family'. *Dad* is concerned with redefining the Fifties male and reintegrating him into the family mainstream. As such its narrative (and those of *Memories of Me* and *Nothing in Common*) is structured around the metamorphosis of its protagonist. Unlike the other films discussed in this chapter, *Family Business* does not wear its heart so openly on its sleeve. Although it is as concerned as any of these films with exploring the relations between fathers and their sons, it is less melodramatic in the way it does so. Partly this is due to the fact that the film's narrative places these relationships into an action-formula through which these relationships are refracted rather than seen via the magnifying lens of *Dad*, *Memories of Me* and *Nothing in Common*. *Family Business* is more subtle in the way in which changes are wrought in Vito McMullen, its version of Fifties Man. In this, such changes as Vito undergoes are similar to those of Max Bazner in *Nothing in Common*—not wholesale but significant, expressed in small ways rather than large.

The relationships in *Family Business* are conflictual but they are built upon or around love between men, genetically and generationally related. There is no doubt that Vito loves his son, Adam, but as is typical of the 'old' male, he cannot express those feelings in personal (feminine) ways—until the very end. He has even greater difficulty with expressing his feelings—other than hostile ones—towards his father and, indeed, never does so until Jesse is dead. The conflict between Vito and Adam is, at first, based in the very fact that the way in which Vito expresses his love for Adam is through his overpowering determination to provide Adam with everything he (Vito) wasn't given by his father. This is, of course, a transposed reaction to his own relationship with his own father. In order to work out his relationship with Adam, Vito must also work through his relationship with his father. The ability to express emotions is less important in *Family Business* than it is in the other films. What is more important is for the son to recognize the father for both who and what he is.

Vito as Fifties man is under attack from just about every conceivable direction. It is little wonder that he is lost. The official voice of Patriarchy, the judge at the trial, accuses Vito of being 'a sorry excuse for a parent'. Vito's wife echoes this claim when she accuses Vito of being too soft, not sufficiently a man in the traditional sense: 'Why are you such a dishrag with Adam?'. Even Jesse taunts him with 'What sort of father slaps a 23-year-old son?' after Adam has defied Vito openly. Jesse also quite accurately points out to Vito: 'That won't get you anywhere' (with Adam). Masculinity as defined by the tenets of the hard-working, emotionally remote (or repressed) father is, yet again, shown to be 'wrong' on just about every count. Fathers are important, to be a father is important, that is what these and other films repeatedly indicate. They are not concerned with demolishing fatherhood, let alone masculinity. But they do echo contemporary concerns when they state, time after time, that the Fifties father (or the yuppie generation father, or the baby-boomer father) is for the most part a failure, even perhaps an irredeemable failure. Even though some of these films may offer some justification for this poor, benighted figure—and *Family Business* does so to a certain extent—they do not offer a case for his continued existence. The degree of change which Vito undergoes in *Family*

Business is demonstrably less than that of John Tremont or Abbie Polin. But the key here is the amount of change which is *demonstrated*, that is made visible. By allowing Adam freedom, it may be argued that Vito, in his way has learnt to free himself of an 'unnatural' preoccupation with the Lawgiving aspects of Patriarchy. Adam has, of course, already freed himself; the real change is that Vito is able to recognize that Adam is entitled to exercise that freedom. As the two go together to the wake for Jesse, Vito asks Adam what he intends to do with the rest of his life. Adam replies that is the first time that Vito has ever asked that question. When Vito acknowledges this and asks again, Adam replies 'I don't know.' Vito, the 'new' Vito, is able to accept that answer.

That Vito loves Adam is manifest but importantly Vito is unable to articulate that love except through attempting to steer Adam in directions which he feels are best for Adam. In a dialogue scene highly reminiscent of that in *Dad* where John attempts to rationalize his 'failure' as a father to *his* son, Billy, Vito says: 'I broke my ass to give you what he never gave me.' Adam retorts, 'I never asked you for anything.' Vito: 'You never had to. You had everything a kid ever wanted. You didn't even need a scholarship. I could have paid...' Adam: 'You never understood me. You still don't.' In distinct opposition to John Tremont, however, Vito makes it unmistakably clear that what he did was for his family and he did not, unlike John, sacrifice family for power, authority, and wealth. (This reflects, presumably, the difference between the fifties father and the yuppie-era father.) It is at this point that Adam openly defies Vito by telling him that there is nothing Vito can do to stop him going ahead with his planned robbery. Vito, frustrated, slaps Adam. The same capacity for violence is manifested soon afterwards when Vito beats up an employee who has been robbing him. The violence erupts when the fired employee makes implied threats against Vito's family. The violence is not directed at the employee so much as it is frustration at Vito being unable to prevent Adam (and Jesse) undertaking the 'caper'. Indeed, at the very beginning of this scene, as Vito enters his office, he says 'That fucking kid', talking about Adam rather than the thieving employee.

That Vito represents the repressed male, unable to give his emotions due articulation, is demonstrated a number of times. He cannot tell Adam that he loves him, and skirts around it at one point when Adam tells him, apropos his maternal grandparents, 'When somebody loves you, you've got a hell of a weapon in the relationship.' The camera which has held both of them in two shot, stays on Vito as Adam moves away. But the closest that Vito is able to come to articulating his feelings at that moment is to call after Adam, 'Hey. Listen, it's supposed to work both ways, kiddo. I mean, if you love someone back, they got an equal weapon, no?' Adam is not unconscious to Vito's meaning: 'That's right, Pop. I guess we got a standoff.'

It is manifest that Vito's concern for Adam is not just or perhaps even that Vito defines himself by the traditional perceptions of masculinity/fatherhood. Despite an implication that Vito is actually excited by the prospect of the robbery (suggested by a slight smile which crosses Vito's face when he hears the details of the caper), he claims throughout that he went on the job to protect Adam. That he does not prevent Adam from being caught is yet another failure of Vito as a father. As Adam is caught by the police, the camera tracks into the watching Vito. The expression of his face registers the hurt and the fear for Adam as much as his own failure. Later, when Vito has returned to his apartment, he is barely able to prevent himself from breaking down as he avoids telling his wife about the caper and Adams arrest. That he does not break down is partly attributable to his desire not to tell his wife, and partly to the definition of masculinity which he lives.

Vito's love for his son causes him to give up to the police both his own father and himself. This apparent act of self-sacrifice drives a further wedge between himself and Adam as it is Jesse who in fact suffers the most, being sentenced to a long jail term while Adam and Vito are free on probation. Adam sees this as an act of betrayal (of Jesse) rather than an act of love on his behalf. Indeed, in a pre-sentence address Adam specifically speaks for his grandfather who he claims 'always respected who I am'. Further Adam, as much as he is the 'new' man of the eighties, can quite confidently state 'My grandpa loves me. He always has. And I love him'. The enormity of Vito's 'sin', in Adam's eyes, is that 'You turned in your own father'. The price that Vito must pay for being unable to express his love for his son in appropriate ways is to be excluded from the life and love of his son. Thus the failure of the traditional definitions of masculinity are made readily apparent.

Yet does Jesse demonstrate any greater capacity for expressing his emotions? What is the fundamental difference between Jesse and Vito as male role models for Adam? From the outset, the narrative is structured in such a way that Jesse and Vito are 'competing' for Adam—that they are competing 'styles' of masculinity. Jesse, for all that he represents an attractive masculinity, cannot in the end represent an enduring masculinity. But his death, in fact, frees both Adam and, more importantly, Vito. Adam must not only become free of Vito through the course of the narrative he must also become free to recognize his own freedom. In a way, each must become free of Jesse. Thus the importance of the concluding sequence in which Vito and Adam together spread Jesse's ashes from the rooftops of Hell's Kitchen. It is then, and only then that Vito is able to embrace and indeed kiss Adam. Here indeed Vito is the more physically expressive, and while Adam places his hand on Vito's shoulder during the singing of 'Danny Boy', it is Vito who covers Adam's hand with his own—a more intimate gesture.

There are moments when Jesse does affect a measure of intimacy with Vito, more so, or at least more physically than he does with Adam. When the caper is still in the planning stage but after Vito agrees to take part, he and Jesse stay in a motel near to the factory they intend to burgle. Here Jesse makes a deal with a pair of hookers, and he attempts to persuade the reluctant Vito to come along. Jesse at first places his hand on Vito's thigh and then begins to fondle him, all the while singing 'It's Almost Like Being in Love'. Any possible homoerotic suggestions are undermined by the fact that moments before Jesse was making arrangements to spend the evening with two female prostitutes. Following Adam's arrest, Jesse and Vito argue over the returning of the stolen 'plasmids'. Vito in his anxiety to release Adam from prison wants to do so straight away, Jesse wishes to move a little bit more thoughtfully. Vito smacks Jesse on the forehead several times, and Jesse responds by leaping to his feet, seemingly about to punch Vito. Instead the two men eyeball each other from very close range, before Jesse unclenches his fist to make a relaxed hand with which he lightly, affectionately taps Vito on the cheek. He then wets a finger with saliva and removes a tiny piece of shaving paper from Vito's lip.

A similar moment occurs when Vito, convinced that Jesse has hidden the plasmids, punches him in the mouth. Jesse responds not by hitting back but by acclaiming the return of the 'real Vito'. It would seem then that even Jesse recognizes the Vito's behaviour as 'Fifties man' is adopted behaviour, not 'natural' or that in which he was brought up. It is social role play. The point is reiterated in a slightly different way when following Jesse's death Adam and Vito finally get together and talk man to man. Here Adam tells him that it is not enough to rationalize his actions by saying everything Vito did, he did for Adam. Adam challenges Vito that if he hated his twenty years in the wholesale meat business, then he did that to himself, and to stop blaming Adam. In other words, Vito took on the role of distant, fifties father voluntarily so to speak. The narrative does tend to argue that the life and example provided by Jesse may have had something to do with it, but it may also be assumed at least that Vito had adopted a role which was socially demanded of a husband-father. In this *Family Business* joins the chorus of disapproval of the fifties-style father, but while this chorus may be raucous it is curiously silent about examining the 'real' origin of this definition of masculinity. Vito McMullen, like John Tremont, thought *that* 'was what a father was—some guy who wore a suit and made a lot of money'. Neither had fathers who corresponded to this image, although Jesse McMullen is distinctly different from Jake Tremont in almost every regard except for the natural intimate affinity he has with his grandson.

I have argued in *Nothing in Common* that sons seem to acknowledge obligations to fathers that require no explanation, and which transcend dislike perhaps even hatred. That this is a socially fixed perception seems beyond question. In *Family Business*, despite all that Jesse represents as 'bad' in Vito's interpretation of their father/son relationship, it seems that Jesse being his father is sufficient to ensure that the bond between them is unbreakable, and that Vito has some sort of obligation towards his father that is not necessarily reciprocal.

In relation to Adam, Vito as a father is not all that difficult to place. He is the familiar father—familiar from both within these films and from cultural perceptions (from which these films arise). Vito is the remote breadwinner, ambitious to see the American dream made real through his son (Adam tells Jesse, 'That's the American way. Each generation does a little better'), whose masculinity is defined by his authoritarian control (or attempts at control) within the family) and who expresses his love for his son through direction and discipline—and 'self sacrifice' in economic terms of working hard to earn the wherewithal to 'give' his son the chance to climb up the American-dream ladder.

Jesse, on the other hand, does not represent to Adam any sort of 'parental' figure—as is made apparent by the manner Adam both addresses and refers to Jesse by his first name. Only towards the end does Adam call Jesse 'Grandpa'; his use of the term in his speech on Jesses behalf to the court is startling because it is unfamiliar. Jesse represents a different type of masculinity, not defined so much by being a variant of 'father' but being a mentor and more especially by being (in a term borrowed from Robert Bly 1988) a 'Wild Man', an unconscious aspect of complete or integrated masculinity absent (according to Bly) from contemporary American males. He is thus explicable more in mythical or socio-psychological terms than socio-cultural ways. The characterization of Vito is, like most fathers in these four films, defined by and through presently held cultural perceptions of masculinity/fatherhood. To Vito, however, Jesse is perhaps the Wild Man but is also and still the Father. (The Wild Man is that side of himself which Vito rejects—or tries to: his acquiescence in the robbery implies he is still in touch with and can be seduced by this side of his male persona.)

Here in *Family Business* as with the other film analysed in this chapter (and other chapters too), women play very little part in the changes that occur in men and between men. They are present but peripheral. Their presence is to nullify any possible interpretation of men's relationships to other men as being, overtly at least, homosexual. Each of the three protagonists in *Family Business* does have a women 'partner' but each woman proves to be either incidental or a hindrance. Each, however, seems to instinctively recognize that of the three versions of masculinity, the three types of male, being 'offered', Adam is the male whom they find most appealing. Elaine, Adam's mother, tells Vito to turn in himself (and *his* stinking father) to the police in order to get Adam released. Jesse's girlfriend tells Vito virtually the same thing. Adam's own girlfriend, Christine, is not consulted. Moreover she is, within the narrative, a transitory figure who exists only for thematic reasons.

As already indicated, Christine's presence may be explained as providing Adam with a needed patina of heterosexuality. Secondly, she provides an opportunity to rationalize Jesse's criminal lifestyle by enabling him, after she has explained how she gets options on apartment leases from terminally ill patients, to make a distinction between illegality and immorality. Even so, together with his mother and Jesse's girlfriend, Christine makes up a 'cross section' of women (all older) who are instinctively drawn to Adam. The childlike, naive, or 'soft' male that he represents is the sort of male women seem to want. Or at least seem to prefer even though it is also the case that Margie is clearly attracted to Jesse and Elaine to Vito. Yet, given a 'choice' they will sacrifice (gladly?) these men for Adam. Their narrative function then is to provide a female perspective and to distinguish between the three types of masculinity on display. Unlike *Dad*, however, there is no strong suggestion that women get between men, or especially between fathers and their sons, preventing them from fully realizing their emotional attachment to each other. Nor do they represent any clearly implied threat of emasculation.

Family Business might almost have been considered as a Coming-of-Age film. The caper and its immediate aftermath is an initiatory trial that Adam has to undergo to 'become a man'. But here instead of the initiation being undertaken to lead Adam away from the 'world of women' to the 'world of men', it serves to lead Adam away from the world of his father to the world defined in part by the Wild Man. As Jesse lies dying in the prison infirmary, he asks Adam, 'You're your own man now, eh?' And Adam replies, 'I'm out from under Vito anyway.' This is where *Family Business* departs company from the other films dealt with in this chapter. Its trajectory for one of its protagonists, Adam, is to allow him to discover, not the feminine side of his maleness, but the masculine side. Vito, however, does follow something of the path of John Tremont, David Bazner and Abbie Polin: he is placed in touch with that feminine side. He has previously had, but denied, the Wild Man—although he reintroduces himself briefly for the purposes of Adam's initiation. The hard shell of his Fifties man masculinity has been cracked at least, and the two 'new' men are able to embrace for the first time while celebrating the life of and the life-force provided by the Wild Man.

These five films 'stack' the odds in their examination of father-son relationships by postulating, either from the outset or as key point of their narratives, a father who is dying. This fact motivates the son's actions (the father's too to some extent) in examining and then altering in the direction of reconciliation and atonement his attitude towards and relationship with his father. In each case, the primacy of the father as The Father is recognised and confirmed; this in a nutshell is what these films ranged across the eighties are responding to in the American *zeitgeist*.

NOTES

1. In fiction, a MacGuffin (sometimes McGuffin or maguffin) is a plot device in the form of some goal, desired object, or other motivator that the protagonist pursues, often with little or no narrative explanation. The specific nature of a MacGuffin is typically unimportant to the overall plot. The most common type of MacGuffin is an object, place or person; other types include money, victory, glory, survival, power, love, or other things unexplained. (http://en.wikipedia.org/wiki/MacGuffin)

REFERENCES

Bly, Robert, *Iron John: A Book about Men* (Reading, MA: Addison-Wesley, 1990).
Mellen, Joan, *Big Bad Wolves: Masculinity in the American Film* (London: Elm Tree Books, 1978).

THREE FILMS, THREE ABSENT FATHERS

INDIANA JONES AND THE LAST CRUSADE (1989)

Throughout the 1980s, Hollywood cinema revealed a consistent concern with father/son relationships, a concern that at times seems almost to have been an obsession. Although father/son relations provide the basic narratives of a number of films (e.g. *Ordinary People* 1980, *The Chosen* 1982, *Harry and Son* 1984, *Dad* 1989, *Memories of Me* 1989), the proof of the strength of this concept is found as much in those films which ostensibly are narratively (and even thematically) concerned with other things.[1]

A film that demonstrates the degree to which this theme had become dominant in Hollywood, and which at the same time reveals important aspects of how this theme is treated, is *Indiana Jones and the Last Crusade*. Given that this film is the third in a series of films whose narratives are based around the exploits of the eponymous hero, and that the first in the series, *Raiders of the Lost Ark*, is one of the most successful American films at the box office, it is reasonable to assume that this, the latest in the series, might well be built narratively around notions of action and adventure and general derring-do.

Indeed, to a large extent, *The Last Crusade* is the narrative formula as before. At least, as before in the first such film. Once again 'Indy' is in pursuit of an archaeological relic of unparalleled spiritual and/or religious significance. This time of Christian importance (the Holy Grail) not Judaic (the Ark of the Covenant) but the overall aura associated with it is much the same, and of course both operate, narratively, as 'macguffins'. And as with *Raiders*, Indy is racing against the pre-war Nazis in an attempt to prevent the relic, and its supernatural powers, from falling into their hands.

Whereas the adventure arguably is the *raison d'etre* of *Raiders*, the narrative core of *The Last Crusade* is not the race to locate the Holy Grail but the relationship between Indy and his (heretofore unknown) father, Professor Henry Jones. The manner in which *The Last Crusade* merely duplicates *Raiders* becomes unimportant because the film's concerns are actually elsewhere. An examination of the nature of the relationship between the two Joneses, and the way in which this is dealt with in terms of the film's structure reveals a great deal about the way in which the theme of father/son relations has been expressed in diverse Hollywood films throughout the 1980s.

A constant of this handling has been to provide as a significant aspect of the narrative trajectory the need and the desire for reconciliation between a father and a son. This reconciliation has, more often than not, been linked with the need for the son to bring about the appropriate conditions for it through an act (or acts) of *atonement*. Much more rarely has the father sought atonement with his son.[2] At the same time, it is seldom demonstrated or suggested that the son is actually blameworthy or has committed a 'sin' that must be expiated before reconciliation is possible. But even where the father is at fault, often for just being a father (that is, acting out the role of a father), it is the son who must seek atonement, usually through a particular action that has no other purpose other than to be a demonstrable act of expiation. This particular aspect, occurring as it does in so many films, implies a social and cultural concern with providing images designed to reinforce an otherwise besieged and embattled patriarchy.

That *The Last Crusade* is 'about' a father/son relation is made manifest in the very opening sequences. A clearly designated prologue introduces the juvenile Indy, thus providing a background not considered pertinent in either of the two preceding Indiana Jones adventures. This prologue is concerned with young Indy trying to prevent the Cross of Coronado, a lost Spanish Conquest treasure, from falling into the 'wrong' hands, and is used to show how several of the famous icons associated with Indiana Jones (the Stetson, the whip) came to be part of his image. However, this is really unimportant. What is important in the prologue is the introduction of the Father, and while the need to introduce the Father is important for the narrative, it is the *manner* of his introduction that is significant.

Henry Jones is established in this prologue as the Father as Law Giver. He exists in the mise-en-scene as little more than an admonishing finger raised to rebuke Indy. Instead of listening to Indy, let alone helping him avoid the treasure-robbers or taking his side regarding the fate of the Cross, he commands Indy (significantly referring to him as 'Junior', as he will throughout the film) to count in Greek before speaking. Throughout this scene, no more of Henry Jones is revealed than this reproving finger, no more is heard than his commanding voice (save for the end of the scene when he mutters over a medieval illumination). At the same time, it is clear that the father 'fails' the son in not listening to him and in not, perhaps, preventing the loss of the Cross. There is more than a touch of irony of course given it is a cross, the essential Christian symbol, which serves to divide father and son, and it will be another Christian icon, the Holy Grail, which will provide the conditions to bring them together again. Nonetheless, it is not the father who seeks to make amends much later but the son.

An ellipsis carries the narrative forward by twenty-six years, and a short sequence has the adult Indy finally retrieving the Cross of Coronado, thus redressing the humiliation of that adolescent defeat. A defeat that was made all the more humiliating through the 'absence' of his father at a crucial moment. The narrative isolation of this one incident, which is all we see of Indy's childhood, means that it stands as the significant event which defines the relationship of Indy to his father until such point as that relationship is reworked by the narrative. It is thus the *disruption* which sets the narrative in motion and which must be redressed before *equilibrium* can be restored. Moreover, the absence of his father is to provide one of two key emphases in the way in which father/son relations structure the narrative that follows. The other is the facing of three challenges in order to ultimately gain access to the Grail, which Indy must use to save his father's life.

At this early stage Indy does not know of any Nazi interest in the Grail and he is brought into this latter-day quest not because of what the Grail ostensibly is but because his father has gone missing while engaged upon the same venture. That it is because of his father rather than whatever other interest that Indy might have in the Grail is clearly delineated by the way in which the camera frames him when his father is first mentioned by Donovan (the art collector who is asking Indy to look for the Grail). First Indy is seen in two shot (with Donovan), dismissing the Grail legend as 'an old man's dream,' presumably a reference to his father and his lifelong obsession. Then as Donovan states that the Grail is 'every man's dream, including your father's I believe', the shot cuts at the mention of his father to a tight close-up of Indy who looks up suddenly, arrested in swallowing a mouthful of champagne. Shortly after, Donovan tells Indy that his father has disappeared while searching for more clues to the location of the Grail.

It is not, however, learning that his father has disappeared that prompts Indy to enter the search—which will be for his father and not initially for the Grail in any case. Indy's motivation is provided in the following scene. He and a friend of his father, Marcus Brody, find Henry's home ransacked. Although clearly puzzled and disturbed, and finding himself in possession of Henry's 'Grail diary' (another macguffin), Indy does not actually voice his determination to go in search of his father until he finds amongst the debris a photograph of himself as a child with his father. What causes Indy to set out on his own 'holy quest' is not the possibility of the existence of the Grail nor what the search for it means (Marcus: 'It is the search for the divine in all of us.') but the image of the father, which is simultaneously that of the Father (Patriarch) in the abstract and Indy's real father in an image frozen at a particular moment in the history of their relationship—in the pre-narrative equilibrium. Marcus's words might be paraphrased by the unspoken 'it is the search for the *father* in all of us' which *The Last Crusade* is really about.

This is reconfirmed in a far less subtle way, following the attempts on Indy's life by the Brothers of the Cruciform Sword (and after an exciting life- and property-destroying chase around Venice, a sequence very much in keeping with the conventions of the genre) when he answers a challenge as to his reasons for seeking the Grail by replying, 'I didn't come to find the Cup, I came to find my father.'

Even before he locates Henry and rescues him from the Nazis, the degree to which Indy is competing with his (absent) father is made clear. He refers to him as 'Attila the professor' and refuses to accept that his father could ever be 'as giddy as a schoolboy' even when he was a schoolboy. When Indy finds the long-sought crusader's tomb, he revels in having done something his father could not (or at least did not): 'he's scared of rats.' And, unbeknownst to either, father and son compete for the same woman, Ilsa Schroeder, who tells Indy that 'you are a great deal like your father' to which Indy retorts, 'Except he's lost and I'm not.'

This sharing of the same woman also introduces a stronger element of Oedipal conflict into the competition between father and son, especially when it is recognized that Henry has had sexual relations with Ilsa first, and that Indy only does so *in his father's absence* and *without being aware* that Ilsa was his father's mistress before becoming his. It is noteworthy that Henry's wife/Indy's mother is totally absent save for a fleeting reference shortly after Henry has chastised the adult Indy for blasphemy. In this thematically charged scene the first mention is made by Indy, who places his mother and himself together in opposition to his father when he insists that neither he nor his mother understood Henry's obsession with the Grail. Henry refutes this by claiming that not only did she accept his 'obsession' but understood it to the point of considering it more important than her own terminal illness. Thus Henry reintegrates her (or her memory) into the patriarchal order and places her in the position of having apparently sacrificed herself to his greater authority.[3]

Competing with the father, absent or otherwise, becomes significantly less important than attempting to impress him and gain his approval after Indy finds him. When Indy machine-guns a bunch of Nazis, Henry says 'Look what you've done' rather than expressing any sort of gratitude for his timely rescue. And later, when Indy has despatched a quartet of pursuing Nazis, he is 'rewarded' only with a stern look of disapprobation from Henry, a look that quickly dissolves the pleased, looking-for-approval expression off Indy's face. Father as Law Giver returns following Indy's exasperated 'Jesus Christ' when Henry insists on going to Berlin after the diary. Henry slaps Indy's face, and again the admonishing finger is raised in stern rebuke.

Although Indy has to rescue Henry again in the course of events, the first part of this narrative trajectory is accomplished. But the disruption that prompted the narrative has not been resolved because the initial disruption is not the disappearance of Henry but the much earlier (and elided) emotional separation of father and son. The importance of father/son relations is not demonstrated merely by bringing father and son together. This is made clear by a scene that takes place in an airship as they leave Germany (having recovered the diary). Here Indy attempts to express his resentment over the way in which their relationship in the past was determined by Henry's 'absence,' of Henry never 'being there' to talk with. Henry in turn defends himself by claiming to have respected Indy's privacy and taught him self-reliance. When Henry challenges Indy's criticism by saying 'Well, I'm here now. What do you want to talk about?', Indy is unable to find anything to say. Reconciliation has not been achieved by simply rescuing Henry—by eliminating the absence of the father. Indy still has to undertake certain labours of expiation, made more potent in this instance by their essentially religious or spiritual nature.

Even so, the degree to which the father and son have moved towards reconciliation, and that they have not finally achieved it, is brought home when it seems that Indy, in rescuing his father (again), has been killed when a Nazi tank with Indy apparently aboard hurtles over a cliff. In opposition to the distinct indifference towards Indy's 'overtures' in the airship, Henry is stricken: 'Oh God. I've lost him. And I never told him anything...Five minutes would have been enough.' (There is a 'pre-echo' of this following the earlier revelation that Ilsa, the woman they have 'shared', is a Nazi, something Henry knew. Henry resignedly tells Indy, 'You should have listened to your father.') What it is that Henry has not told Indy is far from clear, but this emphasizes in a general way the importance of fathers to their sons: fathers are law givers and they are also teachers; passers-on of wisdom, providers of the Law in more ways than one.

The labours are undertaken by Indy to achieve the Grail, not for itself and not for any notions of preventing it from falling into the hands of the Nazis or even those of Donovan (who has his own designs on the cup's promise of immortality), but in order to literally heal his father (shot by Donovan who believes that deed alone will force Indy to act). The importance of the Grail is thus narratively reduced to the device that will save the father, and it is the son, and only the son, who can answer the challenges that bar the path to the Grail and thus to the healing of the father. The probability that the Grail will be taken by the Nazis if Indy returns with it is not even given narrative space.

The closing of the gap between father and son is demonstrated not simply by Indy facing the challenge of the mysterious (and perhaps mystical) devices that guard the entrance to the Grail chamber but is further emphasized by the almost telepathic communication which exists between father and son as Indy attempts to solve the riddles that give the clues to avoiding the fatal traps. In the last of the three tests, Indy is faced with what appears to be an impossibly deep and wide chasm separating him from the Grail chamber. He hesitates: 'Impossible. No one can jump this.' Alerted by Marcus that Henry is close to death, Indy recognizes that the third test demands 'a leap of faith.' Even so he still falters. The scene cuts to a close-up of Henry who intuits Indy's doubt and whispers, 'You must believe, boy. You must believe.' Indy clearly does not hear Henry in the normal physical sense; he hears him in his mind. And steps into the void. This telepathy is present at some level throughout these trials and as noted is not simply one way. Henry reacts to the nature of the tests even though he cannot see them, as with the one which requires Indy to negotiate a series of marked stones by stepping on those which spell 'Jehovah.'

Thus it is that the Holy Grail, which has been given the reputation and reality of enormous supernatural powers (enough presumably for the Nazis to see it as essential—in the absence of the Ark of the Covenant perhaps—in helping them further their ambitions for global domination), is used to heal a (mere?) professor of medieval literature. But of course this use is far more meaningful than that. It is used, this ultimate icon of God's omnipotence, by a son to heal his father, to heal him not simply physically but to heal the emotional rift between them. So that Henry is able, at the end, to offer his newly strengthened right-hand to reach out and prevent his son falling into the bottomless pit (of Hell?). When Henry points out moments later that Indy's real name is the same as his, Henry Jones, the coming together of Father and Son is symbolically complete—two men with but one name. And the Grail, having carried out this task, is in rather profligate style simply thrown away. Its importance to mankind (and the gender designation is deliberate) is to enable son to become reconciled through atonement with father—and the comparison of this version of such reconciliation and atonement with that of the Grail's ostensible original owner adds emphasis to this analysis.

The importance of *The Last Crusade* to any sustained analysis of father/son relations in Hollywood films of the 1980s is not that it is unique but precisely because it is not. The elements of the absent father, the need for sons to seek reconciliation through atonement, the importance of the patriarch, are ever-present (in various forms) in the many films with narratives quite different from *The Last Crusade* and from each other.[4] Of equal significance is the fact that, on the face of it, *The Last Crusade* is an example of a familiar genre—a genre which conventionally has no particular interest in father/son relations—and thus can serve as a indicator of the extent to which this theme has become embedded in the cultural unconscious of Hollywood and, presumably, its audiences.

FIELD OF DREAMS (1989)

Field of Dreams is one of a number of father/son films which were originally written as short stories, novels or stage plays. The screenplay for this film was adapted by Phil Alden Robinson from the novel *Shoeless Joe* by W.P. Kinsella (1982). I do not raise this matter in order to re-activate any hoary debates over the status of written original over celluloid 'adaptation' nor to intervene into the futile field of the comparative study of novel and film. Rather, what is interesting in any comparison between the novel and the film is that the original novel-narrative does not place an inordinate amount of emphasis on the relationship between the protagonist of both narratives, Ray Kinsella, and his father, John. Indeed, within the novel's narrative there are several other strands dealing with characters and relations that did not make it to the screen version of the story. While the plotline concerned with the magical aspects of the baseball field Ray constructs in his corn field are stressed in the novel, the storyline of Ray and his father is the element which is most strongly accentuated in the film. Whether this was a conscious choice or an idea that pushed itself forward out of the cultural unconscious makes little difference. In the seven years it took for this particular story to find its way, *mutatis mutandis*, from page to screen the concept of fathers and their sons had moved from a plot element of no special importance to the forefront of the narrative and the thematic of *Field of Dreams*.

The novel *Shoeless Joe* and the film *Field of Dreams* are both strongly implicated in examining and expressly celebrating the great American pastime, the American cultural metaphor: baseball. What is highly signifying for us is that, for whatever reason, by the time the processes of translation (and transformation) from literary artefact to cinematic artefact had taken place, the main emphasis of the plot and the thematic of the film had become not the cultural (let alone mystical) significance of baseball in American society but the cultural *and* mystical significance of the relationship of fathers and sons in American society. This significance is enhanced not diminished by being equated with and explored through the mythic power of baseball.

In the category of films dealing with expiation and atonement, *Field of Dreams* is one which deals specifically with the son as a socialized 'product' of the '60's. (There are a number of films where the father's actions and personalities are a result of growing up in the '60's. One major example of this is *Running on Empty* [1988].) Ray Kinsella says in extra-diegetic voice-over in the prologue, 'Officially my major was English, but really it was the 60's'. He leaves (perhaps runs away from) home (and father) to attend college at Berkeley; he 'smokes some grass'. The '60s were, for those coming of age during those years, anti-establishment, anti-family, almost anti-everything. It was during this period that Ray grew up and like many of his generation had a falling out with his father for the reason that he was his father and simultaneously the Father—the most obvious representative of the oppressive Patriarchal society the '60s generation were rebelling against. The two fathers—capitalized and non—became, perhaps, conflated into the readily discernible physicality of the literal father.

The introductory sequence shows a number of photographs of Ray's father, John, with Ray providing voice-over narration, furnishing a brief encapsulation of his father's life. He recalls that his father was born in 1896 and wasn't married until 1938. In between he played several seasons of minor league baseball but never made it to the big leagues. Ray was born in 1952, making his father fifty-six at the time of his birth. Ray's mother died when he was three. Ray grows up hearing stories of the 1919 Chicago White Sox told to him by his father. Ray implies that because his father was so old when Ray was born and growing up there is a bitterness concerning his father that has enveloped Ray and has had a lasting effect on his psyche. Thus, it seems, the 'natural' rebellion of son against the father, heightened by the cultural moment of the '60s, is increased by some feeling that Ray was denied the 'right' to grow up with his father and to discover each other during a parallel period of 'development'.

Ostensibly Ray is now—has grown up to become—a loving happy family man who cares deeply about his wife and daughter (notably *not* a son). But when he is working out in the cornfield by himself, he hears (via a voice that only Ray can hear) his first directive, 'Build it and he will come.' This at first leads Ray to attempt to decipher the meaning of this enigmatic command, and when he eventually does, he co-relates his need to build a baseball field to his father's life. While in bed with his wife he says to her: 'I'm thirty-six years old. I have a wife, a child, and a mortgage, and I'm scared to death I'm turning into my father.' His wife Annie asks, justifiably, 'What's your father got to do with all this?' Ray responds:

> I never forgave him for getting old.
> (pauses)
> By the time he was old as I am now, he was ancient. He must of had dreams you know. But he never did anything about 'em. For all I know he may even heard voices too but he sure didn't listen to them. The man never did one spontaneous thing in all the years I knew him. Annie, I'm afraid of that happening to me and something tells me that this may be my last chance to do something about it. I want to build that field. Do you think I'm crazy?

The film does not provide at this point any logic for why Ray should reflect upon his father after being given a ghostly (or heavenly) directive to build a ball park—an action that will require him to plough under acres of valuable corn, placing his livelihood of his family at risk. The only rational connection seems to be that, first, Ray is scared of becoming of 'turning into' his father and that, second and as a corollary, this is a 'spontaneous' act that is clearly contrary to what Ray understands to have been his father's 'nature'.

Annie responds to Ray's *cri de coeur* in a very sensitive and supportive manner. She wants him to follow his dream. Here, unlike most—but not all—of the films in this study the male protagonist is fully supported, even urged on, by a woman with whom he has an emotional connection. In many films, and notably for this chapter's concentration in *Indiana Jones and the Last Crusade*, a women (or women) are hindrances to the coming together of men and need to be dispensed with, thrust aside or rendered powerless. Misogyny is not universal through these father/son films but it is rampant. In *Field of Dreams* Annie, Ray's wife, seems almost to understand what it is that Ray has to do—almost but not quite. Nonetheless, Annie and their daughter, Karin, can both see the phantom ball players from the outset, sharing to that extent Ray's 'vision'.

'Build it and he will come' is only the first of three directives that Ray is given. For unexplained reasons, he has been granted the opportunity to propitiate for his 'sins' against his father. At the time the first command is delivered Ray is certain that the ballpark that he is to build will be a 'sanctuary' for Shoeless Joe Jackson and the other members of the 1919 Black Sox scandal. The vision that Ray has comes to fruition, and Joe Jackson does appear magically out of the corn not as an insubstantial phantom but as a corporeal being who is just as he was in life. Shoeless Joe is eventually joined by his teammates who were also expelled from the game. Ray's actions seem to have had their mysterious but intended effect. Yet after pleasurably watching a practice of the ballplayers Ray is beckoned again by the voice, this time intoning, 'Ease his pain'.

This prompts the second in a series of acts of penance that Ray must perform without quite sure knowing why he must undertake them. Following the receiving of this instruction, Ray intuits that it as the writer Terrance Mann, once a famous and controversial author in the '60s is the 'he' whose pain Ray has been instructed to 'ease'. He later has a dream where he goes to a ball game at Fenway Park in Boston with Terrance Mann. Mann is a public, '60s 'father-figure' who is the antithesis of Ray's father. According to Ray, he was, 'A pioneer in the civil rights and anti-war movements. He knew everybody. He did everything. He helped shape his time. (But) in the end it wasn't enough and what he missed was baseball.' Terrance Mann may represent the opposite of Ray's father, John Kinsella, but they had the common bond of love of baseball.

'At the risk of losing my home and alienating my wife', Ray heads off to Boston from his home in Iowa.

At first hostile and resistant Terry Mann eventually opts to go with Ray to a Red Sox game at Fenway Park. It is at this location that Ray receives his third and final instruction, 'Go the distance'. Similar to Indiana Jones in *Indiana Jones and the Last Crusade*, Ray is tested to see if he is worthy enough to have the opportunity to achieve redemption and atonement with his father. The 'signs' however provide no clue as to the true purpose of Ray's journey and labours. This third test involves Ray, accompanied by Mann, searching for a long-forgotten baseballer, Archie 'Moonlight' Graham, who had once played one innings with the New York Yankees. They track Graham to a small Minnesota town where he had practiced as a doctor for some fifty years and where he has also died some ten years previously. Even so, Ray 'meets' Doc. Graham out walking and offers him an opportunity to fulfil his wish to just once face a big league pitcher. Graham declines the opportunity but as Ray and Mann head back to Iowa, they pick up a young hitch-hiker who tells them he is Archie Graham.

The coincidence of young Graham travelling the Mid-west looking for ball clubs which take on young players reminds Ray that was what he father did at the same age. This prompts Mann to ask, 'What happened to your father?' Ray responds:

> He never made it as a ball player so he tried to get his son to make it for him. By the time I was ten playing baseball got to be like eating vegetables or taking out the garbage...You believe that—an American boy refusing to have a catch with his father?

Ray continues to explain his situation with his father to Terry and ends by saying, 'The son of a bitch died before I could take it back, before I could... (looks down and away) you know.' The masculine side of Ray wouldn't permit him to let Terry know that what he wanted and needed was to tell his father that he loved him. Terry Mann tells Ray, 'This is your penance.' To which Ray replies, 'I know. I can't bring my father back.'

Although Ray has been able to face the memory of his father by this time, and to recognize the wrong which he committed in creating barriers between his father and himself, it is not apparent as yet that the labours which he has undertaken are not simply 'pointless' penances. Pointless, that is, to Ray in a personal sense. As he is forced to ask when each of the penances has been accomplished, and Shoeless Joe, Terry Mann and Archie Graham have each been redeemed by *his* sacrifices: 'what's in it for me?' He is shamed by Joe who asks him if he really did all this for himself and Ray admits that was not the case. Yet each penance was simultaneously for another and for himself, although he did not know it.

The first labour, the building of the baseball field was an opportunity for Shoeless Joe Jackson (and others) to return to playing baseball as young men. But it was also a test of Ray's worthiness to receive, in time, absolution. He puts at risk his family through the probability he will lose his farm. The second labour takes place in order that Terrance Mann might break out of his self-imposed, cynical retreat from the world and again touch the mythical 'goodness' at the core of American society. For Ray, completion of this labour represents his willingness to confront his part in driving the wedge between his father and himself. The third labour allows Archie Graham a 'reward' for his self-sacrifice (choosing medicine over baseball), and for Ray an opportunity to indicate his capacity to allow a similar opportunity—a return to a moment 'misplayed' in the past. In is important to note that Doc. Graham is the only phantom Ray meets who is old as his father was, but also young like Ray's (unknown) father once was.

Upon returning to Iowa Terry joins the small coterie of people who can actually see the ballplayers on the field that Ray has constructed. This group includes Ray, his wife Annie and his daughter Karin. It is Annie's brother Mark who cannot see the baseballers and who provides Ray with the final test of the strength of his conviction in the baseball field which he created. Mark holds the mortgage note on the farm, and threatens that foreclosure proceedings will take place unless Ray will sell the farm to him. This is similar to the final test in *Indiana Jones*, in which Indy must make 'the leap of faith' and step over the edge into an apparently bottomless chasm. Ray too must take a leap of faith: 'people will come' says his daughter. She is supported in this vision by Mann, who espouses the psychic importance of baseball to 'the people'. Ray does go the distance and rejects Mark's offer.

Ray has served his penance and now has a chance to 'right an old wrong.' After Mann accepts an invitation to go into the corn with the other baseball players (the way they enter and exit this world—for the next?) Ray and Annie are left with Joe on the field as twilight falls. A shot of Ray with his arm around Annie cuts to a medium close-up of Joe Jackson, who tells him, 'If you build it (pauses and looks to his right) he will come.' The *he* is Ray's father, John Kinsella. He has been there, seemingly, all the time, amongst the players, 'hidden' behind a catcher's mask and padding. The emotional nexus of many of the father/son films is that moment when the two men join together in a physical sense. It is often an embrace, they may even kiss, or may be something as apparently unassuming as a handshake. Father and son approach each other with an obeisance. John Kinsella makes the first move, offering his hand to his son, without it seems being aware of who he is. His pain has been eased, at least in part; he has had the opportunity to go to the place 'where dreams come true.' As John meets his son, Ray says, 'Karin this is my...this is John.' Ray now as previously is emotionally incapable of addressing his father by or in terms which would unite them. As they say their goodnights, John again offers his hand to his son, there is a two shot of the men followed by a close-up of just their hands clasping. They touch but as yet Ray has not fully acknowledged his father as his father, nor himself as his father's son. As John walks off into the sunset, Ray finally asks, 'Hey *Dad*, you want to have a catch?' The 'Dad' passes easily and without query between them. John responds, 'I'd like that.'

At this point the music that has been in the background—lush strings and subtle woodwinds sounding rather like Copeland's *Appalachian Spring*—swells on the sound track and there follow a number of shots of the two men tossing the ball back and forth. The final shot of the men together is a sweeping camera movement that moves up and away from them, looking towards the horizon, dissolving into a shot of cars heading towards the two men: the people have come. What is it that takes place between these two men that would suggest that all these people would come to see? Have they come to 'see' baseball at its simplest and its purest—another dream on a field of dreams? Or have they come to repeat the reconciliation of John and Ray in their own lives? The film remains totally enigmatic on this point. Its thrust after all his been concerned with a narrative in which a father and a son reach atonement. The 'forgiving' is not really carried out by the father—although there is more than a sense of the laying on of absolving hands in the handshakes between John and Ray. The forgiveness comes from some other, ineffable source, a source which might easily be said to be the cultural unconscious itself.

THE EMPIRE STRIKES BACK (1980) AND THE RETURN OF THE JEDI (1983)

In no other films in my selection of Father/Son films is the need for a father and son to reconcile with each other of cosmic importance, figuratively speaking, than in the initial *Star Wars* trilogy.[5] The very future (or perhaps the past) of the universe itself is at stake in the conflict between and eventually atonement of a father and his son. This places *The Empire Strikes Back* and *The Return of the Jedi*—indeed the whole *Star Wars* trilogy—within the realm of mythology as it is extensively examined by Joseph Campbell. Ancient mythology, or mythologies, (Greek, Norse, Teutonic, etc), do provide, directly or indirectly, precedent and inspiration for the epic narrative of the *Star Wars* trilogy and also many of the incidents, actions and relations between characters of each of the three films. My purpose is not, however, to try and isolate and examine these mythological elements, nor indeed to attempt in anything more than the most passing of ways to draw attention to allusions, references or analogies between other myth-narratives and the narrative of *The Empire Strikes Back* and *The Return of the Jedi*. These two films, I argue, are as much about Father/Son relations as any other films in this study, and it is *because* they are, like *Indiana Jones and the Last Crusade* and other genre-formula films, *unexpectedly* about Father/Son relationships that they are of such particular interest to me.

If it turns out to be something of a surprise to find that the third instalment in the comic book action series *Indiana Jones* is concerned with examining in a quite detailed way the relationship of Indiana Jones to his father, it is perhaps less of a surprise to note that the *Star Wars* trilogy and especially *The Empire Strikes Back* and *The Return of the Jedi* also structure their narratives around that same relationship. Yet it also seems that *Empire* and *Return* are less obsessively concerned with father/son relations than *Indiana Jones and the Last Crusade* because the examination of the relationship is so attenuated. It is spread out over two lengthy film narratives. Further a great deal of the action of these narratives' time and space is occupied with 'peripheral' actions: lengthy battle scenes; various flights, fights and rescues; all involving spectacular technology both fictional and cinematic.

All this action is, in narrative if not commercially orientated senses, motivated by and directed toward the need to bring together the father, Darth Vader, and his son, Luke Skywalker. In *The Empire Strikes Back* it is Vader who initiates actions designed to bring his son to him. In *The Return of the Jedi* it is Luke who consciously seeks out Vader because he is Luke's father. This change is the result of Luke learning that Vader is his father during their first confrontation. Having learnt this, Luke does not deny, disown or attempt to flee from his father (except in the most immediate circumstances of needing to recover from his wounds, physical and psychic). Rather than hate his father as his father seems to hate him, or fear him, Luke is determined to save his father (from the dark side of the Force, from the Emperor who, rather than his father, is the true personification of the dark side). The attraction of the Father is so great that despite the danger to the very foundations of the moral order of the universe, the son must seek atonement with the Father. But of course that very atonement will ensure the moral order of the universe.

The whole point of the narrative of *The Empire Strikes Back* and *The Return of the Jedi* is to bring together the father and son, Darth Vader and Luke Skywalker, with the ostensible purpose of Vader converting Luke to the 'dark side of the Force' or destroying him: of forcing the son to recognize the rule of the Father.[6] That is to say, to align Luke with that which his father represents, the evil aspects of (unrestrained) Patriarchy.[7] *The Empire Strikes Back* does not initially reveal the extent of the 'attraction' between father and son even through it does suggest from quite early on that Luke Skywalker is the object of Vader's 'desire'—that desire being, seemingly, for revenge. Certainly, it is not revealed (even though it is hinted at) that Vader is (or was) Anakin Skywalker until the last few moments of the film. Even so and armed with this knowledge, in retrospect Vader seems to be a mythological ogre-father who wishes to destroy his son before his son destroys him. This seems to invite an Oedipal reading, although there are plenty of other examples of such fathers from Greek and many other mythologies. But there are odd moments when the facade of monstrousness (and facade is literal here given Vader's body is encased in an armour which is both protection and life-support system) breaks down and Vader is revealed to be a father who wishes to save rather than destroy his son. This latter aspect of the relationship appears more strongly within *The Return of the Jedi*, following the first true confrontation in *The Empire Strikes Back*. What seems then to be a classical Oedipal story wherein a father has homicidal designs upon a son who threatens to usurp his powers (or to be in this instance more powerful by having the same power but not using them for evil) is tempered by the revelation of more fatherly feelings (which means in this case more 'feminine' feelings such as we have seen in many films in this study). This apparent contradiction is explained within the film's postulation of the 'Force' which has both good and bad sides. Father and son are placed on opposite sides of this dichotomy although it is also suggested that individuals may 'feel' the pull of both sides of the Force and not just one or the other.

In order to arrive at the 'state of grace' appropriate to confronting his father and to bring about atonement with him (and evidently to face the evil which is his father but is more than his father: the satanic Patriarch, the Emperor), Luke Skywalker must undergo a series of tests in the manner of any mythological or fairy tale hero as outlined by Joseph Campbell in *The Hero with a Hundred Faces* and V. Propp in *Morphology of the Folktale*. In keeping with the adventures of heroes according to Campbell and Propp (and others), the aim of the hero's narrative is to bring about a new order from the chaos of the old or out of that chaos which has arisen from a disturbance of a pre-existing equilibrium.

This is the case with the *Star Wars* trilogy certainly but what is significant for us is that the bringing about of the new order, or most certainly the destruction of the forces of chaos which is the prelude to the establishment of peace and order in the universe, is and can only be accomplished by the coming together of a father and his son, by the recognition of the 'force' of the 'natural' bond between fathers and sons, a 'force' which is greater that the dark side of the

Force of the universe itself. The importance of the events of *The Return of the Jedi* are not the triumph of Good over Evil but the reconciliation of a son with his father between whom the battle of good and evil has been personified. It is a resolution of an oedipal conflict achieved not by the death of the father and his replacement by his son—although Darth Vader does partly interpret the conflict with his son in those terms for a while. Instead the conflict occurs in order for the son to become the object of the father's love rather than the Emperor (or the dark side). This is what Luke requires, not the death of his father (he actively seeks to avoid this throughout) but his love—and in this the *Star War* films show thematic continuity with many other films in this study, especially those films which situate wife/mothers as occupying the same position as the Emperor. Luke Skywalker does not seek to replace or usurp his father in the Emperor's 'affections' (although the Emperor does try to tempt him with this possibility). This is similar to, for example, *Ordinary People* or *Dad* in which respective sons are not involved in replacing their fathers but in expelling their mothers in order that they may become more completely the object of their father's love.

In order to achieve this ideal state Luke Skywalker faces a series of tests—as do Indiana Jones and Ray Kinsella in their respective atonement-narratives. Indeed, it is hard not to see that *Field of Dreams* and *The Return of the Jedi* are closely linked through an inversion of the idea of 'Build it and he will come'. In *The Return of the Jedi* it would seem that by building the Death Star, the Emperor and Vader ensure that Luke 'will come' to his father, to confront his father. This will then form Luke's final test, and his near-death at the hands (literally) of the Emperor will be his final penance, his taking upon himself the sins of his father (and the universe). This manner in which a 'blameless' hero-savoir takes onto himself suffering for others further extends analogies between the *Star Wars* trilogy and the Christian myth.[8]

While it may be argued that Luke's tests begin in *Star Wars* with his leaving home, early Jedi training, and his part in the destruction of the first Death Star, it is not until *The Empire Strikes Back* that it becomes clear that Luke is being tested. Again, some of these tests seem to be simply related to his 'training' as a Jedi Knight. However, soon after his arrival at the home of Yoda, the Jedi Master to whom he has been sent by the ghostly instruction of Obi-Wan-Kenobi, Yoda asks of him, 'Why must you become a Jedi?' Luke replies, 'Mostly because of my father, I guess.' Yet Luke has never known his father, only known of him. And even then that which he has been led to believe is not true: he presumes his father, Anakin Skywalker, to have been killed by Darth Vader. What is on Luke's mind then is the desire revenge the death of his father—certainly an aspect of a father/son relationship: revenge for a death of a father he did not know.[9]

The power of a son's attraction for his father is offered as being a perfectly understood motivation for a particular set of actions. It is at the same moment that a hint is given about the actual relationship between Luke and Vader: Yoda implies Luke is 'like his father', is 'full of anger'. And this hint is amplified when in an initiatory test, Luke enters a cave (a ubiquitous mythological motif) and 'confronts' what seems to be the figure of Vader but which when decapitated reveals Luke's face within the mask. This test and other ones undertaken at Yoda's instruction are only preparatory; they are not the real tests which Luke must undergo before he can achieve atonement.

The first of the real tests involves the necessity of Luke to confront Vader, as indeed will each of the tests. Initially, however, Luke does not know who Vader really is. His determination to face him, despite the objections of Yoda and the phantom of Obi-Wan-Kenobi, is brought about not because he knows who Vader is but because of a need to rescue his friends, most particularly Han Solo whom Vader is torturing in order that Luke may, through the Force, 'feel' Solo's agony and come to his aid. Vader knows who Luke is (although the narrative does not let us know that he knows). Although the narrative of *The Empire Strikes Back* begins with the Empire searching for the location of the rebellious Alliance, at the moment the rebel base is located, Vader asserts, 'I am sure Skywalker is there' not 'I am sure the rebels are there,' thereby indicating the importance of Luke to Vader, an importance which eventually overpowers Vader's allegiance to the Empire's goal of suppressing all opposition. Luke evades the attacking army of the Emperor and has to be drawn to his father by other means. Luke, in this first test, goes to face Vader not because he is his father but because he is, so Luke thinks, the murderer of his father. The importance of the Father is still paramount in Luke's actions.[9]

On the face of it, Luke fails this test. He does not rescue Han, and, more importantly, he is defeated by Vader in face-to-face combat. He is even symbolically castrated by his father when his right hand (his sword hand, so to speak) is struck off by Vader. Luke does not actually fail. The test is not whether he can defeat Vader but that he is able to, firstly, face him, secondly, not be drawn into the dark side, and thirdly, learn that Vader is his father and still resist him. He must first deny his patrilineage before being able to accept his father as his father. This he does. The test has been to see just how Luke can handle this revelation. He flees his father at the end of the test but he does so in order to prepare for the second test. It is at this point that *The Empire Strikes Back* concludes. Narratively, of course, little has been resolved, and indeed little has been revealed. The revelation that Vader is Luke's father explains nothing, least of all why Vader would wish to destroy Luke. In a number of films in this overall thematic category of Father-Son films there are ready assumptions that fathers can and do hate their sons. The condition underpins the Vader/Luke situation here although Vader is characterized as being simply evil, the extent or degree of his iniquity is measured by his desire to destroy his own son. Yet this notion is neither surprising nor unusual. It is equally usual to find sons wishing to reconcile with their fathers even when their fathers seem to wish to destroy them. (For example *At Close Range* [1986] and *Tiger Warsaw* [1988].)

The Return of the Jedi commences with the father still seeking the son. Now, however, there is a subtle change. When the Emperor suggest that Luke must be destroyed, Vader replies in mitigation that 'he is only a boy' and rationalizes his desire not to kill Luke by claiming he could become a valuable ally. It is the first chink in Vader's armour, the first revelation that there is perhaps a father's love beneath his apparent hatred for his son. Later the Emperor himself detects this: 'I wonder if your feelings are clear in this matter'.

The narrative is initially diverted while Luke undertakes to rescue Han Solo. This time the 'renewed' Luke is able to do so and to reunite the band of heroes whose adventures are so closely intertwined with his own. But after doing so, Luke returns to his Jedi Master, Yoda. Here the truth of his patrimony is confirmed as is his need to face the second test, to confront his father again. Only then, Luke is told, can he become a Jedi—in other words, only by confronting his father and in doing so *not* 'become' his father, can he truly become a man. Luke accepts the final test not because he wishes to defeat or destroy his father but because he wishes to save him. He expressly denies any suggestion that he can kill his father and claims 'there is still good in him.' Oedipal conflict is expressly denied. It is love that binds Luke to his father—or to a certain concept of his father, the good that lies hidden within his father.

Although Luke becomes involved in the adventures of the band of heroes and their attempts to destroy the second Death Star, the telepathic presence of his father is too strong, the call to the second test too powerful. This telepathic connection between father and son also occurs in *Indiana Jones and the Last Crusade*. It is something fathers and son share. Here it is present from that point when Vader reveals himself to Luke and after that is omnipresent. Not only can they sense each other but, as we have seen, Luke reaches deeper into Vader's mind and can detect the 'goodness' lurking repressed within that part of Vader that is still Anakin Skywalker. Thus, he leaves the band of heroes, which includes his newly-discovered twin sister, Leia, to face Vader alone. He justifies this by the fact that 'I have to face him. He is my father.' Luke needs not simply to face the father (this would be quite straightforward in Freudian terms) but to 'save' him because he is his father.

Luke faces his father by 'surrendering' and being taken to him. Here he argues for Vader to recognize his 'good side', his feelings for Luke that prevented him from destroying him at their previous meeting. For the first time Vader calls Luke 'son' but claims it is too late for him to turn from the dark side. Luke has to undergo two further tests. He must face and deny the Emperor. And, more importantly, he must once again fight his father, despite himself. In doing the latter, he seems to surrender to the Emperor, to unleash the hate he has for Vader (for his father in Freudian Oedipal terms).[11] Although he inflicts upon his father the same wound as his father had inflicted upon him—cutting off his right hand—he refuses to commit patricide. The Emperor seeks to kill Luke, but his father finds the strength of the good side welling from within and casts the Emperor in to the limitless void. Thus, the son redeems his father from the original sin of being seduced to the dark side, and the father saves his son from physical destruction by the Emperor.

Finally father and son achieve atonement. The human in Vader is reaffirmed by the removal of the vestiges of technology, his life-support helmet, to reveal the man, Anakin Skywalker, within the machine. Here again is the laying-on of hands, this time by the son to the father. And finally, Luke alone provides his father with a Viking-type funeral pyre. He is, however, only cremating the outward remains of his father, more specifically the Darth Vader form of his father. Anakin Skywalker 'lives on' in the phantom manifestations that Luke's mentor/father-surrogates, Obi-Wan and Yoda, have been revealed to occupy. Indeed, at the funeral, the three 'fathers' appear to Luke rather like the Holy Trinity. And it is only Luke who can see them. Not even his twin sister Leia is vouchsafed the (masculine) power to commune with the Three-in-One Father.

The universe has been saved by the reconciliation, the coming together of a father and a son. Each has been healed, and in so being has 'healed' the universal order. Although couched in the language of mythology, *The Empire Strikes Back* and particularly *The Return of the Jedi* rework the cultural concern for fathers and sons that seems obsessively concerned with the need for fathers and sons to come together for both personal and social health.

NOTES

1. A filmography of 1980s films concerned with father-son relations compiled by Neil Rattigan and Thomas P. McManus may be found in *Journal of Popular Film and Television*, Vol.20, No.1, Spring 1992, 21-23.

2. Examples of fathers seeking atonement or forgiveness from their sons are often found in those films that have some background to their narratives in the Vietnam experience. For example, *Distant Thunder* (1988) or *Welcome Home* (1989).

3. It is worth noting in these father/son films of the 1980s the narratives frequently postulate a totally absent mother (e.g. in addition to *The Last Crusade*, *Cloak and*

Dagger 1984, *Reckless* 1984, *Revolution* 1985, *Near Dark* 1987, etc.) Of no little interest is the smaller number of films in which the mother competes with the son for the father's love (e.g. *Ordinary People* 1980, *Dad* 1989). Competition between father and son for the mother is, perhaps surprisingly, seldom a source of major or minor narrative structures, although 'alliances' of mother and son against the father do occur in some films (e.g. *The Great Santini* 1980, *Apprentice to Murder* 1988).

4. Practically all the films I identify have these aspects in varying proportion. Some significant examples are: *The Return of the Jedi* (1983); *A Night in the Life of Jimmy Reardon* (1988); *Dad* (1989); *Field of Dreams* (1989).

5. I am ignoring *Star Wars* not only because it falls outside my self-imposed time span of the 1980s for production and/or release of films but primarily because the importance of the father/son relationship is not apparent in *Star War's* narrative, at least as motivating devices for actions. The existence of a father/son conflict deeply embedded in *Star Wars* can really only be detected through hindsight after viewing the two later instalments in the trilogy.

6. It is no great insight to point out the linguistic similarity of Darth Vader to 'Dark Father'. Robert Bly draws attention to this although curiously he links the father who is the 'tool of the dark side' with the father who is 'more and more enfeebled, dejected, paltry' (1990, 99). This may simply be another example of Bly's failure to read contemporary popular culture accurately. He states in his preface to *Iron John* (1990) that 'images of man given by the popular culture are worn out', a claim this study at least would expressly deny.

7. Unlike creation myths, the 'good' and 'dark' sides of the force in the *Star Wars* do not represent the conflict of feminine and masculine forces. They represent the two sides of masculinity which have been displayed often enough in other films in this study: the stern, unrelenting, patriarchal aspect, and the feeling, caring, nurturing aspect.

8. I don't wish to examine this in detail but I might point out Luke's separation from his father before birth, his wandering in the wilderness, his meeting with and 'baptism' by the John the Baptist figure of Obi-Wan-Kenobi, his tempting by Vader (who plays both Satan and Father), his ability to perform 'miracles' (through use of the Force), and so on.

9. This narrative motivation can be found in films that belong in a filmography of Father-Son films on the 1980s such as *Blue City* (1986), *Cold Steel* (1987) and *Never Too Young to Die* (1986). The reverse – fathers avenging sons – can be found in *Pumpkin Head* (1988) and *Rolling Vengeance* (1987).

10. The importance of the attraction of other males should not be ignored; especially is the attraction between Han Solo and Luke Skywalker. Han saves Luke's life on several occasions and although, for a while, they seem to be rivals for Princess Leia, the true attraction is between the two men. There is a particular moment in *The Empire Strikes Back* when each is about to go his separate way where the camera privileges the looks between them, particularly the way in which Han looks at Luke, that insists on being interpreted as looks of love.

11. Further (perhaps simplistic) Freudian analysis might well see the Emperor as the personification of the Id, Vader as the consequence of the acceptance of the unrestrained Id, Yoda and Obi-Wan-Kenobi representing the Super-Ego and so on.

REFERENCES

Robert Bly, *Iron John: A Book about Men*, (Reading, MA: Addison-Wesley, 1990)

Joseph Campbell, *The Hero with a Thousand Faces*, (New York: Bollingen Foundation, 1968).

V.L. Propp, *Morphology of the Folktale*, (Austin: University of Texas, 1979).

MISCELLANY

LOOKING EAST BUT SEEING WEST—A REVIEW ARTICLE

Robin Allan. *Walt Disney and Europe*. London, John Libbey and Company Limited, 1999.

The relationship of Disney (meaning here, Walt Disney the creator, producer and head of the organisation that bears his name, and that Hydra-headed organisation itself) to the folkloric is an intriguing and vexatious one. On the one hand, there are the animated feature films made from well-known fairy or folk tales—although there are perhaps fewer of these than is sometimes thought: *Snow White and the Seven Dwarfs* (1937), *Cinderella,* (1950), *Sleeping Beauty* (1959), *The Little Mermaid* (1989), *Beauty and the Beast* (1991), *Hercules* (1997), *Mulan* (1998). This is by no means a majority of the Disney feature-length animated films. To this can be added the appearance of use of fairy tales and folk tales in the earlier short cartoons or as part of longer films, such as the 'Johnny Appleseed' section *of Melody Time* (1948) or the 'Uncle Remus' section of *Song of the South* (1946), perhaps too 'The Sorcerer's Apprentice' in *Fantasia* (1940). This last named, 'starring', as it does Mickey Mouse—as an actor playing a role, so to speak—serves however to indicate the other way in which Disney is of interest to folklorists—that Disney itself may well have created folk figures.

Mickey Mouse, it has been sometimes claimed, is likely to remain one of the few visually recognisable icons of the twentieth-century. Mickey Mouse and maybe some other Disney characters are sufficiently embedded in the Western cultural consciousness (and probably, like Coca-Cola, in the cultural consciousness of most of the world as well) to be accorded folk status, despite the fact that they are irrevocably the products of mass culture. As is well accepted, of course, mass culture may produce the objects of popular culture but they are not exactly the same thing, and folk culture since the Age of Enlightenment and the Industrial Revolution has drawn upon the 'products' of both in ways which are affirmative, subversive and aberrant. Because of and despite the enormous 'promotion' of Mickey Mouse by Disney (and not only even most significantly through film alone), he (it?) has taken on the status of a folk figure, who must be akin to, say, Santa Claus. Within its films, Disney has also made use of other folk figures, established outside the Disney 'world' (at least at first), for example, Robin Hood (in *Robin Hood* [1973]) or King Arthur (as a boy in *The Sword in the Stone* [1963]). Indisputably, there are connections of some sort, from several directions simultaneously, between Disney and the folkloric.

Are these connections more than superficial, and do they go further than a form of capitalistic, piratical plundering of folk and popular culture? Robin Allan's *Walt Disney and Europe* seems to offer an opportunity to examine some of these possibilities, given that most of the fairy-tale adaptations by Disney have clear origins in European fairy tales. *(Mulan* is an exception, so too, perhaps, is *Pocahontas* [1995].) Further, the research which forms the basis of Allan's book would seem to offer excellent opportunities to pinpoint the places in which Disney and fairy tales intersect. Prior to Walt Disney becoming 'distracted' by, first, television, second and more importantly, his planning and building of theme parks (the original Disneyland opened in 1955), and third, live-action films, it would seem that all Disney story conferences and production meetings were recorded and transcribed verbatim. Allan has had access to these—whether all or some is unclear, as they are not cited in the 'Select Bibliography—and through them might reasonably be assumed can be found the authentic 'voice' and opinions of Walt Disney. Yet it is debatable whether these are as useful to scholars as, for comparison, the thousands of memos of David 0. Selznick, Disney's being presumably off-the-cuff comments. As Allan points out, as the Disney organisation grew and Walt Disney's personal interest in the animated features shrank, these verbatim minutes also dwindled. It is partly for this reason that Allan's most intense focus is on the early, pre-fifties animated films; Allan also restricts himself for the most part to those films made before Walt Disney's death in 1966, with only limited discussion of animated features made subsequently. This is unfortunate as there has been a burgeoning of Disney animated features since the mid-eighties, averaging a new film every two years or so, many of which have been drawn from fairy and folk tale sources.

There is a sense in which any reader, reviewer or scholar should be wary of books on Disney (or indeed any Hollywood studio) in which the author seems to have been given a high level of co-operation, as has clearly been the case here. Disney, as much if not more than other studios (including some which to all intents and purposes no longer exist), has exhibited a degree of paranoia about allowing itself to be open to the scrutiny of scholars. But, perhaps more with than most other studios, scholars are heavily dependent upon Disney for co-operation, particularly in providing illustrations for published material. One wonders what sort of 'pact with the devil' has to be entered into before the Disney organisation will provide both the illustrations and the permission to use them that most if not all discussions of their animated films must rely upon. Allan acknowledges the Disney organisations and individuals within it, but he does not imply any conditions that might have been set upon what he says in his book. The book is profusely illustrated, and not only with material from the Walt Disney Archive, and this is one of its chief attractions. But any book on the 'art' of Disney must, perforce, be able to reproduce illustrations of that art. 'Art and Disney' has been a recurring subject of studies of Disney—as in the series of books by Christopher Finch for example[1]—and it seems highly likely any such studies must come close to being 'official' Disney publications, or at least 'authorised' ones, given this high degree of co-operation that is essential.

It is not surprising that there is little in Allan's book that is critical of Disney—the man or the organisation. Allan does register Richard Schickel's iconoclastic *Walt Disney*[2], but he dismisses it as the product of 'pique' and as being 'inaccurate'. His bibliography cites Dorfman and Mattelart's *How to Read Donald Duck: Imperialist Ideology on the Disney Comic*,[3] but finds no space to mention their critique—this may be because Dorfman and Mattelart (and Dorfman by himself in *The Empire's Old Clothes*[4]) concentrate on Disney comic books rather than films. They are also interested in the content of Disney productions (and the ideology purveyed thereby), whereas Allan is content to offer a type of production history. It is also a limited history, as Allan has little or nothing to say about the area in which Disney's 'influence' on popular culture might be arguably much greater than the animated films; the comic books and syndicated comic strips; cartoons made for or revived on television; children's literature based (although not exclusively) on the animated films; toys; theme parks; and the huge merchandising industry that surrounds all these things. In keeping with so many books which deal with the 'art' of Disney, that art is seemingly restricted to the animated films; and the 'art' of the graphics of the comic books and children's book illustrations is ignored, perhaps because these images do not resemble 'art' in the same way as the imagery of the animated films can be argued to resemble or even be art.

In his search for European connections in the work of Disney, Allan tends to use the notion of 'European' rather uncritically and to state rather too freely that some aspect or other of a film, a process, a story, a piece of 'art' and so forth is European or shows some European connection without explaining how this is so. For example, he states of the use of Igor Stravinsky's *The Rite of Spring* in *Fantasia,* 'Disney takes European music and transforms it for the New World' (p. 127). That *The Rite of Spring* is somehow unproblematically 'European music' is a given here; the categorisation seems based upon that fact that the composer was 'European' (to the extent that Stravinsky was not American), and that the music was first performed in Paris in 1913. This simply places all of European culture into one apparently monocultural basket, ignoring Stravinsky's specifically Russian origins, ignoring perhaps the specificity of the piece (written for Diaghilev's *Ballet Russes* in Paris—making it either Russian or French or both), ignoring that Stravinsky himself had become an American citizen prior to this film's production.

There is a little too much of this sort of easy connection between the origins of a book, a piece of music, a work (or type of) art, or the birth of the creator of any of these somewhere, anywhere, in Europe and undeveloped claims for this being a significant way in which Disney and Europe 'connect'. E.M. Forster's epigraph to *Howard's End,* 'Only Connect' might do service here as well. This leads to a frustrating sense of unsubstantiated claims. On page 27, Allan states baldly, 'The fairy tale and the European folk tale had been used in some of the *Mickey Mouse* shorts; *(Ye Olden Days* (1933) and *Gulliver Mickey* (1934) are examples)' but does not say which ones or how; is he claiming that *Gulliver's Travels* is a fairy tale or a European folk tale? He goes on:'...but the exploitation of European sources developed with the *[Silly Symphonies]*. In *The Clock Store* (1931) for instance, the ticking clocks are the antecedents for those in *Snow White and the Seven Dwarfs* and more particularly in Geppetto's workshop in *Pinocchio;* another variation on the same theme is *The China Shop* (1934)'. Here he is claiming early Disney is the influence on later Disney without making any case for how, early or late, these are examples of 'exploitations of European sources' or even what those sources might be. European 'influences'—familial, cultural and artistic/aesthetic—are identified by Allan via individuals who worked for Disney and via their art works outside Disney, not all of which found its way fully or unmodified into Disney productions, but this is still circumstantial evidence of influence. In situations where Allan offers direct evidence, this takes the form of comparing various images and drawings, paintings and engravings with similar images found in the Disney archives and, sometimes but not always, in the films themselves. This may argue for a form of (obvious) relationship between Disney and Europe, or it may simply infer it.

Without convincing analysis which demonstrates rather than implies influence, the European 'effect' upon Disney seems to be rather more distant than might be imagined from the title of the book. In a curious way, Allan's discussions seem to demonstrate the opposite to what could reasonably be inferred from that title. In nearly every instance where he discusses narrative or story influences, his examination of the record of story conferences, production meetings and so forth reveal that no matter what the origins—European folk/ fairy tale or, more likely, European literary source—the material was heavily inflected by American popular culture, especially theatre and the like, early silent American films, and perhaps even more by the 'folk' orientated activities that Disney himself experienced growing up in the early decades of the twentieth century in Mid-west American rural locations. Tellingly, Allan cites the case of *Snow White* in which Disney's clear inspiration was a film version seen by Disney as a child in 1916. This example leads to the sort of conclusion about which I am uneasy. Allan states, 'Thus out of popular culture Disney made another product of the same culture', before going to claim that Disney

> imbued the new version with complexities which revived and sustained its popularity. This popularity is due as much to the European origins of the film and the way Disney utilised those origins, as to the responses he and his staff brought to bear upon it (p.37).

I cannot sort out these apparent contradictions; American popular culture produces another artefact of American popular culture which 'sustains its popularity', yet it is the European origins that explain the popularity. I am unable to come to terms with the difference between 'the way Disney utilised these origins' (which caused the film's popularity) and 'the responses that he and his staff brought to bear upon it' (which did not). 'Utilisation' and 'responses brought to bear' seem to me to be the same thing.

The sources of many of the Disney animated features, or the sources of their narratives at least, are stories originating well outside the confines of the cinema, although as Allan frequently notes, many of these stories were inflected and transformed by cinematic influences. Only a minority have origins in clearly accepted European fairy tales *(Snow White and the Seven Dwarfs, Cinderella, Sleeping Beauty, Beauty and the Beast, The Little Mermaid)*. Most of the others have easily identifiable literary sources: Kenneth Grahame, *The Wind in the Willows* (which furnishes the second part of *The Adventures of Ichabod Crane and Mister Toad* [1949], the first part deriving from Washington Irving's *The Legend of Sleepy Hollow); Lewis Carrol, Alice in Wonderland*; Rudyard Kipling, *The Jungle Book*; T.H. White, *The Sword in the Stone; Collodi* (Carlo Lorenzini), *The Adventures of Pinocchio;* James Barrie, *Peter Pan;* Dodie Smith. *One Hundred and One Dalmatians;* Ward Greene, *The Lady and the Tramp;* P.L. Travers, *Mary Poppins,* and of course the fairy tales courtesy of Jacob and Wilhelm Grimm, Hans Christian Andersen and Charles Perrault.

Most but not all these authors and sources are European, but the categorisation is too broad to be useful for analysis. Some are eighteenth-century, some are nineteenth-century, and some are twentieth- century. The majority are English, with only the 'true' fairy tales and *Pinocchio* having origins outside Britain and a handful having origins in America (or American writers).

It is difficult to quite know even with Allan's guidance, what to make of Disney's 'dependence' on European literary sources, beyond an almost sweeping generalisation (which I certainly cannot substantiate at this time) that 'European', or more properly English, writers wrote in ways which suggested, if they did not directly indicate, fairy-tale qualities to their narratives, or some quality of the fairy tale; a willingness to concede imaginative power as much if not more to nature than to culture, an in many instances a ready adoption of anthropomorphism. (The same is true of many of the graphic artists, cartoonists and caricaturists who influenced the Disney 'art' in visual ways.) Is or was there perhaps in the Anglo-European psyche something which disposed it towards a popularised fairy tale form in literature, or at least a certain corner of the field of literature? And was this same quality absent from the North American psyche and literature (other than perhaps in the Native America culture, which, despite *Pocahontas*, Disney has largely ignored in its animated features)? Or are there other reasons why Disney turned its attention to cross-Atlantic sources and not to the local—although the local was not completely ignored: *Tales of the South*, the use of *The Legend of Sleepy Hollow*, 'Johnny Appleseed'. These are intriguing questions that accepting the idea of the 'prestige' attendant upon European literary sources only partly answers; although it is certainly true that the feature length films were 'European' within this limited concept, with the short cartoons—where Mickey Mouse, Donald Duck, and the others of the far-more-familiar Disney anthropomorphised menagerie are endlessly found—are resolutely American) as too are the comic books and comic strips which spin-off from and support the cartoons.

Yet the origins of the animated features are almost the least significant thing about them. Their familiar/European titles may be important, to some extent, in selling the product, but there content is less so. Allan details on a number of occasions the clear evidence that other factors caused considerable changes to the material, changes which ignored or sometimes contradicted the originals. Some of these changes were the consequences of the very practices and demands of animated film making. Most of the changes are attributed, and in most instances by direct reference, to Walt Disney's input, and, strongly related to this, to American popular cultural influences, especially the Hollywood film. Previous Hollywood films, some silent, are clearly identified as points of comparison for purposes of affecting a storyline, shaping a narrative, supplying a character and so on. Allan indeed provides quite a catalogue of these, ranging from the way in which particular actors provided not only the voices but inspiration or even direct aspects of personal appearance for characters in various of the films. He points, quite rightly, to the influence of German expression (in both visual and narrative terms) as it had in turn influenced and been modified by Hollywood practice (particularly via the Horror Film, to which debts can be found in *Snow White* and *Fantasia* in particular).

What Allan only recognises tangentially, but which would repay some close critical examination, is that nearly all the animated features are, in fact,

Musicals in the conventional Hollywood generic sense. This tends to bring me at least full-circle, as I have tentatively argued elsewhere in the pages of *Australian Folklore* ('Magic in the Air—Musicals as Fairy Tales', No.13, 1998. pp. 194-203) that the Hollywood Musical is, in fact, the true twentieth century form of the fairy tale. Disney then is a particular variation and support to this claim; but both the Musical in general and the Disney animated feature are specifically American versions of fairy tale form, American fairy tale creations in fact. Allan's focus (although it is a panoramic rather than a microscopic view) on Disney and Europe serves to suggest the real view should be in the other direction, and that fascinating study along the lines of Disney and America would be infinitely rewarding to folk and fairy tale scholars.

Thus it appears that what is perhaps useful from this is perhaps not what Allan intended: that the fascination with the possibility of making connections between fairy and folk tales and Disney films apparently based upon them **is** that the connections may be much more attenuated than is assumed at first glance. Allan actually makes a case for considering that American folk and popular culture were much greater influences of Disney than the original material he was 'adapting'. This becomes even more apparent when examining what Allan has to say about the European influences on the art (work) of Disney, which is the true focus of this book; stories and narratives, their sources and their adaptation is of rather less interest, and this may go some way to explaining the way in which Allan claims influence without actually testing it. Allan, like many Disney scholars, is more interested in the art of the Disney animated films. If nothing else, the profuse illustrations of the book, including 48 pages of colour plates, would demonstrate this. By using these illustrations, Allan does raise all sorts of intriguing points of comparison, and demonstrates the apparent effect and influence of art, art movements and artists both inside and outside the Disney studio that are European. (There is little or no evidence that Disney was influenced by folk art, only 'high' art.) Disney indeed employed, in most instances for only relatively short times, European artists whose reputations were earned outside the rather restricted arena of commercial animated film production. (He also uses quite a number of American artists as well, of course.)

Allan's research of the Disney archives has produced (and here reproduced) a number of drawings, sketches, full-scale paintings from a variety of these artists, which are associated with one or other Disney production, often from the pre-production level. He draws too upon statements made by and about many of these artists to provide evidence of their effect or influence. But (as in fact any viewer of a Disney film could confirm), if there are influences from European artists in Disney films, these influences are mainly apparent in the backgrounds, in (in filmic terms) the mise-en-scene of the various films' diegeses, and not noticeably in the characters or the characterisations. The colour plates and the interspersed back-and-white illustrations make this clear time after time. With very rare exceptions, characters in Disney animated films are American-ised—even simply American. The drawing of characters is American; in fact they might, over sixty years or so, be said to be almost exclusively Disneyesque, no matter what they are supposed to be according to particular narrative or mood.

With the possible exception of some moments of *Fantasia* (which nonetheless has Mickey Mouse as its most famous image), the 'foreground', the characters of Disney animated films are drawn to a standard that is Disney-American, and not European (or anything else). In most instances, the voices and the speech idioms confirm this. It may well be in recognition of this that Allan devotes three chapters out of his eleven (and one appendix out of two) to *Fantasia:* it is in a way the only Disney film to which clear, unequivocal European influences can be attributed in many of the images both in terms of source and in terms of artistic styles, and all of the music. (Only one other film, *Pinocchio,* gets a chapter to itself.)

What *Walt Disney and Europe* actually does is, contrary to the publisher's jacket claim that it 'is a fascinating study of the way European and European culture influenced Walt Disney and his artists', to diminish these claims. What seems almost self-evident, even to Allan despite his 'meticulous research', turns out, through the discussion and the examinations he offers, to be not really the case at all. The influence of Europe is often, literally as well as figuratively, relegated to the background. What is truly valuable about this book, in addition to its use of so much primary material (and the intriguing possibilities raised by thoughts of unfettered access), is that it may well to serve to direct Disney scholars away from a possibly fruitless search for demonstrable European influences (in artistic styles, in sources of story material, in music) to what strikes me as a much more exciting field of investigation: the interconnections between American popular culture (folk, certainly, but especially commercial culture) and Disney, the way each fed from and off each other, the way in which Disney has become perhaps the major purveyor of folk culture via a specific form of popular/commercial culture, the animated motion picture.

It is not my wish to be unfair to Robin Allan. In fact, those interested in Disney and his/their connection with the folk-loric may well have reason to be grateful for this book. What Allan has done is to make clear that Disney is not simply one (in a long line) of translators of European folk tales (and occasionally those from elsewhere), but, on the evidence of Allan's book, Disney is a major re-writer and re-formulator, even 'creator', of fairy tales in the manner of the Grimm brothers and Charles Perrault. Indeed, although Allan does not write as much, Disney is the greatest creator of fairy tales in the twentieth century.

Arguably huge numbers of people know fairy tales only through Disney, and only know Disney's versions.

Disney is not only a fairy tale creator through those animated feature films based (now, thanks to Allan, obviously based very loosely) in pre-existing fairy tales (via, to varyingly limited degrees, Grimm and Perrault) but also by the very manner in which he/they made fairy tales out of more clearly author-sourced literary material. These have become *the* fairy tales of the twentieth century through Disney's particular and peculiar manipulations of the source material. Disney has provided a consistency to the telling of these different stories, which unites them beyond simply being commodity products of a large-scale capitalist organisation. The value of Allan's work, then, is to turn (or tune) scholastic attention, not to 'Europe' but to America, to the ideologies and practices of Disney (man and organisation), and to both the sources and results of these. Herein, I suspect, lies the most promisingly fruitful area for examining Disney and the fairy tale in the twentieth century.

NOTES

1. Christopher Finch, *The Art of Walt Disney: From the Magic Kingdoms to Beyond*, Bison Books 1958; Harry H. Abrams 1995 and 2011. Christopher Finch, James Earl Jones and Penelope Niven, *The Art of the Lion King*, Hyperion, 1994.
2. *The Disney Version: The Life, Times, Art and Commerce of Walt Disney* (1968); revised editions: 1984, 1997.
3. Ariel Dorfman and Armand Mattleart, *How to Read Donald Duck: Imperialist Ideology in the Disney Comic*, International General, 1984.
4. Ariel Dorfman, *The Empire's Old Clothes*, Pantheon, 1983.

SIFTING THE CINEMA: FOLKLORE, FILM AND HISTORY — A REVIEW ARTICLE

David A. Cook, *A History of Narrative Film*. 3rd edn. W.W. Norton, New York. 1996.

Despite its own folklore, the origins of the cinema were anything but humble. Or if they were humble, they were humble only to the extent that folk culture and folklore are 'humble'. Cinema was to a large extent the product of business, technology and science, and very quickly it was organised as an industry along industrial-capitalist lines, including vertical integration, with control exercised at point of production, distribution and 'consumption' (exhibition), standardisation of product, and in particular centres (notably the United States of America and for a long while Germany), systematic, labour-intensive, 'factory-style' assembly of products. At few points and in few places in its international history was cinema ever a cottage industry.[1]

At the same time that cinema was pursuing and perfecting the practices of capitalistic business and creating as it did so the first true medium of mass culture, it was also forging an unbreakable link with folk culture. From very early on, the production and distribution of films may well have depended upon modern industrial practices but the material from which the product was forged could not be created in the same way and by the same processes. By 'material' is meant, of course, not the physical constituents of film (celluloid, chemicals, dyes, etc.) or the physical machines (cameras, lights, sound recorders, etc), but the content of the motion pictures themselves.

From the very outset of cinema (indeed, from before the outset of cinema if it is accepted that projection is fundamental to the definition of cinema), motion pictures found their materials in the everyday, in the 'folk' culture. Early cinema drew upon the popular entertainment of its time of origin (the late 19th century) and the 'found' world of, obviously, the same time. Popular entertainment forms at the time of the cinema's birth were likely to have strong connections to folklore: sideshows and travelling fairs, the music hall, the popular theatre (with its emphasis on melodrama and pantomime), the magic lantern show of various types of technical sophistication, even medicine shows of the American West, and travelling evangelists[2].

Although momentarily without the capacity for public projection, the cinema began with films made for Edison Kinetoscopes[3]. Films made by the Edison Company—mostly at their 'Black Maria studio' in West Orange, New Jersey—include a number which would seem to demonstrate the pull which folkloric activities already had upon determining or presenting opportunities for motion pictures. The subjects of Kinetoscope films produced in the 1890s include Highland Dancing, performances by Sideshow/Fair performers, Cock Fights, as well as 'everyday' scenes such as Blacksmith's shops, Barber's shops, and so on.[4]

Cinema, as is well known, quickly progressed from the peepshow form of exhibition to liie familiar (and defining) projected form of exhibition. The content of early films remained broadly within the categories of 'capturing' actuality and recording' performances of music hall or sideshow types. Even so, cinema's capacity to tell its own stories, to find its own form was present from the beginning. The Lumiere's famous *L'Arroseur Arrose* of 1896, in which a gardener is tricked into being soaked from his own hose by a boy who first stands on the hose to cut off the water and then steps off it when the gardener looks into the nozzle, is both a cinematic 'story' and a mini–folk tale at the same time.

Both fictional and non-fictional subjects of early films reveal the force of folk culture. Sporting events were an inevitable magnet for the early cinema cameras, and it is instructive to note that some of the earliest films shot in Australia were of horse racing, especially of that great cultural event, the Melbourne Cup (and not only or even specifically of the race itself but of much of the activities surrounding the event).[5] Other early Australian films included material shot at or in relation to cricket matches, football matches and various types of public activities such as military processions, Jubilee celebrations, and most famously the activities associated with the inauguration of the Australian Commonwealth in Sydney in 1901.[6]

It was, however, the production of fictional films which came to dominate cinema everywhere, and it is in the arena of the narrative fictional film that the connections between cinema as a mass/industrial culture and cinema as a folk culture are most important and most complex. Early fictional story films drew upon folk lore quite extensively. In Australia, for example, what is arguably the world's first feature length narrative film, *The Story of the Kelly Gang* (1906), drew upon Australia's pre-eminent folk hero, Ned Kelly, and in ways which followed the folklore of Kelly rather than the historical 'facts'. Bushranger stories were the core of early Australian motion pictures until banned. Bush life' more generally continued to provide the bulk of narratives of Australian motion pictures for a long time, and it arguably still does in significant fashion.

In similar and innumerable ways, the American cinema too found much of its content in folk culture and folk lore. The first Western film, *The Great Train Robbery* (1903), has usually been considered to be based upon the contemporary exploits of the 'Hole in The Wall' gang (i.e., Butch Cassidy and the Sundance

Kid, whose place in folklore was to be reconfirmed in 1969 by the film which bears their names[7]).

The Western is the Hollywood genre in which the effect of folk lore can be most clearly ascertained. The American West had become the object of fictionalisation somewhat before the invention of motion pictures, but not all that long before. Through dime novels and such spectacles as Buffalo Bill's Wild West, the opening and the closing of the American frontier, and the individuals (real and imagined, known and anonymous) who had played some part in it, had passed into the American cultural mythos. The cinema arrived just at the right moment to become the dominant form by which the folk lore of the West was continued, expanded and consolidated. The cinema did not exactly invent the characters and characteristics of the West, but it certainly emphasised some—especially quasi-historical individuals such as Billy the Kid, Wyatt Earp, or Jesse James—and planted particular notions into the folk lore about 'the code of the West', about the particular weapons by which it was enforced, about the costumes that were worn, and indeed about the very landscape itself.

Hollywood's, and indeed global cinema's, relationship with folklore and folk culture is not merely parasitic, to be seemingly leeching the lifeblood of folk culture in order to create the products of mass or popular culture. Nor is cinema's connection with folklore simply that of propagation—adulterated or otherwise to a mass audience. Cinema has also functioned to revive and revitalise folk culture, and, as pointed out above, in many cases to provide the source for much folklore.

Another Hollywood genre demonstrates in rather obvious fashion this relationship between cinema and folk culture: the Horror film. Vampires and werewolves, fear-arousing objects of Middle and Eastern European folklore, have become familiar to many more people in many more parts of the world thanks to the cinema. Knowledge of these creatures, and others besides—zombies, mummies and diverse forms of the 'undead'—has been provided and gained through countless Hollywood (and other originators') motion pictures. It is motion pictures that have provided the folklore as to how these creatures are destroyed: the stake in the heart, the garlic[8]; the holy water for vampires; the silver bullet for werewolves; fire for mummies; a bullet through the brain for zombies, and so on.

The traffic between folklore and the cinema has always been two-way, even if the flow has peaked one way or the other on different occasions. It has not always been quite as obvious as the examples just offered. Folklore and folk culture are more often present in the incidentals rather than in the basic structures of cinematic narratives—always recognising the special cases of fairy tales rendered on screen, and the cultural specificity of particular genres in certain national cinemas. While neither the Western nor the Horror film are any longer (if indeed the latter ever was) the specific preserve of the American cinema, particular national cinemas often tap into their own folk culture to greater or lesser degrees – the fantasy/fairytale genre of Chinese cinema is quite well known in the West, as are ghost stories from Japanese cinema. Folklore inhabits and informs motion pictures at many levels, in many places and at many times.

The 'tracking' of such influences upon the cinema, the study of film history in other words, was until recently the province of film scholars and generally found only in courses in film history within universities, particularly in the United States. It follows that, again until recently, published works of film history were mainly directed at the specialised (if potentially very large) market for texts books for university and colleges courses in film history. Outside occasional film festivals, the general public was unlikely to encounter too many films from the past. There is a certain irony then that it is television—for many of its earliest years looked upon as the implacable enemy and possible nemesis of cinema—that has made the history of cinema (at least as represented by its artefacts, motion pictures) available to an ever-increasing audience. Cable and satellite television, with their insatiable appetite for material and their willingness to seek and exploit niche markets, now provide a scintillating smorgasbord of films old and new, and from all film-producing corners of the world, often through channels dedicated to retrospective or 'world' cinema. In Australia, even before the arrival of cable, SBS were already making available to the *cognoscenti* and the lay-viewer alike, film 'ancient and modern'. This availability has been greatly facilitated with the recent introduction and spread of cable/satellite television.

Film history need not of course concern itself with individual motion pictures themselves, of which there are countless thousands, even hundreds of thousands. Many specialised histories do not; many are focused histories of studios or industries, particular countries or particular times, movements, 'moments' and individuals. General histories must account for all these aspects, or must declare their approach, direction and focus. With the title, A *History of Narrative Film,* David A. Cook does just that. Further, Cook delimits his historical gaze:

> As...we mark the one-hundredth anniversary of cinema's birth..., we should remember that what we celebrate has been overwhelmingly a *narrative* form concerned with individual and collective human destiny. Whether the product of the classical Hollywood paradigm or Zen Buddhist aesthetics, motion pictures have existed for a century mainly as a remarkably effective way for *people to tell stories about people,* (p. xix. Original emphasis.)

People telling stories about people sounds very like a simple definition of folklore.

Cook's third edition of what has become an established text book for film history courses in colleges and universities in the United States and elsewhere offers a comprehensive, even bewildering, coverage of film production since the beginning and in nearly every site in the world in which motion pictures have been made. The scholarship demonstrated in undertaking this task is impressive; the 'Selective Bibliography' alone runs to seventy-five pages. Admittedly what Cook reveals is the tendency towards an Americo-centric focus that other film histories have also demonstrated, a focus that goes beyond simply registering the historical importance that the USA, and Hollywood in particular, may rightfully claim. By the same token, Cook's history does move beyond the orthodox structure of the history of the cinema since the 1890s to allow examination of places and times more often ignored within that orthodoxy. For example, Cook discusses many of the former republics of the Soviet Union separately, recognising both their contemporary autonomous status and also their linguistic and cultural distinctiveness. He extends his coverage equally to non-mainstream film producing countries in Latin America, Asia and Africa.

This Americo-centricity can be demonstrated by examining how Cook discusses Australian cinema, to which he devotes about ten pages (of texts and stills) of the 957 pages of the body of the book. (Glossary, bibliography and index provide another one hundred pages.) This does not seem much but is perhaps quite generous compared with the seven-and-a-half pages given over to post-war Indian cinema, a much more productive film industry. The difference can be accounted for quite simply: Australian films are seen outside Australia to a far greater proportional extent (and probably absolute as well) than Indian films. More than this, however, it is the relation of Australian cinema to the United States that shapes Cook's 'history' of Australian cinema, the bulk of which is concerned with the post-1970 era. Following a succinct summary of Australian cinema prior to the 'Seventies, and a short but accurate accounting of the government intervention which brought about the 'rebirth' of Australian cinema, Cook (with unseemly haste) finds historical significance in the facts that 'In 1981, Australia penetrated the American market with two critical hits' (p.591):

> the following year, the Australian industry achieved a smashing commercial success in the United States with George Miller's *Mad Max II (p.* 592);

> Australia's banner year was 1986 [with] Peter Raiman's *[sic]* tongue-in-cheek *Crocodile Dundee*[9] (p. 592);

by the early eighties, many Australian directors had come to work for the American industry (p.592)

What then follows for two pages of dense text is a catalogue of some of those directors and their American films. This tendency continues even when Cook returns to 'the large number of excellent directors who have chosen to work largely in Australia' (p.593). Cook seems unable to resist this 'Americanization' of historical meaning, since *The Irishman* (1978) is described as a 'Ford-like saga' (p. 595) and *Playing Beatie Bow* (1986) is situated 'in the mold of Robert Zemeckis' *Back to the Future'*.[10] It is at best a moot point as to whether his discussion of Australian cinema in terms of its sometime relations with American cinema is because that is what is historically important about Australian cinema in the global context.[11]

The underpinning that folk lore provides to motion pictures in many parts of the world and at many times is at best only implied in Cook's discussions. And the notion that motion pictures, individually and collectively, may provide new folk lore or modify the pre-existing is not raised at all. Yet, there are moments when these two factors cannot be denied. The clearest example of this is in Cook's final chapter, 'Hollywood, 1965-Present' wherein he makes the case for 'The New American Cinema' commencing with and in many ways being defined *by Bonnie and Clyde* (Arthur Perm, 1967). This film demonstrates excellently the two-way connection between folklore and film. It is based on two historical figures who had already, in their own lifetime and by their deaths, taken on folk-heroic status, particularly in the Depression-era 'dust bowl' states of the American Midwest. In so doing, the film also enhanced the folk status as 'anti-establishment heroes' of the eponymous protagonists and, of course, broadcast this particular image far wider within and outside the United States than perhaps ever before. It is significant then that in historical terms, a film based in folklore should be given a place of fundamental importance in the history of American film and, by extension via the Americo-centricity discussed above, in the history of narrative film more generally.

This is not an isolated incident. Indeed, it can be easily argued that the shape of narrative film all over the world and for most of the one hundred years of its existence was much more profoundly affected by another American film based in folklore. That film was D. W. Griffith's silent epic *The Birth of a Nation* (1915). Cook devotes more pages to this one film than to the whole of Australian cinema, and it is not completely inappropriate to do so. Although based upon a novel, what actually informs *The Birth of a Nation* is Griffith's own knowledge of the folklore of the Civil War, especially Southern folklore. Its view of history is as much if not more the folk memory of the Civil War and its aftermath (and the war had only been fought some fifty years earlier) as it is 'official' history. More examples, though perhaps not quite as demonstrably important, might be found within and beyond Cook's book. In the Australian context, the renaissance of Australian film in the 1970s owes itself to the folklore of the shearer in *Sunday Too Far Away* (Ken Hannam, 1976) (which Cook does not mention) and of the bush in *Picnic at Hanging Rock* (Peter Weir, 1976) which he does. What *A History of Narrative Film* does perhaps more than any other such work available currently or in the recent past is demonstrate the extraordinary manner of the penetration of cinema. Not in terms of the extent to which films are seen in so many places throughout the world, but to the extent in which the ability to make films that speak of the time, the place and more importantly the cultural context of their making has been grasped in so many places at so many times over the past one hundred years. It is clear from Cook's impressive catalogue of places, and of individual film makers and their films, that film functions on a local and a global scale as much more than a mere medium of entertainment, more than merely being the medium of mass-market culture of which it is often accused. This is indeed Cook's thesis:

> the film history represented by this volume... assumes the primacy of human agency among the myriad economic, technological, and social determinants that have made motion pictures the quintessential art form of our century (p. xix).

At times, Cook's concept of 'human agency' seems to be little more than the application of the tenets of the *auteur* theory, to emphasising, that is, the creative and proprietorial role of directors in all times and all places. It is nonetheless possible to see, via the magnitude of the history of narrative film as laid out here, the manner in which the symbiotic relationship between motion picture, human agency, and culture (which in any sense must include the 'folk') is demonstrated. Although this is often ignored, motion pictures function not simply as channels (innocent or otherwise) for the re-presentation of folklore originating somewhere outside the processes of film production, but as originators of folklore.[12]

As the history of film accumulates, one motion picture at a time, randomly even incoherently, on television screens every night of the week, *A History of Narrative Film* provides an admirable way for the individual viewer (and reader) to address that missing coherence. It also invites contemplation, both within and outside the academy, of the sheer breadth and complexity of that history, at the same time as it offers an almost-overwhelmingly detailed description of it.

NOTES

1. This is not to deny that in the past century of cinema and at present some *film making* activity resembles cottage industry, especially a great deal of experimental or avant-garde film making and some independent film making, but by and large the technological basis of cinema and the need for distribution and exhibition of films effectively means film making is film business and not film craft.

2. It is no accident that the earliest cinematic 'entrepreneur' in Australia was the Salvation Army, being both producer and exhibitor of films, religious and otherwise, for its own proselytising purposes.

3. This was a machine which permitted the viewing by one person at a time of a strip of film joined as a continuous loop contained within a closed box. The viewer was required to watch through a 'peephole' as the top of the film passed over a lens. The first public use of such machines is reliably recorded as being April 14, 1894 (Deac Rossell, 'A Chronology of Cinema 1889-1896' *Film History*. Vol.7, no.2, Summer 1995, p,127). It is interesting to note that there is a disputed possibility that Edison Kinetoscope films were projected as early as February the same year (ibid, p. 127).

4. The Edison Kinetoscope films of everyday scenes were not 'actualities' as such but were staged and shot in the Edison studio.

5. Not only in Australia of course. One of the earliest films made in Britain was of the 1896 Derby. The filmmaker seems to have done a better job of actually filming some of the race than does Maurice Sestier, the Lumiere cameraman who filmed the 1896 Melbourne Cup.

6. The processions and ceremonies associated with the declaration of the Commonwealth of Australia, in Sydney on January 26 1901, were filmed by the Limelight unit of the Salvation Army.

7. *Butch Cassidy and the Sundance Kid,* directed by George Roy Hill, 1969.

8. As has often been pointed out, in Bram Stoker's *Dracula,* it is garlic *flowers.* Hollywood's version has become the accepted folklore.

9. The director of *Crocodile Dundee* is Peter Faiman.

10. *Playing Beatie Bow* was released about the same time as *Back to the Future* and was in any case based on a earlier novel by Ruth Park.

11. It ought to be noted that the earliest mention of Australia is in a parenthetical remark in which Cook claims that 'Pathé Freres is credited with pioneering the film industries of Australia...' One wonders who credits Pathé Freres with this. The existing evidence confirms their presence in Australia at an early point, but their contribution seems hardly significant and certainly not worthy of being credited with pioneering the Australian industry.

12. The production 'processes' themselves may be a fertile source of folklore. Apocryphal, publicity and tabloid stories about individuals may take on the status of folklore on occasion. Indeed, it may also be argued that the veiy image of Hollywood which is held at large is more folkloric than actual.

PREVIOUSLY PUBLISHED

'Crocodile Dundee: Apotheosis of the Ocker', *Journal of Popular Film and Television*, Vol. 15, no.4, Winter 1988.

'The Ordinary as Television Spectacle: Oz Soap Opera in the '80s', *Marginal Spaces*, Working Papers Series no.1, Center for Interdisciplinary Research in the Arts, Northwestern University, 1990.

'Fathers, Sons, and Brothers: Patriarchy and Guilt in American Cinema in the 1980s', *Journal of Popular Film and Television*, Spring 1992. Co-authored with Thomas P. McManus..

'*The Demi-Paradise* and Images of Class in British Wartime Films'; 'The Last Gasp of the Middle-Class: British War Films of the 1950s', in Wheeler Winston Dixon, ed, *Re-Viewing British Cinema 1900-1992*. State University of New York Press. 1994.

'Of Horses and Centenaries: Notes on the First Myths about Australian Cinema', *Australian Folklore*, no.12. August 1997.

'Ethnicity and Identity in New Australian Cinema', *Metro Education*, no.13, 1997.

'Sifting the Cinema: Folklore, Film and History—a Review Article', *Australian Folklore*, no.12, August 1997.

'Film' in Philip Bell and Roger Bell, eds, *Americanization and Australia*. University of New South Wales Press, 1998.

'Magic in the Air: Motion Pictures as Fairy Tales', *Australian Folklore*, no. 13. 1998.

'Looking East but Seeing West—A Review Article' *Australian Folklore*, no.15, August 2000.

'Does Dan Die? The Ned Kelly Films and the Question of the Fate of Dan Kelly and Steve Hart at Glerowan', *Australian Folklore*, no.25, November 2008.